21st Century Canadian Diversity

STEPHEN E. NANCOO
EDITOR

Canadian Educators' Press   Mississauga   Ontario

21st Century
Canadian Diversity
  Edited by Stephen E. Nancoo

For information address:
Canadian Educators' Press
100 City Centre Drive
Box 2094
Mississauga, Ontario
Canada, L5B 3C6
Telephone/Fax: 905-826-0578

Canadian Cataloguing in Publication Data

Main entry under title:

21st century Canadian Diversity

Includes bibliographical references
ISBN 1-896191-08-8
1. Pluralism (Social Sciences) - Canada 2. Multiculturalism -
Canada

I Nancoo, Stephen E. (Stephen Emmanuel). II Twenty-first century Canadian
Diversity.

FC105.M8T83 2000   305.8'00971   C99-932691-0
F1035.A1T83 2000

Printed and bound in Canada

CONTENTS

PREFACE

For many of us, the 21st Century represents the future. Now, that future is unfolding before us. For many Canadians, the future is a symbol for change—and there is no better expressive, reflection of that change than in the new Canadian Diversity that surrounds us, from sea to shining sea. This thought-provoking book, **21st Century Canadian Diversity,** brings together these two historically significant streams of thought—the future and Canadian Diversity.

The 21 contributing authors represent a formidable breadth of experience and expertise. They have researched, written, taught or are practitioners in their particular area of interest. They offer their unique perspectives and thoughtful visions of the future and on Canadian Diversity.

We wish, therefore, to thank the following contributors of articles to **21st Century Canadian Diversity**: Pat Bradshaw, Cyril Dabydeen, George Sefa Dei, Stéphane Dion, Nahum Kanhai, Romulo Magsino, Joseph Nancoo, Robert Nancoo, Edite Noivo, Constantine Passaris, Deo Poonwassie, David Roy, Roberta Russell, John Sahadat, John Samuel, Dieter Schachhuber, Roopchand Seebaran, Lloyd Stanford, K. Victor Ujimoto, and David Wicks. Many thanks to *Canadian and International Education* and *Canadian Educators' Press* for permission to reprint articles that appeared in their publications. We also wish to acknowledge the research and editorial assistance of Robert Nancoo and *Canadian Educators' Press*.

This book about the future is written for study and reflection. **21st Century Canadian Diversity** is also a call for action—in the classrooms, in the board rooms, in the public forums and the legislative assemblies. We hope it will challenge students of diversity and of the future to think and act to create a vision of change that embraces the new Canadian diversity.

Stephen E. Nancoo
Editor

INTRODUCTION

Stephen E. Nancoo

21st Century Canadian Diversity challenges the prevailing approaches of looking at Canada. The new millennium has brought in its train an avalanche of commentaries on what the 21st century signifies and holds for Canada and its 31 million people. Missing from many of these analyses is the central role that diversity will play as we progress through the 21st Century.

This book, **21st Century Canadian Diversity**, challenges the conventional way of thinking and acting. In looking at the 21st century, the authors clearly articulate the proposition that as a country with diverse people, we need to face and explore some fundamental questions about the major forces for change within Canadian society. We need to understand how best we can prepare for, influence and shape the 21st century to meet the hopes and aspirations of the diverse Canadian communities.

In looking at diversity and the future, the authors of **21st Century Canadian Diversity** analyze the current state of affairs, explore future challenges we face, create a vision of change for the future, and provide suggestions and possibilities concerning action that could be taken towards a positive, preferred future state.

OVERVIEW

John Samuel and Dieter Schachhuber provide a portrait of diversity issues in Chapter 1, *Perspectives on Diversity*. They look at Canada and its traditional past, the new and emerging future with its increased diversity, the role of immigration, the reasons for, and possible responses to social changes that are occurring and the legislative framework and the common ground in which attempts to accommodate these changes are made.

The mass media perform a powerful and pervasive role in Canadian society. They help shape the national environment in which citizens function and they influence the national agenda that determines and shapes our future. The decisions we make are conditioned by the quality of the information we possess and the mass media are the principal sources, gatekeepers and disseminators of information. Robert Nancoo and Stephen Nancoo explore the role of *The Mass Media in a Diverse Society*, in Chapter 14. They outline the development of the mass media in Canada; place the mass media in the context of the emerging new and diverse Canadian society and examine the impact of the interaction between the media and the changing diverse Canadian society. Finally, they propose a vision for the twenty-first century that seeks to establish a fairer and more equitable relationship between the mass media and Canadian diversity.

In Chapter 3, *Struggle and Resistance: Crafting First Nations in the New Millennium,* Deo Poonwassie and Nahum Kanhai analyze issues that affect the education of First Nation peoples (and generally Aboriginal peoples). An examination is made of recent developments such as the Royal Commission on Aboriginal Peoples and the response of the Government of Canada to the Commission's report, the creation of Nunavut, the Nisga'a agreement and the Supreme Court's Donald Marshall judgement. They look at some of the outstanding issues that are basic to the future relationship of First Nations and the future and suggest ideas relating to the First Nations reclaiming jurisdiction over their destiny in the new millennium.

Stéphane Dion examines *Federalism and Diversity: The Canadian Experience and Unity in Diversity, The Canadian Way,* in Chapters 4 and 5. Dion notes that unity and diversity the Canadian way has two dimensions: first guarantees we give to individual rights and freedoms and second our federal system. He shows how flexible federalism enables provinces which are equal in status to express their own personalities. He believes that the ideal pursued by Canada, through its federative form, its democratic institutions, its charter of rights, its bilingualism and its multiculturalism, is to enable all its citizens to flourish in freedom, taking into account the context in which they are evolving, and respecting their collective loyalties, including the unique character of Quebec society.

The following three chapters, deal with specific manifestations of diversity at work in organizational settings. In Chapter 6, *Managing Diversity*, Stephen Nancoo examines the impact of diversity, offering some theoretical and empirical arguments in favour of diversity, suggests approaches to managing diversity through organizational change and cultivating a culture of diversity in organizations. He makes linkages between diversity and other leadership and management techniques such as total quality, team building and organizatioal learning. He outlines a strategic leadership model for achieving diversity in organizations as well as instruments for creating a culture of diversity.

In Chapter 7, *Women Building Careers in A Diverse Society,* Roberta Russell draws on current feminist and management literature as well as empirical studies to illustrate some of the challenges women face in contemporary work organizations and the way in which some of them are dealing with those challenges. She examines the implications for organizational policy and for training and development practices designed to provide women with a more level playing field in the new millennium.

In their article, *The Oppression of Women in Canada*: *From Denial to Awareness and Resistance,* Chapter 8, David Wicks and Pat Bradshaw outline existing practices of inequality and injustices. After exploring possible causes for the current situation, they delineate strategies of resistance that may lead to a redefinition of the current rules and new opportunities for both men and women.

Two institutions that impact on the lives of Canadians are those of the Police as well as the institution of the Family in society. In Chapter 9, *The Police and the Diverse Society*, Stephen Nancoo examines some of the trends in the internal and external environment and describes their implications for the future of policing. He traces the emergence of a paradigm shift from the traditional form of policing and delineates the nature and characteristics of the new paradigm of community policing. Finally, an integrated approach for public policing in the 21st century is outlined.

In Chapter 10, Edite Noivo looks at *Family Diversity and Cultural Pluralism* by reviewing the transformations that families have undergone in the last decade. She discusses the challenges posed by the present and future diversity in family forms.

Chapters 11, 12 and 13 focus on three significant policy issues that profoundly impact on Canadian Diversity.

Roopchand Seebaran challenges us with a critical examination of *Social Policy and Ethno-Cultural Diversity* in Chapter 11. He describes and analyzes the social policy responses to diversity and develops a framework for advancing more appropriate social polices in the future. He delineates the legislative, demographic, global, development and professional service imperatives that support the implementation of appropriate strategies and social policy goals in the future.

In Chapter 12, *Aging in a Multicultural Society: Public Policy Considerations,* Victor Ujimoto observes that as the population ages the diversity in lifestyles places a heavy burden on health care providers. The problem is exacerbated by health care providers who are governed by outmoded social policies which appear to be more reactive rather than forward looking. He believes that the primary task for gerontologists today is to recognize the cultural diversity of our elderly population. He concludes that there are positive benefits to be gained from an aging heterogeneous population if the elderly are perceived as resources for social change instead of viewing them as a group always in need to compensate for deficits brought about by the process of aging.

In *Promoting Canadian Competence: The Education of A Diverse People,* Chapter 13, Deo Poonwassie delineates why cultural diversity must be a key consideration in the provision of education in Canadian schools. He believes that schools will pay more attention to cultural diversity through curriculum changes although the basic disciplines will take precedence. The inclusive curriculum will be recognized as part of schooling; even so there will be many more private schools based on race, religion and political ideology.

The next three chapters examine the issues of Human Rights, Anti Racism and Multiculturalism. It is envisaged that these three issues should occupy a prominent and enduring place on the agenda for 21st century action.

Identifying Human Rights Issues for the Next Decade, Chapter 14, is the subject of a fascinating study by John Samuel,

Constantine Passaris, Lloyd Stanford and Cyril Dabydeen. They examine the performance of Canadian human rights commissions, and they review human rights in the context of a projected demographic picture, the new economy and its directions, and societal trends. They conclude that, in the paradigm shift currently taking place in a "swim or sink" kind of economy and society, the predictions made at one time that discrimination will decline does not seem to be true anymore. They believe that it is increasingly becoming difficult to achieve equality of employment opportunities in a society that is likely to turn a blind eye on rights violations.

George Sefa Dei presents anti-racism as an educational approach to social change in Chapter 15, *Contesting the Future: Anti-Racism and Diversity.* He looks at the current state of race relations in our diverse society, delineates a preferred future in terms of the creation of an open and equal opportunity society; and sets an agenda as how to go about achieving the preferred future state for the 21st century; that is, the imperative of working collectively and the approaches required for this endeavour.

Romulo Magsino, in Chapter 16, takes a refreshing new look at *The Canadian Multiculturalism Policy: A Pluralist Ideal Re-Visited.* He describes how the policy aims at Canadian unity through the pursuit of principles of equality, freedom of cultural retention, and cultural sharing to promote mutual understanding and appreciation. The policy's goal of unity and the principles surrounding it are justifiable and he advocates for adequate and effective implementation through suitable programs and adequate and efficient resource allocation.

Religion and ethics in a diverse Canada are the themes of Chapters 17 and 18.

John Sahadat, in *Unity in Diversity Not Uniformity*, observes that no one today can speak of Canada as a Judaeo-Christian society and not expect to be contradicted not only because of the empirical data depicting diversity; but also because the indigenous peoples as well as visible minorities have a heightened sense of their rights and freedoms to live out their unique traditions with dignity and to take much pride in doing it. He suggests that our sense of unity without the threat of uniformity will be a good reason for hope of a brighter future with deeper understanding and trustworthy relations.

In *Diversity: A Matter of Ethics,* David Roy explores the many ways in which diversity is perceived in ethical discourse at the beginning of this century, either as a value to be cherished or at the very source of value conflicts that divide society or even threaten to split society asunder. He advises us that if the clash of civilization does come to dominate global politics, ethics itself will pass through a new phase in its evolution. People will be challenged, perhaps more profoundly and broadly than ever in the past, to confront the question of how will it be possible to live with respect for, and in peace with, radically different views of life when these threaten to collide in conflicts that transcend matters of economics, technology and national power.

We conclude with a poem, *Canadian Diversity* by Joseph Nancoo, that dreams of:

"The ennobling necessity
Of harmony in humanity's rich diversity".

What is evident from the contributions by the authors of this book is that diversity is not something we ought to have -- it is something we do have. Whether one sees this challenge of societal change as a threat or an opportunity, the reality is that this diversity will intensify and become more pervasive in our institutions, our cities and our country in the 21st century. Thinking about the years ahead, as explicated in **21st Century Canadian Diversity,** allows us to identify some possibilities, to even change the way we perceive the communities around us and to make those decisions and choices for a more desirable future for Canada and its peoples.

Chapter 1

PERSPECTIVES ON CANADIAN DIVERSITY

T. John Samuel and Dieter Schachhuber

1. INTRODUCTION

Many Canadians ask with considerable legitimacy why and how diversity has become such an important issue. It seems that diversity—along with many related concepts—has become the buzzword of the 1990s, at a time when Canada is getting ready to welcome the 21st century. But behind the buzzword is a reality all Canadians have to deal with: the traditional image and assumptions about Canada no longer work and have to be replaced or modified. Canadian society is changing from stability, tradition, uniformity and acceptance of rules to a society of flexibility, innovation, heterogeneity and individual determination.

Since the 1960s Canada has experienced rapid social change. This change has accelerated in the next two decades and will continue to do so before we reach the 21st century and beyond. Changes that occurred within several centuries are happening within decades now. For instance, today we are all 'minorities' and disability is now seen as a continuum of ability, not as some absolute state of incapacity" (Environics Canada, 1989, p. 6).

This new concern with diversity cannot be based on a mindless and aimless tolerance for everything or anything, nor a gutless abrogation of social standards and personal responsibilities. It has to be based on the need for a rational and moral approach to nation-building, to working towards a common ground which improves the quality of life and maximizes benefits for everyone. The key to successful nation-building is not in the coercive power of the state, or of any majority, or of powerful organizations, or of radical minorities, but in the development of the competencies—the values, skills, knowledge, and abilities required to make a useful contribution in the diverse Canada of today and tomorrow.

What makes the Canada of today different from the past and from many other societies is the means by which this nation-building, this development of the common ground, is to be pursued. The Canadian approach may still be tentative and error prone, but it is clearly based on values and concepts which have long been part of the Canadian identity and which are only now beginning to influence practice: respect for the dignity and integrity of each individual; recognition of collective identities and differences; the right to full participation in society and the responsibility to make a full contribution; a civilized process of ongoing negotiation for a common purpose; public policy which is inclusive; and the responsible personal behaviour required to function in a civilized society.

In this introductory chapter we will look at Canada and its traditional past, the new and emerging future with its increased diversity, the role of immigration, the reasons for, and possible responses to, social changes that are occurring and the legislative framework and the common ground in which attempts to accomodate these changes are made.

2. CANADA PAST, PRESENT AND FUTURE

Diversity is not an entirely new idea. At Confederation, Canada was already diverse in terms of ethnic origins, religions, political views, economic and regional priorities, individual talents. However, we are now facing pervasive qualitative changes which call for new answers and competencies because today's diversity is at the centre of Canadian society—a mainstream characteristic rather than a marginal or a minority concern. By recognizing and addressing diversity as a mainstream characteristic we are foreshadowing the end of hyphenated Canadianism. In a diverse Canada, in an inclusive mainstream, everyone is Canadian.

If Canadian society was not changing there would be no problem, no concern, no need for any government response. But Canadian society is changing: in terms of values, priorities and self-image; in terms of demographic reality, i.e., composition of the labour force, age profile, cultural and ethnic diversity; in terms of gender roles and family priorities; in terms of demands on government for meeting human needs, protecting rights and serving the community. Some of these changes have in fact already transformed Canadian society, and all within barely one generation.

3. "TRADITIONAL" VERSUS "NEW" CANADA

Traditional Canada was more homogeneous, European, white, Christian/religious, male-labour-force dominated in an industrial economy, had English/French as primary languages with a common work ethic, was different from U.S.—monarchy, peaceful, moderate, consensus-seeking, polite—and accepting of authority, traditional, smug, had stable population growth with aboriginal people and minorities outside of an exclusive mainstream. The "new" Canada, on the other hand, is diverse and pluralistic, includes non-whites, is secular with sprinklings of fundamentalism, outward looking, hedonistic, international in a post-industrial economy, wary of authority, has respect for differences, has a low birth rate, aging with rapid economic and social changes, with a focus on individual and group rights.

a. The Traditional Picture

Though this was never entirely accurate, Canada's very European self-image has traditionally been closely tied to the religions, cultures, languages and values of the two "founding" nations. Laws, customs, values, social and political and economic systems were adopted from the two European cultures. Evolution and outside influences created a more specific Canadian identity, but one which still saw itself primarily as European and largely homogeneous. Stability and order have always formed a large part of this identity. Newcomers were pressured to adapt to their new environment. They could retain some cultural, private and personal separateness, but where it counted, most people, regardless of their origins, initially became at least "hyphenated" Canadians and then disappeared into the Canadian mainstream. Their transition was eased by the strong similarities between their own cultures, values and expectations and those of their newly-adopted country. They encountered some hostility and discrimination, had to adapt socially and learn their new political responsibilities. Overall, however, it took them only years, rather than generations to fit in.

Their religion, their skin colour, their particular work ethic, western values, an understanding of industrial society and their experiences with political participation were essentially similar to those of established Canadians. The gap was narrow and could be bridged. Considerable tolerance and even appreciation of ethnic customs allowed for retention of some of their past identity, particularly in food, music, ethnic celebrations and national nostalgia Limited, but benevolent, governmental policies and programs supported efforts to these ends.

Non-Europeans who did not fit in quite as easily came in relatively small numbers, often for a specific and temporary economic purpose which opened the gates just a fraction for them. They rarely moved beyond limited geographic areas. Their numbers and political power were limited and they were slow to organize against often considerable and pervasive discrimination. They seemed willing to pay the personal, social and political costs for the economic advantages they sought and found in Canada. They experienced intolerance and discrimination as individuals and groups. Society at large did not perceive discrimination as a large scale and pervasive social problem which required counter-measures such as anti-discrimination laws or a Charter of Rights and Freedoms.

Given these realities, the need for government action was minimal. Newcomers, given reasonable support and job opportunities, integrated themselves successfully economically but could retain some remnants of cultural identity. They posed few exceptional problems for business and government. Some arrangements had to be made to ensure that newcomers speedily acquired the necessary language and job skills that allowed them to function effectively in the economy and in the labour market. For them, as for all the others, education was presumed to be synonymous with future material and social success. With few exceptions this was borne out in practice.

Aboriginal people were either segregated geographically and culturally or forcibly integrated. Even then, economic separation kept them out of the mainstream. Therefore, they could be largely ignored in the cultural, political and economic evolution of Canada.

b. The New Reality: Diversity

Some aspects of Canada's population diversity can be traced as far back as Confederation with suggestions that Canada has always been a multicultural, or diverse, or an adapting society. However, the challenges Canada faces today have largely been caused by events since World War II.

Europe, or the "old" continent, was the prime immigration source after the war. This changed in the 1960s. Economic growth and political stability restored peace and confidence and kept most Europeans at home. In short, European immigration started to decline in the 60s and 70s. At the same time, the colonial era ended, starting a trend of migration from the Third World which is still continuing to increase. (More on this later.) Political and social unrest, government coercion and economic uncertainty underlie an increasing stream of refugee and economic migrants from areas outside Western Europe. Canada's increasing links with the Third World, its role in the U.N., its political stability and economic prosperity have made it a favoured destination for non-European migration. International pressures for the elimination of discrimination have led to changes in immigration laws. These and other ongoing developments have changed the population face of Canada. Yearly statistics show steady increases in the visible minority population, which now constitutes a sizable minority in the institutions of many urban centres. These new immigrants are introducing new dimensions to Canadian society. Their life experience, their education, their religious practices, and economic and political values are often substantially different from those of mainstream Canada. Their appearance and social behaviour may also set them apart.

Canada's population, the basis of any society, has stopped growing as it used to. It took about 50 years for Canada to grow from 13 million to the current 31 million, but the population will be only at the level of 43 million by 2041, a mere 12 million more in 40 years compared to more than doubling in the last 50 years (Statistics Canada, 1994, p. 66). Two thirds of this growth is expected to come from immigration.

Canada experienced a population growth rate of one percent annually in the decade of 1980-90. In order to maintain that growth rate, immigration annually would have to reach 500,000 by 2030 calculates Ivan Fellegi, the Chief Statistician of Canada (Belous, 1991, p.18). The working age population (18 to 64 age group) would grow by 0.8 percent a year during 1990-2000, but will reach the zero rate of growth by 2010-20 and will decline thereafter.

The slower population growth rate is changing the gender ratio in Canada. In 1983, there were 98 men for every 100 women. However, because of the longer life expectancy of women (over six years more than men) and the aging of the population, by 2011, there will only be 95 men per 100 women (Statistics Canada, 1990, p. 150). The higher age groups will be particularly affected by this phenomenon. In the 65 and over age group, the ratio between men and women will be 7 to 10.

The aging of the population will be an inevitable feature of Canada's demographic future. In the 1986 Census, young people (age 0-17) made up 26 percent of the population and the elderly, 11 percent. By 2036, this would be reversed and the elderly would be a quarter of the population and the young only 18 percent. The median age of the population would rise from 33 years in 1990 to 45 in 2036 (Statistics Canada, 1990, p. 34). The aging of the population would inevitably bring more conservatism to Canadian society (Samuel, 1994). Also it would mean higher costs since to look after a senior the costs to governments will be three times that of a child. (Most of the costs of child bearing and rearing are born by the parents). Higher costs of medical care and of social benefits like pensions for seniors will intensify the struggle for resources between age groups and generations. The fact that Canadians have fewer children and live longer has implications for social policy since the current source of care and support for 80 percent of aged persons comes from the family (Gee, 1990).

Age, sex and lifestyle changes would affect the composition of families. A greater proportion of younger Canadians are choosing to delay marriage, or even to not marry at all. In 1996, 2.6 million persons lived alone and the majority of them were women, particularly women 65 and over. Lone-parent families accounted for 19 percent of all families in 1996 (Statistics Canada, Internet). These trends are likely to continue. As seen in the U.S., between 1970 and 1990, according to the U.S. Bureau of the Census, among whites, lone-parent families (mostly headed by females) rose from 10.1 percent to 23.1 percent while among blacks this was about three times as high.

4. IMMIGRATION AND THE COMMON GROUND

Although immigration presents many challenges, few of Canada's core values are seriously threatened despite expressions of views to the contrary. Historically, Canadians have not developed a well-defined, ethnically-based or ideological identity, but rather see themselves as a "civic" nation based on common goals, values and social institutions. Integration attempts to strike a balance among these values, the cultural distinctiveness of the French/British groups and the values of new immigrants. The modern requirement is to develop a truly integrated and participatory society. This implies adjustments on the part of both immigrants and of Canadian society. Realistically, the onus to adapt and integrate will always be on newcomers, no matter how elaborate and prominent the notions of diversity and multiculturalism may be. The key to success will lie in Canada's ability to ensure open and equal access to all its institutions.

a. Immigration and Population Growth

Immigration has always been a very visible component of Canada's population profile. At the time of the 1996 Census, over one person in six was foreign-born and one third of the population was either foreign-born or had at least one foreign-born parent. Net international migration has accounted for almost a quarter of Canada's post-war population growth. When population growth occurs more through immigration than through natural increase, it has a larger impact on society and on the structures through which new members (births and immigrants) are integrated into society. It is not surprising, therefore, that in the 1990s Canadians and their governments are questioning and discussing immigration issues and are debating how to manage the emerging diverse society so that everyone can fully participate and contribute.

b. Immigration: A Balancing Act

Immigration levels are determined by a number of influences such as demographic, economic, labour force, social/family (family reunification) needs, humanitarian principles (acceptance of refugees) and the ability to absorb, integrate, and settle newcomers.

Hard trade-offs often have to be made among these influences and a very difficult balancing act needs to be performed. They determine who will be admitted into Canada, how many, and how their efforts to integrate into Canada will be supported. Since the choices are sometimes incompatible, e.g., labour force requirements vs. refugee emergencies or family reunification priorities, the debate will be an ongoing one.

Canadians need to realize that there is not necessarily a destructive conflict between diversity and preserving core national values. Immigrants come to Canada because they recognize and value the country's stability, tolerance, and institutions. In most cases, immigrants want to fit into Canadian society and they want essentially the same things native-born Canadians want: to build a prosperous, secure, peaceful life for themselves and their families.

5. DIVERSITY AND ITS ACCEPTANCE

Despite occasional outbursts against cultural diversity, studies show that Canadians who approve of such diversity "is more than twice the percentage not in favour of the idea of Canada as a diverse society (69.3% vs 27.3%)" (Berry and Kalin, 1993, p.6). The falling fertility rate and the low rate of population growth in Canada, combined with high population growth in developing countries and the consequent push for settlement in immigrant-receiving countries have resulted in higher levels of immigration in Canada. Immigration levels rose from 88,000 in 1984 to about 250,000 in ten years and then declined to 174,000 by 1998. Immigrants came from almost every country in the world. According to Statistics Canada, because of the country's low fertility rate, to maintain a population growth rate of one percent annually, 200,000 immigrants were required in 1991. But this number will increase to 320,000 in 2011 and 560,000 in 2036 (Statistics Canada, 1990, p. 32).

a. Ethnicity

Immigration over the decades has drastically changed the ethnic make up of Canada. In 1881 ethnic groups other than British or French were only 10 percent of the total population (Samuel, 1990, p. 3). In 1991, the same groups were 42 percent of the population. According to cautious estimates based on conservative assumptions, the visible minority population increased from 6.3 percent of the population in 1986 to 9.1 percent in 1991. Under certain assumptions it is projected to reach about 15 percent by early in the century (Samuel, 1992, p.17). The total visible minority population in 1996 was 3.2 million and this is expected to increase to over 8 million by 2016. According to the 1996 census, the ethnic Chinese population was the largest visible minority group (860,000) followed by South Asians (671,000) and Blacks (574,000). The fourth largest group was West Asians and Arabs followed by Filipinos, Latin Americans and Southeast Asians. Apart from the total numbers, a most significant feature of the settlement of visible minorities in Canada is that they live mostly in census metropolitan areas. In Toronto they were 40 per cent of the population in 1996 and in Vancouver over one third, while in Montreal, Edmonton and Calgary visible minorities were about a fifth of the respective metropolitan areas' population. Depending upon future immigration levels, these numbers will be significantly larger in the 21st century. However, ethnic boundaries are shifting due to intermarriage, cultural integration, the emergence of a Canadian identity (those who reported their ethnicity as "Canadian" in the censuses multiplied manyfold in the ten years between 1986 and 1996), and increasing pride in ethnic identity. For instance more and more Canadians seem ready to reveal their ancestry.

b. Religion

Until 1971, the proportion reporting "no religious affiliation" was relatively stable at less than 0.5 percent until 1971 but it rose to 12.5 percent in 1991 (Government of Canada, 1993, p. 2) While those reporting "Catholic" increased from 38.7 percent to 45.7 percent between 1921 and 1991, the percentage of Protestants decreased. Though still small in actual numbers, between 1981 and 1991, Buddhists, Muslims, Hindus and Sikhs doubled or tripled (Ibid., p.3).

c. Disability

In 1986 1.4 million persons in the 15-64 age group reported a disability (Statistics Canada, 1996, p.29). This number is projected to rise to over 2 million by 2016. The rate of disability increases with age and two out of five 65 and over had at least one disability (Minister of Supply and Services Canada, 1986 p.4). More women than men report having a disability, with mobility limitations mentioned most frequently. Adults reporting a disability tend to have received less formal education than others. Among those of working age (15-64 years), almost half the persons with a disability are on the job market compared to three quarters of the able bodied. As can be expected, persons with disability have a much higher unemployment rate and a lower income than the Canadian population in general. Committee after committee of federal and provincial governments have urged "urgent measures" to integrate persons with disabilities into the evolving labour market, though relatively little has been achieved so far.

d. Aboriginals

In 1996 about a million Canadians reported to have aboriginal blood and more than three-quarters of them lived off reserves. Three out of five aboriginals were in the labour force. They had much higher unemployment rates and lower levels of income. Socially, they had the highest rate of welfare dependency, highest suicide rate and a proportionately much larger rate of incarceration. Because of high birth rates and falling death rates, their numbers are growing rapidly. According to Statistics Canada projections, by the beginning of the century, they will be four percent of the population (Hagey, et. al., 1989, p.5).

e. Women

Gender roles have changed dramatically in the last few decades and will continue to do so into the 21st century. More and more women are entering the labour force, have become career oriented and have joined men in every realm of human activity. In 1962 there were only 1.8 million women in the labour force, a participation rate of only 29.0 (Labour Canada, 1973, p.3). By 1996, almost 9 million women were in the labour force, a participation rate of 65.5 percent according to Statistics Canada.

6. REASONS FOR SOCIAL CHANGES

It is legitimate and logical to ask, "Why has Canadian society changed so much?" There are five main reasons behind the emergence and recognition of diversity.

a. Moral and Social Reasons

Canada's social values and its population would have changed even without the impact of immigration. The epochal events of the 1960s changed social priorities worldwide. As a result, equality, justice, human and group rights, individual dignity, rights to full opportunity and full participation heavily influence business and government decisions. This means people demand to be treated as respected individuals, often challenging established traditions. The individualism of the 1960s and 1970s became enshrined in human rights laws, ombudsman's acts, redress, and complaint mechanisms and in the Canadian Charter of Rights and Freedoms in the 1980s. The reality of diversity was recognized in employment equity legislation and multiculturalism acts. But astute leaders and managers didn't need legislation to realize that their world was changing. The education system, public services, the big corporations all have run into the reality of the new market place in which each individual voice demands to be heard. Significantly, the changes within Canada are paralleled by similar upheavals world wide.

b. Demographic Changes

Recent population statistics and even very cautions projections highlight two major developments: First, there has been a steady and significant decline in the fertility rate which inevitably raises questions about population growth and the long-run viability of Canadian society and the economy. In the late 1950s a woman completing her reproductive life would have had 3.9 children (Samuel, 1981, p.9). Today this has declined to only 1.7. To replace the existing population Canada needs 2.1 children per woman (One to replace the father, one to replace the mother and 0.1 to replace all those who do not want to or cannot, have children.) But Canada's fertility rate has been below the replacement rate since 1972.

Second, there has been a steady and dramatic shift in the origin (or source countries) of immigration, from Europe to Asia, South America, the Caribbean and Africa. During the postwar period, until the sixties, the proportion of immigrants arriving from non-traditional sources was extremely small. By 1974 however, these sources contributed 46 percent of immigrants and by 1996, this has increased to 80 percent.

A major part of Canada's population growth now comes from immigrants of different and changing cultural ethnic and religious backgrounds who have to be integrated successfully into Canadian society. Furthermore, fertility rates among the aboriginal peoples are dramatically higher, ensuring at least a numerically greater presence and a higher visibility of aboriginal people in Canada, aside from their growing demands for recognition, economic and social improvement and self-determination.

A declining, or low, fertility rate is tacitly assumed to be a problem to Canadian society. Population growth is conceived to be good and desirable and population decline as a harbinger of a general decline though there is surprisingly little debate on the logic of this popular notion. At least superficially, there are rather obvious connections between the fertility rate and three other factors, all of which relate to the status and independence of Canadian women. The increased education levels of girls and women, their rising participation rate in the labour force and increasing average income levels have enhanced women's self determination and their economic independence and have given them significant roles outside the family. The changing status of women is itself an indication that the traditional mainstream has expanded, includes new actors/actresses and is striving to accommodate diversity.

7. BUSINESS NECESSITY

Business and government, as employers and providers of products and services, are waking up to the reality of diversity and its impact on the conduct of business and government. Diversity is entirely compatible with democracy, with the goals of business, with the Canadian sense of justice, fairness and equality and is increasingly recognized as an important part of Canada's national identity. In its most practical sense, workforce diversity is seen as a key to success in increasingly open and integrated global markets. Advantages can be found in three areas:

a.   Employers in all fields have access to the employment skills of the total labour force and are assured an adequate labour supply. During the 1990s and well into the next century better than two thirds of new entrants into the labour force will be aboriginals, ethnic and visible minorities and women who bring the flexibility, the new skills, the community involvement and the cultural understanding required to do a competent job in a diverse society.

b.   By addressing the different needs of all population groups, product design and service delivery will be effective and appropriate to the identified needs. Conflicts and waste will be reduced or prevented. Cooperation between clients and business and the agencies of government will be increased. The boundaries between customers and providers of goods and services are becoming blurred by the need to deal effectively with diversity and change. The bottom line has become an effective teacher.

c.   By responding to the increasing diversity in Canadian society, business and public institutions develop the flexibility and problem-solving ability required in a global environment and in serving a changing, unpredictable and demanding world.

It is necessary to assure that the work environment provides the same challenges and opportunities for all employees, male and female, minorities, and persons with disabilities. Such diversity will challenge some old but untested assumptions and lead to better business decisions. "...The more diverse the decision-making group process, the more likely that group will avoid the wrong or disatrastrously wrong decision" (Foster, 1987, p.12). Referring to American businesses it has been stated that "American businesses that fail to employ and develop people representative of diverse communities and countries are, in effect, choosing to restrict severely their client and customer base. On the other hand, companies whose management validates and articulates a strong commitment to employee diversity—and competence in managing that diversity—have a business policy designed to position them for a greater market share at home and abroad" (Foster et al., 1988, p.39). A Wall Street Journal article pointed out that "diverse task teams charged with developing domestic and international markets are more aware of market opportunities and threats than homogenous task teams...A balance of values is needed around the conference table to solve business problems" (Ibid).

8. GLOBAL COMMUNICATIONS EXPLOSION

Not only are there constant changes and shifts in population and new patterns of communications and intercultural relations, there is a much higher level of knowledge about them. Nothing is an isolated or local incident any more. Any weakness and conflict (also every opportunity and success), now become known internationally and may lead to an immediate response. The information age makes every one aware of the wide and complex range of individual needs and characteristics as well as the constantly growing common interest. Therefore, the media, politicians, public institutions, business, law-enforcement agencies are now always visible in their actions and have to be seen to be dealing effectively and competently with the issues arising from diversity. Visibility and accountability also have become an effective teacher.

Post-industrial technology, post-modern values and the evolving global village call for a radical change in organizational culture and individual adaptability. New technologies and new forms of organization make an appropriate and effective response to diversity a practical possibility. Strong networks, co-operation, personal creativity, judgement, and responsibility are crucial to success in post-industrial society and in an open global economy. Organizations are developing the ability to adjust and adapt, to make instant and local decisions which are based on actual reality, rather than driven by old habits, inflexible rules and irrelevant systems which are blind to diversity, incentives and individual needs.

9. POSSIBLE RESPONSES TO DIVERSITY AND CHANGE

There are three different ways both individuals and organizations can respond to the social changes now happening in Canada. Unfortunately, only one of them works. Fortunately, we are beginning to agree which one it is.

a. The Natural Response

The first and usual human and organizational response to substantial change is rigidity, passivity and rejection. Initially, we want to refuse to accept any need and responsibility for change and adaptation, simply because we are comfortable in our habits, secure in our knowledge of what works and feel little incentive to go forward into the unknown. We want to change only if two things are clearly demonstrated:

i.   Our old ways are too costly, irrelevant, ineffective or even damaging to our own interests; and/or

ii.   The new ways and solutions have been clearly and reliably demonstrated to be efficient, relevant, effective and supportive of our interests.

Our willingness to change can be increased if we receive public and organizational support, and the tools, knowledge and resources required to undertake change. In the long run rigidity and rejection is self-destructive, it causes conflict, wastes resources and impedes progress. The job does not get done; poor decisions lead to poor results.

b. Discrimination

The normal response to change, i.e., rejection and rigidity, cannot be sustained forever. Frustration will rise, the old methods will increasingly fail. The ensuing fear and uncertainty may lead to active discrimination against those we see as causing all the "trouble". Anyone different may be rejected as an outsider or as an unreasonable intruder whose influence has to be challenged and limited. Scapegoating and blame-fixing are the first step toward active discrimination and all the costs and conflicts it entails. Rational debate will be impaired by emotions and tribalism. Discrimination imposes costs and suffering on the victims without gaining any real and lasting advantages for anyone else and is clearly incompatible with the values and goals of modern society.

c. Adjustment/Adaptation to New Reality

The inadequacy and inappropriateness of resistance and discrimination have already become apparent. Real answers are being sought and found. The answer inevitably is based on the need to take personal and institutional responsibility for implementing the necessary changes in personal behaviour, in political processes, in management decision making, in organizational systems and in service delivery. This means development of the skills and competencies required to get the job done efficiently and effectively in changed circumstances.

10. THE LEGISLATIVE FRAMEWORK

In a more homogenous and unchanging society, a constitution or charter may protect legal, political and civil rights but make little mention of so-called human or minority rights. Not surprisingly, the British North America Act, until 1982 the de facto constitution of Canada, contains little protection against discrimination on the various grounds listed in today's Canadian Charter of Rights and Freedoms or Canada's assorted federal, provincial or territorial human rights acts.

In recognition of Canada's diversity, the social changes which have occurred over the past 25 to 30 years have now also become reflected in legislation. Much of Canada's anti-discrimination and human rights legislation flows from its obligations as a signatory of U.N. rights covenants and declarations. Thus Canada's legislation meets both domestic, social and political needs as well as international obligations.

a. The Canadian Charter of Rights and Freedoms

The *Canadian Charter of Rights and Freedoms* guarantees the rights and freedoms set out in it subject only to such reasonable limits prescribed by law as can be demonstrably justified in a free and democratic society. The fundamental freedoms (a) freedom of conscience and religion; (b) freedom of thought, belief, opinion and expression, including freedom of the press and other media of communication; (c) freedom of peaceful assembly; and (d) freedom of association are implicitly freedoms of individual identity and a recognition of diversity. Furthermore, the equality rights section guarantees that every individual is equal before and under the law and has the right to equal protection and equal benefit of the law without discrimination and in particular, without discrimination based on race, national or ethnic origin, colour, religion, sex, age or mental or physical disability. This section in essence states that governments may not discriminate against individuals in laws, policies and public programs. Clearly, such a provision is required only in a society which recognizes the reality of diversity.

b.   Human Rights Acts:

Human Rights Legislation at the federal and provincial levels, which more accurately could be called "anti-discrimination law", prohibits discrimination on a number of identifiable grounds, including race, national or ethnic origin, colour and religion and other immutable characteristics which differentiate individuals from each other. It proscribes discrimination in matters relating to employment, in the provision of goods, services, facilities and accommodation.

c.   Employment Equity Acts

The Employment Equity Act, passed by the federal government in 1986, was the first law of its kind in Canada. It addresses the need to overcome the discriminatory effects of past practices, policies and systems in employment. The stated purpose of this Act is to achieve equality in the work place so that no person shall be denied employment opportunities or benefits for reasons unrelated to ability. The practical long term outcome of this Act, and similar legislation in the provinces is to make the workplace as diverse as the workforce from which the workers are drawn. An Act to revise and strengthen the Employment Equity Act at the federal level was passed in 1995.

d.   Multiculturalism Acts

According to the *Canadian Encyclopedia*, Multiculturalism, as a term, first came into vogue in the 1960s to counter "biculturalism", a term popularized by the Royal Commission on Bilingualism and Biculturalism. Its use has spread from Canada to many countries, notably Australia. Several European countries like Holland and Germany seem to be interested in following Canada's example.

The term, multiculturalism, is used in at least three senses: (a) to refer to a society that is characterized by ethnic or cultural heterogeneity, (b) to refer to an ideal of equality and mutual respect among a population's ethnic or cultural groups, and (c) to refer to government policy proclaimed by the federal government in 1971 and subsequently by a number of provinces.

The Canadian Multiculturalism Act was passed unanimously by both Houses of Parliament in July 1988. Several provinces have followed suit. These acts promote a society whose institutions are open to the participation of, and contributions from, the cultural and racial diversity of all people. It is a logical extension of the body of anti-discrimination legislation in Canada over the last twenty years. Provinces have in place a wide range of related policies, bodies and legislation which deal with issues related to cultural diversity, race relations, and multiculturalism. Several municipalities, particularly Toronto, have come up with a wide range of policies to promote multiculturalism and healthy race relations.

Multiculturalism recognizes that diversity in race, culture, ethnicity is now, and will be, a fundamental characteristic of Canadian society and of its national character. It confirms that only a positive pluralism will ensure that Canada will gain all possible advantages from this diversity. This means that everyone has a right to their beliefs, private practices and a right to state their beliefs and opinions while granting others the same rights; in cultural matters this means no coercion into a single cultural standard and a co-operative, respectful approach to solving differences among, and between, individuals and the larger community, regardless of group characteristics.   Above all, it means the full participation in all aspects of Canadian society for all Canadians, regardless of culture, ethnic or national origin, religion, race and colour.

The bottom line of multiculturalism is to ensure **full participation and full contribution** by **all** Canadians. In this context it is important to remember that "if the need to feel worthy is a fundamental human requirement, it is satisfied in considerable measure by belonging to groups that are in turn regarded as worthy. Like individual self-esteem, collective self-esteem is achieved largely by social recognition. Everywhere...collective social recognition is conferred by political affirmation. For this reason, struggles over relative group worth are readily transferred to the political system" (Horowitz, as quoted by Cairns, 1989, p. 113).

Much of the criticism of multiculturalism centres on the much less important and rapidly-fading focus on superficial folkloric "culturism" which has virtually disappeared as a policy or government concern. According to Abu-Laban and Stasiulis "a policy of multiculturalism allows for some ideological space to pursue demands for affirmative action, and for more representative and responsive institutions within areas such as education, health care, and policing. Further, it also allows for a more inclusionary definition or discourse about membership in the Canadian political community that grows in importance as Canada becomes more ethnically and racially diverse as a result of immigration through the 21st century" (1992. p. 381). It is to be hoped that any revisions to legislation will focus on the positive nation-building energies which motivate all Canadians, no matter their origin.

11. COMMON GROUND

In all of this it must of course be recognized that any society can only function effectively if there is wide ranging agreement on the common ground which unites its people. Canada's economic, political and legal systems, the role of government, of the justice and education systems, and a uniquely Canadian relationship between citizens and governmental authorities and respect for human dignity and individuality have all been shaped over a long common history and are therefore typically Canadian. Changes can only be made through legal means and in a manner consistent with a liberal democracy. Participation in this society requires acceptance of legal authority, commitment to the work ethic, acceptance of personal freedom and responsibility, as well as the granting of the same rights, privileges, justice and liberties to others. Furthermore,

Canada has deeply ingrained informal practices and rules of behaviour which are essential to the smooth functioning of society and which change slowly and only by broad consensus.

It is clear then, that multiculturalism and acceptance of social diversity do not allow for the creation of myriads of little fiefdoms which grate against each other on the northern part of North America. Multiculturalism is an idea, a policy and a program which assure that the largely personal and private aspects of culture and religion are not limited unnecessarily and unfairly, do not become the basis for restrictions or discrimination, but rather that they become the spice of life, enriching the lives, community and cultural understanding of all Canadians.

Canada's growing diversity is often seen as a challenge to its unity and identity. Diversity, however, has always been an integral part of Canada's identity as a nation. Immigrants always have had to integrate into existing society and accept the core values, norms, and symbols which define Canada. That Canadian national values and national identity are imprecise and subject to debate and change is part of the national character. In the years since confederation, some basic values and expectations have clearly been established. Evolution and change will inevitably occur, but slowly and over time, maintaining a continuity of values and norms—a necessity and a responsibility—if a modern, civic nation is to provide leadership to the community of nations, as it has done in recent decades.

REFERENCES

Abu-Laban, Yasmeen and Daiva Stasiulis. (1992). "Ethnic Pluralism Under Siege: Popular and Partisan Opposition to Multiculturalism". *Canadian Public Policy*. XVIII:4, December.

Belous, Richard S. (1991). *Demographic Currents: Trends and Issues that Face the United States, the United Kingdom and Canada.* British North American Committee, Occasional Paper No.7.

Berry J.W. and Rudolf Kalin. (1993). "Multicultural and Ethnic Attitudes in Canada: An Overview of the 1991 National Survey", *Paper presented to Canadian Psychological Association Annual Meetings*, Montreal.

Cairns, Alan C.. (1989). "Political Science, Ethnicity and the Canadian Constitution" in *Federalism and Political Community: Essays in Honour of Donald Smiley*. David P. Shugarman and Reg Whitaker (eds). Peterborough: Broadview Press.

Environics Canada. (1989). The Focus Canada Survey: Immigration, Multiculturalism and Population Policy, Toronto: Mimeo

Foster Badi G., "Workforce Diversity and Business", *Training and Development Journal*, April.

Foster, Badi G. (1987). "Re-Education for Work in the 21st Century", Keynote address to the *Seventh General Conference of the World Future Society Education Sector*. Cambridge, Ma.

Gee, Ellen M. (1990). "Demographic Change and Intergenerational Relations in Canadian Families: Findings and Social Policy Implications", *Canadian Public Policy*, XVI:2:191-199.

Government of Canada. (1993). *Religion in Canada, 1981-1991*, Ottawa: Heritage Canada

Government of Canada. (1993) *Canadian Diversity: Facts and Figures*, Ottawa: Heritage Canada

Hagey, Janet, Gilles Laroque and Catherine McBride. (1989). *Highlights of Aboriginal Conditions, 1981-2001, Part III*. Ottawa.

Halliday, Bruce. (1993). *Profitable Choices for Everyone: Report of the Standing Committee on Human Rights and the Status of Disabled Persons*. Ottawa House of Commons.

Jain, Harish. (1990). *Employment Equity: Issues and Policies, Part I* Ottawa: Canada Employment and Immigration Advisory Council.

Labour Canada. (1973). *Women in the Labour Force*. Ottawa: Women's Bureau.

Minister of Supply and Services Canada. *1986 Profile of Disabled Persons in Canada*. Ottawa.

Samuel, T.John. (1994). *Quebec Separatism is Dead*. Ottawa: John Samuel & Associates Inc.

Samuel, T. John. (1992). *Visible Minorities in Canada: A Projection*. Toronto: Canadian Advertising Foundation.

Samuel, T. John. (1990). "Social Dimensions of Immigration in Canada", Paper presented at the International Conference on

Race Relations: Policies, Practices and Research in 1990. Toronto: York University.

Statistics Canada. (1999). 1996 Census information on the Internet.

Statistics Canada. (1996). *Projections of Persons with Disabilities at Work, Canada, Provinces and Territories, 1991-2016,* Ottawa.

Statistics Canada. (1994). *Population Projections for Canada, Provinces and Territories, 1991-2016*, Ottawa.

Statistics Canada.(1990). *Women in Canada: A Statistical Report*, Ottawa.

Chapter 2

THE MASS MEDIA IN A DIVERSE SOCIETY

Robert S. Nancoo, Stephen E. Nancoo

INTRODUCTION

The mass media perform a powerful and pervasive role in Canadian society. They help shape the national environment in which we function and they influence the national agenda that determines and shapes our future. The decisions we make are conditioned by the quality of the information we possess and the mass media are the principal source, gatekeepers and disseminators of information.

This chapter will examine the mass media in the diverse Canadian Society. This study will briefly outline the development of the mass media in Canada; place the mass media in the context of the emerging new and diverse Canadian Society and examine the impact of the interaction between the media and the changing, diverse Canadian society. Finally the article will delineate some recent developments and propose a vision for the twenty-first century that seeks to establish a fairer and more equitable relationship between the mass media and Canadian diversity.

The mass media—press, radio and television—are important institutions in Canadian society. They are more than merely conduits of news, information and entertainment. The mass media are institutions in their own right in constant interplay with other structures, institutions and the public creating and re-creating change. Viewed in such a way, the media become a formidable force in modern democratic societies. Indeed, the pivotal role of the media in Canadian life is recognized and enshrined in the *Charter of Rights and Freedom* that proclaims the freedom of the press and other media (Constitution Act 1981, Part I, Schedule B (Charter of Rights and Freedom), 2 (b).

In delineating the reasons for the universal importance of the media, McQuail (1993) advances the following propositions:

> The media are a growing and changing industry providing employment, producing goods and services, and feeding related industries; they also comprise an institution in themselves, developing their own rules and norms that link the institution to society and to other social institutions. The media institution is, in turn, regulated by society.
>
> The mass media are a power resource—a means of control, management and innovation in society, which can be a substitute for force or other resources.
>
> They provide a location (or arena) where, increasingly, the affairs of public life are played out, both nationally and internationally.
>
> They are often the location of developments in culture, both in the sense of art and symbolic forms, but also in manners, fashions, styles of life and norms.
>
> They have become a dominant source of definitions and images of social reality for individuals, but also collectively for groups and societies; they express values and normative judgements inextricably mixed with news and entertainment (p.3).

DEVELOPMENT OF THE MASS MEDIA IN CANADA

In Canada, changes to and growth of the mass media are linked to changes in "economic and social structure and developments in technology" (Singer 1995, p.2). Vipond (1992, p.10) expressed a similar view that the principal factors that led to the rise of the media were "external influence, industrialisation, urbanisation, technological change, and the growth of the working class and increased literacy and leisure." In this section, we would outline the rise of newspapers, radio and television in Canada.

Newspapers

Newspapers were the first influential form of the mass media in Canada. Wilfred Kesterton and Roger Bird (1995, p. 30) classify the development of the newspaper into five convenient, historical periods. During the First Period (1752-1807), the newspapers provided official information, foreign news, government announcements and information and advertisements. The pioneer printer editor also served as King's Printer, the revenue from which supported the continuance of the newspaper.

The Second Press Period, (1807-1858), according to Kesterton and Bird (1995, p. 33) saw a dramatic increase in population, the growth of towns, industries and wealth. With these increases came a dramatic rise in the number of newspapers and communities served by newspapers. They noted that in 1857 a total of 291 papers were published in the provinces then constituting British North America. Vipond (1992, p. 2) observed that at this time "virtually every paper...most issued weekly or bi-weekly was allied with either the Conservative or Reform (Liberal) cause, aiding and abetting the favoured party's stance, and then benefiting from the patronage of government printing or advertising contracts when it won power."

In the Third Press Period (1858-1900), Kesterton and Bird (1995, p. 34) write that "everywhere tiny villages and hamlets sprang up, and almost immediately newspapers appeared to serve these fledgling communities" in the new Pacific settlements, the Prairies and B.C. interior. By the end of 1900, there were 1227 newspapers and periodicals and a population base of 5,592,299.

Accelerating the growth of the economy and consequently newspapers were the installation by mid-century within the country of both railway and telegraph. Popular dailies became increasingly independent and often supported popular, reformist causes. Vipond (1992, p. 13) indicated that "above all, these newspapers featured diversity in their contents, so as to appeal to as much of the heterogeneous population of the modern Canadian city as possible."

In the Fourth Press Period (1900-1952), Kesterton and Bird (1995 pp. 36-37) observed a qualitatively different type of growth and prominence of newspapers arising from "soaring circulation and from the emergence of the newspaper as a giant business enterprise." One of the causal factors of this development is the dramatic increase in population such that the years 1941-51 saw the greatest absolute growth in population for any decade in Canadian history. Indeed, by 1951, Canada's total population grew to 14,009,655, and quite significantly 8,268,253 (61.6%) lived in urban centres where the large newspapers flourished.

With the increase in population and newspapers' circulation there was also an emerging revolution in technology. Newspaper production became more costly because of the expensive equipment needed to serve the increased readership, resulting in a greater concentration of control in the hands of fewer and fewer publishers and owners. "In 1930, 116 dailies were controlled by 99 publishers; by the beginning of the Fifth Press Period in 1953, 89 newspapers were controlled by 57 publishers, with 11 publishers accounting for 42 dailies, or about half the total" (Kesterton and Bird, p. 38).

The offset press, and now satellite and computer technologies have revolutionised newspaper quality and production and have facilitated an even greater concentration of ownership of newspapers. Today, there are now eight newspaper groups: Thomson, Hollinger, Toronto Sun Publishing Corporation, Quebecor, Gesca, Irving, Armadale and the Burgoyne Group. Although, there is greater competition for the advertising dollar, especially from television, this has not prevented news organisations from making healthy profits. There is, however, the expressed misgivings by some media critics over the concentration of ownership and the emerging trend of cross ownership between media corporations and other forms of corporations.

Of some countervailing significance is the tendency in large metropolitan centres to have community newspapers. By 1993, there were some 1150 such newspapers, with 683 of them holding membership in the Canadian Community Newspapers Association and a combined weekly circulation of 5,741,000. What is also of profound significance is that immigrant communities are being served by the **ethnic media**, which appear to flourish in the large metropolitan centres, especially Metropolitan Toronto and Vancouver. These new voices and alternative responses are emerging in the diverse communities. The gathering strength of this assertion of the presence of diversity is a direct and creative responses by new voices to the challenges posed by the perceived sense of undrrepresentation in terms of coverage and hiring by the mainstream news media.

Unlike broadcasting, newspapers in Canada, from their inception to the present time, have enjoyed a great degree of independence from governmental regulation. From the beginning, newspapers were founded and closed, bought and sold by private enterprise. Those newspapers that have prospered and continue to survive have always been owned by the private sector. Of a truth, the history of newspapers in Canada appeared to follow the unquestioned dictum that a free press needs free enterprise.

Radio Broadcasting

Radio broadcasting began shortly after the First World War, around 1920 when the Marconi Company in Montreal launched its experimental station XWA. By 1923, over thirty stations were in operation. Given the size of the country, its small population and its regional dispersion, one can see the attractiveness of radio, which like the railroad was an important link from sea to sea. Not surprisingly therefore is the fact that by 1950 almost all Canadian homes had at least one radio.

In 1932, acting upon the recommendation of the Aird Commission, a Radio Broadcasting Act was passed that created the Canadian Radio Broadcasting Commission. The Act gave the CRBC power to broadcast, and to license and regulate private stations. In his speech to the House of Commons, Prime Minster R.B. Bennett said:

> ... this country must be assured of complete control of broadcasting from Canadian sources, free from foreign interference or influence. Without such control radio broadcasting can never become a great agency for communication of matters of national concern and for the diffusion of national thought and ideals and without such control it can never be an agency by which national consciousness may be fostered and sustained and national unity still further strengthened. (Canada, House of Commons, 1932, 3035).

In 1936, the Canadian Broadcasting Corporation was created by the Canadian Broadcasting Act. The new legislation gave the CBC more autonomy but also ensured a role for the private sector, thereby committing both public and private broadcasters to the goal of national unity.

Between 1936 and 1950, radio coverage increased from 50 per cent of the population to 90 per cent of the population. Both the public and private stations are expected to "safeguard, enrich and strengthen the cultural, political, social and economic fabric of Canada". (Broadcasting Act, 1991, clause I). The Act also specified a special role for CBC "to contribute to the shared national consciousness and identity," "strive to be of equivalent quality in English and in French" and "reflect the multicultural and multiracial nature of Canada." (Broadcasting Act, 1991, Section 3(1) (m).

"The question is the State or the United States?" (Nolan, 1986, p.31). An excellent summation of the nationalist claim for public broadcasting and protection from US programming!

Television

In 1952, the first two CBC television stations, CBFT Montreal and CBLT Toronto began broadcasting. Although, the intention was that the public sector would be the main supplier of TV services, private broadcasters—The CTV, a private English network an Tele Metropole a private French-language network in Montreal, were established. With the advent of cable companies and satellite broadcasting corporations—Time Warner, CNN and other private US corporations CBS, ABC, NBC) the private television stations are in the ascendancy over public broadcasting networks, the CBC and educational television stations.

Today's TV viewer is faced with a plethora of choices in which the defining issue is not merely whether it is public or private broadcasting, but more importantly how little of it is Canadian programming and how many of the programs emanate from the United States of America. We have moved from a public versus private industry into a penetrated TV industry where the production and distribution systems are overwhelmingly American. Even the exhibitions of television programs—the local TV stations—are overwhelmed by the presence of the American networks and pay services.

Advertising

Advertising is the principal source of revenue that supports newspapers, private radio and television. The obsessive need to maximise circulation and audiences to attract advertisers and advertisements often take precedence over the need to communicate or educate the reader on the great issues of the day. Equally important is the view that advertising content has not kept pace with the significant social and cultural transformations occurring within Canadian society especially in relation to women, aboriginals and visible minorities.

"Advertisers can influence content in at least three ways—through the advertising copy itself, by linking advertising copy to other content, and by influencing the gatekeeping decisions of owners and publishers" (McPhail and McPhail, p. 132). It is of some importance therefore that a brief examination should be made of the impact that media advertising exercise in relation to diversity.

Research studies have indicated that women and visible minorities do not fare very well in media advertising. Underrepresentation and stereotyping of women in advertising have frequently been identified as legitimate cause for complaint and concern by media researchers and feminists alike.

Shari Graydon (1995, p. 143) noted that Media Watch have identified the following four problematic trends in media advertising:

> Objectification — equating women with objects is dehumanising and encourages the notion that women can be bought, owned, and disposed of.
> Irrelevant sexualization — using women's bodies in a sexual way in order to attract attention perpetuates the attitude that women's primary function is to serve men sexually.
> Infanticization — presenting women as silly, childish, and coy, or passive and vulnerable, waiting to be rescued (especially in contrast to men, who are generally

portrayed as strong, serious, and assertive) undermines women's need for independence and reinforces the perception of women as victims.

Domestication — defining women always in relationship to their husbands, children, or parents, and showing them predominantly in a home environment, denies the complexity of women's lives and their contributions to society. (These categories represent a condensed version of trends described in Media Watch's *Objective Letter Guide* 1992, p. 4).

Erin Research's 1988 content analysis for the CRTC revealed that: advertising in Canadian TV included fewer female characters than male, fewer women over 35; fewer female voice-overs, a strong tendency to associate women with home and family roles and women were more likely to appear in ads for household consumer goods. Women were less likely to appear in political announcements or automobile ads.

Stereotyping and under-representation also characterised the approach by advertisers vis-à-vis visible minorities. The Canadian Advertising Foundation established a Race Relations Advisory Council in 1990 with a view of promoting "a more proactive involvement and contribution by the advertising council". Even so, it is noticeable that visible minority groups remain largely invisible in Canadian advertising.

Owaisi and Bangesh (1978, p. 21) noted that less than one per cent of ads from TV, newspapers and magazines and catalogues included visible minorities. When they were used, more often than not "the bulk of visible-minority-group representation, blacks as well as Asians, is (in) the role of hungry, needy people receiving hand-outs." Such stereotyping appears to be the dominant feature of visible minority group representation in television commercials.

Although the Canadian population is aging, the elderly are also underrepresented in advertising commercials. Like visible minorities and women, the elderly when they do appear in advertisements are stereotyped by associating them with certain products.

THE PHILOSOPHY OF CANADIAN MASS MEDIA

The significant role and influence of the mass media and communications in Canadian society was cogently articulated in the philosophical and empirical writings of important Canadian thinkers. Harold Innis (1950) and Marshall McLuhan (1960) and more recently Wallace Clement defined the seminal influence of communications in shaping the nature of societies.

Carey (1967) indicates that:

> Innis and McLuhan, alone among students of human society, make the history of media central to the history of civilisation at large. Both see the media not merely as technical appurtenances to society but as crucial determinants of the social fabric. For them, the history of the mass media is not just another avenue of historical research; rather it is another way of writing the history of Western civilisation (p.5).

Innis delineated the interconnectedness between the vitality and durability of countries and the modes of communication that dominated within them. For Innis, communication technology is the prime determinant of institutional, cultural and social change. He "was the first to undertake a macro-level examination of the link between the media and culture. He laid the intellectual foundation for the field and many of his concerns are reflected in Canadian cultural policy debates" (McPhail and McPhail, p. 64).

McLuhan alerted us to the differences between hot and cold media, the notion that the medium is the message and the role of electronic media and communication in the creation of the global village. For McLuhan:

> all media work us over completely. They are so persuasive in their personal, political, economic, aesthetic, psychological, moral, ethical and social consequences that they leave no part of us untouched, unaffected, unaltered. The medium is the message. Any understanding of social and cultural change is impossible without a knowledge of the way media work as environments. (McLuhan, 1967, p. 26).

It is the view of Wallace Clement (1975 p. 325) that "together the economic and media elite are simply two sides of the same upper class" holding between them "two of the key sources of power—economic and ideological—in Canadian society and form the corporate elite".

Clement encourages us to:

examine the way that news is selected, interpreted, and presented, and its potential for affecting our perceptions of reality. Public awareness can motivate the media to present the diversity of opinions and issues so necessary to the effective functioning of liberal democratic societies.(McPhail and McPhail: ibid. p. 71).

Of some significance in relation to our discussion of the mass media and their relationship with the diverse, pluralist society. "Clement argued that if the media are to present a balanced picture of reality the media elite must be separate from other elites and must represent all the major groups in society. Only then can the media provide a pluralistic and detached analysis of other elite activity." (McPhail and McPhail, ibid.)

THE MASS MEDIA AND PUBLIC POLICY

Our review of the development of the mass media and the philosophical and empirical writings of Innis, McLuhan and Clement elucidated the potential of the mass media's critical influence in the national scheme of things. The Special Senate Committee on the Mass Media (The Davey Report), titled *The Uncertain Mirror* (1970, p. 11), acknowledged the important contribution of the media in helping Canadians "define who and what we are." As such, there have been royal commissions, committees and tasks forces to examine and formulate media and communication policy within the framework of national identity, unity and the promotion of a distinctive national culture.

The Davey report (1970, p. 6) expressed concern that "control of the media is passing into fewer and fewer hands" and the logical "outcome of this process is that one man or corporation could own every media outlet in the country except the CBC. The committee believes that at some point before this hypothetical extreme is reached, a line must be drawn." The report noted that the print media were "becoming increasingly concentrated in the hands of a smaller and smaller privileged group of businessmen".

The Canadian Government's interest in the role of the printed media could be traced to the Massey's Commission and gained impetus with the publication of the Davey report. But it was the closure of the *Ottawa Journal* and the *Winnipeg Tribune* coupled with the sales between Thomson and Southam that left Southam as the sole owner of the only English language daily in Montreal and Ottawa and the two dailies in Vancouver and Thomson the owner of the only daily in Winnipeg that led to the creation of the Kent commission.

The Kent report expressed grave concerns with the ownership concentration trend that would lead to a diminishing of journalistic diversity, and the real fear that the journalistic process was being sacrificed on the altar of the corporate hierarchy of values in terms of business cost. Further the exercise of power was "subject to the indifference or to the whim of a few individuals, whether hidden or not in faceless corporations." (Royal Commission on Newspapers, *Report,* p. 89).
The Commission's Report admonished:

> Freedom of the press is not a property right of owners. It is a right of the people. It is part of their right to free expression, inseparable from their right to inform themselves. The commission believes that the key problem is the limitation of these rights by undue concentration of ownership and control of the Canadian daily newspaper industry (p. 1).

Recent acquisitions of Southam by Conrad Black's Hollinger and concern over the threat of the demise of the news agency Canadian Press (CP) in 1996 reawakened the concern over the concentration of ownership. Dalton Camp (*Toronto Star*, September 29, 1996, p. B3) observed that at last count Black owned "58 of Canada's 104 daily newspapers. He also owns *Saturday Night* magazine. He is on track to own more. The way things are going, Canadian journalism—the print end of it, at least—could well become the private fief of one man."

Notwithstanding Camp's stand and the Council of Canadians challenge to Hollinger's takeover of Southam, the temper of the times suggests that complaints about newspaper concentration have become more muffled and do not resonate among working journalists and other critics with the same righteous indignation as was the case a couple decades or more ago.

In the newspaper field, both the Senate Special Committee on the Mass Media (1970) and the Royal Commission on Newspapers (1981) commented on how the trends towards conglomerates adversely affect the quality and diversity of news. It is in the broadcasting field, however, that the most strident approach has been taken. This vigilant stand is assumed because broadcasting is viewed as "not just an element or section of culture" but as "the most powerful manifestation or mirror of culture... It has become the national performance stage, and the national forum of information and debate (Juneau, 1986, p.4).

The three recurring, interconnected themes of nationalism, economics, and technology are the leading factors in the development of broadcasting in Canada.

In 1929, the Royal Commission on Radio Broadcasting, the Aird Commission made recommendations on how radio may best and most effectively serve the national interest. The Special Committees on Broadcasting in 1932 and 1935 examined the private-public sector roles in terms of developing nationality.

The then emerging field of television, the powerful medium that combines the dual qualities of radio and video led to the creation of the Royal Commission on National Development in the Arts, Letters and Sciences (Massey Commission, 1951) which was mandated to review how television can be developed nationally. The Royal Commission on Broadcasting (the Fowler Commission, 1957) asserted that "as a nation, we cannot accept, in these powerful and pervasive media, the natural and complete flow of another nation's culture without danger to our national identity (Canada, Royal Commission on Broadcasting 1957, p. 8).

More recently, the Task Force on Broadcasting Policy (The Caplan-Sauvageau Task Force) followed the same tendencies of previous reports by postulating that the Canadian broadcasting system "should offer, so far as possible, a truly Canadian service for those millions of Canadians who have demonstrated their belief in one" (Canada, Task Force 1986, p. 21). In assessing the role of broadcasting, the Task Force emphasised the need to "safeguard, enrich and strengthen the cultural, political, social and economic fabric of Canada" (p.152).

Two particular concerns, within the general context of broadcasting and the imperatives of national unity and identity, are the issues of addressing the distinct needs of Quebec and francophones and that of the people of the North. Ever since the Aird Commission the province of Quebec exercised its provincial rights under education and culture to have a protective eye in the field of broadcasting.

The Task Force on Broadcasting Policy (1988) made recommendations to give the North and its peoples greater participation and access in radio and television broadcasting. Further the Standing Committee on Communications and Culture argued:

> Our recommendations are designed to place aboriginal broadcasting, especially native-language broadcasting, on a firm foundation that will enable it to continue to flourish in Canada's north and expand to meet the needs of the native populations elsewhere in Canada (Standing Committee 1988, p. 275).

In terms of programming, the 1991 Broadcast Act requires the broadcasting system to "provide a reasonable opportunity for the public to be exposed to the expression of differing views on matters of public concern" (Statutes of Canada 1991, Ch. 11, Section 3(i).

The Broadcasting Act provides a framework for the broadcasting system to exercise its social responsibility. For example, Section 3(1)(d)(iii) provides for "the development of Canadian expression by providing a wide range of programming that reflects Canadian attitudes, opinions, ideas, values and artistic creativity." National unity and identity considerations are provided for in the urging to ensure the safeguarding, enriching, and strengthening of the cultural, political, social, and economic fabric of Canada, Section 3 (1) (d) (ii). There can be no mistaking of the Act's intentions in relation to diversity as Section 3(1) (d) (iii) also provides for "the needs and interests, and reflecting the circumstances and aspirations of Canadian men, women and children, including equal rights, the linguistic duality and multicultural nature of Canadian society and the special place of aboriginal peoples within that society."

In the Broadcast Act (1991), the government calls for programming at the CBC which would reflect the multicultural and multiracial nature of Canada (Section 3(m) viii. To reinforce the global nature of this direction, the Act also indicated that the programming by alternative television services should reflect Canada's regions and multicultural nature (Section 3(r) (iii).

Of private broadcasters, it was noted that where the Commission considers it appropriate, they will originate programming, including local programming and in particular provide access for underserved linguistic and cultural minority communities (Section 3(t) iv).

The Act also made provision for the needs of Aboriginal communities viz: "Programming that reflects the aboriginal cultures of Canada should be provided within the Canadian broadcasting system as resources become available for the purpose" (Section 3(o).

The CRTC has promulgated regulations that prohibit the broadcast of "any abusive comment... that, when taken in context, tends or is likely to expose an individual or a group or class of individuals to hatred or contempt on the basis of race, national or ethnic origin, colour, religion, sexual orientation, age or mental and physical disability." (CRTC, *Television Broadcasting Regulations* 1987 as amended in 1991, 5(b); and CRTC *Radio Regulations* 1986 3(b), as amended in 1991).

Many of the goals enshrined in the Broadcasting Acts and accompanying regulations have not been realized. Inspite of this, the succeeding Acts and the numerous studies that have been made in the area do point to a set of enduring values that should guide broadcasting in the future. Thus a common theme in all examination of broadcasting policy is the persistence of the notion of broadcasting as an instrument of national unity and national identity, both important issues to all members of the diverse Canadian society.

THE MASS MEDIA AND DIVERSITY

In the preceding sections, the outline of the rise and development of the Canadian mass media viewed geography and demographics as two powerful factors that shaped Canadian communications and the media systems. These two factors continue to persist and exert powerful influences in the media today. The most powerful demographic factor is the changing face of Canadian society, especially in the large metropolitan cities of Toronto, Montreal and Vancouver where we see people of every creed, race and linguistic group making our societies even more diverse and multicultural.

Canadian society is changing: in terms of values, priorities and self image; in terms of demographic reality, i.e. composition of the labour force, age profile, cultural and ethnic diversity; in terms of gender roles and family priorities; in terms of demands on government for meeting human needs, protecting rights and serving the community. Some of these changes have in fact already transformed Canadian society, and all within barely one generation. In other words, diversity is the new law of life and living in Canadian society.

Diversity is not something new. Indeed, much of our sociological and historical analyses are premised on the description of Canada as a mosaic as compared to notions of the melting pot evolution of society which has traditionally been associated with the United States. According to the historical version of the melting pot theory it was suggested that immigrants to the United States would ultimately lose their identity, culture and language and adopt the prevailing, dominant culture, customs and language of the United States. The historical reality is that there is in the United States a high degree of cultural persistence to the extent described by Wilson and Gutterez (1985) as a huge salad, in which each group retains its individual characteristics and identities while interacting with other groups to form the whole nation.

In Canada, the official policy of **multiculturalism** is a perceptive response to the current and historical reality of our **mosaic character**. There is agreement with the hypothesis that future demographic changes will continue to define Canada as a diverse, multi-cultural, multi-racial, multi-religious and pluralistic society.

In recognition of Canada's diversity, the social changes which have occurred over the past 25 to 30 years have now also become reflected in legislation such as the Canadian Charter of Rights and Freedoms or Canada's assorted federal and provincial or territorial human rights acts.

Notwithstanding the changing face of Canada or the well intentioned legislation that legitimises multi-culturalism and diversity, the rhetoric of social justice for the diverse groups that constitute Canada is a far cry from the reality of daily practice. Indeed recent research makes a telling commentary of the great distance and divide between the goals of media organisations on the one hand and the aspirations of our diverse communities, especially aboriginal and visible minorities on the other. (Nancoo and Nancoo, 1996).

The first major problem that critics of the media repeatedly identify is the underrepresentation of minorities both in terms of content as well as employed personnel in newspapers, radio and television. Segments of our diverse population, visible minorities and aboriginal are underrepresented and unreported by the mass media, except in cases of conflict and crime and the sports pages. It is hard to justify this exclusion from mainstream media since the ethnic media outlets in the major metropolitan centres are filled with a multiplicity of news stories about visible minorities in a variety of areas of human activity.

In advertising, there are few visible minorities in the press, radio and TV. Based on this thirty-year longitudinal study, Robert MacGregor (1997) shows how visible minority women are underrepresented in Canadian print advertising. He further points out that the roles played by visible minority women continued to be narrowly and stereotypically defined, with minimal change over the thirty year period. MacGregor notes that to the extent that viewers and readers of advertisements have their beliefs, attitudes and behaviours possibly affected by what they perceive in the media, relations between the races and sexes may be affected by advertising's limited and often stereotyped portrayals of visible minorities. Similarly, Doreen Indra (1997) demonstrates how South Asian women have been excluded in the Vancouver press.

The report of the House of Commons Special Committee on Visible Minorities in Canadian Society *Equality Now!* indicate that a survey of English-language broadcasting disclosed that visible minorities represented 9 percent of the characters in dramas, 2 percent of news anchors, 4 percent of reporters, 5 percent of guests on news features, and 6 percent of music and variety show participants. In its 1993 study, the Canadian Daily Newspapers Association revealed that of those responding to their survey, only 2.6 percent of newsroom staff were visible minorities. While there are indications that there are marginal improvements to these figures, underrepresentation of visible minorities is still an inequitable and unjust fact of life in the mass media.

Generations Research (1988) reported that 74 per cent of major prime time TV characters were "North American White" and that "the large majority (who weren't white) were Black American found primarily in the U.S."; and that Canadian television news focuses on negative or specifically cultural images accenting differences and excluding visible minorities from more than general coverage (Jiwani, 1988). As a minority group, for example, South Asians (at times referred to as East Indians) are rarely if ever seen in mainstream television advertising and programming. Given their growing numbers and their purchasing power, greater representation of this group as well as other visible minority groups makes good advertising and business sense.

In an empirical study of "Visible Minorities and Native Canadians in National Television News Programs" Perrigoe and Lazar (1992, p. 271) concluded that "the involvement of non-white Canadians in routine news stories continues to be significantly less than their current representation in Canadian demographics."

Fleras (1992) offered the explanation that "a further problem is the absence of racial minorities in creative positions (such as those of director, producer, editor or screenwriter). Fewer still are employed in the upper levels of management where key decision-making occurs. The experiences of racial minorities are thus distorted or attenuated" (p. 412).

In a study of billboard advertising in Montreal, Niemi and Salgado (1989) found visible minorities featured in only one billboard from a total display of 163. They concluded that such under-representation of minorities tend to "deny their existence, devalue their contribution to society, and trivialise their aspirations to participate, as fully-fledged members" (pp. 28-29).

This marginalisation is not restricted to visible minorities. For example, Fletcher, Marino and Everett, in "News Coverage of

Disabilities and Disabled Persons in the Canadian Media," a study presented to the House of Commons Standing Committee on the Status of Disabled persons, (Ottawa, April 1988) found that the media content relating to persons with disabilities was "sporadic, limited and distorted." Other studies on the natives, the young and old are quite similar as noted by Eileen Sanders (1991, p.273). "Such exclusion argued Niemi and Salgado (1989, p.21) create "feelings of rejection, of marginality, and of non-belonging".

Through the eyes of the media, aboriginals and visible minorities are often regarded as a "social problem". This means that the marginalised groups are portrayed as either people who have problems or create problems for "mainstream society". Fleras (1995) observes that

> First Nations are portrayed as a threat to Canada's territorial integrity (the Lubicon blockade in 1988) or national interests (the Innu protest of NATO presence in Labrador); a risk to Canada's social order (the Oka crisis); costly (over \$5 billion in federal expenditures); an economic liability (the massive land claims in the North); a crisis for the criminal-justice system (disproportionate numbers incarcerated); and a medical concern (suicides and rehabilitation) (p. 414).

In her excellent article on *Rights and Warriors: First Nations, Media and Identity*, Gail Guthrie Valaskakis (1997) observes that in the heat of the moment and the aftermath of Oka many questions were raised about the role, nature, and function of the media in a democratic society. She makes the critical observation that writing in the media has not followed the lead of current literary, artistic and ethnographic critique to include the meaning and role of representation and cultural appropriation.

Haroon Siddiqui (1993, p.D-1) pointed out that visible minorities are portrayed in the media as a "dazzling array of trouble spots:... stumping immigration authorities, cheating on welfare, or battling among themselves or with their families." It is not made known whether dysfunctional behaviour is more or less than what prevails in mainstream communities and Siddiqui observed that not much space is devoted to the broad range of interests and activities of visible minorities outside their ethnic group.

Stereotypical images of disadvantaged groups are not uncommon. Fleras (1995, p.416) observed that both in the St. Regis-Akwesasne Reserve which involved conflict between pro and anti-gambling factions there were examples of the media portrayals in terms of "age-old stereotypes... dusted off and circulated for the benefit of audiences who were fascinated and horrified by the vision of Mohawk against Mohawk."

The net result of this unbalanced negativism is, as *Report on Equality Now* (1984) indicated that "alternating between denying or exaggerating their presence, the media create a strong psychological barrier between visible minorities and the rest of Canadian society." They are, to quote another observer, "described in the context of having problems in need of solutions that expend an inordinate amount of political attention or a disproportionate slice of national resources."

Fleras (1995, p.417) attributes the negative media minority relations to issues of "institutional resistance and media logic" and "the dynamics of discrimination." The argument has also been advanced that many studies on the media and the diverse society "have been equally negligent in ignoring the media as institutions with distinctive agendas and organisational priorities. Refusal to insert a "media dimension" into this research can only lead to further delays in securing a multicultural balance between media goals and minority aspirations" Fleras (1994, p.268).

This comment invites two questions? Should the media be pushed by researchers or pressure groups in exercising sound, critical judgement in performing their mandate and responsibilities in terms of their traditional and time-honoured role and functions? Or should they of their own volition come to an ethical and professional recognition of the inherent flaws in the performance of their responsibilities?

While the media unfailingly uphold the libertarian principle to ensure their freedom, much of the public policy debate have unambiguously informed and reminded the media of their inescapable social responsibilities. Secondly, how does the historical development of the media in practice, the issues that the media have traditionally confronted, the thinking of our media theorists and the public policy outputs of task forces and commissions inform and illuminate the media relations with the diverse Canadian society, especially the disadvantaged groups within the mosaic?

Researchers have often pointed to the fact that the media have been viewed traditionally as a pivotal player in the debate on national unity and the creation of a distinctive national identify. On both fronts it will be an intellectual failing of the mainstream media not to recognise the changing nature of Canadian society and the necessity for the media to be more inclusive of all groups that are strenuously striving to be an integral part of the national mosaic. Far too often the mainstream media appear to be more interested in maintaining the "status quo" and consequently "other voices often go unheard" and newcomers tend to be "consigned to the margins of media content" (Fletcher, 1995, p.242).

As part of its social responsibility and in pursuit of the public interest, the mass media of their own volition need to insert those self-correcting mechanisms in their institutional structures and to reorder their priorities to mirror the presence of all the constituent parts that form the national community. After all, it is the media that take pride in their self-description as "the fourth estate" and as the "watchdog" over the "public interest". Nothing less should be expected of organizations which continuously and aggressively seek to set and interpret the national agenda.

Recent Developments

To their credit, the mass media have made some progress in addressing the issues of diversity.

Employment equity hiring is one of the criteria the CRTC employs in the renewal of licences. And both the Multiculturalism Act and Employment Equity Act expect federally regulated agencies like CBC radio and television to make progress towards minority employment.

Eighteen per cent of the editorial positions at CBC are held by visible minorities. CBC has an internship program for women, aboriginals and visible minorities. At City TV, about 30 per cent of the employees are visible minorities. The CTV has a five year plan which it hopes will increase its visible minority representation. CTV also has an internship program.

The Broadcasting Act of 1991 has promoted the idea of giving greater expression to programs concerning visible minorities. The Canadian Radio-Television and Telecommunications Commission (CRTC) strongly advised both the Canadian Broadcasting Corporation and the Canadian Television Network to "recognize the changing demographic reality of Canada and the concerns of ethnic minorities (in its) mainstream programming..." (Decision 87-200, 1866, p.26). The networks were asked to:

> balance the representation of multicultural minorities in the mainstream programming of both the English and French television networks, in a manner that reflects realistically their participation in Canadian society, and so as to eliminate negative stereotypes. (Decision 87-140, 1987, p.55).

The responses of both the CBC and CTV supported greater involvement of individuals from various ethnic groups in their programming. The CTV (1986, p.280) told the Commission that:

> CTV supports the principle of the development of Canadian broadcasting services which are designed to reflect the cultural and linguistic plurality of Canada and recognises that these factors are an essential part of the social structure of the nation.

The *CBC* (1986, p.107), in its response to the CRTC said: "The CBC's commitment to multiculturalism is pervasive" and in a brief, significantly titled *A Broadcasting Policy Reflecting Canada's Linguistic and Cultural Diversity* to the CRTC stated:

> The CBC... continues to affirm and reflect in its programs the multicultural riches and multi-racial characteristics of Canadian society in keeping with the Corporation's obligation to "contribute to the development of a national unity and provide for a continuing expression of Canadian society". Schedule planners and program staff are expected to demonstrate continuing awareness of, and sensitivity to, this aspect of the CBC role. (CBC, 1985, p.533).

As well the Canadian Association of Broadcasters (1988) noted that its members have a critical role to play in depicting the changing cultural face of the country:

> Within their portrayal of ethnic minorities in information and entertainment programming, radio and television stations can affect the attitudes of mainstream society towards these groups. At the same time, the manner in which particular ethnic group is portrayed can be a significant factor in developing the self perception of ethnocultural groups as they integrate into society (p. 7).

In terms of television broadcasting, *City-TV* in Toronto and *Vision TV* have been blazing new trails in the area of diversity issues. Both in terms of programming and hiring of minorities, one can find the many dimensions of the Canadian mosaic represented. In Toronto, *CFMT* also does a significant degree of diversity programming. Many ethnic groups also buy time and take to the TV screens on weekends with an explosion of entertainment and news programs that serve the needs of the diverse groups that make-up Canadian society. In Toronto, *CHIN* and *CHUM* radio stations play an important role in the airing of programs sponsored by different ethnic groups.

Newspapers like the *Toronto Star* and *Montreal Gazette* have increasingly featured stories about the diverse communities. Furthermore, alternative responses are observed in the newspaper field where the ethnic press give expression to the divergent views and news of minority communities. Statistics Canada data show 131 minority newspapers being published in the year 1989. One of the first ethnic group to have established itself with a number of ethnic newspapers is the Chinese. There are three Chinese language dailies that publish in Vancouver and Toronto. *Maclean's* recognized the potential of this market through its publication of a Chinese edition. The *Vancouver Sun* has taken a step forward in reprinting in English letters to the *Ming Pao Daily News*, a Vancouver based Chinese newspaper. The vigorous role the ethnic press play is evidenced by the fact, for example, that although Canadians tracing their origin to the Caribbean are numerically small, in the metro-Toronto area there are at least six ethnic newspapers competing for the attention of members from the Caribbean community. This type of competition in the ethnic press is also observed among other ethnic groups from other geographical areas.

The aboriginal groups have made some strides in their control of the media. TV North Canada, Northern Natives Broadcasting Access Programs and Watawau are examples of broadcasting systems controlled by our native populations. There are also aboriginal newspapers that are meeting the needs of native communities.

Minore and Hill (1997) documents how the Northern Native Broadcast Access Program (NNBAP) facilitates the production of regional radio and television shows by Native communication societies in northern areas of seven provinces and the territories. Of special significance is the operation of the Wawatay Communications Society, set up by the Nishnawbe-Aski Nation, which has helped in establishing community radio stations.

Quite significantly, another landmark event was the approval by the CRTC of the Aboriginal Peoples Television Network (APTN), which opened its primary production centre in Manitoba in 1999. The creation of APTN will provide an aboriginal focus on events, culture, news and views not only for Aboriginal peoples but for the non-Aboriginal majority as well. APTN can help to shape the attitudes of the public by providing interpretations of history and "facts" through Aboriginal lenses. (See Chapter 3, in this Volume.)

The comments by Perrigoe and Lazar (1992) about the mainstream mass media nevertheless still hold true. They argue that the:

> mass media can play a pivotal role in helping to enlighten both official and public awareness about the nature of historical grievances and about the character, culture, and aims of native peoples. The enormous potential for the mass media to be a front-runner in the forging of amity, tolerance and understanding between Native Peoples and other social groups in Canada should be fairly self evident... However, the mass media coverage of native peoples have probably operated more as a steadfast

obstacle to, rather than a significant purveyor of mutual
cultural acceptance and co-operation (p.273).

The report card shows that the mass media are slow
learners in the lessons of mainstreaming the new diversity. This is
the unfortunate conclusion notwithstanding the historical evidence
of the role of the media in the development of the country and the
national necessity and moral imperative to adequately reflect the
heterogeneous community. At a time of downsizing in news
organizations, scarce resources, global and technological
competition, the challenge of ensuring some semblance of balance
to the multi-faceted, media-minority-diversity issues becomes even
more challenging. The dream of a society where the full gamut of
the diverse potentialities of all will be represented remains
eminently worthy of the best efforts of all; especially, we need the
best and committed efforts of those who currently own, control,
exercise power over, work for and represent the mainstream, mass
media.

The Future

It is difficult to predict the future, especially when
demographics, technology, ideas about the media and their
relationship with the diverse communities, and Canadian society
change so rapidly. However, on the basis of "what has been" and
what is currently happening, we are able to create a vision of what
is desirable in the 21st century. Certainly we are able to propose
what the preferred state of the future should look like.

We have outlined "what is currently happening" in the
media and in the diverse Canadian society. Today, the modern
Canadian society is very different from the "modern city" during
the early development of the media in the late nineteenth and first
half of the twentieth century. In the 21st century, predictions are
that the nature and rate of changes in the modern Canadian city are
likely to be even greater. Indeed, modern Canadian cities like
Toronto, Vancouver and Montreal are becoming increasingly a
microcosmic reflection of the rainbow-type quality and
heterogeneous diversity of the global village. The portrait of the
new diversity reveals significant dimensions in terms of age,

education, gender, culture, ethnicity, race, the physically challenged and values.

The consensus of the research findings (Nancoo, 1996) is that as of today, the mainstream Canadian mass media do not accurately reflect or represent this new diversity either in terms of content or personnel.

For those interested in the field of mass media and their inter-play with diversity, as well as those committed to issues of social justice and enhancing diversity, we need to undertake more research as well as to incorporate in our agenda a program of action. In terms of the preferred and desirable future, there is still much to be done in the areas of curriculum development, and social activism that ensures a more positive relationship and representation of the diverse Canadian communities.

In regard to curriculum development, the new diversity that characterises so much of Canadian society sends a powerful message to communications, journalism and media educators in our universities and colleges. If we are to accept the projections that diversity will become even more pervasive, then programs in communications, the media and journalism should initiate courses or integrate content into their existing courses that give recognition to this "new diversity" and its significance for the media and Canadian society.

On the issue of research, much of the literature on the media and diversity are largely American. Research rooted in the experience of the challenges and responses in Canadian society and institutions need to be explored.

The notion of the global village arose from the genius of the Canadian imagination through the writings of McLuhan. With globalization, the competition of market forces are such that Canada and its communication industries would only be able to ignore diversity at their own peril.

The many trips by Canada's Prime Minister Jean Chretien to China, India and other Asian nations underlines the pivotal role of commerce and international trade to Canada. It also provides the mass media with compelling lessons to assess their relationships, especially in terms of their representation of the diverse communities. Such a move is good for journalism and the media as well as publishers and owners. Embracing diversity makes good business sense for all.

The technological revolution is moving apace. It is suggested that 75 per cent of the future work force will be involved in information related jobs. Within this framework a new underclass would be created. National unity and a common identity become more difficult to forge when there are deep chasms between groups of people in a multiplicity of areas. As a consequence, the new technologies should be used to build bridges and a sense of common understanding in the forging of a coherent identity and shaping of a stronger community.

We are in the information age. For example, The School of Journalism at the University of Western Ontario recently merged with the university's departments in library information and computers. The post-mass media era, witnesses an influx of the technological tools of cyberspace, such as personal computers, telephone and fax modem. Cyberspace is where the personal communications, images, sounds and news meet via the computer. The internet in terms of capacity and population has revolutionised communications nationally and internationally.

The Globe and Mail is printed in many locations across Canada, employing satellite transmission of finished pages to remote printing plants. The Globe's four page FAX summary is available to anyone anywhere in the world through a fax machine. Daily newspapers now provide public telephone information services in a growing number of areas such as sports scores, weather, road conditions etc. The Ottawa Citizen accepts letters through e-mail. A number of other national and international newspapers are also on the internet.

In Canada cable TV systems are now operating. News services such as Cable News Network (CNN), Headline News and CBC Newsworld and CTV function around the clock. CPAC reports live news events without editing. On a recent visit to Trinidad one of the writers of this article had no problem in looking at the United States television stations for most of the day. The programs were the same US television programming one finds in the Metropolitan Toronto area.

The advances in technology have occasioned a number of media related developments. The new technology spawned a diminishing of the boundaries between print, radio, television and telecommunications. The new technology makes it easier for the transnational media-giants to operate, consequently diminishing notions of cultural sovereignty and to some extent diversity itself.

The new technology that have fostered the growth of media giants also resulted in organisations which are vertically integrated across production lines and horizontally between different types of media and different types of business. These developments do not spell the demise of traditional mass media, which will continue to exist. They, however, do call for a greater degree of responsibility in order to respond effectively to the new challenges spawned by what has been variably described as the new media or the post mass media milieu. In this context, McQuail (1994) proposes that the reworking of the media will need to be framed by a new public interest vocabulary gathered around such matters as freedom, diversity, information quality, social order and solidarity and cultural order.

On the question of diversity, McQuail (1994, p.247) suggests that, when applied to media systems and content, the main elements are that: Media should reflect in their structure and content the various social, economic and cultural realities of the societies (and communities) in which they operate in a more or less proportional way.

- Media should offer more or less equal chances of access to the voices of the various social and cultural minorities which make up a society.
- Media should serve as a forum for different interests and points of view in a society or community.
- Media should offer relevant choices of content at one point in time and also variety over time of kind which corresponds to the needs and interests of their audience.

McQuail notes that diversity also lead to certain results such effecting social change by giving access to new voices, provide a check against misuse of freedom because of ownership concentration, promoting understanding between groups and thereby limiting social conflicts and adding richness and variety to cultural and social life.

Indications are that the new technologies and new forms of media will only widen the inequalities and discrepancies that are currently so prevalent. It is of the utmost importance, therefore, that our mainstream mass media organisations strive towards creating a corporate culture that embraces diversity. This means that mass media organizations must recognise diversity through their commitment to an inclusive culture that respect and give meaning to the demographic realities of Canadian society by initiating tangible steps in the area of adequate representation in hiring and fair portrayal through balanced coverage of diversity groups and issues. In this way, and in the public interest, the mainstream mass media will work towards nurturing and strengthening the diverse mosaic that is Canada.

REFERENCES

Camp, D. (1996). *Toronto Star*, September 29, p. B3.

Canada. House of Commons. Standing Committee on Communications and Culture. (1988). A broadcasting policy for Canada. Ottawa: Supply and Services.

Canada. House of Commons Special Committee on Visible Minorities in Canadian Society. (1984). *Equality Now.* Ottawa: Queen's Printer.

Canada. Task Force on Broadcasting Policy. (1986). *Report* Ottawa: Supply and Services.

Canada (1981). Royal Commission on Newspapers (Kent Report). Ottawa: Supply and Services.

Canada 1981 Constitution Act, Charter of Rights and Freedom.

Canada. Special Committee on the Mass Media. (1970). *Report.* Vol. 1. *The Uncertain mirror*. Ottawa: Queen's Printer.

Canada. Royal Commission on Broadcasting. (1957). *Report.* Ottawa: Queen's Printer.

Canada Royal Commission on Radio Broadcasting. (1929). Ottawa: Edmund Cloutier.

Canada. (1932). The Special Committee on Radio Broadcasting. Canada. Royal Commission on National Development in the Arts, Letters and Sciences (Massey Report). (1951). *Report*. Ottawa: Queen's Printer.

Canada. *Canadian Broadcasting Act*, (1936). Ottawa: King's Printer.

---*Broadcasting Act*, (1958). Ottawa: Queen's Printer.

---*Broadcasting Act*, (1968). Ottawa: Supply and Services.

--- *Broadcasting Act* (1991) .

Canadian Association of Broadcasters (CAB) (1988) *A Broadcaster's Guide to Canada's Cultural Mosaic* Programming Opportunities and Community Relations, May, Ottawa.

Canadian Radio Television and Telecommunications Commission (CRTC) 1987a. Decision 87-200.

---(1987b). Decision 87-140.

---(1986a). Multicultural Broadcasting in Canada. Presentation by Frank Spiller Associates for the CRTC, Ottawa, Ontario.

---(1986b). Brief by National Capital Alliance of Race Relations. Quoted in CRTC Decision 87-299 regarding CTV licence renewal, June 30.

CBC (1986). License Application, June.

---(1985).Submission to CRTC Proposal for an Ethnic Broadasting Policy for Canada. Ottawa, Ontario. Section 2(I) 30.

Carey, J.W. (1967). Harold Adams Innis and Marshall McLuhan. *Antioch Review* 27:5-39.

Clement, W. (1975). *The Canadian corporate elite: An analysis of economic power*. Toronto: McClelland and Stewart.

Constitution Act (1981) Part 1 Schedule B, (Charter of Rights and Freedoms), 2(b).

CTV (1986). License Renewal Application. June 30.

Erin's Research (1988).

Everett, Robert and Frederick J. Fletcher (1995). "The Mass Media and Political Communication in Canada" in *Communications in Canadian Society* Toronto: Nelson.

Fleras, A. (1995). "Please Adjust Your Set": Media and Minorities in a Multicultural Society" in Singer (ed.). *Communications in Canadian Society.* Toronto: Nelson.

Fleras, A. (1994). "Media and Minorities in a Post-Multicultural Society: Overview and Appraisal" in J. W. Berry and J.A. Laponce (ed) *Ethnicity and Culture in Canada*, Toronto: University of Toronto Press.

Fletcher, Marino and Everett. (1988). "News Coverage of Disabilities and Disabled Persons in the Canadian Media" Ottawa: House of Commons Standing Committee on the State of Disabled Persons

Generations Research Inc. (1988). *The Portrayal of Canadian Cultural Diversity on Canadian Network Television*. Secretary of State. Ottawa.

Gernier, Marc. "The Centrality of Conflict in Native Peoples Coverage by the Montreal Gazette: War zoning the Oka Incident " in *Critical Studies of Canadian Mass Media.*

Grantzberg, G. (1987). Report on the Portrayal of Visible Minorities by Manitoba Television" Manitoba Intercultural Council, January.

Graydon, Shari (1995). "The Portrayal of Women in Media: The Good, the Bad, and the Beautiful" in Benjamin Singer (ed.), (ed.), *Communications in Canadian Society.* Toronto: Nelson.

Hackett, R. A. (1989). Coups , earthquakes and hostages? Foreign News on Canadian television" *Canadian Journal of Political Science*, 22(4) December :809-25.

Indra, D. (1996) "The Invisible Mosaic: Women, Ethnicity, and the Vancouver Press," in *The Mass Media and Canadian Diversity*, Chapter 5. Mississauga: Canadian Educators' Press.

Innis, H.A. (1972). *Empire and communications.* Toronto: University of Toronto Press.

---(1964). *The bias of communications.* Toronto: University of Toronto Press.

---1956 *Essays in Canadian economic history.* Toronto: University of Toronto Press.

Jain, H. (1992). "Employment Equity and Visible Minorities: Have the Federal Policies Worked?" Canadian Labour Law Journal, Vol. 1, p.388.

Jiwani, Y. (1988) "The Mediation of Inequality: VisibleMinorities in Canadian News Media." Unpublished. Simon Fraser University.

Juneau, P. (1986). Address to the annual conference of the International Institute of Communications. 11 September. Edinburgh, Scotland.

Kesterton, Wilfred and Bird, Roger. (1995). "The Press in Canada: A Historical Overview" in *Communications in Canadian Society.* Toronto: Nelson.

Lorimer, Rowland and Jean McNulty. (1987). *Mass Communications in Canada* Toronto: McClelland and Stewart.

MacGregor, R. "The Distorted Mirror: Images of Visible Minority Women in Canadian Print Advertising" Chapter 4 *The*

Mass Media and Canadian Diversity. Mississauga: Canadian Educators' Press.

McLuhan, M. (1962). *The Gutenberg Galaxy*. Toronto; Universityof Toronto.

---(1964). *Understanding the media The extensions of man*. New York: McGraw Hill.

---(1967). *Understanding the media*. New York: McGraw Hill.

McPhail, Thomas L. and McPhail, Brenda M. (1990). *Communication: The Canadian Experience*, Toronto: Copp Clark Pitman Ltd.

McQuail, Dennis. (1993). *Mass communication theory*. 2nd ed. Beverly Hills: Sage Publication.

McQuail, D. "Mass Communication and the Public Interest: Towards Social theory for Media Structure and Performance" in David Crowley and David Mitchell (eds.) *Communication Theory Today*. Stanford: Stanford University Press, p. 236-253.

Minore, J. B. and Hill, M. E. (1997) Native Language Broadcasting An Experiment in Empowerment. In. *The Mass Media and Canadian Diversity*. Mississauga: Canadian Educators' Press.

Nancoo, S. E. and Nancoo, R.S. (1996). *The Mass Media and Canadian Diversity*. Mississauga: Canadian Educators' Press.

Nancoo, S. E. and Chacko, J. (1993). *Community Policing in Canada*. Toronto: Canadian Scholars Press.

Nancoo, S. E. (1978). The mass media and electoral campaigns. *The Indian Journal of Political Studies*. Vol. 2. No. 2. July 1978.

Niemi, Fo and Salgado, Mario. "Minorities in Billboard Advertisements in Montreal's Subway Stations" *Currents* 5, no.3 (1989): 27-28

Nolan, M. (1986). *Alan Plaunt and the Early days of the CBC Radio*. Toronto: CBC Enterprises.

Owaisi, L. and Bangesh, Z. (1978). "Visible Minorities in Mass Media Advertising" *Report* to the Executive of Canadian Consultative Council on Multi-Culturalism.

Perrigoe, Ross and Lazar, Barry (1992). "Visible Minorities and Native Canadians in National Television News Programs" p.259-272 in Marc Grenier (ed.) *Critical Studies of Canadian Mass Media.* Butterworths, Toronto, 1992.

Pike, Robert M. "Canadian Broadcasting: Its Past and its Possible Future".

Porter, J. (1965). *The vertical mosaic.* Toronto: University of Toronto Press.

Raudsepp, E. (1996). "Emergent Media: The Native Press" In. S. Nancoo and R. Nancoo (ed.) *The Mass Media and Canadian Diversity.* Mississauga: Canadian Educators Press.

Sanders, E. (1991). "Mass Media and the Reproduction of Marginalization," in Fletcher, F. (ed) *Reporting the Campaign: Election Coverage in Canada* Toronto: Dundurn Press. pp. 273-321.

Siddiqui, H. (1993). "Media and Minorities: Failing to Mix the Message". *Toronto Star*, 24 April 1993.

Singer, Benjamin. (1995). *Communications in Canadian Society.* 4th ed. Toronto: Nelson Canada.

Valaskakis, Gail Guthrie.(1996). "Rights and Warriors: First Nations, Media and Identity". In S. Nancoo (ed), *The Mass Media and Canadian Diversity.* Mississauga: Canadian Educators' Press.

Vipond, Mary. (1992). *The mass media in Canada.* Toronto: James Lorimer & Company, Toronto.

Wilson, Clint and Frank Guttirez (1985). *Minorities and the media: Diversity and the end of mass culture.* Beverly Hills: Sage Publications.

Chapter 3

STRUGGLE AND RESISTANCE: CRAFTING FIRST NATIONS IN THE NEW MILLENNIUM

Deo H. Poonwassie
Nahum Kanhai

To be a stranger in one's own land is not a self-imposed ordeal. Except for the deviant, people do not normally create conditions for sadism, masochism or nihilism in modern times. Scanning the global landscape of Aboriginal realities, we encounter situations of economic poverty, unemployment, genocide, xenophobia, cultural erosion, loss of language, isolation, loss of pride; and the list can go on. These conditions may be seen, for example, among the Aboriginal peoples of Australia, Fiji, South and Central America, some areas of North America, Western Europe, Russia, Indonesia, and China. Colonization is at the root of these alienating experiences whether it is internal or external. In the case of Canada, the history of colonization is the story of exploiting, subduing, and oppressing the Aboriginal peoples of this land. But in spite of this onslaught from Western Europeans, Aboriginal peoples have survived and are no longer politically passive. They are re-grouping and reclaiming their rights using the methods condoned in our society.

This chapter is an overview of issues that affect the education of First Nation peoples (and generally Aboriginal peoples). It will highlight major documents in the development of a historical relationship with government, the present approaches to education, and aspects of educational development for the future.

For our present purposes it is necessary to define some terms that will be used throughout this chapter. Over a period of time different terms have been used to describe the original peoples of this land. **Indian** was the common acceptable term used to refer to all original inhabitants. This term is still used legally as **Status Indians** to mean "a person registered or entitled to be registered as an Indian according to the *Indian Act* (as amended by Bill C-31 in June 1985)", (INAC 1994-95 pp. 2-4). **Aboriginal** refers to the descendants of the original peoples of Canada and includes Indian (Status and non-Status), Inuit, and Metis, (*The Constitution Act, 1982*). **First Nations** includes all groups that belong to the Assembly of First Nations and others who are *treaty* or *status* Indians. This term came into popular use since 1982; in this paper the term "Indian" will be used in the legal sense especially when referring to events before 1982. Regardless of the terms used, it must be made clear that First Nations people are not a homogeneous group and, while there is much in common, there are differences in language, religion, traditions, and aspirations.

Significant Historical Events

The *Indian Act* of 1868 has precipitated living conditions of Indian peoples for over a century. This act was designed to control, protect, assimilate, and "civilize" these peoples not for their benefit, but for the protection of European immigrants and their interests in the development of this new country. Indeed the government positioned itself politically in 1857 when an *Act for the Gradual Civilization of the Indian Tribes* was passed. The purpose here was to assimilate the Indians so that they may survive; in addition they were encouraged to surrender their Indian status and become enfranchised. The government was very active in passing legislation to "keep the Indians in their place". A comprehensive *Indian Act* was passed in 1876; this document included every aspect of the Indians' life such as health, education, land ownership, alcohol consumption, governing structures, management and investment of funds, and the loss of status for women who married non-Indian males.

The *Indian Act* was revised in 1951; this revised version was similar to the 1868 vintage, but it emphasized: "1. Defining status more precisely. 2. Facilitating enfranchisement. (and) 3. Allowing more responsibility to local bands", (Frideres, 1983, p.30). *The Indian Act* has restricted the activities and development of Indian people; yet it is the chief instrument for holding the Federal government to its written promises and a springboard for reinterpretation and modernization of agreements. This piece of legislation is seen as a hammer of oppression; "it has become the most vicious mechanism of social control that exists in Canada today" (Frideres, 1983, p. 33). The *Indian Act* was amended further in 1985 (Bill C-31) allowing Indian women to marry non-Indian men and retain all their rights as an Indian person. Again, this further supports the view that the Federal Government has direct control over the lives of these peoples.

The decade of the 1960s witnessed a flurry of activities in Canadian Society; social movements seeking justice, peace, equality, and racial harmony dominated the social and political landscape. In 1967 a significant report in two volumes entitled *A survey of contemporary Indians of Canada: A report on economic, political, educational needs and policies* was published. Hawthorn, the main author, provided a realistic but dismal picture of social and economic conditions on Indian reserves. Schooling for Indian children was inadequate and inappropriate: the curriculum was alien, the routines were different, and the stereotype of "dull retarded without ambition" worked against these students. The report provided a list of 41 recommendations on education, the central theme being integration of Indian children into the public school system (Kirkness, 1992. p.107).

Prime Minister Pierre E. Trudeau was elected in 1968 with the promise to create a "just society". In reconciling this promise, Indian Affairs recognized that Indians were not being treated fairly and the new government moved to review its policies. The liberal ideology recognized individualism over group rights and employing this principle, the Minister of Indian Affairs and Northern Development, Jean Chretien, tabled a "Statement of the Government of Canada on Indian Policy" in the House of Commons in 1969. This became known as the "White Paper".

The White Paper proposed several changes: (a) the legislative and constitutional bases of discrimination should be removed; (b) the Indian Act should be repealed; (c) Indians should receive services like other Canadians through the same agencies and governments; (d) the Indian Affairs Programme within the Department of Indian Affairs and Northern Development (DIAND) was to be abolished; (e) the control of Indian lands should be transferred to Indian people. The mood of "power to the people" which was prevalent in the 1960s was reflected in these proposals, but further analysis reveals that the White Paper was "designed more to protect the government from external criticism than to meet the aspirations of Canadian Indians as these were perceived by Indians themselves" (Ponting and Gibbins, 1980, p.27). The White Paper was in effect proposing the abolishment of Indian Reserves and the transfer of all responsibilities to the provinces and other Federal departments. The reactions from Indian people were fast, furious, and vociferous.

The White Paper was attacked on the basis that it would "mean cultural genocide and an abrogation of the treaties" (Wuttunee, 1971. p.38). The charge against the White Paper was headed by Harold Cardinal, President of the Indian Association of Alberta, and in 1970 presented the Red Paper, "Citizens Plus" to the Prime Minister, it began:

> To us who are Treaty Indians there is nothing more important than our Treaties, our lands and the well being of our future generations. We have studied carefully the contents of the Government White Paper on Indians and we have concluded that it offers despair instead of hope." (Quoted in Wuttunee, 1971. p.41).

The Red Paper rejected every aspect of the Government's White Paper mainly on the grounds that the Federal Government was relinquishing its fiduciary responsibilities to the Indian people. In the same year (1970) the Union of B.C. Indian Chiefs produced "A Declaration of Indian Rights - the B.C. Indian Position Paper". In this paper the Chiefs rejected the White Paper and proposed that Indians control their own destiny through the administration of their own programs—a step towards self-determination. Their statement was even more forceful—"The Federal government seems intent on raping our culture and unique status, on wanting to destroy our identity as Indians. We reject this philosophy and demand our rightful place in society as INDIANS", (Quoted in Wuttunee, 1971, p.62).

Probably the first major response to the White Paper was

Harold Cardinal's (1969) *The Unjust Society*; in it he writes:

> Now, at a time when our fellow Canadians consider
> the promise of a Just Society, once more the Indians
> of Canada are betrayed by a programme which offers
> nothing better than cultural genocide. (The White
> Paper) is a thinly disguised programme of
> extermination through assimilation. For the Indian to
> survive, says the government in effect, he must
> become a good little brown white man. (Cardinal,
> 1969, p.1.)

These are harsh words, but from the history of the Indian peoples in
Canada, these sentiments represent a reality held by many of them.
As can be expected, Cardinal attacked the White Paper with facts,
figures, a recounting of a history of wretchedness, and above all a
justified accusation of Federal government betrayal.

The reaction to Cardinal was recorded by another Indian,
William Wuttunee, in his book *Ruffled Feathers*. In the introduction
to this book Johanna Wenzel writes:

> Many Canadian Indians are working hard at
> resolving their present-day difficulty in finding a
> place as individuals in the Canadian mosaic.
> However, still more native involvement and opinions
> are needed as the Twentieth Century races ahead,
> threatening to leave behind those who bemoan unjust
> treatment by white settlers and legislators. And that's
> what *Ruffled Feathers* is all about. It is also a rebuttal
> to Harold Cardinal's Unjust Society. (Wuttunee,
> 1971, p.v.)

Wuttunee takes every issue mentioned by Cardinal and gives
the opposite point of view. They do, however, agree that the Indian
people have not been treated fairly. They depart when they consider
solutions—Cardinal seeks to improve conditions for Indians through
slight modifications of the existing governing structures. Wuttunee
suggests that Indians should take more responsibility for their lives
and have less dependency on the federal government. Herein lies the

two major approaches to the improvement of living conditions for Indians in Canada.

The late 1960s and early 1970s saw concerted efforts by the Indian peoples and the government of Canada to influence the directions of official policy and action that affect the destiny of Indian peoples. Indians saw education as a key instrument in any form of development, especially if self-government was to be achieved. The National Indian Brotherhood (N.I.B.), through an intensive consultation process with its constituencies, formulated a policy paper in 1972 entitled *Indian Control of Indian Education*. In the conclusion it is clearly stated that "there is difficulty and danger in taking a position on Indian education because of the great diversity of problems encountered across the country" (p.30). Hence, this policy paper is based on two fundamental principles of education—**parental responsibility** and **local control.**

For too long Indians have been removed from shaping the form of education for their children. We have seen the use of boarding schools, industrial schools, residential schools, and public schools; in addition the influence of religion in the education of Indian children have had lasting effects, some of them devastating, even fatal. Indians felt very strongly that they should have decision-making powers (not merely advisory) in areas such as budgets, curriculum, staffing, physical facilities, and governance. "In a letter to the President of the National Indian Brotherhood dated February 2, 1973, the Minister gave official recognition to **Indian Control of Indian Education,** approving its proposals and committing the Department of Indian Affairs and Northern Development to implementing them". (National Indian Brotherhood, 1972, p.iii).

Implementing the proposals of the document was endlessly tied up in government bureaucracy. For example, DIAND began planning for implementation, but neglected to involve the Indian people—this was a violation of a basic premise stated in the document! The government produced a series of policy statements in the form of E. Guidelines (Ward, 1986). A joint NIB/Cabinet Committee was established to discuss implementation plans and phases. The first meeting was aborted; by 1978 the NIB decided to terminate its participation in this joint committee because there was no legislation forthcoming to amend the *Indian Act* which would enable implementation of the proposals. In 1982 the NIB drew up plans for implementation of the proposals and presented them to the government, who thought they were good plans but had no money to do the job. Meanwhile, the government was working with individual Bands to transfer some power for making decisions for the local control of education, thus undermining the position of the NIB as co-ordinator of this effort. (Ward, 1986). Since 1982, there has been an acceleration in transferring administrative aspects of education to the Bands that made such requests. A significant restructuring of the National Indian Brotherhood occurred in 1982 when it became the Assembly of First Nations (AFN).

Intermittent Improvements

Over centuries of dealings between the governments and First Nations there is an accumulation of distrust and suspicion. This is seen in broken promises (e.g. treaties), the lack of will to modernize agreements (the *Indian Act*), and the perpetuation of poverty in First Nations communities (reserves). In 1990 four major issues emerged that highlighted the conditions facing First Nations peoples (Poonwassie, 1991). The Donald Marshall Inquiry found that the **judicial system** of Nova Scotia was racially prejudiced against First Nations peoples. (Mannette, 1992.) Indeed, a major project—the Aboriginal Justice Inquiry—was in progress in Manitoba at this time. When it was completed in 1991, it contained an indictment of the justice system as it was applied to the Aboriginal peoples of Manitoba.

The second issue concerned Aboriginal rights in the Canadian Constitution. Elijah Harper, an Indian MLA from Manitoba, refused to give consent to the Meech Lake Accord because Aboriginal rights were not outlined in the proposed constitution. Third, the issue of land claims was highlighted in the Oka Crisis. This renewed accusations of racism, oppression, perpetuation of poverty, and denial of civil rights. Finally, the historical abuse of Indian children in residential schools surfaced as the Grand Chief of the Assembly of Manitoba Chiefs admitted that he was abused in a residential school. These issues are alive and prevalent today; some efforts, though sporadic, are being made to address them and education is still seen as an instrument for creating better living conditions for First Nations peoples in Canada.

First Nations are gradually, but surely taking control of education for their people. Some statistics from INAC's *Basic Departmental Data, 1998* reveal that:

(a)   For Kindergarten, Elementary, and Secondary Schools, Enrolment grew from 85,582 in 1988/89 to 115,796 in 1997/98; this was an increase from 80.9% to 81.3%. (Table 3.1: p.29).

(b)   For Post-secondary Institutions, enrolment increased for registered Indians from 15,572 in 1988/89 to 27,100 in 1997/98. Those numbers can be higher because these figures represent only those students funded by DIAND; some students find alternate funding. (Table 3.3; p.31).

(c)   The full-time post secondary enrolment for registered Indians was 6.6% (12,551 aged 17-34) in 1994-95 and actually dropped to 6.5% of the population aged 17-34. For all Canadians there was an increase from 10.4% in 1994/95 to 13.1% in the same age group. (Table 3.4; p.32).

(d)   In 1988/89 there were 280 Band-operated schools; in 1997/98 there were 448. This shows an increase of 60%. (Table 3.6; p.34). A Band-operated school is defined as a school whose services are delivered by an Indian Band.

(e)   Kindergarten, elementary, and secondary school students from reserves attend four different types of schools: Federal, Provincial, Band-operated, and Private. In Federal Schools, the enrolment was 16.1% in 1988/89 and 1.5% in 1997/98. Provincial Schools saw a drop from 47.9% in 1988/89 to 38% in 1997/1998. Private Schools have a small proportion from 1990/91 to 1997/98. (Table 3.7; p. 36). Clearly the trend is towards Band-operated schools and some form of Indian control of their education.

It is important to note the use of the term "**Band-operated** schools" by INAC instead of "**Band-controlled** schools". It would appear that in the former, the implementation/administration of schools is carried out at the local level, but major policy decisions are made elsewhere; if the latter term was used, it would indicate not only implementation/administration but also actual jurisdiction over policy matters. This is a crucial distinction when considering forms of self-government and self-determination of First Nations.

While these figures show promise of increased accessibility to education, the reality of quality of life is rather the opposite. Suicides and deaths in First Nations communities remain high compared to the Canadian average and life expectancy is six years less than the Canadian population. Economic development in the communities still cannot alleviate massive unemployment which ranged from 58% in Saskatchewan to 18% in Newfoundland in 1996. These are average figures which when examined closely can reveal unemployment in some communities up to 80%. (INAC, 1998.)

First Nations are forging new relationships with the Federal Government; it is difficult, but progress is being made. It is unfortunate that in order to be heard First Nations must resort to extreme actions such as the Oka Crisis, blockades, marches, and sit-ins. Compared to other parts of the world, First Nations peoples in Canada are peaceful and patient.

In education many laudable achievements have taken place. Some examples are the establishment of the First Nations House of Learning on the University of British Columbia campus; the Saskatchewan Federated College (affiliated with the University of Regina); and the Special Premedical Studies Program at The University of Manitoba which has graduated about 20 medical practitioners. Many universities have established departments of Native Studies with responsibilities for teaching and research. Post-secondary institutions have established access programs for Aboriginal peoples to enter universities and community colleges; some special programs designed mainly for Aboriginals provide training in professions such as Law, Dentistry, Medicine, Pharmacy, Medical Rehabilitation, Engineering, Social Work, and Education. Indeed many Aboriginal students do not need the facilities of Access programs and are successful in regular entry programs. Aboriginal academics with graduate degrees have formed a research organization call *Mokakit Education Research Association,* (a Blackfoot term, which means **to strive for wisdom**). The *Canadian Journal of Native Education* publishes research and other articles about Aboriginal education.

Given the history and conditions through which Aboriginal peoples have survived, their achievements in other fields are equally phenomenal. In the field of the visual arts, Daphne Odjig, Norval Morrisseau, Jackson Beardy and Kenojuak are some of the best artists of national and international repute; and in architecture there is the creative Douglas Cardinal. In entertainment Thompson Highway, Tom Jackson, Buffy Sainte-Marie, Graham Green, Kitten and Tina Keeper have shown outstanding talent. In politics there is Elijah Harper, Ovide Mercredi, and Ethel Blondin who have been exceptional role models; and in business, success stories are exemplified in the fortitude of Matthew Coon Come and Frank Hansen.

The accomplishments of Aboriginal peoples are many by any standards. However, most important and remarkable is their tenacity for survival against extremely strong forces of destruction. With the deliberate attempts to assimilate, isolate, and even exterminate, these peoples have overcome the pressures of cultural extinction. The renaissance and cultural rebirth have begun, and the movement towards self-determination is gaining momentum. The Federal Government and peoples of Canada must recognize these achievements and directions and assist in this process.

Recent Developments

The Royal Commission on Aboriginal Peoples (RCAP) was established on August 26, 1991. The Report of this Commission, in five volumes, was published in 1996. After five years of intensive and extensive research on all aspects of Aboriginal living conditions, hopes and dreams, this Report can justly be hailed as the most comprehensive written account about Aboriginal peoples in Canada.

These five volumes covered all aspects of Aboriginal Peoples lives including history (especially the emasculating relationship between Aboriginal and non-Aboriginal people); the treaties signed between nations; the restoration of families (values, communities, education); the question of Aboriginal identities; and the real possibility or renewal (implementation plan, public education, financial costs).

As a response to the RCAP Report, the Government of Canada responded with a document: ***Gathering Strength: Canada's***

Aboriginal Action Plan (1997). The Plan has four objectives: renewing the Partnership; Strengthening Aboriginal Governance; Developing a New Fiscal Relationship; and Supporting Strong Communities, People and Economics. Clearly the response is well-written; but the implementation will require considerable effort on the part of the Federal Government and the Aboriginal Peoples of this land. The financial cost seems enormous, but if this is not allocated in future national budgets, the human costs will be incalculable.

Information provided by INAC as "backgrounder" pamphlets to the *Gathering Strength* publication reveals that the Aboriginal population will grow by 1.7% with 2.3% growth on reserves; the majority of the First Nations population is under age 25. The implications of this demand planned economic development and improved access to education. The snail pace of movement to meet these demands will continue to maintain "Third World" conditions in First Nations communities, and the gap between the "haves" and "have-nots" will continue to grow.

On April 1, 1999, the map of Canada changed to include a new territory: Nunavut. In 1993, the Nunavut Act to create Nunavut, and the Nunavut Land Claim Agreement Act were enacted by Parliament; in 1994 the Nunavut Implementation Commission was established to advise the Federal Government on various aspects of creating this new territory. On April 1, 1999, Nunavut was officially created, and with an area of 2 million square kilometres and a population of 25,000, it is an example of modern treaty-making and self-governance. This new Territory is not proclaimed as an Aboriginal Territory; however, since 85% of the population is Inuit and the majority speaks Inuktitut, the new political/geographical entity is defacto Aboriginal. This could be an example of successful self-government within Canada.

After many years of negotiations and several millions of dollars in expenditures, a final agreement with the Nisga's people to reclaim 2,000 square kilometres of land in northwestern British Columbia received parliamentary approval. The agreement provides powers of self-government similar to municipal governments and $490 million in cash, grants, and government program funds (National Post, October 22, 1999. p. A7). The Nisga'a people relinquished claims to a much larger land base and removed themselves from the Indian Act. Their agreement has been hailed as a landmark in modern treaty-making, but many have labelled it a "race-based" treaty; it has had its detractors in British Columbia and in the Opposition Reform Party of Parliament. This is yet another example of First Nations' struggle for self-government and recognition as a people.

As Aboriginal peoples in general, and First Nations in particular, seek justice through settlements in courts, the fight for rights, inherent and legislated, becomes highly intense. On September 17, 1999, the Supreme Court of Canada acquitted Donald Marshall Jr. for fishing without a licence on the basis of treaties signed between the Mi'kmaq and the Crown in 1760-1761. As a result of this 5-2 ruling by the court, the Mi'kmac of the east coast of Canada decided to fish lobster outside the designated lobster fishing season. The ensuring violent clashes between Aboriginals and non-Aboriginals highlighted centuries-old injustices meted out to aboriginal peoples. Non-Aboriginals claimed that their livelihood and those of their children were imperilled because of the possible depletion of the lobster stocks that will happen if the Mi'Kmaq are allowed to fish year-round. On the other hand the Mi'Kmaq claimed that they had the legal right to fish at anytime and that their living conditions were scandalous for centuries. Now that the Supreme Court has recognized their rights they intend to exercise them. From these extreme interpretations from both sides a compromise of regulated fishing was reached.

The importance of this ruling regarding the use of natural resources for First Nations to afford a "reasonable living" must be recognized. The living conditions (health, housing, employment, education) of First nations have been below the national average for centuries. Although the legal channels for improving these conditions of abject poverty are arduous and expensive, it appears that this is the only path left for Aboriginal peoples. Even then the imperatives of a neo-colonial mentality will be implemented by the majority society through unequal power, new rules, negotiations, and advantageous interpretations of the law. The path of Aboriginal justice is paved with impediments of high financial costs, racism, and inequality.

The CRTC approved the request of the Aboriginal Peoples Television Network (APTN) to be carried on basic cable throughout Canada on February 22, 1999. APTN opened its primary production centre in Winnipeg, Manitoba, in September 1999. Media, especially in the form of television, is a powerful force in our culturally diverse nation. The creation of APTN will provide an Aboriginal focus on events, culture, news and views not only for Aboriginal peoples but for the non-Aboriginal majority as well. APTN can help to shape the attitudes of the public by providing interpretations of history and "facts" through Aboriginal lenses. The possibilities for projecting positive role models, educating viewers and promoting Aboriginal cultures and languages both nationally and internationally are limited only by imagination and creativity. The Aboriginal producers, directors, actors, and technicians are rising to these challenges and they will claim the 21st century as their own. (For further details see RCAP, Vol. 3. pp.620-632) These developments in 1999 only point the way to what will be a most eventful and strident new millennium. The die is cast and the progress of Aboriginal peoples will increase but not without struggles. There will be instances of both peaceful resistance and violent conflicts but the move towards self-government will continue.

The Future

There are many outstanding issues that are basic to the relationship between First Nations and others. Mercredi and Turpel (1993) point out five key areas: (a) The Indian Act of 1876 is an archaic document that must be revised to remove injustices and to include the realities of First Nations aspirations. (b) Agreements entered into by the Canadian government and First Nations should be honoured without the expensive and time-consuming litigation processes. (c) Disputes over natural resources and conserving the environment need to be settled, taking into consideration the values and culture of First Nation peoples. (d) The social, spiritual, economic, cultural, and psychological effects of a history of oppression, degradation, and assimilation are surfacing in social problems such as family violence, substance abuse, depression, suicide, poor housing, inadequate health services, and anomie among First Nations peoples. These situations are explosive and must be addressed. (e) The abject poverty and soaring unemployment in First Nations communities create conditions that are prevalent in the least developed countries of the world.

First Nations peoples have called international attention to their cause, and they have sent delegations to the United Nations and to the Queen of England. When it comes to the living conditions of First Nations peoples, Canada is on record for violating basic human rights. Indeed, when Bishop Desmond Tutu visited Indian reserves in Quebec in 1990, he compared them to homelands in South Africa. Canada is a member of the G-8, a club of the richest and most industrialized countries of the world, and it has been rated as the best country in the world by the UN for its quality of life. Clearly this does not apply to First Nations; this is deplorable and must be corrected.

First Nations peoples are working desperately to improve their poor living conditions; a major direction is the achievement of self-government.   Their claim to the **inherent** right to govern themselves is rooted in their history. In the new millennium, many more promises will be made by the Federal Government and the long and arduous process towards self-government will continue.

Economic determinism and the values of "economism" are making inroads and influencing directions in many Aboriginal communities. The diminishing prospects for constitutional talks on Treaty and Aboriginal rights and the glacial pace of movement on the R.C.A.P recommendations heighten fears about Aboriginal prospects and are forcing communities to look in other directions.

Economic development and Aboriginal entrepreneurship ranging from mining interests to gaming are having greater appeal to many leaders than the indefinite wait on governments' readiness. In fact Aboriginal eagerness for shorter routes to economic self-sufficiency has also been an opportunity for the Federal Government to be active without addressing the more contentious issues of collective inherent rights.

The current trend look much like a grooming of Nations for life in the corporate world. A major step in this direction was taken with the passing of Federal legislation in 1999 of an Act Providing for the Ratification and Bringing into Effect the Framework Agreement on First Nations Land Management. By virtue of this Act, Indian bands can utilise collective lands as legal instruments equivalent to co-lateral in commercial transactions. The implications of this legislatively-facilitated basis of Indian land tenure include permitting what had been vehemently resisted in the rejection of the white paper of 1969, which said: "that control of Indian lands should be transferred to Indian people" (Statement of the Government of Canada on Indian Policy, p.6). Indians responded in the Red Paper with the notion that "the legal title has been held for us by the Crown to prevent the sale or breaking up of our land" (1972, p. 6).

In addition to the weakening of the basis of Indian land tenure the government is engaging in dismantling the Indian Act by also re-municipalizing Bands with new Federal enactments. This trend provides enjoyment of a wider range of devolved administrative roles and greater facility in the pursuit of investments, economic and social development as provided with the new Land Management Act (1999) and federal transfer agreements between the Ministry of Indian Affairs and Indian Bands. Many leaders now embrace this shorter route to alleviating suffering while others are holding out for long term solution based on constitutionally protected self-governments.

A corporate proto-type is fast influencing both modalities for survival as well as legal and political status of Aboriginal people. Which approach will best ensure Aboriginal peoples interests and intergenerational well-being in the new millennium?

A key instrument in creating a strong people is an appropriate system of education. First Nations recognize this and have produced many policy statements regarding this issue such as *Indian Control of Indian Education* and *Tradition and Education Toward a Vision of our Future*. These documents point in one direction—First Nations must control the education of their people. After being dependent on an imported education system, First Nations have made successful efforts to create and control their own system in order to develop the strength, pride, and competence for survival in a highly technological society. Still there is much that is left to be done.

First Nations must decide the form and content of their education and government structures. Kindergarten, elementary, and secondary education must meet the needs of the communities and the society in which they live. The cultural base, including language, must be re-established to provide the proper balance necessary for survival in a changing world. Many First Nations are already controlling the direction of education in their communities; however, this will increase at an accelerated pace as self-government becomes a reality. The curriculum is a crucial issue, and while history and culture of First Nations form integral parts of the programs, basic skills in computing, reading, and writing will also be given equal weight in designing curriculum. First Nations youth must not be trained to be disadvantaged in a world where knowledge is growing exponentially; the skills of learning to learn must be an essential part of their education.

Post-secondary education is crucial to the development of any form of self-reliance within nations. At the community college level, the skills required to be good trades people are packaged to meet the standards required for providing competent services. Tradespersons such as plumbers, carpenters, electricians, builders etc. become indispensable if a viable infrastructure is to be created in First Nations communities. Where would such training be available? In urban centres or in First Nations communities? Is it possible to have regional community colleges (and branches) that would meet these needs?

First Nations peoples have already recognized that university education is crucial in realizing their dreams. Efforts are constantly made to have more of their peoples receive degree training. It is therefore important for First Nations to establish their own colleges and some day their own universities. The potential and needs are there. (For a detailed account of research findings on education, see RCAP, Vol. 3, Ch. 5.)

The arts and entertainment areas will grow in the near future. Theatre, movies, and music will continue to develop new talent as young First Nations people find room for self-expression. More artists and sculptors will continue to find a niche for their exquisite works nationally and internationally. These aspects of culture have not been sufficiently emphasized in plans for self-government; the efforts have been concentrated on the language, customs, and spirituality of First Nations.

As First Nations youth become more educated and grounded in their traditions, they will understand the importance of political power in their communities and in society in general. The future holds promise that the power of political intervention will become the pursuit of young leaders; this will be necessary if First Nations self-government is to become a viable reality.

All aspirations of First Nations will be determined through successful negotiations and not through violence (although it appears that some forms of violence such as Oka, tends to raise the consciousness of both Canadians and First Nations). Non-Aboriginals are not leaving this land and Aboriginals are not leaving it either, nor will either group be exterminated. It is crucial that the Canadian government and people seize this reality and show the world that justice and fairness are still important values when negotiating with Aboriginal peoples.

Much attention has been given to the process of empowerment and it is indeed a powerful concept. However, it must be clear that a person cannot be truly empowered by some one else; others may **create the conditions** for empowerment but only the individual can empower him/herself. This self-empowerment is a lasting personal achievement grounded in the individual psyche that prevails regardless of the difficulties that are encountered in the future. This chapter has highlighted some of the problems, issues, and possibilities for First Nations. From a participant-observer stance, it appears that First Nations visions are now clearer as the fog of inertia is lifting, and further progress is immanent as we begin the new millennium.

There appears to be a heightened consciousness among First Nations peoples; this is evident in increased political activity, concentrated litigation on land claims, accelerated programming for spiritual healing, diversification in community economic development and a major thrust in providing appropriate education. The future of First Nations, through this century, will be moulded by the quality of First Nations Leadership and their resistance to the new colonialism. The stage is set for the reclamation of self-government and this momentum will be maintained by a clear vision of destiny and sustained focused negotiations. Action to support negotiated agreements will be executed by trained and educated **Aboriginal personnel**; this direction will require an education system that is controlled by Aboriginals in order to provide suitably qualified experts for new challenges. While there will be power struggles and regional differences, First Nations will undoubtedly reclaim jurisdiction over their destiny in the new millennium.

REFERENCES

Cardinal, H. (1969). *The unjust society.* The tragedy of Canada's Indians. Edmonton: Hurtig Publishers.

Charleston, Mike. (ed.)(1988). *Tradition and education: Towards a vision of our future.* Vol. 1-3. Ottawa: Assembly of First Nations.

Frideres, J.S. (1983). *Native people in Canada. Contemporary conflicts.* Ontario: Prentice-Hall, Canada.

Government of Canada. (1999). *An Act Providing for the Ratification and Bringing into Effect the Framework Agreement on First Nations Land Management.*

Hawthorn, H.B. et. al. (1966-1967). *A survey of contemporary Indians of Canada. Vol. I & II.* Indian Affairs Branch. Ottawa: Queen's Printer.

INAC. (1994). *Indian and northern affairs Canada and Canadian polar commission.* 1994-95 estimates. Ottawa: Government of Canada.

INAC: Indian and Northern Affairs Canada. (1998). *Basic departmental data.(1998).* Department of Indian Affairs and Northern Development. Ottawa: Minister of Government Services, Canada.

Indian Chiefs of Alberta. (1972). *Citizens Plus.* Edmonton: Indian Association of Alberta.

Kirkness, Verna J. (1992). *First Nations and schools: Triumphs and struggles.* Toronto: Canadian Education Association.

Mannette, Joy. (1992). *Elusive justice: Beyond the Marshall inquiry.* Halifax: Fernwood Publishing.

Mercredi, O. & Turpel, M.E. (1993). *In the rapids navigating the future of First Nations.* Toronto: Viking.

Ministry of Indian and Northern Affairs. (1969). Statement of the Government of Canada on Indian Policy. Government of Canada: Ottawa.

Minister of Supply and Services. (1996) *Report of the Royal Commission on Aboriginal Peoples.* (RCAP). Ottawa: Government of Canada.

Minister of Supply and Services. (1997). *Gathering Strength. Canada's Aboriginal Action Plan.* Ottawa: Government of Canada.

National Indian Brotherhood. (1972). *Indian control of Indian education*. Ottawa: National Indian Brotherhood.

National Post. October 27, 1999. p.A7

Ponting, J.R. & Gibbins, R. (1980). *Out of irrelevance*. Toronto: Butterworths.

Poonwassie, D.H. (1991). "Issues in teacher education for Aboriginal peoples: A Canadian perspective." *Florida Journal of Teacher Education*. Vol. VII. pp. 3-15.

Ward, Margaret S. (1986). "Indian education: Policy and politics 1972-1982." *Canadian Journal of Native Education*. Vol. 13. No. 2. pp. 10-21.

Wuttunee, W.I.C. (1971). *Ruffled feathers*. Calgary, Alberta: Bell Books.

Chapter 4

FEDERALISM AND DIVERSITY: THE CANADIAN EXPERIENCE*

Stéphane Dion

Federalism is a system of government that has a number of advantages in terms of governance, management of the economy, democratic life, and influence on the international scene. The world's largest democracies are federations, as are many of the most prosperous countries. But the true genius of this form of government lies in its ability to reconcile diversity in unity. And it is this ability that I want to talk about today.

Because federalism is flexible and can adapt to different contexts, our countries have obviously developed different approaches and mechanisms. I do not claim to be a specialist on your federation, so I will limit my remarks to describing how we in Canada try to reconcile diversity in unity. I will leave it to you to determine which ideas are applicable and which are not to the very different context of Mexico. I hope you will find my remarks to be of some relevance in your search for what you call the New Federalism in Mexico.

Unity in diversity the Canadian way has two dimensions: first, the guarantees we give to individual rights and freedoms, and second, our federal system. At an international conference in Puebla on *The Americas in Transition: Challenges of a New Millennium*, I spoke mainly about the first dimension: the very Canadian way in which the primacy of individual rights is established while taking account of collective identities. This article talks about the second dimension. I will show how our flexible federalism enables provinces which are equal in status to express their own personalities.

Federalism and Diversity

Most federations have significant differences in the character of their constituent states: size, wealth, language, ethnic or religious make-up. This is true of Mexico and of Canada as well. At the same time, the best established federations tend to give their constituent units roughly the same constitutional powers. This is true of the United States, Australia, Germany, and Switzerland. Despite huge differences, for example, between Alaska and California, or between Quebec and Prince Edward Island, the constitutional powers of these state or provincial governments are essentially the same.

Of course, it is not inconceivable that a federation could have some asymmetries in the basic powers assigned to different states or provinces. But the functional significance of such asymmetries would depend on the extent of the differences, the political weight of the state or states with the extra powers and the possibility of other states having the extra powers if they so chose.

Spain, for example, has experimented with asymmetries, and there appears to be a tendency for units that have had fewer powers to seek the greater powers of the bigger states.

Inevitably, an extremely asymmetric regime gives rise to questions about the role that elected representatives from different states play at the centre. If the federal government is responsible for education in some states but not others, must the federal Minister of Education be from a state where it has this responsibility? Should representatives from all states vote on federal educational matters? Can very differentiated roles for representatives at the centre be sustained over time? These issues go to the heart of the representative nature of the central federal institutions.

Thus while some asymmetries may fit particular circumstances, there is room for deep scepticism about a federal architecture which is too asymmetric.

This raises the question: how can very different constituent units be content with the same constitutional status? How can federalism be flexible enough to respect both the principle of equality and that of diversity?

Federations use three methods to achieve this end. The first is financial asymmetry. This consists in establishing intergovernmental transfer mechanisms that are specifically designed to assist the less wealthy components of the federation. The objective is to ensure that, despite the inequality of their autonomous revenues, the components are more equal in actual fact.

The second method is constitutional asymmetry. In this case, the Constitution recognizes certain specific arrangements that meet the needs of some of the federation's components without challenging the equality among them.

The third method may be called optional asymmetry, which stems from the different relations that develop between the federal government and other governments within the federation. Some may choose to exercise all of their constitutional responsibilities, while others prefer to assign some of them to the federal government.

Compared with other well established federations, Canada practises these three forms of asymmetry to a considerable extent (Watts, 1998, p.100). Our country does so while respecting the equality of status of the provinces.

1. Financial asymmetry

The Canadian federation has an intergovernmental financial redistribution mechanism that is undoubtedly unequalled in scope in any other federation. Section 36 of the *Constitution Act, 1982* commits the federal government to help equalize the field so that all provinces have "sufficient revenues to provide reasonably comparable levels of public services at reasonably comparable levels of taxation."

This principle, which has been called a "pillar of modern Canadian federalism" (Milne, 1991, p.295) is an overt recognition of the natural differences (such as size, population, wealth, etc.) that exist among the constituents units of our federation. It is strongly and consistently supported by Canadians from have and have-not provinces alike.

2. Constitutional asymmetry

All of our ten provinces have broadly the same constitutional powers. It is true that, in the period from 1905 to 1930, the newly created provinces of Alberta and Saskatchewan did not have the authority over natural resources that resided with the other provinces. This was a significant source of grievance on their part which was only resolved through giving them the same powers as the other provinces. As for our northern territories, vast, with a limited population and very dependant on federal aid, they do not have the constitutional status of provinces.

There are very significant "asymmetries" of other types in terms of special provisions for individual provinces within the Canadian constitution. The historic constitutional protection for denominational (that is to say, religious-based) schools, for example, has varied a good deal between provinces, depending on their character and earlier history. And at the provincial level, only the government and legislature of New Brunswick is officially bilingual, while in Quebec and Manitoba, the minority languages of English and French respectively, have some important constitutional protection. Only Quebec uses civil law while the rest of Canada uses common law, and three of the nine seats on the Supreme Court are therefore kept for civil law lawyers from Quebec. In the same vein, the Constitution Act, 1867 addressed the possibility of unifying private law in the common law provinces, which implicitly excluded Quebec and protected its civil law tradition. Under the Constitution Act, 1982 the Government of Quebec has the right to limit access to English schools for as long as it deems this to be desirable in order to protect the French language in our North American context.

3. Optional asymmetry

Optional asymmetry takes many forms in Canada. These asymmetries have arisen over time, because the provinces have chosen to use their powers in different ways. Some provinces, Quebec first and foremost, have used many more of the possibilities provided for in the Canadian Constitution. A number of federal government policies encourage this flexibility.

For example, most of our provinces have integrated their personal and corporate income tax regimes with the federal regime, but Quebec has kept both distinct and Ontario has a separate corporate tax regime. Similarly, the tax collection arrangements for provincial taxes vary across the country, with the federal government collecting provincial income, corporate or sales taxes in some provinces but not others.

Our immigration regime is managed differently in Quebec than in the other provinces because the government of Quebec has concluded a bilateral agreement with the federal government in this area of joint jurisdiction. Pensions, also a joint jurisdiction, are managed by the federal government outside Quebec while in Quebec the province manages a regime that is closely coordinated with the federal one. Both Ontario and Quebec have their own police forces, whereas the other provinces contact the Royal Canadian Mounted Police to do provincial policing.

Some human resources programs paid for by the federal government have had their management transferred in different degrees to the provinces, depending on the arrangement they have preferred with the federal government. For example, recent job training agreements gave the provinces the choice between extensive autonomy or co-management of programs with the federal government. The Government of Newfoundland opted for co-management, while the Government of Quebec chose autonomy.

Finally, Quebec and New Brunswick have the status of participating governments within the *Organisation internationale de la Francophonie*, which is not the case for the other Canadian provinces.

The flexibility of Canadian federalism thus allows for extensive optional asymmetry in comparison with what is generally found in other federations. The key point of these asymmetries is that they do not reflect differences in underlying constitutional powers but demonstrate the flexibility of the federation in terms of the practical use of these powers.

Conclusion

This is the Canadian way of seeking unity in diversity. The result is that the provinces' equal status is not to be confused with uniformity. It is very much in keeping with the pluralist quest for public service quality. This is the ideal of our federation. I am not saying that it has managed to achieve the ideal perfectly. I am saying that pursuit of that ideal is the very essence of our federation.

Canadian federalism is not set in stone. No federalism should be. It is continually evolving, along with the different needs of our populations. A number of the intergovernmental arrangements I have described may vary in the future, and others may be added, but the Canadian federation will always have the same objective: to make it possible to pursue common objectives through diversity of experience. Is this not the objective you are pursuing in Mexico through your New Federalism?

This objective is pursued in Canada through determination and considerable discussion. The debate is often heated. Our Prime Minister, the Right Honourable Jean Chretien, likes to say that Canadians have two convictions. The first is that Canada is the very best country in the world. The second is that their province does not get its fair share within the federation.

These debates, these discussions, this pluralist quest, can all seem complicated and difficult sometimes. But it is precisely from this constant synergy that Canadians draw the vitality that gives them their enviable quality of life. They could not do so in disunity, nor if Canada were a unitary country rather than a decentralized federation. More and more Canadians, particularly Quebecers, are coming to realize this.

Of course, there is no single model of federalism. Our federalism is not the same as Mexican federalism or American federalism, for example, because our contexts and the challenges we face are very different. Nevertheless, federalism is likely one of the best responses to ensure that diversity is the very opposite of a problem, a threat or a source of division, and is instead a strength which helps a country to prosper in unity.

Endnotes
*This is an address delivered by the Hon. Stéphane Dion at El Colegio de Mexico, Mexico on October 1, 1999.

REFERENCES

Watts, Ronald. (1998). *Comparing Federal Systems in the 1990's.*
        Kingston: Queen's University.
Milne, D. (1991*).* "Equality or Asymmetry: Why Choose?", in
        Ronald L. Watts and Douglas M. Brown, eds. *Options for a
        New Canada.* Toronto: University of Toronto Press.

Chapter 5

UNITY IN DIVERSITY, THE CANADIAN WAY*

Stéphane Dion

South Asia: eight countries.

Afghanistan: two official languages (Pashto and Dari) and three major ethnic groups (Pashtuns, 38%; Tajiks, 25%; Hazaras, 19%).
Bangladesh: 83% Muslim, 16% Hindu.
Bhutan: 59% Bhote, 20% Ngalops, 25% Nepalese.
India: 25 states, 7 territories, three major ethnic groups, six main religions, 18 official languages.
Maldives: Indians, Sinhalese, Arabs.
Nepal: one official language, Nepali, but some dozen other languages are also used.
Pakistan: Punjabis, Sindhis, Pathans, Baluchis.
Sri Lanka: Sinhalese, 74%; Tamils, 18%

I am not surprised that federalism and multiculturalism, as means to achieve the peaceful cohabitation of different populations within a single state, is of great interest to South Asia specialists, such as yourselves.

The cohabitation of different populations within a single country may well be the main issue of the new century, not only in South Asia but elsewhere in the world as well. A 1997 Carnegie Corporation report states that since the end of the Cold War, the number of conflicts within states has greatly exceeded the number of conflicts between states. In addition, a study published by the United States Institute of Peace Press has identified 233 ethnic or religious minorities that are calling for improvements to their legal and political rights, many of which are in South Asia.

According to Professor Daniel Elazar (1994), President of the Jerusalem Center for Public Affairs, there are 3,000 human groups in the world who are conscious of a collective identity. And yet, there are not even 200 states in the UN. To each people its own state, a slogan reiterated once again by Lucien Bouchard on June 5, 1999, ("[sovereignty] responds to a need of almost all people on earth") [Translation], is an impractical idea that would fragment the planet. As former United Nations Secretary-General Boutros Boutros-Ghali (1992, p.9) has stated: "Yet if every ethnic, religious or linguistic group claimed statehood, there would be no limit to fragmentation, and peace, security and economic well-being for all would become ever more difficult to achieve."

In other words, we need to invent Canadas throughout the world. They will be different from ours, to be sure, but they will pursue the same ideal: mutual assistance of different populations within a single state, which see their living together as the development of a more complete citizenship, closer to universal values. As Indira Ghandi once said, Canada is the proof that "diversity not only enriches but can be a strength." Our country, Canada, is largely seen throughout the world as a model of openness and tolerance, and is admired for its capacity to unite different populations.

It is easy to imagine the world's reaction if Canada were to break up. It would be said that this defunct federation had died from an overdose of decentralization and tolerance--in short, from an overdose of democracy. Don't be so tolerant, as decentralized, as open as Canada has been, or else your minority or your minorities will turn against you, jeopardize the unity of your country, and perhaps destroy it: that's what would be said.

The very reason I entered active politics is that I want to hear the opposite. I want to hear people say, throughout the world: We can be confident in our minorities, and allow them to flourish in their own way, because in that way they will strengthen our country, just as Quebec strengthens Canada.

The Canadian unity debate is universal in scope. If a country as fortunate as Canada fails to maintain its unity, Canadians will have sent a very bad message to the rest of the world at the beginning of the new millennium.

I am going to describe the Canadian method for cohabitation of different populations, as I see it, and will leave you to determine which elements of it can be transposed to the extremely varied contexts of South Asia, and which cannot. I will also explain why, in my opinion, the solution to our unity problem lies in further developing this Canadian method, rather than abandoning it.

1. The Canadian way to encourage cultures to live together

The Canadian system is based first and foremost on individual rights. Only flesh-and-blood people exist in a tangible way, only they are capable of feelings, freedom, happiness. That being said, individuals maintain or develop affinities on the basis of sharing common traits. Some of those affinities relate to language, culture and religion, and are expressed as collective identities.

The Canadian ideal consists of seeing these differences between groups of citizens not as a problem, but instead as a strength, which, rather than separating citizens, allows them to pursue together the plural quest for what is just and good. The promotion of collective identities or affinities in Canada does not mean the negation of individual rights. It is meant to help Canadian citizens to develop and flourish. It in no way weakens the feeling of a common Canadian identity. On the contrary, Canadians' acceptance of their plural identities nourishes within them a genuine love for their country.

In this sense, Canadian multiculturalism is not a series of closed ghettos, and it must not become one. It expresses the conviction that human beings are better served by cultural exchanges than by cultural assimilation or separation. Canada was the first country in the world to adopt a multiculturalism policy and continues to play a leading role in this regard, for which it received high praise from UNESCO in 1996.

The quest for a better autonomy for Aboriginal peoples must not mean that the individuals that make up those peoples have fewer rights than other Canadian citizens. They too are protected by the *Canadian Charter of Rights and Freedoms*. But this status of autonomy must enable these Aboriginal populations to deal with the specificity they have inherited from their history and the political status that was imposed on them.

The notion of founding peoples would be unacceptable if it meant that Canadians of British or French origin ought to have more rights than other Canadians. But it draws its meaning from the fact that Canada has the good fortune to have two official languages that are also international languages, windows on the world. With regard to the more fragile situation of French, Canada has inherited from its history the good fortune, the privilege and the duty to promote French and French-language cultures in Quebec, in Canada as a whole and throughout the world, and to make this heritage accessible to Canadians of all origins.

The notion of distinct society, or a society with a unique character, cannot give Quebecers more rights or privileges than other Canadians. Possible constitutional recognition of this notion could not give the Government of Quebec more powers than the other provincial governments, without it being known in advance what those would be. This notion means that the Canadian federation must be flexible enough to address the varied needs of its federated components, including the unique character of Quebec society.

That unique character is easy to identify: Quebec is the only province where Francophones and Anglophones alike can be described both as a majority and as a minority. Francophones are the majority in Quebec, but are a minority in Canada and a very small minority in North America. Quebec Anglophones are certainly part of the majority in North America and Canada, but in Quebec, where they live and work, they are a minority. The pursuit of the harmonious cohabitation between Francophones and Anglophones in Quebec is taking place in the unique context of Quebec society. It is incumbent on governments and the courts to take that unique character into account. And that is just what the Supreme Court of Canada does, according to one of its former chief justices, the late Brian Dickson. For all practical purposes, potential constitutional recognition of Quebec's specificity would merely formalize existing practice.

The Canadian federation, and in particular, the division of constitutional powers between the federal and provincial governments, are not organized on the basis of collective identities, defined in terms of peoples or nations. Rather, it is individual rights that still and always are paramount: the objective, as set out in the Constitution, is that the federation ensure that all citizens, to the greatest possible extent, have access to public services of comparable and optimal quality. But that quality is achieved in different ways, depending on the different contexts of each province. It is important that each province have the means to pursue that quest for quality, and this is the basis for the extensive redistribution mechanisms to benefit the less wealthy provinces.

The provinces have equality of status. There is only one status for provinces in Canada, not two or three—either you are a province, or you are not. In law, they all have the same constitutional responsibilities. In practice, however, some provinces, particularly the province of Quebec, have used the potential afforded them by Canada's Constitution much more than other provinces have. A number of federal government policies encourage this flexibility. For example, the recent job training agreements allowed the provinces to choose either extensive autonomy or co-management of programs with the federal government. The Government of Newfoundland chose co-management, while the Government of Quebec chose autonomy. The flexibility of Canadian federalism thus allows for a de facto asymmetry that is quite pronounced in comparison with what is generally found in other federations.

We can see that the provinces' equality of status is not to be confused with uniformity. It is perfectly in keeping with the plural quest for high-quality public service.

This is the Canadian way of seeking unity in diversity. It is based on the primacy of individual rights. But it does not establish these rights in the abstract; it takes into account the diverse realities of which individuals are a part. Our multiculturalism, our bilingualism and our federalism all give tangible expression to the way individual rights mesh with collective realities.

2. The Canadian method and the challenge of separatism

There and those who say that the existence of a separatist movement in Quebec is proof that Canadian federalism doesn't work. I say that's inaccurate: Canada is undeniably a country that works in comparison with others, in the sense that it provides its citizens with one of the best qualities of life in the world. That quality of life stems in large part from a spirit of tolerance, openness and mutual trust between different populations that is hard to find elsewhere. Canada can and must be improved, but we shall do so even more effectively once we have resolutely decided to stay together.

To improve Canada, we need to build on its diversity and to see it as a strength. But we cannot build on its diversity while denying its most fundamental dimension: the inalienable difference which makes each individual, each person, a unique human being. To renounce the primacy of individual rights, to organize the country primarily along the lines of collective representations of identity as defined by public authorities, which they would refer to as peoples, nations or what have you, to submerge individuals into these collective entities, is not building unity in diversity. It is proposing an artificial uniformity within each of those collective constructions.

There are those who claim that Quebecers, Quebec Francophones, at least, look uniformly to their provincial government, whereas Canadians in the other provinces look to the federal government. And so the Canadian federation should be recognized in accordance with those supposed preferences: centralize Canada outside Quebec and hand over to the Quebec government a large number of the responsibilities currently assumed by the federal government.

But such a simplistic vision of things is not borne out by opinion polls. Quebecers are not uniformly lined up behind their provincial government any more than other Canadians are the centralizers they are made out to be. For example, an EKOS poll in November 1997 indicated that better cooperation between governments is the preferred solution of 51% of Quebecers and 60% of Canadians outside Quebec, compared with decentralization to the provinces, favoured by 38% of Quebecers and 22% of Canadians outside Quebec, and centralization toward the federal government, the choice of 8% of Quebecers and 18% of Canadians outside Quebec.

Canadians throughout the country prefer better cooperation between the two orders of government rather than radical centralization or decentralization. Decentralization has more support in Quebec than it does elsewhere, but even in Quebec, the most popular choice is that of better cooperation between governments.

Another false solution, akin to the previous one, is what I called internal separatism. This consists of giving the separatists part of the powers they are calling for, in the hope that they will get to the point where they lose their appetite for separation. For Canada, which is already a very decentralized federation, this would mean gradually handing over almost all public responsibilities to the Government of Quebec. By doing so, it would be hoped that the vast majority of Quebecers would be satisfied with this extensive autonomy, and that the hardline separatists would be marginalised.

In my opinion, it would be a mistake to pursue such a strategy. Every new concession made to appease the separatists would lead Quebecers to withdraw ever further into their territory, to define themselves by an exclusive "us", to see other Canadians increasingly only from afar, and to reject the Canadian government and common Canadian institutions as a threat to their nation, a foreign body. The division of powers between the two orders of government is not a bargaining chip that can be used to allay separatism.

Internal separatism is a strategy doomed to failure. It cannot make a country work in unity. What the separatists want is not piecemeal powers, yesterday job training, tomorrow an enhanced role at UNESCO. What they hope for is for Quebec to be a separate country. They want to cease being Canadian. Lucien Bouchard said so yet again as recently as June 5: "A people must conduct itself as a people and manage its own affairs within its own state." (Translation)

The separatist leaders' ideology of exclusive nationalism consists of presenting our Canadian dimension as something foreign to ourselves as Francophone Quebecers. Something foreign and unnecessary, and worse, something harmful and threatening. That's why the separatist leaders don't want to ask a clear question on secession: they know that their exclusive nationalism is rejected by a clear majority of Quebecers. The main obstacle to their project is that the vast majority of Quebecers feel that they are Canadians too. That is confirmed by all the opinion polls: something like 80% of Quebecers feel that they have a Canadian identity in addition to their Quebec identity. Quebec nationalism is generally open to the Canadian dimension and the Quebec dimension alike.

Quebecers in general see themselves as a people, but they also see themselves as belonging to the Canadian people, and they don't have a problem acknowledging the existence of more than one people in Quebec. Many remain attached to the French-Canadian people. They appreciate these different identities and make them their own, and are wary of exclusive conceptions of the nation.

Quebecers clearly feel that the reason we have a federation is not so that we can withdraw farther away from one another. It is so we can pursue common objectives together, through the diversity of our experiences and institutions and the plurality of our identities.

Conclusion

Georges-Étienne Cartier believed that Canada should be a political nationality, where different populations can work together in all confidence for the common good, without having to fear the melting pot of uniformity. That was an innovative idea at the time. Assimilation was actively promoted throughout the Western world in the 19th century by those with a liberal spirit, for example through one-size-fits-all mandatory schooling. They saw it as a precondition for ensuring equality of opportunity among individuals.

Assimilation has existed and still exists in Canada, but on the whole it has failed. Francophone and Anglophone had to learn first to tolerate one another, then to better respect one another, and then to extend one another a helping hand. This difficult learning process, including its darker pages, made them better disposed to welcome new citizens from every corner of the globe.

Canada is still a political nationality. The ideal pursued by our country, through its federative form, its democratic institutions, its charter of rights, its bilingualism and its multiculturalism, is to enable all its citizens to flourish in freedom, taking into account the context in which they are evolving, and respecting their collective loyalties, including the unique character of Quebec society.

I am not saying that Canada has managed to achieve this ideal. I am saying that the pursuit of this ideal holds the key to strengthening our unity. I also believe that this ideal is universal in scope, and that the pursuit of this ideal may help countries that, in contexts more difficult than our own, in South Asia and elsewhere, need to achieve harmony among their populations, and to seek, in some way, their own Canada.

Endnote

* This is an address delivered by the Hon. Stéphane Dion to the South Asian Council of Canadian Asian Studies Association, in Montreal on June 10, 1999.

REFERENCES

Elazar, Daniel J. (1994). *Federalism and the Way to Peace.*
          Reflections Paper no. 13, presented at Queen's University.
Boutros-Ghali, Boutros. (1992). *An Agenda for Peace.* New York:
          United Nations.

Chapter 6

MANAGING DIVERSITY

Stephen E. Nancoo

INTRODUCTION

The face and fabric of the Canadian workforce are changing. Fundamental demographic changes that are fueled by changing immigration patterns, an aging population and the influx of women in the workplace are creating a more diverse workforce and workplace. Already a fact of organizational life, a portrait of the new workforce reveals significant new dimensions of diversity in terms of age, education, gender, cultures, race, values and the physically challenged. Trends indicate that this diversity will become more pervasive, providing organizations, their leaders and managers with enormous challenges and opportunities well into the twenty-first century.

Historically, a defining difference between the Canadian and United States experience is the comparison between the mosaic (Canada) versus melting pot (United States) description of these two countries. In the United States, however, the melting pot theory that was very popular in the first third of the twentieth century is now less popular in the United States. Indeed, the social psychologist Triandis (1994) makes a compelling case for "additive multiculturalism" that allows for a policy that elicits increased appreciation of U.S. minorities and their ethnic identities. It is interesting, therefore, that although the case for additive mulitculturalism is of relatively recent origin in the United States, most of the published research and writing on diversity reflect the US experience. In terms of the Canadian experience, there is a paucity of research and writing in the area of managing the diverse Canadian workforce, a fact cogently documented by a number of scholars, in a recent issue of the *Canadian Journal of Administrative Sciences* (Burke, 1991; Kirchmeyer and McLellan, 1991; Joy Mighty, 1991).

This chapter examines the impact of diversity, offers some theoretical and empirical arguments in favour of diversity, suggests approaches to managing diversity through organizational change and cultivating a culture of diversity in organizations. Finally, linkages between diversity and other leadership and managerial techniques will be made and their meaning for the future of organizations and organizational learning are explored.

Impact of Diversity

Given that diversity is an organizational fact of life, the question as to how mangers and leaders are harnessing the capacities and talents of this diverse workforce suggests a need for empirical answers. Based on her research, Russell (*Women Building Careers in a Diverse Society*, Chapter 7, in this volume) identifies barriers women encounter in their efforts to build careers in contemporary work organizations. Some of the common approaches used to manage minority and other cultural groups are also faulted by researchers (Kirchmeyer, McLellan, 1991, Joy Mighty, 1991).

One of the approaches employed by organizations in managing diversity is through a homogenization of their workforces. This approach advances a monocultural view of organizational life that ignores potentially valuable new perspectives and interests, deprives the organization of value added human capital, suppresses constructive conflict and places enormous pressure to conform to established practices thereby stifling creativity and innovation (Brown, 1983; Fernandez, 1981).

There are telling findings based on the limited research in the Canadian milieu. Reitz (1988) found that among minorities there were patterns of wage inequality, a slower achievement of upward mobility and an underutilization of their knowledge and skills. Burke (1991) noted that minority managers experienced more discriminatory treatment and greater resistance to equality. He also found that organizations that provided a more favourable climate for minority managers and professionals may experience benefits among white males as well. Zureik (1983) concluded that while Canadian managers view race and ethnicity to be irrelevant to promotional opportunity, minority group members have to be better performers in order to succeed in organizations.

In a review of the research literature, Kirchmeyer and McLellan listed the following organizational barriers encountered by members of minority groups: isolation from key information and informal networks in organizations, withholding of challenging assignments from minorities, less autonomy and less discretion for minority workers as compared to non-minority workers, low supervisory expectations of the abilities of minorities and a lack of mentoring or sponsoring of members of minority groups.

Advantages and Disadvantages of Diversity

Diversity shows mixed results in organizations. On the disadvantageous end of the spectrum, evidence suggests that intercultural conflict and diverse subjective cultures may lead to reduced cohesion Other diversity effects include conflict and stress (Fernandez, 1991), ineffective group interaction (Fenelon and Megatree, 1971); the potential for lower productivity and morale (Solomon, 1989). What, therefore, can an organization gain from diversity? In making the case for treating diversity as a necessary part of business strategy, Morrison (1992, pp.18-28) identified a number of tangible benefits accruing from diversity. These include:

1. Keeping and gaining the market share. A diverse workforce will be valuable in building sales, capturing diverse markets and providing better customer service, increasing the organizational competitiveness and facilitate the penetration of an increasingly global marketplace.

2. Cost savings. Morrison's survey revealed that "many executives believe that an effective approach to fostering diversity will save money over the long term and often even in the short run."

3. Increased productivity. Although it is difficult to assess the impact of diversity on productivity, Morrison found that many organizational executives expect greater productivity from employees who enjoy coming to work, who are relaxed instead of defensive or stressed in their work setting, and who are happy to be

working where they feel valued and competent. Another group of researchers concluded that there is a positive relationship between employees' perception of being valued and cared about by their organization and their attendance, dedication and job performance (Eisenberger, Fasolo and Davis-LaMastro, 1990). Donna Thompson and Nancy diTomaso (1988) argue that a multicultural approach has a positive effect on employees' perception of equity, which in turn affects their morale, goal setting effort and performance. Organizational productivity is consequently improved. Cox and Blake (1991) present evidence linking diversity to enhanced creativity and innovation. The Eisenberger group also found that employees who felt valued and cared about by their organization were more innovative without any direct reward of personal recognition. Birnbaum (1981) and Ziller (1972) showed that heterogeneous groups (in terms of race, age, values, background, training and so on) are more productive than homogeneous groups. A number of executives interviewed by Morrison were convinced that diversity would enhance their organization's ability to find innovative solutions to business problems and to create a wide range of goods and services.

4. Better Quality Management. By enlarging the pool of talent from which to choose there is a greater likelihood that the quality of management will be improved.

Other researchers have found that heterogeneous groups tend to be more creative than homogeneous groups, consequently leading to higher quality decisions (McGrath, 1984; Triandis et. al, 1965; Willems and Clark, 1971). On the other hand, homogeneity leads to group think and poor decision making (Janis, 1982).

Jain (1992) makes a significant statement in regards to the positive impact of diversity on economic relations. He postulates:

> Since commerce and trading with other nations are becoming the mainstay of Canada, and international competition is on the rise, managers of Canadian organizations will increasingly work with their counterparts from different countries, cultures and ethnic and racial groups. Canadian organizations and management must of necessity utilize talent regardless of gender and colour to remain competitive, to survive and to grow. Managing a

diverse workforce therefore, has become a critical issue if Canadian organizations are to gain and retain a competitive edge.

This idea is reflected in Canada's strategic direction in terms of its trade policy as exemplified by Prime Minister Jean Chretien's trade trips to India, China and Latin America.

Most importantly, organizations, both public and private, should in the final analysis internalize the diversity agenda because of, what I would describe as, the ethical imperative: that is doing it because it is the most appropriate and the right and fair thing to do (For a perceptive account of the relationship between ethics and diversity, see essay by David Roy, Chapter 15 in this Volume).

Inspite of the obvious advantages that could be derived from a diverse workforce, Morrison concludes that there are important barriers manifesting mindsets that are out of tune with today's workforce and the organizational demands for successful, well-performing organizations. What is needed therefore is for organizational managers and leaders to engage in strategic and determined efforts at changing the culture of their organizations to reflect the values of diversity.

Organizational change

To initiate, sustain and effectively manage and value diversity require fundamental organizational change, that is, a change in the culture of the organization. This observation is based on this author's involvement in training managers and leaders from different levels of organizations (from supervisory to executive) from every Canadian province over the last fifteen years. Leaders initiating organizational change must undertake three related processes: 1. Leaders must have a clear vision of an ideal or desirable future state. Leaders must ensure that through a process of dialogue with stakeholders, their vision must become a shared vision. 2 Leaders must make a realistic assessment of their organization's current situation. 3. Leaders and organizational members must deliberately plan to close the gap between the present state and the ideal future state. In the transitional period, visionary leaders should develop goals and formulate strategies for moving the organization from the present to the future state.

Understanding the state of the present organizational culture is a necessary first stage. Changing the culture is what is required in managing and leading the diversity advantage into the future.

Creating a Culture of Diversity

Loden and Rosener (1991), and Gardenswartz and Rowe (1993) are among the advocates emphasizing the importance of creating a culture of diversity within organizations. They write: "When valuing diversity becomes the norm, not the exception; when others are part of the mainstream and no longer on the periphery; when the organization automatically utilizes the talents of all employees—then the ultimate goal will finally be achieved, and full lasting benefits of the culture of diversity will be apparent to everyone"(p.215).

Three phases of creating a culture of diversity, as proposed by Loden and Rosener, are:

1. Setting the stage by endorsing the value of diversity and communicating this value throughout the organization.

2. Education and change implementation practices through a systematic process of awareness and culture change. This would include awareness education, diversifying decision making groups, creating structures to support organizational change and developing coaching and tutoring mechanisms.

3. Ongoing maintenance of the culture change by the development of on-going activators that ensure that valuing diversity remains a high priority.

Creating a corporate culture that embraces diversity is also proposed by Lee Gardenswartz and Anita Rowe (1993, pp. 385-412). They emphasize the importance of nurturing an inclusive organizational culture and introduce assessment tools for measuring the degree of openness in an organization's climate. Recognizing that the resistance to change is a factor in an organization's cultural rigidity, they argued for planned steps to be taken in the transition from a monocultural to a multicultural organization.

Their prescription for a successful diversity effort is for a battle that must be waged on the individual as well as the organizational fronts. In terms of organizational action, they identify the need for (a) creating involvement and commitment at every level of the organization, (b) teaching cross cultural management, (c) building valuing diversity into the bone marrow of the organization (d) accepting the demographic reality (e) making rapid change the constant and, (f) being willing to pierce the power structure.

Jamieson and O'Mara (1993, pp. 34-41) advanced a case for changing the management mindset and introducing a "flex management" model that prescribes new directions for managing the diverse workforce. They identified four strategies: matching people and jobs, managing and rewarding performance, informing and involving people, and supporting lifestyle needs.

In a flex management approach, they explained, by changing an organization's polices and systems, one can also change organizational values. These values are a new corporate mindset based on individualizing, providing choices, seeing people as assets, valuing differences, encouraging greater self-management, and creating flexibility.

Morrison (1992, p.160) recommends a five step action process for developing diversity in organizations:

- Discover diversity problems in your organization.
- Strengthen top management commitment.
- Choose solutions that fit a balanced strategy.
- Demand results and revisit the goals.
- Use building blocks to maintain momentum.

Linkages between Diversity and Approaches to Leadership and Management

For diversity initiatives to survive and flourish, they must be integrated with other leadership and management processes. There are complementary linkages between valuing diversity and contemporary leadership and management practices as strategic planning, total quality management, team building, empowerment and creating a learning organization.

Strategic Planning and Leadership

Strategic planning is the process whereby organizational leaders in partnership with stakeholders determine the vision, mission, values and goals of the organization and how to achieve them.

Leaders transform their organizations by formulating a compelling shared vision of what the organization is capable of becoming. The idea is to create an ideal preferred future.

Leaders also need to do an environmental assessment to form an understanding of the organizations' current status in terms of their strengths and weaknesses, threats and opportunities

---

A Strategic Planning and Leadership Model

(1)

Where we are?
Assessment
of current
situation.

(2)

Where we ought to be?
Create a VISION of an
ideal, preferred future.

(3)

How do we get there? How do we
achieve our VISION? Organizational
culture change. Strategic leadership
to create mission, values, goals and
action plans to achieve and institutionalize the ideal preferred future
of diversity.

Having established the gap between where the organization is and where it ought to be, leaders must strategically lead and manage the process in order to effect the necessary organizational transformations. In so doing they need to elaborate their mission and values and develop goals and action plans to achieve the vision as illustrated in the Strategic Leadership and Planning Model above.

Total quality management (TQM) is a process of continuous improvement, evaluation and adjustment to ensure that the customer/client receives the highest quality service or product at the lowest cost. Thomas (1991) identified several commonalties between TQM and managing diversity. For example: both TQM and managing diversity are rooted in the possibility of organizational competitiveness. TQM places a high emphasis on employee involvement. Similarly, managing diversity is premised upon the empowerment of the diverse community of employees so that their full potential will be tapped. Furthermore, like managing diversity, total quality management is for the long term. Total quality management and managing diversity programs both call for fundamental organizational culture change to successfully implement these programs. Thomas writes that "when managing diversity is integrated with total quality, the most significant implementation challenges that remain with total quality are more successfully addressed"(p. 165).

Team building. Fostering teamwork is all about getting people to work together toward common goals. Effective teamwork is built on the foundation of cooperative—a sharing of the work—and collaborative—a sharing of the power or authority—relationships.

There is a belief that fostering teamwork and self managing teams enable an organization to achieve its goals in an effective manner. "When properly designed and appropriately nurtured, these teams provide a substantial competitive advantage in the marketplace, as well as a human or social advantage in the workplace" (Jamieson and O'Mara, 1991, p.130).

Self managing teams have the potential of providing the organization with a competitive advantage in the marketplace through enlightened customer/client practices. Equally important, they also have the capacity of providing for human and social advantage through employee satisfaction.

There is a school of thought which suggests that developing quality teams is becoming more difficult. Fernandez and Shaw believe that this difficulty stems from the fact that "customer and employees are becoming more diverse. Quality teams are likely to consist of people who differ in race, ethnic background, gender, age, sexual orientation and other dimensions. They maintain that the difficulties are surmountable if organizations train their people to understand and respect their diversity, as well as to understand teamwork and other tools for innovation" (Canervale and Stone, 1994).

Empowerment: Empowerment is a central tenet, a core value in the managing/leading diversity paradigm. Managing diversity is a critical determinant of the success of efforts to empower employees.

Rosabeth Moss Kanter (1984) advanced four principles that empower others: (1) Give people important work to do on critical issues. (2) Give people direction and autonomy over their tasks and resources. (3) Give visibility to others and provide recognition for their efforts. (4) Build relationships for others, connecting them with powerful people and finding them sponsors and mentors.

Building a Learning Organization

Developing and nurturing a learning organization is the glue that integrates the total quality management, teamwork, empowerment and managing diversity processes.

Peter Senge et. al. (1994, p.6) describes the core elements of the learning organization as:

> **Personal mastery** — learning to expand our personal capacity to create the results we most desire, and creating an organizational environment which encourages all its members to develop themselves toward the goals and purposes they choose.
>
> **Mental models** — reflecting upon, continually clarifying, and improving our internal pictures of the world, and seeing how they shape our actions and decisions.
>
> **Shared Vision** — building a sense of commitment in a group, by developing shared images of the future we seek to create, and the principles and guiding practices by which we hope to get there.
>
> **Team Learning** — transforming conversational and collective thinking skills, so that groups of people can reliably develop intelligence and ability greater than the sum of individual members' talents.
>
> **Systems thinking** — a way of thinking about, and a language for describing and understanding, the forces and interrelationships that shape the behaviour of systems. This discipline helps us see

how to change systems more effectively, and to act more in tune with the larger processes of the natural and economic world.

The relationship between organizational learning and managing diversity is evident. For client/customer centred organizations, where it is imperative to identify the processes that are fundamental for the continuous improvement of the product and service necessary for client/customer satisfaction, it is more likely that the multi-cultural workforce will lead to the realization of the shared vision of a competitive advantage in the global marketplace. We are witnessing a significant internationalization of the workforce and internationalization of cultures within organizations. Organizations and their members have to learn to adapt to this internationalization of culture. They will be able to effectively do so if there is a commitment to the valuing of the diverse workforce, which will be at the heart of the organization of the future. Those who embark on the journey of developing learning organizations which lead, manage and value diversity and capitalize on harnessing "the whole gamut of human potentialities" in their diverse workforce will be better able to adapt productively and creatively to the changes and challenges of the new millennium.

Conclusion

In this Chapter, I have attempted in a preliminary way to capture the essence of managing/leading diversity. We have observed that the Canadian workforce is changing, with significant new dimensions in terms of age, education, gender, culture, ethnicity, race, values and the physically challenged. The organization of the future is also changing in terms of our understanding, the structure and culture of organizations. Inspite of this, we have noted the limited amount of research in the Canadian literature on diversity within our public and business organizations. Even so we recognize the advantages of diversity and the need to create and nourish a culture of diversity within organizations of the future so that the full potential of the diverse workforce can be harnessed to the benefit of the organization as well as Canadian society. We also made linkages between diversity and such contemporary leadership and management practices as total quality management, teamwork and empowerment. Finally, we have emphasized the need to develop and nurture strategic leadership with strategic planning tools as well as establish learning communities to institutionalize the values and culture of diversity. This development would enable us to adapt and benefit from the changes and challenges that are an inherent part of the internationalization of the organization culture and the realities of a diverse workplace which will become increasingly more pronounced in the 21st century.

References

Birnbaum, P. (1981)."Integration and Specialization in Academic Research." *Academy of Management Journal,* 24.

Brown, L. D. (1983). *Managing conflict at organizational interfaces.* Reading, MA: Addison-Wesley.

Burke, R. (1991). Managing an Increasingly Diverse Workforce Workforce: Experiences of Minority Managers and Professionals in Canada. *Canadian Journal of Administrative Sciences,* 8 (2), 108-120.

Cox, T. H., and Blake, S. (1991). "Managing Cultural Diversity Implications for Organizational Competitiveness," *Academic of Management Executive,* 1991. 5, 45-54.

Cox, T. and Finley Nickeson, J. (1991). Models of Acculturation for Intra-Organizational Diversity, *Canadian Journal of Administrative Sciences*, 8 (2), 90-100.

Eisenberger, R., Fasolo, P. and Davis-LaMastro, V. (1990). "Perceived Organizational Support and Employee Diligence, Commitment and Innovation." *Journal of Applied Psychology,* 75, 51-59.

Fenelon, J. R. and Megatree, E. I. Influence of Race on the manifestation of Leadership. *Journal of Applied Psychology*, 55, 353-358.

Fernandez, J.P. (1991). *Managing a Diverse Work Force: Regaining the Competitive Edge*. New York: Lexington Books.

Gardenswartz, L. and Rowe, A. (1993) *Managing Diversity*. Illinois: Business One Irwin.

Jain, H C. (1992). Employment Equity and Visible Minorities: Have the Federal Policies Worked? *Canadian Labour Law Journal,* Vol. 1, p. 388.

Jamieson, D. and O'Mara, J. (1991). *Managing Workforce 2000.* San Francisco: Josey-Bass Publishers.

Janis, I.L. (1982). Groupthink in J. L. Gibson, J. M. Ivancevich, & J.H. Donnelly (eds). *Reading in organizations.* Plano, TX: Business Publications.

Joy Mighty, E. (1991). Valuing Workforce Diversity: A Model of Organizational Change. Canadian Journal of Administrative Sciences, 8(2), 64-70.

Kirchmeyer, C. and McLellan, J. (1991). Capitalizing on Ethnic Diversity: An Approach to Managing the Diverse Workgroups of the 1990s. *Canadian Journal of Administrative Sciences,* (8), 72-79.

Loden, M. and Rosener J. B. (1991) *Workforce America! Managing Employee Diversity as a Vital Resource.* Illinois: Business One Irwin.

McGrath, J. (1984). *Groups: Interaction and performance.* Englewood Cliffs, NJ: Prentice Hall.

Morrison, A. M. (1992) *The New Leaders*, San Francisco: Josey-Bass Publishers.

Senge, P., Kleiner, A., Roberts, C., Ross, R.B., Smith, B.J. (1994). *The Fifth Discipline Fieldbook.* New York: Doubleday.

Thomas, R. (1991). *Beyond Race and Gender.* New York: AMACOM.

Thompson, B. L. and DiTomaso, N. Eds. (1988). *Ensuring Minority Success in Corporate Management.* New York: Plenum, 1988.

Triandis, H.C. (1994) *Culture and Social Behavior.* New York: McGraw Hill Inc.

Willems, E.P. and Clark, R. D. (1971). Shift towards risk and heterogeneity of groups. *Journal of Experimental Psychology*, 7, 304-312.

Ziller, R.C. "Homogeneity and Heterogeneity of Group Membership." In C. G. McClintoch (ed.) *Experimental Social Psychology.* New York: Holt, Rinehart & Winston.

Chapter 7

WOMEN BUILDING CAREERS
IN A DIVERSE SOCIETY

Roberta J. Russell

In a recent interview Betty Friedan, commenting on the direction the feminist movement has taken, said "What concerns women most is jobs—getting them, keeping them, getting promoted in them" (Wente, 1993). The focus of this paper is the career advancement of women, the barriers that limit that advancement, and the ways in which individual women and organizations have already or can in the future deal more effectively with those barriers.

This paper draws on current feminist and management literature and from two studies conducted by the author in the early 1990s of middle managers in the fields of public administration and education to illustrate some of the challenges women face in contemporary work organizations and the ways in which some of them are dealing with those challenges. The paper examines:

- the ways in which their careers develop, particularly the barriers they encounter in their efforts to build careers,
- the ways in which they individually address some of these barriers and change organizations in the process, and finally,
- the implications for organizational policy and for training and development practices designed to provide them with a "more level playing field", to use a popular sports analogy, in the 21st century.

This paper uses data from two studies of women and men administrators in education and public administration to illustrate some of the points being discussed. The participants for one study (Russell, 1993) were randomly selected from school systems in eastern Ontario and middle managers in the public service based in the National Capital Region while participants for the other study of visible minority administrators (Russell and Wright, 1992) came from school systems in Halifax, Ottawa, Toronto, Winnipeg and Vancouver. Sixteen of the forty-three administrators (21 females and 22 males) individually interviewed were visible minorities. Each of the studies also made use of focus groups and interviews with "elites" (Marshall and Rossman, 1989), people considered to have a good understanding and/or valuable "insider" knowledge of the relationship between career development and gender and race. These elites included employment equity officers, human resource specialists, editors of books or leaders of task forces related to the subject, and union representatives.

The interviews with individual managers focused on biographical information and early career experiences; views of mentoring professionalism, success and opportunities in contempo-rary organizations; and strategies used for coping with barriers. Focus groups (Krueger, 1988; Morgan, 1988a) and elite interviews were conducted during the design phase to generate insights and vet the interview guide and after data collection to vet preliminary findings. Standard qualitative methodology for the analysis of long interviews (McCracken, 1988) and focus groups (Krueger) were utilized.

In examining issues related to women in the workplace, and particularly women in management, one of the great challenges one faces is the difficulty of imagining what the post-2000 work world will look like. In a survey Decima Research conducted for Maclean's at the end of 1994, 69% of Canadians interviewed said that everything was changing so fast that they found it hard to imagine life 10 years from now. The news media contributes to this uncertainty with diverse and often contradictory reports on the status of women in the workplace. Within the same week one may see newspaper articles to the effect that the glass ceiling is beginning to shatter and that women are advancing on all fronts, that the work outlook is bleak for women, that a woman's work is never done because women do twice as much around the house as men, or that the "new economy" is hitting female employees particularly hard. Obviously, women's careers is a complex subject.

Michael Fullan (1993) argues that we need a new mind-set for contending with the complexity of the dynamic and continuous forces of change which are being experienced at all levels of society. "The solution", he says, "lies in better ways of thinking about, and dealing with, inherently unpredictable processes" (p. 19). In the late 1970s Rosabeth Moss Kanter (1977) introduced a "new mind-set" to the way we look at the experiences of women in the workplace. She helped us get away from the "Us versus them" (men versus women) approach to focus on structures and the ways in which they can shape career outcomes.

In spite of all the uncertainty, there are some things we do know. The number of women in Canada's workforce is increasing. While access is improving, women continue, despite credentials as good as or better than their male peers, to be differentially rewarded for their contributions (Beauchesne, 1995). Thus, while the challenge of "getting in" has largely been addressed, "getting on" within the organization continues to be a problem for many women (Peitchinis, 1989). Even in fields and organizations where women have tended to dominate numerically, such as education, public administration, and banking, they continue to experience organizational life from the bottom of the organizational hierarchy. In addition, the optimism of the early 1980s about women's career opportunities has been tempered by the organizational downsizing and delayering of recent years.

Available statistics on women in fields as diverse as banking, academe, school systems, politics, and government demonstrate that only modest progress has been made over the past twenty years. In Canada, women still constitute a minority of university presidents; members of the federal cabinet; upper level executives in banking; executive level managers in the federal government, and members of the Senate. The growth of women managers has not been proportional to the overall influx of women into the workforce. The fact that the numbers of women middle managers in both government and education are increasing may appear to be reason for optimism until one considers that both organizations are among the most "women friendly" in our society, having traditionally employed a higher proportion of women than most other organizations. In addition, most of these women are relatively recent appointees to their positions and their numbers are increasing very slowly. Some estimate that if gains proceed at the current rate it may take another twenty or more years for women to achieve equity with men in the workplace.

The Literature: Career Development and Career Barriers

It was not until the 1970s that there was much consideration given by researchers to the study of women managers. Early in the 1960s, Packard (1962) could write that he was being reasonably accurate in his use of language when he referred to executives as "he", since women so rarely attained top executive jobs. He went on to describe women as "perhaps the most discriminated against of all minority groups in industry" (p.35). Writing nearly 25 years later, Yeakey, Johnston and Adkison (1986) noted that despite the fact that "occupations, industries, and organizations have exhibited patterns of racial and sexual stratification that have persisted historically" (p.111), studies of organizations had virtually ignored this fact. By the early 1980s, however, Albrecht (1983) wrote that women in management was a rapidly emerging issue and predicted that it would "probably become one of the key social issues in business for the rest of the century" (p.93).

With the increased research attention to women in the workplace, it has become clear that by almost any measure used, women are underrepresented in the senior levels of work organizations in North America, even at the level of middle management. While there have been extraordinary changes in the status of women in North American society since the beginning of the 1960s, the careers of those women who did advance in work organizations tended to plateau at the middle management level. My rationale for focusing on middle managers was my belief in the need to better understand the career plateauing phenomenon, the glass ceiling, experienced by many women at that middle management level.

According to Florence Bird (Personal communication, March 14, 1990), Chair of the Royal Commission on the Status of Women in Canada (Supply and Services Canada, 1970), members of the Commission had assumed that once women reached middle-level management positions they would routinely move up to the senior levels of organizational management. This has not happened.

Women managers have also tended to occupy positions in such areas as personnel and human resources, elementary education, public relations and communications, the so-called "velvet ghetto" (Ghiloni, 1987). While such positions were initially seen as representing progress for women, they appear to isolate or ghettoize women from mainstream organizational issues and operations and to restrict them to areas seen as ones to which women are naturally better suited. That isolation appears to limit their access to the experiences and information needed to develop the organizational overview necessary to upward mobility in the organization.

Organizations have traditionally been seen as passive and neutral, a view suggesting that any barriers women or others experience are the result of their own deficiencies. This perspective reflects a classic "blame the victim" (Ryan, 1971) view of the world and promotes "a kind of self-help for women" approach (Marshall and Mitchell, 1989, p.2), advising them to behave more like men in order to succeed. Wright (1988) critiques that approach, saying that "according to this view, claims that women can obtain power and authority by learning to behave more assertively naively overlook the effects of organizational structure on people's careers" (p.173).

A more contemporary perspective sees institutions as actors in their own right and not simply as the sum of outside forces or their members. Added to that perspective is the view that differences in career outcome are best explained in terms of differential access to opportunities and experience (Kanter, 1977), that what an individual brings into the organization is considerably influenced by such socially constructed institutional factors as training, orientation, and other factors related to the way in which the workplace is organized.

Earlier approaches to explaining differences in male and female career outcomes focused on differences in the ways men and women work and used those differences to justify the underrepresentation of women in leadership roles. In recent years there has been increased awareness of the fact that women and men in organizations have been given different opportunities to build careers (Morgan, 1988b; Rees, 1990; Task Force on Barriers to Women in the Public Service, 1990; Bank of Montreal, 1991).

An extensive body of literature has developed which documents the barriers women experience in their efforts to advance their careers in organizations (Kanter, 1977; Stokes, 1984; Shakeshaft, 1987; Morrison, 1992). Research (Kanter, 1977;

Fernandez, 1981; Ortiz, (1982) suggests that the experiences of workers within the same occupational groupings and within the same organizations may differ significantly, that these differences are based on gender and racial discrimination, and that this more fully explains what Asplund (1988) describes as "careers in slow motion"—the slow ascent of women and minorities up the organizational hierarchy—than have previous theories. Recent studies by the U.S. Department of Labour (1991) and the Government of Canada (Task Force on Barriers, 1990) document the fact that the credential building experiences and career enhancing assignments available to men are too often unavailable to women. A number of barriers to their being provided such opportunities have been identified. Key among these are men's preference for working and socializing with other men which tends to isolate women from important information supply networks (Kirp, Yudof, and Franks, 1986; Russell, 1993) and the "spotlight effect" (Asplund, 1988) experienced by non-traditional managers, "being noticed more, watched more, and judged more" (Morrison, p.64) than their white male colleagues. Others have written about the role chance plays in the development of women's careers (Young, 1991) and that it is the norm for women's careers to develop in a non-linear pattern (Clark, Caffarella, and Ingram, 1993). Denied the developmental experiences their male colleagues can take for granted, how do women cope?

A 1991 report by the Bank of Montreal on the advancement of women in its organization also illustrates some of the career advancement barriers which women experience in organizations. The Task Force report, based on responses from nearly 10,000 employees to an intensive questionnaire, is important because the problems it identifies are ones which have increasingly become the focus of other organizations and researchers trying to understand the experiences of women in work organizations. The report identified several assumptions or myths (p.6) which have been used to explain women's underrepresentation at senior levels as follows:

— women employees are too young or too old to compete for promotions. In fact, the average age of women employees of the bank was 37 compared to 38 for men.

— women are less committed to their careers because they have babies and quit. The study reported that women had longer service records than men at every level except senior management, where they are relative newcomers.

— women need more education in order to compete. At the non-management and junior management levels which are perceived as the feeder routes to senior levels, more women than men had degrees.

— women don't have "the right stuff" to compete successfully. More women than men figure in the top two tiers of performance.

— time will take care of women's advancement to senior levels of the Bank. The Task Force concluded that time is not the solution. It estimated that at the present rate of their progress, women would represent only 18% of executives and 22% of senior managers by the new millennium.

Kanter (1977) used the term "token" to describe people who are alone or nearly alone in a peer group. The rarity of their type in the group puts tokens in the position of representing their ascribed category to the group, locking them into pre-determined roles (e.g. woman-engineer). It is important to distinguish between this use of the term, token, and "colloquial references to the selection or placement of individuals solely on the basis of their membership in one or another demographic group" (Rebne, 1988, p.86).

According to Kanter (1977), the way in which group structures shape interaction contexts and influence particular patterns of male-female interaction can contribute more to a better understanding of the subject of gender and the workplace at this point in history. An advantage to this approach, she suggested, was that it made it possible to "generalize beyond male-female relations to persons-of-one-kind and persons-of-another-kind interaction in various contexts" while at the same time enabling researchers to untangle what is unique about the case of male-female interaction in work organizations. According to Laws (1975), "tokenism is likely to be found whenever a dominant group is under pressure to share privilege, power, or other desirable commodities with a group which is excluded" (p.51).

The manner in which organizations address issues of diversity today is the product of a long historical tradition. Dalton (1959), in his classic study of male managers documented the tendency on the part of managers to recruit people like themselves.

Writing in the 1930s, one of the fathers of management theory, Chester Barnard (1938), had justified this tendency, considering "associational attractiveness as exceedingly, and often critically, important" (p.146). By "associational attractiveness", Barnard said that he meant social compatibility and he went on to say that if homogeneity of race, class, religion, education, customs, etc. is missing in an organization "(m)en often will not work at all, and will rarely work well" (pp. 146-7). Packard (1962) suggested that such thinking has helped to establish white Protestant males as the "in-group" and gatekeepers to management in most large North American institutions (pp.39-40).

In addition to the difficulty of being seen as a representative of a group rather than as an individual, Bogart (1990) has documented the toll which "micro-inequities", the daily injustices they experience, take on the energy and confidence of tokens. Fernandez (1981) points out that "as tokens, every action is performed under the critical scrutiny of nontokens" (p.96), what Kanter (1977) describes as "performance pressure", Asplund (1988) refers to as the "spotlight effect", and Milwid (1990) terms "living under scrutiny" (p.39). As research by social psychologists demonstrates, one's performance may be considerably limited under such conditions (Goffman, 1963; Kleck and Nuessle, 1968).

The research on gender and the workplace fairly consistently confirms that men interact with men and women interact with women. While some suggest that this relates to fear of gossip or concerns about "ambiguity of intent" (Marshall, 1979), it seems possible that it may also be related to the common understandings, "consciousness of kind" (Bernard, 1981), that individuals of the same gender share, creating higher levels of comfort for same gender interactions. According to Shakeshaft (1987), male managers are reluctant to provide women with critical feedback on the quality of their work, in effect denying them knowledge that will help them correct deficiencies in their performance, an important element in organizational socialization. The result for women is that they are denied opportunities to learn about the organization.

These studies suggest that the expectations and attitudes conveyed by male gatekeepers in organizations rather than the actual performance of women may better explain the slower than expected progress of women into management and up the organizational hierarchy. Once identified as token, organizational expectations are adjusted to fit the stereotype held of the group of which the token is a member. In the case of women, research suggests that this may take the form of limiting access to as full a range of organizational socialization experiences as is necessary to acquire the knowledge and experience required for upward mobility in the organization (Schein, 1973, 1976; Ortiz, 1982).

To summarize then, there is a significant body of literature with a fairly lengthy research tradition and linked by a common thread of understanding which turns the focus of problem definition away from "victim-analysis" and "its preoccupation with the wounds, defects, and personalities of the victimized" (Ryan, 1971, p.119) to aspects of organizational functioning (Kanter, 1977). Many of the organizational structures and the experiences those structures shape, which Kanter and others discuss as ones women have greater difficulty in gaining access to, relate to organizational socialization.

Token status limits one's access to experiences and opportunities important to fitting into and advancing within organizations. These experiences and opportunities generally fall under the conceptual umbrella of organizational socialization. Organizational socialization has been described as a process of "being taught what is important in an organization or some subunit thereof" (Schein, 1977, p.211); as a "subjective process ... that happens to people as they move through a series of structured experiences and internalize the subculture of the group" (Lortie, 1975, p.61); and as "a process typically thought of as occurring at the time of organizational entry" (Pfeffer, 1982, p.96). Marshall (1977) emphasizes the power of this process to create organizational insiders and outsiders, describing the socialization process within organizations as "a selection process no less than a job interview" (p.4).

Marshall and Mitchell (1989) describe the "career environmental message" for women as one in which they can expect occupational segregation and the pressure of tokenism (Kanter, 1977), and where they can expect to work in "a culture whose norms were developed with the expectation that males will fill most positions" (p.4). They and others describe these norms as including the belief that military and team sports views of the world are most appropriate (Cava, 1988; Morgan, 1988b). The few women who move into the senior levels of management are women who are able to survive isolation, "fit into a foreign culture", and act and talk in ways abnormal for them (Marshall and Mitchell). Even when women encounter individual males who are supportive of their career aspirations, problems remain. Chase and Bell (1990) caution that "(w)hen gatekeepers (hirers) hold positive attitudes toward women, but are blind to the processes that re-create men's dominance of positions of power, then they may be helpful to individual women and at the same time participate in processes that reproduce men's dominance" (p.174).

According to Fernandez (1981), "(t)he informal system is at the heart of the middle management functions and grows still more critical with every step up the corporate ladder" (p.55) and it does not get easier for women and minorities as they move up in the organization. "If anything, reaching the upper levels makes exclusion more apparent and more painful since fewer same-race (or same sex) individuals are in those levels who can be used as sounding boards and support systems" (p.55), he says. They may feel even more "excluded because they naively believe when first entering the system that they will be judged on the basis of ability and work performance and thereby included in the informal networks". It becomes obvious, he says, that "total conformity" is "the prerequisite for admission to the club" but "race and sex are unalterable" (pp.55-6).

Others suggest that whether this socialization is gained through mentoring (Kanter, 1977; Epstein, 1988), buddy systems (Cooper and Smith, 1990), formal training programs (Asplund, 1988), or informal interactions with more experienced managers and senior executives (Fernandez, 1981; Shakeshaft, 1987), women will have fewer such experiences than will their male peers.

The preceding examination of existing research on women's career experiences, particularly their organizational socialization, suggests that many of the career experiences which have helped equip men to gain access to and to function effectively at the most senior levels of organizational life are ones which women are much less likely than their male colleagues to receive. At the same time, researchers and organizations are unlikely to understand or give consideration to the management skills women may have acquired through family or community volunteer work experiences (Young, 1991).

Research Results: Career Development and Career Barriers

Women managers in these studies, both educators and public servants, provided numerous examples from their careers to support the view that differential work assignments had represented a major career barrier for them.

As other research (Fernandez, 1981; Asplund, 1988) suggests, women interviewees tended, more than men, to assume that hard work and a high level of performance would be rewarded by promotions. While these women may have been naive about how promotions are decided, male interviewees, too, reported having been naive about such things at the beginning of their careers. Men, however, learned fairly quickly, most often through their informal networks, that other factors such as who you knew and visibility within the organization were important, too. Once they determined the role these factors played, they appeared to have more ready access than women did to the information and experiences needed in order to advance their careers. Women have been criticized for tending to focus more on credentials than on networking and career enhancing experiences, but it is possible that they focus on those aspects of their work lives over which they believe they have some control. They do not need anyone else's support or permission to register for training courses, particularly if they pay for the courses themselves, as women are more likely than men to do (Asplund, 1988). As one of the female educators interviewed said about the credential-experience issue, because women are too often denied the opportunities to practice the skills they will need in order to advance, they are likely to be credential rich, but experience poor.

Exposure to management through special projects or committee work, an "apprenticeship by observation", had been critical for many of the women interviewed. As one woman school principal described it, seeing management up close through such experiences creates an ambition for it, encouraging women who may never have considered a management career to develop interest in it. According to another, a woman manager in the public service, building a successful career benefits from participation in "special projects where you can be seen" and can learn. She was the youngest of all the women interviewed but she had a very good sense of how one advances, knowledge which seems to have come from a boss-mentor she had very early in her career. She credited his advice and coaching with giving her a slight advantage over her peers which helped her move ahead of them.

The informal system is at the heart of middle management functioning and becomes even more critical as one moves up the hierarchy. Women interviewed were often naive about the informal side of organizational life which, as tokens and outsiders, they rarely got to witness. The glass ceiling experienced by many women is, perhaps, best understood in this context. Women can get to middle management positions through hard work and determination, but something else is required beyond that level. As Fernandez (1981) suggested, that something else appears to relate to the kind of insider knowledge and broadly based and influential networks which produce the comfort level with organizational politics and power needed to function at the most senior levels of an organization.

One factor which appeared to provide visibility within the system was mentioned by several educators. It is, perhaps, best described as a "surprise factor", breaking a pattern or doing the unexpected. A couple of the examples provided included a male perceived by his colleagues as bookish or scholarly choosing to work with students who had difficulty in learning and a woman who was a specialist in a particular field choosing to move to a school which was very poorly equipped to support that specialization. They described such choices as providing them with career challenges, but acknowledged that such choices also served as "attention getters" for them, increasing their visibility.

The isolation described by several women and the male resistance to being managed by a female which one woman manager described are likely to limit performance without the mediating benefits of other factors such as a mentor. Three of the women managers described experiencing tokenism which appeared to have been tempered by considerable support from male mentors.

Several of the women interviewees talked about what it took to succeed. According to one, both self promotion, something she said she was good at, and visibility are important. Another appeared to intuitively understand the importance of packaging and promoting oneself although she did not explicitly label it as such. A third woman described looking for assignments that would provide her with greater visibility and mobility. While women need visibility, the women interviewed tended to be less conscious than males of the need for it and their male supervisors, unconsciously perhaps, limited women's opportunities for obtaining it.

Supervisors still tend to think of men first when assigning staff to serve on task forces, special projects, etc. It is in these discretionary areas, in the assumptions on which individual decisions and choices are made by a boss, where women experienced the greatest barrier. One women manager reported that people had assumed without consulting her that because of family responsibilities she was not in a position to accept an assignment in a regional office, experience which can contribute significantly to career advancement in the public service. When opportunities for promotion were available women were less likely to be considered by their supervisors as serious candidates for promotion, even when they were the most qualified in terms of experience and credentials.

Gender based differences in opportunities for organizational socialization or learning were played out in terms of exclusion and privilege, women tending to be excluded from a wide range of such experiences while men received "taps on the shoulder" and various special opportunities, sometimes even when their qualifications did not meet the formal requirements for the job. Women were aware that they needed to be perceived to have paid their dues by systematically serving in each position as they moved up the hierarchy. One man, who had skipped a stage most people assume to be a necessary one on route to the position he now occupies, said that despite this, he knew everything he needed to do his new job. Women, on the other hand, had to "cover all the bases". As one woman said, "I don't think there's anything I didn't do".

In relation to organizational socialization experiences, one of the most surprising results of these particular studies was just how little encouragement and support it took to make a difference in some of these women's careers. While several of the women interviewees had had mentors over a number of years, others described how a few words of encouragement or advice at a critical point made a great difference in their career aspirations and confidence levels. This suggests that translating a belief in women's leadership potential into supportive action need not entail a huge amount of a supervisor's time or an organization's resources. The men interviewed, not only had more and a wider range of organizational socialization experiences, they were more likely to have been the recipient of these experiences without having had to actively pursue them.

While the myth (Bank of Montreal, 1991) that women are less motivated than men to aspire to management careers has been the explanation given for their underrepresentation in management level positions, several men interviewed for this study said that they had not been motivated initially to become managers until someone suggested to them that they consider it. Someone "turned them on" to the possibility by saying that they would be good at it or, even better, told others in the organization that they would be, as one woman's principal did for her. As she described it, he provided the "pre-publicity" which set the stage for her advancement. As a result, others in the organization started seeing her as having management potential, setting the stage for her to launch herself into a management career.

Participants in these studies, both male and female, provided considerable support for the view that, while women may be "indebted to individual men who have provided encouragement and support", they remain "psychologically separate from the dominant culture of their organizations" (Milwid, 1990, pp.5-6), "are not accorded team member status" (Stokes, 1984, p.24), and are marginalized in the life of organizations (Kanter, 1977). As a result they will have unequal access to opportunities for socialization to organizational norms and culture. While women middle managers described their early efforts to get noticed and promoted, men provided numerous examples of the relative ease with which they were able to achieve recognition and advancement.

A significant number of male interviewees provided specific examples of the organizational limits which continue to be placed on women's careers within their own organizations. While both groups of women middle managers interviewed, saw systemic discrimination as a major barrier for women, all of them remained optimistic about their own chances of career success. Energy and optimism appeared to be important qualities for those people who succeed in becoming managers.

Addressing Career Barriers and Changing Organizations

In times of crisis, women appeared to be quite prepared to devote whatever time was required to deal with the crisis in a way which was non-confrontational and which preserved relationships. Several of the women interviewed for these studies described using specific mediation strategies to reduce conflict. Women managers were much more likely than their male colleagues to describe investing energy and time in trying to maintain and preserve relationships in this way. While a number of women managers talked about their work in building and maintaining good relationships between individuals, work groups, and organizations, few of the male interviewees focused on relationships in this way. Two women labeled these activities as "fence mending" and "bridge building" work.

In describing how they handled conflict and crisis, women talked about bringing people together to work out a solution, the importance of people having involvement in the process, and of developing skills in staff and students that will serve them well beyond the current crisis. In discussing how they handle a crisis, women described approaches characterized by persistence, an effort to understand opposing points of view, and attention to detail. Males tended to describe using a more aggressive approach, one which not one of the women interviewees described using.

A number of women described using humour as a way of managing difficult situations. These women appeared to use humour both to reduce the stress caused by discrimination and to try to help other women who will follow in their footsteps by educating male colleagues and supervisors. Most of the examples provided by female interviewees would qualify as what has been described as "humour of survival" (Ken Louch, CBC Newsworld, 1992). Their humour was often self-deprecating and not at the expense of others, what has been described as typical of "women's humour" (Cyrette, 1995). A woman school principal said that she was incensed by some of the discrimination she experienced, but that "when you react to them you play into their hands". Instead she advised using such techniques as saying "the things before they say them". Sitting through meetings with male colleagues who were making decisions on assignments to task forces and special committees and who rarely considered women for such assignments, she might say "(o)h, you don't want to let a girl do that". Using humour in this way, she says, helps the men save face and, more importantly, reduces the behaviour. She described women's humour as more inclusive than men's humour which she sees as tending more often to be sarcastic and directed against others. The descriptions provided by women interviewees suggest that humour is often their way of resisting the role of victim. Rather than simply suffering in silence, women may feel they take some control of a difficult situation when they use humour in this way and men may perceive these women as less formal and less "foreign" to the culture of the organization, as someone who "fits in". One woman who used such humour cautioned that it must be used with care to avoid alienating people with whom you need to be able to work.

Related, perhaps, to the capacity to use humour is the ability to play roles and games and to bend rules. While one woman who had a background in amateur theatre described using such techniques, men were much more likely than women to do so. Perhaps, it requires the confidence of the organizational insider to use such techniques. A number of women interviewed expressed resentment of what they describe as men's ability or willingness to bend rules and play games, complaining that it was unfair.

Women's use of humour was just one example of what might be termed survival strategies. Other strategies they described using included creating networks of women experiencing similar challenges to share strategies for succeeding, identifying role models, actively searching for and lobbying for stretch assignments and opportunities to see the organizational "big picture", putting a positive spin on marginality, and refusing to give up during difficult times in order to demonstrate to those women whose careers would follow theirs that it can be done (Russell, 1995).

In dealing with a crisis or major problem, women managers were more likely than their male colleagues to invest considerable time and effort in gathering information, engaging staff and colleagues in identifying solutions, and in trying to preserve relationships between individuals and between sectors of an organization. Men tended to involve fewer people, but to have more ready access to organizational insiders, and to act much more quickly. The speed with which they described being able to respond to a crisis situation appears to relate to this more ready access to powerful insiders. While there were significant differences in the ways in which men and women behaved in such situations, these differences can be expected to become less pronounced in workplaces of the future as women make greater gains toward insider status and men develop a wider range of perspectives and styles.

Implications for Organizational Policy, Training, and Development Practices

Where do we want to be in the early 21st century? How can we get there? Organizations have adopted various strategies for change. The Ontario Ministry of Education (OME), for example, decided in 1990 to set targets for administrative positions in Ontario school systems. Specifically, the OME established a goal of 50% representation by women in these positions by the year 2000. With that target in mind boards across the province have engaged in a variety of activities designed to help make that happen, but as Taylor (1992) points out, they have a long way to go before those targets are met. The federal government (Task Force on Barriers, 1990) and the Bank of Montreal (1991) are using other approaches to achieving equity for its women employees. There is no one way of achieving equity for women in the workplace. The following ideas for supporting organizational change, which come from the research literature and from people interviewed for my own research, have implications for work organizations.

Many of the stories women told in describing their careers are stories of how they overcame barriers. While important, it is easy to become so focused on these individual survival stories that one forgets the organization and the role organizations have played in supporting the barriers these women describe experiencing. However, individual actions do not change systems in any significant way, and as research demonstrates, structural and systemic barriers represent a formidable limitation to the advancement of women's careers. The way in which the organizational socialization of workers is influenced by gender presents one of the best explanations to date for the underrepresentation of women at the middle management level of organizations and the glass ceiling which prevents their rise to more senior levels.

Awareness of informal systems

Organizations need to devote resources to helping newcomers better understand the informal side of organizational life. The purpose of this should not be to help women behave more like men, but to help them develop a more realistic understanding of organizations in order to plan their careers in an informed way. This has implications for management training, as well, since managers will need to better understand how traditional organizational practices have worked against the full participation of many workers, both male and female. Coupled with this awareness, managers need to be trained to more effectively assist employees to develop careers whether that development involves lateral or upward movement and to respect the choices employees make.

Innovative Staff Development Models and Practices

There is less need to invest resources in inventing such models since they are already being used by some of the more progressive organizations in North America, including individual businesses, universities, federal and provincial government departments, school systems, and universities. Many existing models and practices would transfer, often with need for little adaptation, to other organizations. Among some of the models and practices suggested by this study are formalized mentoring programs, buddy systems, more systematic and prolonged orientation programs for newcomers, and anti-sexist peer support systems for males.

Training Versus Experience

One of the fears which some women reported having about advancement was that they did not know what happens at the level above them and were not sure they had the skills or experience to survive at that level. For some women, this lack of knowledge about the next level above them may serve as a self-imposed ceiling preventing their career advancement. Overcoming these fears or lack of confidence might best be accomplished through such experiences as job-shadowing of more senior staff or short courses in specific skill areas such as financial management rather than training programs which focus on building confidence or on assertiveness training.

Making the Management of Change More Inclusive: Enlisting Allies in Working for Change

As Asplund (1988) suggests, there is a clear need to involve all employees, not only human resource specialists and members of the affected group, in work to find solutions to the career barriers experienced by some groups. Involving males increases their investment in and commitment to change and provides allies who have much to share and to teach.

It is difficult to know from interviews alone whether the more progressive views expressed by many males interviewed actually get played out in the work world, but the fact that the awareness is there is encouraging since a first stage in the process of societal or organizational change is the recognition that a problem exists. These attitudes appeared to be influenced by the career challenges being experienced by their wives and daughters as Schein (1973) and Jardim and Hennig (1990) predicted. This is also supported by a recent poll conducted by the New York-based Families and Work Institute (Dorning, 1993). Several men interviewed fit in many ways the profile of men one might expect to have very traditional views of women in the workplace. In fact, they were among the most sensitive of all those interviewed, male and female, in terms of their understanding of the concepts of systemic discrimination. They could describe in significant detail the kinds of barriers which exist for women and how these barriers serve to limit women's career advancement. The wife of one woman interviewee's mentor, for example, had experienced considerable discrimination early in her career and several other men interviewed have daughters but no sons.

Men may need considerable support in order to effectively engage in meaningful change efforts, however. Since their careers probably advanced in the more open organizational climate of the

1960s and 1970s, they may not be particularly effective in coaching others to advance in today's workplace where opportunities are more limited and where advancement is more formalized, especially if their advice is based on their own experience.

Personnel Policies and Support from the Top

As women managers described the ups and downs of their careers, it became clear that one of the consistent features of the most positive experiences described was the commitment of senior officials who have the power necessary to translate commitment to change into action for change. Such messages from the most senior levels of an organization are difficult for employees to ignore.

Because, as one woman pointed out, the systemic discrimination which reduces women's access to a wide range of socialization experiences is largely unconscious and invisible, it is particularly difficult to address. Unenlightened leaders and decision makers may subtly sabotage the best of selection procedures and other measures designed to help advance the careers of women. Organizational efforts to increase equity must focus on organizational leaders, not only on the victims of discrimination, in order to "direct attention, confidence and support for these changes" (Stokes, p.23) by adopting a system of management accountability for the improvement of conditions for women.

The federal government has initiated a wide range of initiatives in response to the Report of the Task Force on Barriers to Women in the Public Service (1990). A major effort has been devoted to making managers at all levels accountable for employment equity, making it a management issue not a women's issue.

New Directions

The role of informal processes in shaping access to career opportunities and career outcomes is profound and deserves more study. Statham, Miller, and Mauksch (1988) stress the need for more qualitative research in order to improve our understanding of these dynamics. As demographic change reshapes the employee mix in organizations, it will become increasingly important to better understand the role organizational socialization plays in the career outcomes of women and other newcomers to organizational management, such as visible minorities, and to develop strategies for directing the process more effectively rather than leaving it to chance.

Female Designed Models for Structuring and Managing Organizations

Lenz and Myerhoff (1985) present an optimistic view of ways in which women's values are quietly revolutionizing the workplace by introducing a humanizing quality to the work environment. While one may wonder whether they would be as optimistic today as they were in the mid-80s, there are still many signs that women are leaving their mark on the culture of the work world. In my own research men report adopting different ways of working based on their observations of how women perform some of these roles or tasks differently.

While women appear to be more prepared to try new organizational and management models (Helgesen, 1990; Fisher, 1991), a few men are beginning to do things differently as an expression of their dissatisfaction with traditional management styles (Fisher, 1991). A manager in the public service who admired the methods he saw his women colleagues using lamented the fact that the "system" does not provide support for people like himself who would like to learn to use a more participatory leadership style and team approaches. He expressed the view that women more "naturally" use these methods effectively, but that men like himself needed some support in order to do the same.

While it would be misleading to suggest that there are styles and models which are strictly male or female, the examples men and women participants in this study provided about their own career experiences provide strong support for the view that there are particular models and styles with which women tend to be more comfortable. Whether their capacity to try non-traditional approaches is conscious or simply the product of their marginal and token status is not clear. It may simply be that as outsiders, largely unschooled in male management models, they resort to what they know, a more relationship and people centred approach.

While men are much less likely to use and to discuss such approaches, a few indicated a strong interest in learning more about them. More systematic studies of ways in which women prefer to manage and of women's work groups would make a valuable contribution to organizational and leadership theory.

Assumptions About Careers

Much of the career literature promotes a three-to-five year plan approach. That is, major writers in the field promote explicitly the view that employees have a three-to-five year period in which to get noticed and fast tracked by their employers and implicitly, for the most part, that this period is at the beginning of one's working life. This perspective does not contribute to effective career planning for women. Several women participants in this study described dropping out once or several times to care for children or to follow a husband's career. One woman manager had been out of the work force for twelve years. Few career analysts have looked closely at what women are doing during those periods out of the work force and the role that parenting and community volunteer work can play in helping them to, not only maintain, but add to the bank of skills they had when they dropped out. Women's careers may have multiple paths, as they move in and out of the paid work force or make lateral career moves between organizations or paid and volunteer work during their early parenting years.

Responsibility to Others

Like the women interviewed by Milwid (1990) who agreed to be interviewed in order "to give the next generation an insider's perspective on making it in a man's world" (p.35), women interviewees spoke often about their responsibility to other women whose careers will follow theirs. A woman principal acknowledged the importance of having extremely competent women in these pioneering roles, saying that it was easier for her because her predecessors were so competent and that we can't afford any women "duds" yet. This need to excel to counteract the myth that women are asking that male workers be displaced in favour of less qualified women creates additional performance pressures (Kanter, 1977) for these women pioneers.

The participants of this study and the research literature are agreed that support networks, male and female, are extremely important because "if institutions do not insure survival, support systems must" (Stokes, 1984, p.25). A number of organizations have provided support for women's networks in the form of space for meetings, resources for newsletters, and staff time for coordination. These networks provide valuable assistance to newcomers having difficulty adjusting to the organizational culture. A systematic examination of the various forms networks take and the relative value of each in providing support to members of various groups would provide valuable direction on how to best allocate limited resources to meet needs.

The experiences of women building careers in organizations and the impact of increasing numbers of women employees and women managers on the ways organizations function is worthy of increased research attention.

Conclusion

Organizations now have a better understanding of the processes which come into play in organizations when members of groups which have traditionally existed as "outsiders" to organizational life, such as women, the disabled, racial minorities and aboriginal Canadians, attempt to become "insiders". The conceptual framework used based on Kanter's work and developments in organizational socialization provides a framework for looking at issues related to women's career development. This framework makes it possible to study the impact of socially constructed gender, race or other limitations which come into play when new types of workers holding different cultural values and life experiences begin to move into organizations rather than in terms of men against women or one racial group(s) against others. As Rebne (1988) notes, Kanter's work "does not oblige us to make the uncharitable assumption that male faculty (or other colleagues) actively discriminate against women in the manner proposed by the nonstructural theories" (p.84). The focus of the problem becomes socially constructed organizational structures and processes, rather than individuals or groups of individuals. This makes it possible to see everyone as having a role to play in finding solutions to the problem.

REFERENCES

Albrecht, K (1983). *Organizational Development: A total systems approach to positive change in any business organization.* Englewood Cliffs, NJ: Prentice-Hall

Asplund, G. (1988). *Women managers: Changing organizational cultures.* New York, NY: John Wiley & Sons.

Bank of Montreal. (1991). *The Task Force on the Advancement of Women in the Bank.* Toronto, ON: Bank of Montreal.

Barnard C. (1938). *The Functions of the Executive.* Cambridge, MA: Harvard University Press.

Beauchesne, E. (1995, March 29). *Bias lowers women's pay StatsCan study suggests.* The Ottawa Citizen, A1, A2.

Bernard, J. (1981). *The female world.* New York, NY: The Free Press.

Bird, F. (1990). *Personal Communication*, Ottawa, March 14, 1990.

Bogart, K. (1990, April). *Critical issues for the 1990s: The underrepresentation of women and minorities in academic educational programs.* Paper presented at the 1990 annual meeting of the American Educational Research Association, Boston, MA.

Cava, R. (1988). *Escaping the pink collar ghetto.* Toronto, ON: Key Porter Books.

Chase, S.E. and Bell, C.S. (1990). Ideology, discourse and gender: How gatekeepers talk about women school superintendents. *Social Problems*, 37(2), 163-177.

Cooper, R. and Smith, B.L. (1990, October). Achieving a diverse faculty. *AAHE Bulletin*, 10-12.

Cyrette, C. (1995, February). Women and their wicked healing wit. *The Business and Professional Woman,* 50(3), 2.

Dalton, M. (1959). *Men who manage: Fusions of feeling and theory in administration.* New York, NY: John Wiley and Sons, Inc.

Epstein, C.F. (1988). *Deceptive distinctions: Sex, gender and the social order.* New Haven, CT: Yale University Press.

Fernandez, J.P. (1981). *Racism and sexism in corporate America: Changing Values in American business.* Lexington, MA: Lexington Books.

Fisher, K. (1991, September 19). *The changing male manager.* Presentation of the Canadian Centre for Management Development, Ottawa, ON.

Fullan, M. (1993). *Changing forces: Probing the depths of educational reform.* Bristol, PA: The Falimer Press.

Ghiloni, B.W. (1987). The Velvet Ghetto: Women, power, and the corporation. In G.W. Domhoff and T.R. Dye (Eds.), *Power elites and organizations* (pp. 21-36). Newbury Park, CA: SAGE Publications.

Goffman, E. (1963). *Stigma: Notes on the management of spoiled identity.* Englewood Cliffs, NJ: Prentice-Hall.

Helgesen, S. (1990). *The female advantage: Women's ways of leadership.* New York, NY: Doubleday.

Jardim, A. and Hennig, M. (1990, November). The last barrier: Breaking into the boys club at the top. *Working Woman,* 131, 132, 134, 164.

Kanter, R.M. (1977). *Men and women of the corporation.* New York, NY: Basic Books, Inc.

Kirp, D.L., Yudof, M.G., and Franks, M.S. (1986). *Gender justice.* Chicago, IL: University of Chicago Press.

Kleck, R.E. and Nuessle, W. (1968). Congruence between the indicative and communicative functions of eye contact in interpersonal relations. *British Journal of Social and Clinical Psychology,* 7, 241-246.

Krueger, R.A. (1988). *Focus groups: A practical guide for applied research.* Newbury Park, CA: Sage.

Laws, J.L. (1975). The psychology of tokenism: An analysis. *Sex Roles,* 1(1), 51-67.

Lenz, E. and Myerhoff B. (1985). *The feminization of America: How women's values are changing our public and private lives.* Los Angeles, CA: Jeremy P. Tarcher, Inc.

Lortie, D.C. (1975). *Schoolteacher: A sociological study.* Chicago, IL: The University of Chicago Press.

Louch, K. (1992, March 4). Television interview, *On the Arts.* Toronto, ON: CBC Newsworld

Marshall, C. (1979). *The Career socialization of women in school administration.* Unpublished doctoral dissertation, University of California, Santa Barbara, California.

Marshall, C. and Mitchell, B. (1989). *Women's career as a critique of the administrative culture.* Paper presented at the annual meeting of the American Educational Research Association, San Francisco, CA.

Marshall, C. and Rossman, G.B. (1989). *Designing qualitative research.* Newbury Park, CA: Sage

McCall, M.W., Jr., Lombardo, M.M., and Morrison, A.M. (1988). *The lessons of experience: How successful executives develop on the job.* Lexington, MA: Lexington Books.

McCracken, G. (1988). *The long interview.* Newbury Park, CA: Sage Publications.

Milwid, B. (1990). *Working with men: Professional women talk about power, sexuality and ethics.* Hillsboro, OR: Beyond Words Publishing, Inc.

Morgan D.L. (1988a). *Focus groups as qualitative research.* Newbury Park, CA: Sage Publications.

Morgan, N. (1988b). *The equality game: Women in the federal public service (1908-1987).* Ottawa, ON: Canadian Advisory Council on Status of Women

Morrison, A.M. (1992*). The new leaders: Guidelines on leadership diversity in America.* San Francisco, CA: Jossey-Bass Publishers.

Ortiz, F.I. (1982). *Career Patterns in education: Men, women and minorities in public school administration.* New York, NY: J F Praeger.

Packard, V. (1962). *The pyramid climbers.* Greenwich, CT: Fawcett Publications, Inc.

Peitchinis, S.G. (1989). *Women at work: Discrimination and response.* Toronto, ON: McCelland and Stewart, Inc.

Pfeffer, J. (1982). *Organizations and organization theory.* Marshfield, MA: Pitman Publishing Inc.

Rebne, D. (1988). Occupational differences in women's research production. In R.M. Schwartz (Ed), *Women at work* (pp.68-93). Los Angeles, CA: Institute of Industrial Relations, University of California.

Rees, R. (1990). *Women and men in education: A national survey of gender distribution in school systems.* Toronto, ON: Canadian Education Association.

Russell, R.J. (1995). Learning from survivors: Women leaders who have stayed the course share their stories. In Cecilia Reynolds and Beth Young, (Eds.), *Women and Leadership in Canadian Education.* Calgary, AB: Detselig Press.

Russell, R.J. (1993). *Experiencing and exercising power: Men and women middle managers in education and public administration.* Unpublished doctoral dissertation, University of Ottawa, Ottawa, ON.

Russell, R.J. and Wright, R. (1992). The socialization experiences of visible minority women in educational administration positions. *CanadianEthnic Studies*, 24(3), 127-136.

Ryan W. (1971). *Blaming the Victim.* Brattleboro, VT: The Book Press.

Schein, E.H. (1977). Organizational socialization and the profession of management. In B.M. Shaw (Ed.), *Psychological foundations of organizational behaviour* (pp.210-232). Santa Monica, CA: Goodyear Publishing Co, Inc.

Schein, V.E. (1973). The relationship between sex-role stereotypes and requisite management characteristics. *Journal of Applied Psychology*, 57(2), 95-100.

Shakeshaft, C. (1987). *Women in education administration.* Beverly Hills, CA: Sage Publications.

Statham, A., Miller, E.M., and Mauksch, H.O. (Eds.) (1988). *The worth of women's work: A qualitative analysis.* Albany, NY: SUNY Press.

Stokes, M.J. (1984). *Organizational barriers and their impact on women in higher education.* Washington, DC: National Association for Women Deans, Administrators, and Counselors.

Supply and Services Canada. (1970). *Report of the Royal Commission on the Status of Women in Canada.* Ottawa, ON: Information Canada.

Task Force on Barriers to Women in the Public Service. (1990). *Beneath the Veneer.* (Vols. 1-4). Ottawa: Supply and Services Canada.

Taylor, A. (1992). Employment Equity in Ontario School Boards. *Canadian Women Studies*, 12(3), 52-55.

U.S. Department of Labor. (1991). *A report on the glass ceiling initiative*. Washington, D.C.: U.S. Department of Labor.

Wente, M. (1993, November 13). "How to be 72: A lesson from Betty Friedan", *The Globe and Mail, A2.*

Wright, L.M. (1988). *The use of power at work: The power tactics of university administrators*. Unpublished doctoral dissertation, University of Pennsylvania. Ann Arbour, MI: UMI Dissertation Information Service.

Yeakey, C.C., Johnston, G.S., and Adkison, J.A. (1986). In pursuit of equity: A review of research on minorities and women in educational administration. *Educational Administration Quarterly*, 22(3), 110-149.

Young, B. (1991, June). *On Careers: Themes from the lives of four Western Canadian women educators*. Paper presented at the annual conference of the Canadian Society for the Study of Education, Queen's University, Kingston, Ontario.

Chapter 8

THE OPPRESSION OF WOMEN IN CANADA: FROM DENIAL TO AWARENESS AND RESISTANCE

David Wicks, Pat Bradshaw

Introduction

Suggesting that women have occupied disadvantaged positions in the workplace is not a moot point: the cause of women's oppression, and the ways to eliminate discrimination against women, however, remain contentious. The main assumption underlying the arguments in this chapter is that the current and future situation for women in Canada is dependent upon deeply entrenched, and largely unconscious, cultural values and norms. These taken-for-granted and socially constructed rules have led to the oppression of women,[1] and unless these rules, however informal or invisible are made explicit the status quo will likely remain unchanged. One need look no further than the presence of large ethnic groups and communities in Canadian cities to see how many pressures toward cultural reproduction exist, even when individuals are far removed from their home countries and national cultures. While this chapter attempts to present a vivid picture of the inequality and injustices that exist, we do not want to present a totally hopeless future scenario. After describing the current situation in Canada and exploring possible causes for it, we begin to identify strategies of resistance which may lead to a redefinition of the current rules, and new opportunities for both women and men.

"Rules of Thumb"

Part of our approach is to explore norms and rules which guide, often unconsciously, our behaviours. An evocative example of a socially created rule originated in 1767 in England as the "rule of thumb" when common law permitted a husband "to chastise his wife with a whip or rattan no wider than his thumb". Why, we ask, would they need such a rule? Did they think that their wives should be treated in such a way as to have some protection from excessive abuse? Did they not want to leave marks of this abuse for others to see? Did they want to save the lives of these "possessions" who did so much of the work? We do not purport to know the answers to these questions, but we started to ask ourselves whether new rules of thumb have emerged to guide the way women in Canada are treated within our patriarchal system.

For example, are there rules of thumb that say:
- Women may work in greater numbers (the participation rate of women was 58% in 1991 and is expected to increase to 63% by the year 2005), but it is what group of women one belongs to which determines how many women will work (aboriginal women had a paid labour force participation rate of 40% in 1986 as compared to 56% among non-aboriginal women and for immigrant women the participation rate was 54%).[2]
- Women may work when the demands of the capitalist system call for it, but they will be primarily restricted to traditionally female occupations such as teaching, nursing, clerical, sales and service jobs (71% of working women are employed in these jobs as compared to only 30% of men). Immigrant women should primarily be limited to non-clerical, product fabrication, sewing and data entry jobs.
- Women's earning will be substantially less than men's (in 1992, women's full time earning averaged 71.8% of men's).
- Women should take the part-time jobs so that men can work full-time (women held 70% of part-time employment in 1991 and this has been stable since 1976, part-time work represents 25% of the employed female work force while it represents only 9% of the paid male labour force. For young women, aged 16 to 25, part-time work is becoming increasingly common, in

1971 26% of this group worked part-time while in 1991 this has risen to 43%)

- We will allow women to unionize, but this rate should be limited to 30% (as compared to 37% of men) and few women should be appointed to leadership positions within the unions.
- Keep most women out of pension plans (only 39% of women were enrolled in a pension plan in 1990 as compared to 50% of men).
- Only one woman in four should be physically abused by her spouse (51% of Canadian women have experienced at least one incident of physical or sexual violence since the age of 16, 25% of all women have experienced this type of violence at the hands of a marital or common-law partner. 38% of all women murdered in Canada in 1992 were killed by a current or estranged male partner.)
- Let women do paid work and contribute more to the family employment income, but don't let them forget that traditional women's work in the home (women's contribution to family employment income has increased from 29% in 1971 to 36% in 1991 while they still do the majority of the household work, on average women in dual careers work an extra 30 twenty-four hour days each year compared to men (Hoschchild, 1990). If all the work in the home that women perform were counted it would contribute another 39% to the GNP (1986 figure).
- Let women with young children work (between 1976 and 1991, the participation rate of women with a youngest child under three increased from 32% to 62%), but don't provide them with adequate day care to allow them to take advantage of the limited opportunities available to them. (In 1991, there were 2.2 million children under 12 who required at least 20 hours of day care per week. With an estimated 330,000 spaces across Canada, only 15% of these children would be served by licensed day care arrangements).
- It is not our responsibility to worry about poverty among women who are retired or single parents. (In 1987 the average income for women over age 65 was $13,596/ year. While 62% of single parent mothers with children under 18 lived in poverty in 1991, 80% of these women earn under $30,000/year).

Like many cultural norms, or rules of behaviour, these types of rules of thumb become so much a part of the fabric of our social lives that we take them for granted. We as a society conspire to keep the silence about the plight of women while the metaphorical as well as physical, beating continues. The screams from the victims of this abuse are not heard as we all live in complicity, accepting the socially defined rules which legitimate and control many of the visible markings of the beatings. The rules are now more subtle and harder to name, and the scars are more on the emotional and psychic levels, with the psychological trauma only now being identified (Goodman et. al., 1991).

One of the most insidious ways of disguising these victims is developing a second set of rules of thumb. These are one which present the illusion of Canadian women's success, advancement and conquest. They are rules which permit a select group of Canadian women to work in the corporate and government worlds, to run their own businesses, and to sit on corporate boards. These successes are permitted in order to perpetuate the mythology of Canada as a "democratic", "fair", and "progressive" country in which meritocracy is the only determinate of an individual's ultimate success (female or male). Any of us, according to this myth, can be president of a company, own a business, and join the elite clubs if we are only smart enough, work hard enough, and are prepared to "play the game" and network with the "right people".

The rules of thumb which permit our society to perpetuate this mythology look something like this:

- Let some women sit on boards of directors (but keep it to about 6% of the total number of directorates).
- Let some women hold managerial positions (but limit their involvement to about 14% of all managerial jobs in the federal government, 10% of senior managerial jobs in the private sector and 1.6% at the vice-presidential level and above in corporations).
- Select women for executive positions who are primarily single and do not have children, because spouses and children might distract them (95% of male executives are married as opposed to only 58% of female executives, similarly 90% of male executives have children as opposed to only 48% of the female executives).

- Pay female executives less than males (in Canada female vice-presidents earn 46% less than men in the same jobs (Auster, 1993).
- Let more women into managerial levels, but keep them segregated in support and staff jobs such as personnel or public relations.
- Institute sexual harassment policies, but don't eliminate the problem completely. (It is estimated that 49% of working women in Canada will be sexually harassed at some point in their working lives).
- Let women start their own companies (research shows that women in Canada are starting their own businesses at three times the rate of men, primarily in the retail and service sectors, that they are often discriminated against by lenders, work long hours, continue to meet traditional family responsibilities, and feel isolated from support networks. Many entrepreneurs in Canada are born outside the country, 16% overall. Annual incomes for 80% of female entrepreneurs, in one study (Belcourt et al., 1991), were below $50,000 a year and one-third of the sample received no salary. Male business owners report annual earnings 66% higher than earning reported by female business owners).

Some will argue that these are not rules, that things are improving for women, that it truly is a system of equal access for all, and that any remaining inequities are being legislated out of existence. We simply do not agree. We see these as socially constructed rules; such rules have been institutionalized to the extent that they are not acknowledged, let alone challenged. The deep structures of power, as they affect the 51% "minority" of women in Canada, are firmly entrenched. At the beginning of the the millennium, we see little cause for optimism. The way out of this disaster is to break the existing "conspiracy of silence", to explore the rules which enforce the status quo, and then to find the points from where resistance is possible. The change must start with brutally accepting/acknowledging the horror of the current system, increasing the consciousness of, and bringing into clear sight, the current cultural norms and "rules of thumb" and their consequences.

Creation of Rules of Thumb

In this section of the chapter we would like to explore various explanations for the existence of cultural norms and rules which perpetuate the entrenched discrimination against women in Canadian workplaces. We will focus on women and work because it is the area in which we have done research and study; this is neither a reflection of the seriousness of the problems for women in other contexts and spheres of life, nor is it a statement of the importance of this issue over others. The creation of rules and practices of discrimination and systemic inequities for women in one context are a mirror reflection of the creation of similar rules in other contexts. The holographic nature of the patriarchy is evidenced by the embeddedness of the values and rules at all levels of analysis from interpersonal, to family, to group and organization, to society as a whole. By attacking the perception that all women have an equal chance to succeed in the workplace, we hope to also expose the entrenched nature of the problems women face, and debunk the myth that anyone can succeed based on merit and/or ability alone. The issues are much more deeply entrenched and must be understood at all levels.

Edgar Schein (1985) presents a view of how culture can be analyzed based on cultural characteristics at a variety of levels. We feel that this type of approach is an excellent way to study the creation of discriminatory rules and practices, viewing them as cultural phenomenon that have been perpetuated throughout the 1900s. More specifically, in analyzing the rules of a particular group, three fundamental levels at which culture manifests itself should be distinguished. These levels, moving from surface to deeper levels, are (i) observable artifacts, (ii) values, and (iii) underlying assumptions.

When first entering a social system it is relatively easy for the newcomer to observe cultural artifacts. For example, included in this category is everything from the way secretaries dress, to the language used in day-to-day work, and the "girlie" calendars in the shipping/receiving area. The problem with directing attention to only artifacts is that while they can be objectively observed, they are not always easy to decipher. While the examples of artifacts presented here leave little doubt that a sexist work environment exists, consider the case of organizations where these types of artifacts are not present. Does this suggest that a non-sexist environment exists? We would suggest not, rather that further analysis of deeper cultural levels is necessary in order to fully capture the normative or acceptable behaviours in a given contest. Of course one of the inherent problems with attempting to study cultural artifacts is the possibility of making incorrect inferences from them. We would suggest that by gaining an understanding of the deeper levels of the organization's culture, connections between assumptions, values and artifacts can be made, providing more accurate or defensible interpretations of the visible structures and processes that have become a part of organizations' day-to-day operations.

Through a more in-depth observation of organizational members, one can study a culture's values (sometimes referred to as ideologies or norms). By attempting to understand why behaviours happen the way they do, insight into how people feel and think is gained, which contributes to an understanding of the visible artifacts. Complete understanding, however, will not be gained until the deeper levels of the culture are analyzed.

Only through intensive observation and focused questions can one seek out and decipher the taken-for granted, underlying assumptions and rules that determine perceptions, thought processes, feelings and behaviour. Once underlying assumptions become understood, it becomes much easier to decipher the meanings implicit in behaviours and artifacts, leading to the opportunity to address how cultural patterns are originally formed, and consequently can be changed in the future.

Deeply held assumptions often start out historically as values, but become institutionalized, or ingrained in the organization's culture as they become incorporated into standard operating procedures, programs. etc. The characteristic of such assumptions that make them most salient, in our opinion, to the study of sex-based inequality is that they are no longer questioned, and consequently become less and less open to discussion, and therefore change. By attempting to position sex-based discrimination, both systemic an systematic, as a cultural phenomenon, it becomes increasingly obvious why it is so difficult to break the patterns of cultural reinforcement, and effect change in a direction which treats women and men more equitably.

Increasingly it is being suggested that organizational cultures are inherently gendered. Only recently has empirical support been found for this contention, but theorizing of this nature has been on the fringe of mainstream organizational research for over ten years. Organizational theory in general is sexist, either neglecting issues of gender, or treating gender as a variable that can be manipulated to increase profitability. As such, the dominance of masculine ways of thinking and behaving have taken a central place in both management theory and the workplace, leading to a somewhat pessimistic view of change in our opinion. If the dominant cultures in business schools and organizations are firmly grounded in male-centred practices, then the opportunities for the concerns of marginalized groups to take a central role are likely to be few and far between.

Albert Mills (1988), a researcher in the area of organizational culture and gender, suggests that a gender-based perspective of organizational analysis is imperative, yet rarely performed. By suggesting that organizational culture provides a useful concept for the analysis of gender, we are attempting to draw attention to the relationships between sociocultural influences and organizational structures and practices. By understanding the ways organizations perpetuate discriminatory practices and behaviours through cultural mechanisms, we begin to make sense of the ubiquity of organizational cultures which typically favour maleness. As a result, organizations socialize their members to adopt particular gender identities, and develop policies and practices which conform to sex-biased values.

If organizational cultures are characterized by a masculine ethos as we suggest, then understanding the day-to-day work activities of the organization becomes an important area of study. Normative, taken-for-granted behaviours are a natural result of the assumptions and values of a culture which are transmitted to their members through a socialization process. As such, daily activities are dictated not only by formal structures, but also informal norms typically defined in terms of gender and sexuality. It has been argued that the barriers to women's equality rest with the criteria used to recruit and promote within organizations. While not suggesting that this argument has no merit, we would further suggest that, as well as scrutinizing the processes and criteria of selection and promotion, that other, perhaps less formal or observable, rules or procedures determine and constrain the behaviour of organizational participants. More specifically, a liberal view neglects the negotiated and culturally mediated character of rule use, and gives primacy to formal, sanctioned rules as determinants of organizational structures and practices. In contrast, we suggest that it is not only (nor primarily) the **formal** rules that present the major obstacles over which women must overcome, rather the assumptions of the efficacy of such rules, combined with other assumptions of "appropriate" behaviours on the part of individuals.

Sara Delamont (1989) uses the concept of the "Saturn's rings" phenomena to depict the typical focus on formal structures, while simultaneously ignoring hidden or covert assumptions concerning the desirability of certain behaviours. What this image attempts to demonstrate is how the dust of an organization's formal rationality can hide the gendered values and taken-for-granted assumptions, leaving only the technical rules or components visible. As a result, the structure **appears** to be the component which determines women's career progression, and the culture of the organization is left, often unacknowledged, in the background. From this perspective it is clear that structures (representing only artifacts) are not the appropriate target for change if sex-based discrimination is deeply-embedded in the cultural rules of most organizations. We must begin to dig deeper to understand and alter the values and assumptions which legitimate the presence of discriminatory practices. The "bureaucratic solution" to gender oppression clearly does not address the male-defined structure and essence of work roles, and subsequently the criteria by which performance is evaluated. It seems obvious, therefore, that the deeper cultural levels that are most central to cultural change remain unquestioned and unchanged.

In a recent empirical study we have found that, on average, current cultural values in a large sample of Canadian organizations can be described as largely consistent with a masculine ethos or ethic. This is not surprising, and is entirely consistent with descriptions of our patriarchal world as similarly rational, objective, intellectual and analytical. The results of this study support the contention that cultures of organizations are inherently gendered in ways that systematically privilege typically masculine values over characteristically feminine ones. These findings demonstrate the pervasivenes of such patterns, and also the range of differences across a variety of organizations. We also found that these patterns are reinforced by the values reflected in existing reward structures, suggesting that change, in order to facilitate the integration of women, requires a shift in these values toward ones which are more valuing of diversity in all its richness (Bradshaw and Wicks, 1994).

The ubiquity of a masculine ethos in organizational cultures is a logical consequence, in our opinion, of the dominance of modernist thought in the social and natural sciences, built around ideals of rationality, objectivity and value-neutrality. While few would argue that these ideals are undesirable, we question both their applicability to certain types of knowledge claims and their venerated paradigmatic status. For example, what constitutes "good leadership" or "effective decision-making" are evaluated and defined in terms of their compatibility with the ideals of modernist thought. As a result, some forms of leadership, decision-making, and communication hold a privileged position over all others based on their adherence to a set of ostensibly "rational" criteria. What we suggest is that these types of ideals are in fact exclusionary; they are best suited for knowers who have, or who are capable of achieving, a "view from nowhere". These ideals simultaneously assume an essential human nature, with substitutable knowers who are capable of transcending contextual and experiential differences. The problem with such essentialist positions is the neglect of the plethora of routes to knowledge claims that will likely result from differences in socialization, experience, moral development etc.

One need look no further than the business schools to see the reinforcement of modernist thought in action. By teaching students "how" to manage, we assume an essential nature of superiors and subordinates, and communicate the appropriate ways to manage under a variety of situations. Words like "intuition", "idiosyncratic", "sensitivity", and "emotion" are strangely absent from management education, indicating the veneration of modernist thought, and the associated ideals, as the sole route to knowledge claims. When we observe that the ideals of modernist thought are those typically associated with masculine, it appears as no surprise that organizational cultures are dominated by characteristically masculine values. Only recently has feminist scholarship begun to be incorporated into organizational theory literature. This inclusion, albeit extremely low in concentration, has brought a voice to the previously silenced "other" perspectives within our field, confronting the assumptions upon which mainstream (or perhaps malestream) organizational research rests. Feminist perspectives of organizational theory attempt to expose the male-centred world views, and their effects on the understanding of gendered relationships, knowledge structures, and male domination in the workplace. By virtue of incorporating masculine systems as normal and rational, organizational theory produces, and reproduces, certain ways of understanding organizational life. We suggest that it is precisely these understandings which contribute significantly to the underlying assumptions of individuals, all of which contribute to a culture characterized by the masculine ethos.

Implications for Change — Strategies of Resistance

Given our portrayal of work places as fundamentally oppressive to women (for the most part), from where do the possibilities for change arise? As we have previously suggested, the bureaucratic solutions typically favoured by organizations and governments are destined to failure. By addressing only the manifestation of gender biases, no fundamental, long-lasting change is expected. Only by addressing deep seated values and assumptions and unspoken rules of thumb can change be effected which will reduce, and eventually eliminate, the systemic and systematic discrimination against women. What we advocate here are two strategies of resistance which challenge inequitable treatment, sentiments, and beliefs of women and men.

One strategy for altering pressures to comply to sex-based norms and rules (either consciously or unconsciously) is the displacement of the dominant discoursed, part of what Michel Foucault calls "an insurrection of subjugated knowledge" (1972, p.81). By viewing the voices of opposition as **opportunities** for altering the existing structures of power, new discourses may be able to reveal the politics embedded in the dominant discourses by presenting an opposition, not simply a passive reaction, to them. While we have suggested that modernist thought occupies a dominant position in management theory and practice, clearly there are oppositions to its venerated status. By having a discourse of opposition (for example a radical feminist discourse) based on specific experiences of a subjugated group, yet connected to others through a nexus of discourses vying for dominance within a discursive field, resistance of this nature can render the dominant discourses obsolete, revealing the partiality of their ostensibly "universal" claims of "the best way" to manage.

A second strategy of resistance involves challenging the existing power structures by confronting them with speech and actions that embody a "reality" totally incongruent with that currently in place. Western culture has been referred to as one of domination; individuals look for powerful individuals to whom they defer their authority, and consequently obey. Domination, however, is only a "system", and as such requires individuals to comply in order for the system to maintain its dominance. Domination, is not a natural state, but one that requires choices over time; without suggesting that women "naturally" comply to men's whims, we do want to suggest that domination can be "undone" by consciously recognizing the choices we all make, and recognizing that we always have the opportunity to act differently. Raising the level of consciousness of the ways in which our alternative courses of action are pre-determined by cultural influences is an important step in identifying the oppressive nature of many cultures. Only by being aware of how we comply can we act consciously to question the very structures and processes which provide both the opportunity for success/advancement, and the threat of internal self-destruction.

Once consciousness has been raised, we must begin to refuse the pressures to comply, and question the "authority" of the taken-for-granted aspects of organizational life that guide daily practices. In order to do this, individuals must organize, because a critical mass will be required in order to change the deeper cultural phenomenon of values and assumptions. Refusal to comply means, among other things, refusal to remain within the constructs or confines of thought that are labelled "acceptable" or "normal". Clearly cultures provide strong forces towards conformity to a normative display of behaviours and attitudes; if an organizational participant must always pass an internal test of what others think is "reasonable", oppressive cultures will remain. Only over time can a new "reality" be created, based upon, for example, more egalitarian principles or ideals of sustainability.

In today's workplace we see a range, or continuum, of tactics of resistance. While these range from conformity and "fitting in" to overt defiance of "unquestioned" authority, we suggest that only by attempting to address the deepest cultural phenomenon can long-term change occur. This presents a somewhat fatalistic view of women in the workplace, but it is also one supported by a variety of empirical research. What we do **not** want to suggest, however, is that change agendas are entirely futile. In fact we suggest quite to the contrary; change can arise from the actions of any one of us. It takes the questioning of the fundamental ideals that have structured thought and organizations, and active resistance to the deep-rooted values and assumptions which privilege male-centred norms at the expense of all others. As Kathy Ferguson (1993) suggests, the typical response of women who attempt to claim entry into the worlds that men have reserved for themselves (for example the corporate boardroom) is to demand access by yelling "me too!". While there may be valid political reasons for taking this position, "the response challenges only the answers to the 'woman question', not its terms" (1993: 2). In short, we need new rules of thumb which are not built on a hierarchy with male-defined (or phalocentric) values at the pinnacle.

Endnotes

1.   We recognize that cultural values and norms do not only affect women as a group, and that oppression on the basis of, for example, race, class, and homosexuality are also problematic in our society. The oppression of women presents an interesting case to study, however, because unlike the other groups mentioned above, women actually represent a majority (albeit a small one) in the Canadian population. In fact, feminist theory has provided the foundations for social change for a variety of marginalized groups, and we hope to continue to provide broad implications for social change by addressing the oppression of women. Clearly parallel arguments could be made for other groups, and perhaps arguments that would be more easily heard in the dominant discourses.

Visible, overt discrimination is something everyone observe and understand; cultural oppression that operates tacitly is a much more serious problem.

2.   Most statistics were obtained from Statistics Canada publications, identified in the references section of the chapter.

REFERENCES

Auster, E. (1993). "Demystifying the glass ceiling: Organizational and interpersonal dynamics of gender bias". *Business and Contemporary World.* Vol. V, no. 3, 47-68.

Belcourt, M., Burke, R., Lee-Gosselin, H. (1991). "The glass box: Women Business Owners in Canada". Canadian Advisory Council on the Status of Women.

Bradshaw, P. and Wicks, D. (1994). "Investigating the gendered nature of organizational culture". Working Paper, York University.

Canadian Human Rights Commission. (1983). "Unwanted Sexual Attention and Sexual Harassment: Results of A Survey of Canadians". Ottawa: Ministry of Supply and Services.

Delamont, S. (1989). *Knowledgeable Women.* London: Routledge.

Ferguson, K.E. (1993). *The man question: visions of subjectivity in feminist theory.* Berkeley, CA: University of California.

Foucault, M. (1972). *Power/Knowledge: Selected interviews and other writings.* New York: Pantheon.

Galarneau, D. (1994). "Female baby boomers: A generation at work". Ottawa: Statistics Canada, Minister of Industry, Science and Technology and Prentice Hall.

Ghalam, N. (1993). "Statistics Canada Target Groups Project: Women in the Workplace". Ottawa: Minister of Industry, Science and Technology.

Goodman, L., Koss, M., Fitzgerald, L., Russo, N. and Keita, G. (1993). "Male violence against women: Current research and future directions." *American Psychologist*, October, 1054-57.

Government of Canada. "Earnings of Men and Women". Ottawa: Statistics Canada, Labour and Household Surveys Analysis Division, 1991, 1992, 1993.

Hoschild, A. R. (1990). *The Second Shift.* New York: Avon.

Lero, D. (1994). "110 Canadian Statistics on Work and Family".
    Ottawa: Canadian Advisory Council on the Status of
    Women.

Longair, J. (1990). *Canadian Directorship Practices: A Profile*. A
    Conference Board of Canada Report, March.

Mills, A.J. (1988).   "Organization, gender and culture".
    Organizational Studies, Vol. 9, 351-369.

Ontario Women's Directorate, (1992). "Infoflash: A Fact Sheet on
    Women in Ontario". No.3, March.

_____. (1993). "Wife Assault: Dispelling the Myths". October.

Schein, E.H. (1985). *Organizational culture and leadership*. San
    Francisco, CA: Josey-Bass.

Statistics Canada. (1993).   "The Daily Statistics Canada: The
    Violence Against Women Survey".   Thursday, November
    18, Catalogue number 11-001E.

"The Boys Club".   *The Financial Post Magazine*.   September
    (1993), Pp. 16-24.

Chapter 9

THE POLICE AND THE DIVERSE SOCIETY: TRENDS AND PROSPECTS IN THE 21ST CENTURY

---

*Stephen E. Nancoo**

Introduction

Issues having to do with the police and the diverse society profoundly impact on all of us as citizens, taxpayers, practitioners and potential victims. Some of the compelling, policing questions we need to address in the 21st Century are: What will the crime and societal environment be like in the 21st Century? What emerging future conditions are likely to affect policing? How are we to prepare for the future of policing in a diverse society? What are the contours of a potentially effective police service delivery model that would meet the safety and security needs of a diverse community? What are the contours of a potentially effective police service delivery model that would meet the safety and security needs of a diverse community?

Futures Research

For a long time, the arrival of the 21st Century has stood for the future and what we shall make of it. In preparing for that future, futurists have written a number of significant studies: Toffler (1990); Naisbitt and Aburdene, (1990); Kennedy, (1993) and David Foot (1996). Within recent times, increasing attention is also being paid to the future of policing. In terms of American policing, Bayley (1994) provides an interesting comparative analysis and a blueprint for the future of policing as one of society's most basic institutions; Klofas and Stojkovic (1995) take a look at the much broader canvas of the future of crime and justice. In the Canadian context, the most significant works that command our attention are: Normandeau and Leighton, (1990) was a path-breaking work which influenced the work of Canadian policing in the 1990s and; Nancoo (1993) offered a significant contribution in promoting community policing and strategic leadership as the instruments creating much-needed transform-ational change within policing.

Even in the best of times, musing about the future is a difficult task in which one could either overlook profound issues or engage in an exercise of pure fantasy. Futurists are certainly restricted by the realization that the future is neither fixed nor predetermined, the future is not predictable, and individual choices and actions can influence and change the future (Tafoya, 1986, p.202).

This chapter will examine **The Police and the Diverse Society: Trends and Prospects in the 21st Century.** First, we will review some of the trends in the external and internal environments and analyze their implications for the future strategic direction of policing. Second, we would explore how as part of the strategic planning process, visioning may influence the outcomes and our conclusions about the future. Defining the police mission and clarifying values become fundamentally important exercises in the context of setting the future, strategic direction of policing the diverse society. Considering these processes, we would trace the emergence of a paradigm shift from the traditional form of policing, and delineate the nature and characteristics of the emerging paradigm of policing.

ENVIRONMENTAL SCANNING
External And Internal Trends

In a world where the rate of change is accelerating, monitoring the environment allows one to proactively anticipate and creatively manage rapidly increasing changes. Environmental scanning provides futurists with a method of identifying future trends that fundamentally influence or alter an organization and its environment. Demographics, aboriginal issues, ethnicity and immigration, economics, political and social forces, organization, management and technology are some of the identified trends that are shaping the future of the diverse Canadian society, policing and police organizations.

Demographics

The aging population: Low fertility and increasing life expectancy trends suggest an aging of the Canadian population. The number of seniors (the 65 and over age group) will rise from 3.2 million in 1991 to 5.0 million in 2011, an increase of 56.3 percent. (George et al., 1994, p.71). This is much higher than the rate of growth of the total population during the same period. Changes in the population would see the emergence of a labour force consisting of and older Canadians and more women.

Aboriginal Peoples: With an average life expectancy that is shorter than the Canadian average and a fertility rate about fifty per cent higher than the rest of the population, the Aboriginal population is becoming younger. Aboriginals, who saw a rapid decline of their population from one hundred percent following the arrival of the colonizers, are now increasing in their proportional representation of the Canadian population. With half of the native population living in urban centers, indications are that an increasing number of young native persons will move to urban areas in the future. A serious social issue for all Canadians is the fact that there is currently an over-representation of Aboriginal peoples in prison. "Public inquiries in Alberta, Saskatchewan and Manitoba found that the aboriginal people were more likely than non-Aboriginals to be denied bail, to be held in pre-trial detention, to be charged with multiple offenses, to be given little time with their lawyer and to be incarcerated upon conviction" (Policing in British Columbia Commission of Inquiry, 1994).

Ethnicity and Immigration: Canada encompasses a diversity of racial and ethnic groups, which can be broadly classified as: the aboriginal peoples, charter groups (descendants of British and French) and ethnic minorities (visible and non visible minorities). The aging of the Canadian population motivated the public policy decision to increase immigration levels, which also saw a dramatic shift in the dominance of source countries for our immigrants. For example, whereas in the 1960s immigration to Canada consisted of people mainly from the United Kingdom,

United States and Europe, changes in immigration laws in 1968 facilitated the arrival of people in Canada from a wider range of countries, especially Asia, Latin America, the Caribbean and Africa. (See Chapter 1 for an explication of immigration patterns.)

The trend toward an increasingly diverse society as evidenced by the greater number of languages, cultures, religions, national and racial origins will likely increase. The total visible minority population in 1996, for example, was 3.2 million and this is expected to increase to over 8 million by 2016. Another significant trend is that the majority of new Canadians tend to settle in the densely populated metropolitan centers of Toronto, Vancouver and Montreal.

The family: The structure of the Canadian family is in a state of flux. Most Canadian families have two incomes, with both spouses working. Projections are that there will be a continuing increase in the number of single parent families, the majority of whom will be headed by women.

Technology: The technological revolution is altering social organizations with the explosive growth in computers and computer literacy and advances in artificial intelligence and mass communications. The organization, national and global electronic infrastructures, the information superhighway, will continue to reshape what we do and how we do it.

Globalization: Globalization is a defining feature of the world in which we live. With globalization, there is the growth of the information economy, the trend toward electronic commerce, the digitalization of cultural products and the "death of distance". In economic and social terms, we have created a global "ecology" in which events in one part of the global system are felt everywhere. (*Canada 2005*, 1997, pp.12-13).

Internal and Other trends: Other significant issues and trends that are impacting on the police in its operations within the diverse Canadian society include a growing demand for police accountability, competition for scarce financial resources, a growth in private policing, the changing nature of crime trends, regionalization of small police services, greater civilianization of personnel and a reorientation of the nature, content and methods of training and greater demand for services to victims of crime and disorder.

Implications For Policing

Each of the identified environmental trends will have profound implications for the police and the diverse society. Accompanying the **aging of the population** will be an increase in the fear of crime among the elderly. The fear of crime is as real as crime itself. In 1993, 57% of women aged 65 and over reported feeling unsafe and alone in their neighbourhood. It is also predicted that by the year 2041, 23% of the population will be over 65. As a consequence, there will be an increase in non-crime related calls for service from the police. Because of their greater vulnerability, the elderly will increasingly become the targets of incidents of fraud and non-violent offenses.

Mirroring this societal trend, police services are also aging, resulting in the forecast that clusters of police officers will opt for early retirement in the first decade of the twenty-first century. As a consequence, police organizations will have an opportunity to redress the underrepresentation of certain groups through the recruitment of qualified women and visible minorities. This organizational population aging will result in the possibility of an increase in the number of women and other underrepresented groups in senior policing positions.

In relation to the **aboriginal people** condition and its implication for policing and police organizations, the report, *Closing the Gap* states that there is "an overwhelming desire among aboriginal people for greater control over policing in their communities and for the development of programs tailored to their particular cultures and values" (*Policing in British Columbia Commission of Inquiry,* 1994). Informed observers have expressed a cautionary note that the traditional model of policing may not meet with the needs and values of aboriginal people (Depew, 1993; *Policing in British Columbia Commission of Inquiry*, 1994). The public policy conclusions suggest, therefore, a continued implementation of the trend towards a recognition of aboriginal people right to establish their own policing objectives (*Policing in British Columbia Commission of Inquiry*, 1994) and the creation of independent, aboriginal policing services.

From a philosophical standpoint, it is expected that aboriginal policing organizations will embrace community policing as the model that is most consistent with their traditions and history (Depew, 1993; Nancoo, 1993). The future national thrust in aboriginal policing is appropriately captured in the comment: "We believe it is important to establish a good relationship between police forces and aboriginal people. The objectives of our recommendations are to foster the establishment of effective Aboriginal police forces, staffed with officers who will be sensitive to Aboriginal people, and to improve the manner in which non-Aboriginal forces serve Aboriginal people. Such forces, using a community policing approach, will provide services that are culturally appropriate and support the deep commitment to justice that was frequently raised with us by aboriginal presenters" *Policing in British Columbia Commission of Inquiry*, 1994).

The ethnic, cultural, linguistic, religious and racial diversity occasioned by **immigration** and an increasing number of visible minorities present a challenge for policing and police organizations. Commissions of Inquiry in various provinces have identified the need for improving race relations between the police and minorities as a priority. Consequently, organizations will have to effectively respond to the greater need for cross-cultural sensitivity and race relations training. There is also the need for strategies by police services that provide for greater participation by minority groups in the policing of our diverse communities. Recognition of this need is manifested in the philosophical commitment to the idea that the police should be representative of the community it serves (*Ontario Police Services Act,* 1990; *Policing in British Columbia Commission of Inquiry,* 1994) and the establishment of community advisory groups and other mediating mechanisms to facilitate effective relationships between the police and ethnic communities will continue (Samuel, 1995; Normandeau and Leighton, 1990, Nancoo, 1993; Canadian Association of Chiefs of Police, 1992).

The changing family structure of two working parents and the increasing trend towards single parent families headed predominantly by women suggest a number of challenges for police work and police organizations.

The implications for police work are: (1) An increasing number of unsupervised "latch key kids," creating additional work for the police. (2) The elderly will require a wider range of police services because of fewer offspring caring for the aged. (3) Higher rates of crime against vulnerable groups, such as women, children and the elderly. (4) Fear of residential break-ins at unoccupied or unsupervised homes is likely. (5) The increase of women in the workplace will probably lead to an increase in crime for women as well as by women, especially white collar crime. Police departments will of necessity have to forge strategic partnerships with other organizations and agencies providing services to victims, vulnerable groups at risk of victimization, and offenders under community supervision.

Crime Trends indicate that a major concern is the intolerant level of violent crime committed by our youths. In some urban centres, youth gangs are rearing their ugly heads and violence in schools will be a serious concern for educators and law enforcement officers. Recent shootings in schools in Alberta, Toronto, and Orleans are anathema to the learning and educational process and the safety and security of our school children and immediate efforts to eradicate this form of violence is a societal necessity. It is imperative that police organizations establish partnerships with the schools and the communities to reverse these unfortunate trends.

As **technology** changes, new crimes and new methods of combating crime emerge. For instance, the computer has given rise to computer crime. The computer will greatly accelerate the globalization of crime leading to increased corporate crime, fraud, and money laundering.

On the other hand, the computer also helps in catching conventional criminals; data on criminal styles of operation have provided suspects and led to arrests and convictions in many cases. Gene Stevens (1990, p.99) predicts that:

> computer assisted analyses of everything from hair and blood to mud and stains have led to the apprehension and conviction of increasing number of offenders. Within, the overwhelming chores such as assigning officers to patrol based on incidents of crime. One of the most intriguing uses of the computer is to develop "profiles" of criminals. From a few clues—the injuries inflicted on the victim, the mode of entry into the house, the place and time of the crime etc.—computers are being used to identify the age, sex, hair-color, heights, weight,   educational   level,   psychological

characteristics, home town, speech pattern, motivation of the perpetrator in the case.

With **globalization** we are also experiencing crime on a global scale. There are the threats of the drug trade, extortion, trafficking in luxury motor vehicles, financial crimes, international hate crimes, terrorism, illegal means of migrations, transnational organized crime, fraud against governments, organizations and individuals, the serious problem of the child sex tourism trade and the multifaceted cyberspace crimes.

With globalization there needs to be a re-definition of community and community policing to embrace a global dimension. Canadian police organizations will have to establish global partnerships to cope with the problems of global crime. The exchange of police information and personnel with international partners should become more commonplace. The training of Canadian police personnel with an international perspective would better prepare our organizations for the threats posed by global crime.

In terms of the diverse society, hate crimes are becoming an emerging issue of concern and it is the view of some that action is necessary in order to prevent perpetrators from abusing the information highway with their message of hate. Keeping abreast of technological innovations to prevent and detect crime will motivate police services to provide officers with specialized training as well as enhance the trend towards civilianization with the requisite specialized expertise.

Private Policing

Although the major thrust of this article is with public police, one cannot escape dealing with the inexorable growth of private policing and its impact on public policing and society at large. It is currently estimated that there are twice as many private police as public police in Canada.

The growth of private policing, part of the general trend towards the pluralising of policing, have consequences for the level of public safety, for access to public security, for human rights and for accountability (Bayley and Shearing, 1996).

Although the pluralising of policing has increased public safety it does not do so under market circumstances to all members of the community since it is customized to those who pay for the services. Nor is private police held to the same level of accountability as public policing thereby making private police more security conscious than rights conscious. Bayley and Shearing suggest that:

> If we are right that governments cannot provide satisfactory public safety, that neighbourhoods will have only haphazard success in doing so, and that mass private property will continue to dominate urban space, then market-based private security will inevitably increase relative to public policing. It may even begin to cannibalize public policing if affluent people become more reluctant to pay twice for safety. It follows, therefore, that there will be no avoiding the emergence of dualistic policing stratified by race and class. The affluent will be protected by private security agents organized by interest groups and operating according to preventive principles backed up by the requirements of specialized membership or participation; the poor will be protected by a weakened public police operating according to principles of deterrence based on procedurally limited law enforcement. Western democratic societies are moving inexorably, we fear, into a Clockwork Orange world where both the market and the government protect the affluent from the poor—the one barricading and excluding, the other by repressing and imprisoning—and where civil society for the poor disappears (pp.601-602).

Given the scenario advanced above, I propose to delineate an agenda for change in Canadian public policing which provides for the safety and security of all the people in all our communities. This agenda for change envisions an important role for public policing that is consistent with both the needs of the citizens and values that are in keeping with the traditions of our democratic society.

Vision, Mission And Values: Creating A Desirable Future

Given the conclusions based on our review of some of the environmental trends and their implications for public policing, the question of where are we going could be predicated on two differing viewpoints. On the one hand, we could assume that the future will merely be an extension of the past or that we are the mere pawns of an uncertain future. Alternatively we could through deliberate choices attempt to invent or create the desirable future through visioning and strategic planning. What is needed is understanding and planning. Understanding of trends and events that will shape the future is required. Planning is required to effect the changes that are needed to influence the trends and future (Sapp, 1992, p.196.) Some police organizations—Hamilton-Wentworth Regional Police, Toronto Police Service, Peel Regional Police, North Bay Regional Police, Sudbury Regional Police, Ontario Provincial Police, Waterloo Regional Police, Ottawa-Carleton Regional Police, and Calgary Police, to name a few—have begun the process of developing strategic plans, a trend which is likely to increase as police organizations grapple with the future (Nancoo, 1993).

Creating a Vision

Visioning starts the strategic planning process because it serves as a driving force in inventing the organization's future. Futurists who begin the strategic planning exercise through an envisioning process believe that the times demand transformational leaders who will focus on the designing and creating of an ideal, desirable future. Such "leaders look forward to the future. They hold in their minds visions and ideals of what can be done... Leaders breathe life into visions. They communicate their hopes and dreams so others clearly understand and accept them as their own. They show others how their values and interests will be served by the long term vision of the future" (Kouzes and Posner, 1987).

Progressive chiefs of police and police organizations have begun the process of deliberately engaging in the setting of their own organizational vision statements. Hamilton-Wentworth Regional Police, Royal Canadian Mounted Police (RCMP), the

Ontario Provincial Police (OPP), Toronto Police Service, Peel Regional Police and Waterloo Regional Police are cases in point. Also one Provincial Government, Ontario, outlined a vision of policing, referred to as the six principles of the *Ontario Police Services Act*. These principles are:

1. The need to ensure the safety and security of all persons and property in Ontario.

2. The importance of safeguarding the fundamental rights guaranteed by the *Canadian Charter of Rights and Freedoms and the Human Rights Code, 1981.*

3. The need for cooperation between the providers of police services and the communities they serve.

4. The importance of respect for victims of crime and understanding of their needs.

5. The need for sensitivity to the pluralistic, multiracial and multicultural character of Ontario society.

6. The need to ensure that police forces are representative of the communities they serve.

In addition to the six principles, the *Ontario Police Services Act* requires police organizations to provide the following core police services: crime prevention, law enforcement, assistance to victims of crime, public order maintenance, emergency response, and administration and infrastructure.

Defining the Police Mission

In the 21st century, police organizations and their stake-holders will have to develop well-defined, focused mission statements. Since there are competing policing strategies, a clear mission statement which outlines the organizations raison d'etre will influence the organization's macro-strategy, resource allocation and style of policing. To illustrate, the mission statement of the Hamilton-Wentworth Regional Police Service "is to serve and protect in partnership with our communities". Such a mission statement connotes its distinctive model and style of policing, something quite different from the sort of mission statement of an organization beholden exclusively to the traditional para-military model of policing.

Values

All decisions are based on values and a fundamentally important aspect of organizational excellence is an emphasis on values-driven decision-making. Values are "enduring beliefs that a specific mode of conduct is preferable to an opposite or converse mode of conduct or end-state of existence" (Rokeach, 1977). Values should guide the behaviour of an organization and its employees.

Police organizations are beginning to make explicit their values, which will determine, among other things, the style in which policing will be pursued and the acceptable modes of conduct and behaviour of their employees. With the rapidity of societal change, formulating and publishing these values will provide a useful anchor for policing organizations and their personnel.

A number of common themes have emerged among police organizations that have taken the critical step of developing values statements. Some of these commonly shared values among disparate police organizations are to: protect human life as the highest priority, perform duties with the highest ethical standards, share responsibility with the community for improving the quality of life, working in partnership with the community to prevent crime, treat victims of crime with compassion and sensitivity, empower employees; create a professionally, effective and satisfying police service and seek excellence in each activity undertaken, efficient response to community demands, using only the minimum force required in carrying out duties, respect for and value of equitable treatment to all individuals of the diverse society, and a commitment to continuous learning and improvement.

In creating a vision, defining the mission, clarifying the core organizational values and in formulating strategic plans to effect organizational change, a police service must inform itself of the total quality management and quality leadership approaches. Essentially the total quality management and quality leadership approaches embrace the following fundamental characteristics:

1. Customer/client focus: Everyone in the organization determines who the customer/client is. The analysis of the vision, mission, values, core competencies the the organization's strengths

and weaknesses, opportunities and threats, are essential to identifying the customer/client needs that must be served.

2. Total involvement: Everyone works to satisfy the customer/client through continuous improvement processes. Making all managers and employees part of the improvement process increases the acceptance of change.

3. Continuous improvement processes through problem solving and fact based decision-making. A problem-solving approach encourages the use of data to drive decision-making. The emphasis on measurement of customer-client needs and expectations and the measurement of the capability of meeting those needs form the basis of Total Quality Management (Domb, 1993; Couper and Lobitz, 1991; Nancoo, 1993).

In the 21st century, the quality movement will of necessity assume new dimensions. The first quality revolution focused on the product. This was followed by the addition of customer and client satisfaction to the quality movement. Quality relationship with employees is the next frontier of an integrated quality movement involving the components of product/service client/customer and empowered employees in the 21st Century.

Towards A Paradigm Shift In Policing

Consistent with the conclusions emerging from the strategic planning process is an increased recognition in the policing community that a shift from the predominantly traditional form of policing to a new paradigm of policing is necessary. Scholars and practitioners in both Canada and the United States have underlined the serious shortcomings of the traditional model of policing that continues to be the **modus operandi** of many North American police departments.

On the basis of research over the last 20 years, American scholars and progressive practitioners have identified the limitations of the traditional model: as "its predominantly reactive stance toward crime control; its nearly exclusive reliance on arrests as a means of reducing crime and controlling disorder; its inability to develop and sustain close working relationships with the community in controlling crime; and its stifling and ultimately unsuccessful methods of bureaucratic control" (Moore, 1994)."

In a Canadian context, the strategic planning process with

its drive towards creating a vision, defining the police mission scanning the environment and clarifying the values of police services focused attention on the inadequacies of the traditional method of policing. These processes also underlined the need for new approaches to policing and advanced the case for fundamental organizational change to police organizations.

What should the future of public policing in the diverse Canadian society look like?

Researchers have observed that a paradigm shift from the traditional form of policing to community policing is developing in the philosophical thinking, strategies and operational practices of a number of pioneering police services. Variously described as community-based policing, or community-oriented policing, community policing is portrayed as the official morality with respect to policing in Canada (Clairmont, 1993), the most progressive approach to contemporary policing (Normandeau and Leighton, 1990), the dominant ideology and organization mode of progressive policing (Murphy,1993), the new orthodoxy for cops (Rosenbaum, 1994), and a paradigm shift (Nancoo, 1993).

For the 21st Century, there is growing consensus that community policing will be the operating philosophy of most Canadian police organizations. One could quite legitimately ask why is this the case after only a brief courtship with the American-style 'professional' or "traditional" model of policing?

As more and more police organizations embark upon strategic planning and environmental scanning of their communities, they are coming to the inescapable conclusion that community policing is an idea whose time has indeed come. This is the case of the Ontario Provincial Police(OPP), Edmonton Police Service, Hamilton Wentworth Regional Police, Peel Regional Police, Waterloo Regional Police Service, Sudbury Regional Police Service, Winnipeg Police, The Royal Canadian Mounted Police(RCMP), and the Ottawa-Carleton Regional Police Service, to identify a few.

In the long term, as we move from strategic planning to strategic management and total quality management, police organizations will strive to institutionalize the community policing paradigm. This belief is premised on the view that both total quality management and community policing share the same underlying conceptual frameworks of client focus and client satisfaction, problem solving and widespread employee involvement and participation.

Unlike the United States with its continuing debate on differences between community policing and problem oriented policing, in the Canadian environment problem solving is conceptually and operationally considered as an integral part of the community policing philosophy. Enlightened police chiefs have given their support to this idea as evidenced by the community policing model adopted by the Ontario Association of Chiefs of Police (OACP) sub-committee on community policing.

The environmental scanning processes which involve the participation of both the public and the politicians who have supported the democratic notions of partnerships and account-ability, concepts integrally linked to the community policing paradigm.

There is increasing confidence among police organizations because, according to Bayley (1994) Canada has considerable experience with community policing that is readily available within many police organizations. This is especially the case as it applies to rural policing, which as noted by Murphy (1993) "traditional small town police may soon discover that they have all along been slightly ahead of their time."

To some extent as well, Canadian police executives could not be indifferent to the debate on community policing that was taking place in the United States. Without a critical research body in Canada, and in light of this country's close geographical proximity to the United States, Canadian policing is inevitably susceptible to the transnational influences of American policing ideas, ideologies and strategies. This transnational influence is facilitated through American financed and sponsored conferences and the considerable United States governmental-supported research on community policing as well as such organizations as the International Association of Chiefs of Police and the Police Executive Research Forum.

More importantly however, one should not lose sight of the fact that in embracing community policing, Canadian police chiefs were also attempting to recapture their policing roots. Like many other institutions, Canadian policing was a beneficiary of the British traditions—the traditions of Robert Peel and his principles, and the traditions of such organizations as Metropolitan London

Police and the Royal Irish Constabulary—because of this country's political and institutional connections with Great Britain during colonial times. These traditions include at least an awareness of Peel's principles one of which articulates the prophetic dictum that the role of the police is "to maintain at all times a relationship with the public that gives reality to the historic tradition that the police are the public and the public are the police; the police being only members of the public who are paid to give full-time attention to duties which are incumbent on every citizen, in the interests of community welfare and existence." (Nancoo, 1993.)

To understand the future, it is also necessary for us to understand the past and the present. It is not unexpected therefore that in their attempt to shape their future by an appeal to their historical past, Canadian police organizations are also being pushed by the reformist temper of contemporary times, as is illustrated by the community policing recommendations from commissions of inquiries and task forces. For example, *Ontario Report on Race Relations and Policing Task Force* (1989) and the *British Columbia Commission of Inquiry into Policing* (1994), both proponents of community policing, were themselves significantly influenced by today's reality of an increasingly diverse society and the reflections of citizens-advocacy groups representing various segments of this diverse society.

While the majority of police services proclaim community policing as the most appropriate approach to preventing and solving problems of crime and disorder, this is not always the case in practice. Indeed there are virile pockets of resistance to the idea in some police organizations. Furthermore, the nature of policing, even in the realm of community policing, is significantly different from Peel's conceptualization a century ago. The new conceptualization of Community policing involves a wider set of variables in relation to community partnerships, community safety concerns, victims assistance, empowered employees and a movement away from the para-military style and structure of police organizations.

The coming to terms with the philosophy and practices of community policing and attempts at a re-conceptualization of what community policing is all about constitute a re-inventing of community policing—paralleling the reinventing of government themes in the public administration literature—and consequently my labeling of community policing as **the new paradigm of policing**. Bayley reflected that Canadian policing faces a confrontation of paradigms—reactive containment of crime by the "thin blue line" versus proactive problem solving through the mobilization of community resources. And the widespread public proclamations of police organizations "that we have community policing too" coupled with the demands of advocacy groups allowed one researcher to conclude that "the rise of community policing represents today one of those significant changes **a paradigm shift**" (Nancoo, 1993).

What augurs well for the future is that organizations are undertaking fundamental organizational change through their efforts at strategic planning that deliberately seek to establish strategic alliances with the communities in community policing initiatives. Peel Regional Police noted in its environmental assessment (1994) that in keeping with the mission and values statement, "we are committed to community oriented policing through the practice of problem oriented policing and the development of community partnerships." Hamilton Wentworth Police Service, which has institutionalized the strategic planning process as its modus operandi, has community policing as a central tenet in its Strategic Plan. Toronto Police Service Beyond 2000 document outlines neighbourhood policing as its vision of the future.

The Nature Of Community Policing

Community policing is primarily a philosophy of policing. There is remarkable consensus on the philosophical basis of the paradigm of community policing as evidenced by researchers and writers from the United States of America, Canada and Britain (Bayley, 1994; Trojanowicz and Buceroux, 1990; Nancoo, 1993). Pivotal to this philosophy is the fundamental notion of a co-operative partnership between the police and the public in pursuit of the peace, safety and security of our communities.

The elements of this strategic partnership find expression through consultative and collaborative patterns of partnership behaviours between the police and the community. Organizations involved in the strategic planning and strategic management process are expected to engage in extensive consultations with their communities through focus groups, town hall meetings, surveys, and advisory committees. Collaborative efforts are intended to form strategic alliances with members and agencies of the community in pursuit of the goals of crime prevention and control of crime and disorder.

Given the growing diversity of our population, policing organizations of the future will seek increasingly innovative ways in encouraging citizens to become more involved in, and responsible for policing neighborhoods and communities. Included in this notion of partnership is the democratic principle that while the police should be immune from political interference in its investigations, the police are indeed accountable to the community and its democratic institutions in its policy formulation and decision-making processes.

To accommodate the changes envisaged by the community policing philosophy, the structures and institutions of policing must be changed. "A police organization that is heavily invested in the professional model of policing—with a centralized hierarchical and bureaucratized command structure—will have difficulty creating an environment that is conducive to community policing strategies and that encourages creative problem solving" (Rosenbaum, 1994, p.124).

Moore and Stephens (1991, p.103) postulate that to change to community policing, "the administrative structure would have to be changed from a functional organization to a geographic one to enable the police to develop the rapport they need with local community groups. The centralized decision-making structure would have to yield to a much flatter, more decentralized style to acknowledge the reality of the organization's dependence on the initiative and discretion of its front-line officers, and to exploit their skills."

In Canada, structural changes and decentralization and re-engineering the police functions are now taking place. Ontario Provincial Police, Hamilton-Wentworth Regional Police, Toronto, Edmonton Police Service and Ottawa-Carleton Regional Police Service are among some of the police organizations that have restructured or reengineered their police organizations.

To accommodate community based policing principles, the following organizational changes are recommended:

More decentralization — management decision-making and routine police operations are moved to a community neighborhood or beat level.

Less bureaucracy — decision making becomes more participatory.

Less hierarchical organization — create fewer ranks and fewer levels of organization (*British Columbia Commission of Inquiry into Policing*, 1994:C-7).

Canadian policing experience reflects a wide range of implementation programs and tactics in its movement from a primarily reactive, legalistic and bureaucratic model of policing to a preventive, proactive-reactive, balanced, community based style of policing. It is accepted in the community policing lexicon in Canada that problem solving or problem oriented policing is a critically important strategy in implementing community policing. Problem oriented policing involves a process where problems are systematically defined and researched, then alternative solutions are explored and implemented.

Unlike conventional policing responses that deal with individual incidents, problem oriented policing search for the basic problem that produce the incidents. Problem oriented policing attempt to define common underlying problems that relate to repeated calls for service. "Conventional police response is to the symptoms and not the basic causes of crime, with the result that crime problems remain unresolved and continue to demand police responses. Community policing is aimed at dealing with the whole problem." (*Policing in British Columbia Commission of Inquiry*). Calgary, Edmonton and Peel Regional Police Services are examples of police services that have been internationally recognized for their problem-oriented policing. Ontario Provincial Police, Ottawa-Carleton, Vancouver and Montreal Urban Community Policing have initiated problem oriented programs.

Hamilton-Wentworth Regional Police introduced a priority service-calls system, a victims assistance program—which earned them the prestigious Weber Seavey Award—and a framework for continual community-based consultation processes. Waterloo Regional Police initiated a community development and community mobilization program, while Fredericton has installed a storefront operation Peel Regional Police has a well-thought out Crime Prevention through Environmental Design (CEPTED), which earned them the Weber Seavey Award, and problem-oriented policing program. Toronto Police Service's policing document 2000 provides for community policing arrangement, including provisions for structural change and decentralization. For some time now, Toronto experimented with foot patrols, storefronts and mini stations. Halifax reorganized into three neigbourhood zones with consultative committees and village constables. Halton Regional Police has developed its own style of proactive-reactive policing. Many police services like Sudbury, Sault Ste. Marie, Durham, Vancouver, Victoria, Winnipeg, Kingston, Calgary, Guelph, Belleville, Thunder Bay and Peterborough have introduced a variety of community policing programs while Edmonton has been described as the Mayo clinic of community policing in Canada. In addition to the many municipal services, both the OPP and the RCMP are implementing community policing in small towns in Ontario and various parts of the country. The challenge for policing organizations in Canada is to move beyond the individual programs to a service-wide philosophy of community policing.

The Ontario Association of Chiefs of Police sub-committee on Community Policing has adopted a model of community policing which states: "Community Policing is not a program; it is a way of doing business—a philosophy"

The model provides for five components to community policing. These are:

Enforcement:
- Focusing on community safety concerns and serious violent crime.
- Enforcement activities that optimize service to the community. Focused enforcement in response to community safety concerns and violent crime. Both Toronto Police Service and the Ontario Provincial Police have sophisticated computer models of enforcement within a community policing framework. By the year 2001, the OPP will implement its Community Policing Network (COP NET) service wide.

Community development:
- Community led initiatives that contribute to solving crime and public order problems.

- The Police and the communities engage in partnering arrangements that span the areas of social, economic and other areas of development.
- Encouraging communities that become full partners in initiatives intended to identify and address some of the root causes of crime. Waterloo Regional and Vancouver have innovative community development programs.

Community-police partnerships:

- Developing and maintaining partnerships in the community at both the front-line and corporate level, permitting meaningful community input into all aspects of policing.
- Maintenance of public order, the prevention of crime, and the response to crime are the shared concerns and responsibilities of the community and the police.
- Permanent mechanisms to permit meaningful community input into all aspects of policing in a community. Numerous Canadian police organizations have created productive partnerships with communities across Canada.

Police service reengineering:

- Affecting organizational change to support contemporary management styles and processes.
- Change management to revise police services structures, human resources, administrative processes and operational policies. Strategic planning for effective police services.
- Technology enhancement and streamlining administrative processes, quality initiative, performance measurement and best practices. For example, Hamilton-Wentworth embarked upon a reengineering process to fundamentally redesign the organization's structure, processes and service delivery.
- Hamilton's reengineering process is the catalyst to transform the organizational culture from a traditional, command and control policy driven operation to a culture that is strategic, value based and community driven.

Police learning and Problem Solving.

- To provide for the: development of systems to ensure continuous learning opportunities.
- Delivery of problem-oriented policing training for front-line officers. Peel Regional Police and Calgary Police both won the Herman Goldstein award for problem-oriented policing. Both

of these organizations also place a high emphasis on continuous learning. Peel also extended its problem oriented policing capacity through its systematic application of Crime Prevention through Environmental Design and Crime Prevention through Physical Design.

- A widely accepted problem-oriented model is SARA, an acronym which stands for scanning, analysis, response and assessment. The OPP employs the PARE model which stands for problem identification, analysis, response, and evaluation. The RCMP developed its own CAPRA model, which translates as Clients, Acquiring and Analyzing information, Partnership, Response and Assessment.

Three recent conferences, chaired by Stephen Nancoo, explained the five aspects of the OACP-adopted community policing model to more than 300 senior police officers in Ontario. Among those explaining and providing best practices applications of Enforcement, Community Development, Partnerships, Reengineering and Police Learning and Problem Solving aspects of the integrated model were: Ken Robertson, Chief of Hamilton-Wentworth and President of the Ontario Association of Chiefs of Police; Larry Gravill, Chief of Waterloo Regional and President of the Canadian Association of Chiefs of Police; Steven Reesor, Deputy Chief of Toronto Police; Dan Parkinson, Superintendent of Peel Regional Police; Kevin McAlpine, Chief of Durham Police; Mike Boyd, Deputy Chief of Toronto Police; Brian Cunningham, Deputy Chief Waterloo Regional; Dave Klenavic, Chief of Belleville; and Brad Nudds, Superintendent and Director of the Community Policing Centre of the Ontario Provincial Police. New police recruits to the Ontario Police College are also exposed to this model. Certainly in Ontario, it would appear that the dominant police service delivery model in the 21st Century would be the OACP model which provides an integrated policing approach embracing the notions of enforcement, community-police partnerships, police service reengineering, community development and police learning-problem oriented policing.

As mentioned previously, in the twenty-first century, the notion of community policing has to make a visionary leap to embrace new directions that transcend the narrow jurisdiction of a police organization's geographical boundaries. In an era of globalization, the redefinition of community should be conceived in terms of establishing partnerships with neighbouring police organizations as well as global police organizations. Certainly, police leaders need to become more actively involved in national and international police organizations in order to have a common platform for discussion and action on the impact of global factors on the local and national crime scenes.

Conclusion: Leadership and the New Policing Paradigm

This chapter identified some of the major trends and challenges for policing and the diverse society in the 21st Century. Much is changing in policing, including a change to the community policing paradigm. The success of the police in seriously addressing the challenge of change and the issues that present themselves in the future will depend upon the quality and courage and values-driven transformational character of the police leadership. The critical dimension in the successful and acceptable paradigm shift to community policing resides in great measure on the long term, sustained commitment to innovation and change by the police leadership. Quality policing will come from a visionary leadership and the active participation of a trained and empowered workforce in the service of and in partnership with the citizens of a diverse and democratic society. The determination to make a significant difference in environments rife with turbulence and change, problems and pressures, threats and opportunities is the essence of the leadership challenge in the new millennium.

*The views expressed in this paper are those of the author and not necessarily of any organizations with which he is associated.

REFERENCES

Bayley, D. (1991). *Managing the Future: Prospective Issues in Canadian Policing.* Ottawa: Ministry of the Solicitor General of Canada.

Bayley, D. (1994). *Police for the future*. New York: Oxford University Press.

Bayley, D. and Shearing, C. (1996). The Future of Policing. Law and Socierty Review, Vol. 30, (3), pp.585-606.

Clairmont, D. (1993). Community-Based Policing and Organizational Change. In Chacko and Nancoo (Eds.) *Community Policing in Canada*. Toronto: Canadian Scholars' Press.

Couper, D. and Lobitz, S. (1991). *Quality Policing: The Madison Experience*. Washington: Police Executive Research Forum.

Deming, W. E. (1986). *Out of the Crisis*. Mass: MIT.

Depew, R. (1993). Policing Native Communities: Some Principles and Issues in Organizational Theory. In Chacko and Nancoo (Eds.), *Community Policing In Canada* (pp. 251-268). Toronto: Canadian Scholars' Press.

Domb, E. (1993). Total Quality Management. In William Bean (Ed.). *Strategic Planning That Makes Things Happen*. Massachusetts: HRD Press.

Foot, David. (1996). *Boom, Bust and Echo - How to profit from* the *coming demographic shift*. Toronto: Macfarlane, Walter and Ross.

Kennedy, P. (1993). *Preparing for the twenty-first century*, Toronto: Harper Collins Publishers.

Klofas, J. and Stojkovic, S. (Eds.). (1995). *Crime and Justice in the year 2010*. California: Wadsworth Publishing Company.

Kouzes, J .M. (1987). *The Leadership Challenge*. San Francisco: Josey Bass Publishers.

Metropolitan Toronto Police Service Environmental Scan.

Moore, M. H. and Stephens, D. W. (1991). *Beyond Command and Control: The Strategic Management of Police Departments*. Washington D.C. Police Executive Research Forum.

Murphy, C. (1993). The Development, Impact and Implications of Community Policing in Canada. In Chacko and Nancoo (Eds.) *Community Policing in Canada*. Toronto: Canadian Scholars' Press.

Naisbitt, J. and Aburdene, J. (1990). *Ten Directions for the 1990s, Megatrends 2000*, New York: William Morrow and Company, Inc.

Nancoo, S. E. (1993) The Future: Trends and Issues in Community
    Policing. In Chacko and Nancoo (Eds.). *Community
    Policing in Canada.*, Toronto: Canadian Scholars' Press.

Nancoo, S. E. (1995). Strategic Planning in Ontario Police
    Services, mimeo.

Normandeau, A. and Leighton, B. (1990). *A Vision of the Future of
    Policing in Canada.* Ottawa: Ministry of the Solicitor
    General of Canada.

Ontario Police Services Act. Toronto: Government of Ontario.

*Ontario Report on Policing and Race Relations and Policing Task
    Force,(1989).* Toronto: Government of Ontario.

Peel Regional Police Environmental Assessment (1994).

Policing in British Columbia Commission of Inquiry.(1994).
    Closing the Gap. Victoria: Government of British
    Columbia.

Report of the ADM Sub-Committee (1997). *Canada 2005: Global
    Challenges and Opportunities.* Ottawa: Government of
    Canada.

Rokeach, M. (1973). *The nature of human values.* New York: Free
    Press.

Rosenbaum, D. (Ed.). (1994). *The Challenge of Community
    Policing.* California: Sage Publications.

Sapp, A. D. (1992). Alternative Futures. In Larry T. Hoover (Ed.).
    Police Management Issues and Perspectives. Washington:
    Police Executive Research Forum.

Stevens, G. (1990). Crime and Punishment : Forces Shaping the
    Future. In Edward Cornish (Ed.) *1990s & Beyond.*
    Maryland: World Future Society.

Seagrave, J. (1997). *Introduction to Policing in Canada.*
    Scarborough: Prentice Hall

Tafoya, W.L. (1986). *A delphi forecast of the future of law
    enforcement.* Doctoral Dissertation, University of Maryland
    College. Ann Arbor: University Microfilms International.

Toffler, A. and Toffler, H. (1990). *Powershifts: Knowledge,
    wealth, and violence at the edge of the 21st century.* New
    York: Bantam Books.

Trojanowicz, R. and Bucceroux, B. (1990). *Community Policing.*
    Ohio: Anderson Press.

Chapter 10

FAMILY DIVERSITY
AND CULTURAL PLURALISM

Edite Noivo

INTRODUCTION

Dual career families, Native families, reconstituted families, immigrant families, single-parent families, rural families, ethnic families, aged families working-class families, which are we referring to when speaking of "Canadian families"? In a society where there are nearly as many different family forms as ethnocultural groups making it, "Canadian Families" are intrinsically linked to concepts of plurality and pluralism. Furthermore, each family type may be differentiated in terms of the diverse experiences it represents, or according to gender, social class, ethnicity and age differences. In all cases, major social transformations have occurred around and within "the family,"[1] altering its structure, roles and practices, and will likely continue to do in the future. At the beginning of a millennium, many of those remaking the ongoing changes both in the ethnosocial composition of the population and in the family realm manifest apprehension and anxiety. Thus, in recent years not only have families changed but how we look at them has also changed. Envisaging a twenty-first century multiracial, multiethnic Canadian society of multiplex family forms, many are articulating concerns over national unity, cultural identity, and new trends in marriage and parenthood.

In what follows, we will review the recent changes in the socio-demographic composition of Canada as well as the trans-formations which family functions have undergone in the last decades. Some discussion over the challenges posed by the present and future diversity in family forms, a global phenomena not restricted to advanced or post-industrial societies, then follows. However, due in part to the limited attention minority group families have received and given the fact that an increasing number of Canadians will be living in ethnic minority family households, our ultimate focus is placed on ethnic families. Often problematized and believed to portray distinct family values and practices which may contrast with Canadian norms, these families are often regarded as traditional and fixed entities resisting change. Assessed from a "social problems" perspective, they are generally viewed as restricting the social and economic integration of its members into mainstream society. Depicted as if "living in the past," immigrant and ethnic families are also projected as more cohesive and stable, having extensive supportive kin networks, greater respect for the elderly and showing a stronger familist orientation and less dependency on public services.

Either perceived under nostalgic and mythical visions of premodern family forms or censured for failing to integrate Canadian cultural norms and practices, these families' realities continue to elude our understanding. However, in 1991, 31% of all Census respondents declared an ethnic origin other than French or English, 37% of Canadians aged 15 and over had at least one foreign-born parent, and over one million families communicate in a non-official language (Statistics Canada, 1993). Consequently, it is becoming increasingly difficult to overlook the ethnocultural diversity of Canadian families. The fact is that, unlike the predicted end of "the family" and of "ethnicity," both seem here to stay. Indeed, these are and will likely remain two of the most salient features of our 21st century society. Accordingly, an enhanced analysis of each is reached by integrating both realities. In the process, we will hopefully determine that the ethnocultural diverse families represent a rich and invaluable means from which to assess the present and future plurality of family forms, practices and experiences. For, if all families are mediators between the individual and society, ethnic families act as bridges between societies, and within them, between distinct cultural groups. In the end, because the legitimation and integrity of nation-states also depend on their ability to incorporate and represent all constituting ethnic groups, the integration of these families into mainstream society is no negligible issue.

The Changing Face of the Canadian Population

To understand the current Canadian demographic composition, we must step back and observe that at the time of its state formation (1867-1914), Canada already envisaged large scale immigration as a means to increase its labour force. Indeed, up until the First World War, net migration contributed to 62.3% of the population growth (Satzewich, 1993). After the Second World War, and despite highly fluctuating levels, yearly arrivals range between 200,000 and 300,000 (Statistics Canada, 1991). This, according to many, makes Canada a country of immigrants and is behind its steady demographic growth and multiethnic composition. However, given the widely documented past restrictions in the national origin of those admitted to this country, up until 1962 the vast majority of immigrants (over 90%) were Europeans.[2] Since both founding fathers were also of European ethnic stock, it is not surprising that by 1971 only 4% of Canada's population had roots elsewhere. This means that until the seventies, this country was almost exclusively made up of "White" Christians who spoke and lived in one of the several European languages and cultures, namely English, French, German and Italian.[3]

Since then, or throughout the eighties, a significant shift in the origin of newcomers occurred, so that by 1989 one half of all immigrants were Asians. Briefly, as family immigration decreases and independent applicants are favoured, even though many citizens of the U.K. continue to arrive, newcomers are now, Vietnamese, East Indians, Chinese as well as from the Caribbean, Central and South America, the Middle East and North Africa. At this point, two remarks are noteworthy. The first is that recent immigrants are generally younger than those arriving decades ago. For example, in 1989, 56% were under 30 and 80% were under age 40 (ibid.) The second is the overwhelming concentration of immigrants in Toronto, Vancouver, and to a lesser degree in Montreal. This explains how Canada's largest city has changed, to the point that in 1991 its ethnic minority population (62%) outnumbers dominant group residents. But Toronto is not alone in this; Vancouver is also home to more minority members than mainstream Canadians (61%), and let us also note that in both cities, 17% of their ethnic residents are considered "Non-Whites"(ibid.).

In confirming that Canada's ethnic demographic composition has substantially changed, the above statistics simultaneously
indicate that ethnic populations must be included in this as in
similar social analyses. Over fifty ethnic groups are here to stay
and likely to survive across generations (Reitz, 1980). What
appears to lag behind is our acceptance that our society has become
so ethnocultural diverse that, in many schools, neighbourhoods and
major cities across the country, people from all Continents,
religions and speaking many other mother tongues, as a group,
outnumber those of English and French origin. It follows that in
the public sphere as in family households, most Canadians
experience intercultural relations in some form or another to the
point that we are all eventually confronted with questions of
reshaping our ethnocultural identities, symbols and practices.

Changing Family Forms

No one questions that, in Canada as elsewhere, fundamental family changes have occurred in the last fifty years. Divorce
rates, nonmarital cohabitation, single parent families, homosexual
couples and childless marriages, in addition to new patterns of
sexuality and courtship are sufficient evidence that the structure,
functions and basic character of "the family" have been revolution-
ized. Preceding such transformations were significant historical
changes in the size, composition and role of families. Seeking to
account for the latter, the author of *World Revolution and Family
Patterns* (Goode, 1963) remarks that changes in the economic and
ideological systems inevitably alter family structures. Accordingly,
increased industrialization, urbanization, social mobility and indiv-
dualism are said to have operated profound changes in family and
kinship and to account for the dominant model known as "the
nuclear family."[4] With it, a perfect "fit" was attained, which led
Parsons (1971) to call it the "the normal family." Thus, not only
was it presumed by functionalists and society at large that
"normal" people would seek to constitute such a family, but that it
procured members the satisfaction, intimacy and meaning to their
lives. When, only a few years later, signs that such a model did not
really seem to fit with the realities of large populations, including
women, not to mention the needs of industry for female labour,
questions arose as to whether ordinary families had the material

and emotional resources to carry out the designated "functions". One corollary was that "the family" came to be seen as undergoing a crisis (e.g., Lasch, 1977).

Predictably, accounts of the "crisis" and whether contemporary families are de facto functional or dysfunctional, and for whom, vary substantially from one theoretical perspective to another.[5] An unforgivable oversimplification would nonetheless deem that, whereas for feminists the core problem lies in patriarchy and to victimize women the most, for the Marxist minded, the root lies in capitalist relations and the economic system, which is said to injure working class families the most. Functionalists, on the other hand, regard that changes in family and gender roles, in addition to economic problems and public intervention in the family sphere is where the responsibility lies. Noticeably, what analysts of all brands have in common is a tendency to focus on the structural properties of "the family," and—overwhelmed by changes in our social organization—to question whether it can or cannot carry out its functions. For all of them, families refer primarily to reproductive groups charged with socialization and cultural reproduction. The more progressive of them, all too eager or politically involved in struggles for desirable options to the dominant model, tend to mistakenly take new living arrangements as evidence that such alternative forms are finally materializing.

A resulting problem is that in all cases, families continue to be viewed as absorbing the troubles produced elsewhere and are conceived as victimized entities that are defencelessly acted upon. As if families were unable to produce their own tensions and interpersonal conflicts, or as if members always act under conditions in which they have no choice, without constructing part of their realities. In short, by disregarding the changes which families have undergone across the centuries, little attention is paid to the extraordinary ways in which families have adapted to new economic structures and persisted in critical times and transitions periods. However, among a number of historical strategies developed to overcome the austere material conditions hindering family life, members often resort to migration. Instead of abandoning their family projects and lifestyles, they seek more favourable economic settings to pursue them. Understandably, those overlooking such facts are likely to question whether the presumed endangered and fragile institution of "the family" will make it to the next century, and if so, what will it look like.

To tackle that question, we believe that one must forcibly distinguish between marriage and "the family" as these terms are no longer synonymous. In other words, whether we take the second to mean an institution or a relationship, the above often exist separately as in the case of single-parent families and childless couples. Marriage, it is generally agreed, refers to a contractual union between spouses, namely wedlock. Questions arise in cases in which reproduction does not take place, such as voluntary childlessness. "The family" is significantly more polysemous, and its multiple forms along with the realization that beyond relationships and shared activities, it is essentially a *process* (Harris, 1990, p.70), renders it nearly undefinable. Indeed, those attacking monolithic past definitions call for a broad definition in which family refers to a social group which may or may not include two spouses, children and whose members may or may not share residence or even cohabit (Eichler, 1988, p.4). Besides including almost everyone, this less established denotation poses problems, for example, the fact that the rearing of children generally requires propinquity between the rearers and the reared. In addition, it does not reflect the "reality" that generational repro-duction occurs mainly within familial households. Averting the ongoing debate over grand definitions, what we need to remember from this, is that families include a variety of forms in which domestic groups hold, experience and nourish familial relation-ships with in-members.[6]

Once we accept the separation between "marriages" and "the family", we are then ready to question the extent to which delaying or declining to contract marriage, or to dissolve it through legal divorce, may actually indicate a diminished commitment to marriage, but not to family life. Actually, the idea that high divorce rates represents more of a dissatisfaction with one's marriage or partner than with that institution has gained wide acceptance, particularly in light of relative high rates of remarriage. In Canada, for example, although an estimated 40% of all marriages end in divorce, remarriage is frequent, as 32% of all marriages are remarriages (Statistics Canada, 1993). Thus, this seems to suggest that individuals are not really rejecting marriage but rather their partners. That they are expressing a greater dissatisfaction with prescribed roles and traditional practices than with the marital lifestyle *per se*.

Statistics showing that one third of all couples aged 25 and younger are living in a common-law relationship also suggest that many are feeling more comfortable with nonmarital cohabitation. Yet in 1991, there were only 4.1% common-law couples with children living in Canada (ibid.), which means that most eventually contract marriage. Still within this issue, the argument that nowadays individuals are giving higher priority to "independence instead of marriage (...) personal pleasure instead of nurturance" (Orthner, 1990, p.95) seems rather weak, as it appears that individuals actually want both. For example, Statistics Canada reports that in 1991, 86% of those aged 15 to 24 declare an intention to have children. Likewise, 87% of Canadians feel that family is becoming more important.[7] However, there is also indication that while the majority of business and professional people in this country are said to be willing to devote more time to family life at the cost of career advancement, a significant one third would probably not, and less than 20% of respondents seems unhesitatingly willing to do so.[8]

Unquestionably, Canadian society is largely family centered. But as Mellman et al. (1990) claim of North Americans, while family is highly valued and children seen as the greatest source of personal gratification, pleasure and meaning in life, most individuals find the quality of the family relations more important than the formal status of the family. In other words, they emphasize the relational more than the institutional side of it. In fact, more and more family observers share the opinion that the emphasis is not on family, nor on children, nor on marriage, but on relationships. To understand that, let us pursue our analysis by integrating the above data to the presumed importance we place on "relationships".

Partly due to the decline of community ties (Nisbet, 1953), increased individualism (Bellah et al., 1985), the reduction of kin ties (Harris, 1990), the relegation of intimacy and nurturance to the private sphere (Sennett, 1974), and also due to the widely disseminated therapeutic orientation found in psychological literature or articulated by helping professionals, it is undeniable that an unprecedented societal focus is being placed in relationships. Moreover, as Morgan (1991, p.128) points out, the marital relation is not another or a simple relationship but "the relationship." Once marriage has shifted from a social role paradigm to a personal relationship paradigm, the emphasis is no longer in role relations but on relationships. But since the latter are infinitely more complex, the stability or durability of marriage are the price to pay.[9] Clearly, "the relationship" has been affected by other styles and sets of relationships, such as therapeutic and parent child. In addition, marriage "as best friends" has become a common expectation, as it is generally associated with higher levels of communication presumed to create and sustain intimacy. In short, as individualism expands, social ties weaken, and affection and solidarity in the public sphere are harder to find, individual seek involvement and closeness in "the relationship" which becomes increasingly expected to make up for all. It is thus not so much a lack of motivation, as often conceived, but an increased commitment to attain "the good relationship" that leads individuals to make, break and remake marriages. In that sense, marriage cannot be viewed as a threatened institution, although now one for the benefit of the individual and not the other way around. Taking Goldscheider and Waites's claim (1991) that it is not a matter of "no families" but of "new families" one step backwards, we may say that it is not a matter of no marriages but of new marriages.

But, most married partners live in familial households and have children. In 1991, in Canada, 62% of all married persons were parents and so were 52% of the divorced, and 13% of all families are single-parent families with dependent children (Statistics Canada, 1993). Thus, one question frequently raised is whether, in the search for satisfying relationships, children and their needs are not being sacrificed. In other words, are those contemplating divorce attentive to the social, economic and emotional costs their children will likely pay? The impacts of unstable marriages, divorce and remarriage on children have been widely dealt with (see for example, Walczack and Burns, 1984; Wallerstein, 1985; Wallerstein and Blakeslee, 1989) and will not be discussed here, although some comments on post-divorce parent-child relationships will be made further on. Nonetheless, beyond the criticisms that new family trends are showing more narcissism than a commitment to nurture children, there seems to be consensus that children are not receiving sufficient parental attention and nurturance.   Claiming that American society has never been collectivist, but has always stressed independence and self-sufficiency, Orthner (1990, pp.99-100) notes that "three out of four adults believe that the problems affecting children today are worse than when they were young." According to him, "the public wants to see renewed attention to fostering commitments and caring for children."

Such a perspective is also shared by those concerned with the impact of the culture of work on families, and of the money economy and consumerism on family life (Bellah 1990). However, it is also possible that this issue is more pertinent to middle-class contexts. A central concern is that in single-parent as in dual career families, members are spending less and less time together. "For all the talk about the importance of children" write Hochschild and Machung (1989 p.231), "corporations have done little to incorporate the needs of working parents" and "the job culture" they go on to say "has expanded at the expense of a "family culture". In partial agreement with that, Bellah (1990) argues that it is not so much the working time but the extra work - for the sake of consuming yet more - that is the central element in reducing family time.

In the case of divorced families, in which children are physically separated from a parent, usually the father, the focus is placed on the importance of father-child contact. It is noteworthy to observe existing class and gender differences. Briefly lower-class fathers are said to have lesser contact with their children than do fathers from the upper classes. In addition, there seems to be significantly less contact between fathers and daughters than fathers and sons (Walker, 1994). Explanations for the above are claimed to lie in the lower material life conditions and lower communication skills of these fathers, as well as on their reported malaise with the new weekend father role (ibid.)

Regarding the above, we want to add two comments. The first applies to the widely held idea that children in divorced families lose not only daily access to one parent but lose contact also with members of their wider family (Clulow, 1991). Yet, contrary to such belief, it seems to us that whereas lower fertility and higher divorce rates result in a shrinking number of family members, these are largely counterbalanced by the duplication of parents and relatives brought about by divorce and remarriages.

This is to say that in reconstituted families, most children have two sets of parents, grandparents and cousins, in other words, lots of ties. On this aspect, we might add that changes in family practices, roles and relationships have evolved more rapidly than how we conceive or refer to them.

Our second comment pertains to the relationship between family and work. Basically, a previous remark concerning working parents leads us to add that whereas "the family" has adapted to changes in the public sphere, the reverse remains to be done. For example, schools and health care institutions still expect working parents to be available in the daytime. Thus, while employers need to understand the need for flexible working schedules for parents of young children, "the school of the 21st century" must enlarge its services to include parental supportive services and child care (Zigler and Gilman, 1990). Clearly, an impending major transform-ation is the increasing number of individuals who will work from their own households. But whereas many anticipate an easiness in balancing work tasks and family responsibilities, it remains to be seen whether the opposite is not more likely. The stresses of attending to both children and paid work, or the hardship of managing interrupted schedules, have already been remarked in cases of student mothers and independent professionals whose workplace is the familial household. Surely, such trends are more likely to affect middle-class families first. The Canadian working class of the 21st century is rather more likely to encounter cyclical unemployment, relocation, involuntary part-time work and income cuts. All these are known to increase anxiety, depression and stress, which negatively affect the quality and satisfaction with family life. In short, economic instability and material deprivation generally increase the likelihood of divorce and strained family relations.

Canadian Ethnic Families

Given that "ethnic" has become as much a popular, complex and reifying term as "family" and that both are largely ideologically and politically charged, conceptual clarifications are needed before using the notion of "ethnic families." Firstly, while the proposition that we are all ethnics is tautological, the idea that some of us are ethnics while others are not is untenable. An alternative may be to regard "ethnicity" as a social construct which is latent and which tends to come forth in contexts whenever individuals—who either perceive themselves or are perceived by others as being culturally or racially different—come into contact. However, as history has shown, this attribution is generally made by (dominant) group(s) who hold the political power to designate others as ethnics. This is not to say that hegemony alone creates the ethnicisation process. For ethnicity is mainly embedded in identity formation and maintenance and is thus based on an ethnic identification.

Yet an ethnic identity is another multi-faceted and unfixed entity which also depends on a situation or social context. This means that not only does societal saliency of ethnicity vary significantly, both in historical and spatial terms, but that individuals may equally choose to emphasize their ethnic identity in some situations and to downplay it in others (Royce, 1982). Also, while most people have a single ethnic identity, others, like children of intermarriages, hold double or triple. In addition, as part of our understanding of social diversity we need to keep in mind the differences between "white" and "non-white" ethnics. This is because racialized members may not hold a distinct ethnic identity but nonetheless be perceived by others as different and also because most cannot easily manipulate their physical traits.

Briefly, although ethnicity may be conceived as social and political manoeuvre for the purpose of sustaining social stratific-ation, insofar as it is commonly rooted in a distinct culture and identity, it may also be an instrument for group survival and political demands for social equality. Actually this has been evidenced both in Canada as elsewhere, in that ethnic identification and pride as well as group persistence have triumphed over cultural homogenization or assimilationist pressures. In fact, contrary to the recommendations made by celebrated Canadian sociologists, in the past as in the future, few are willing to shed away their cultural differences so that *The Vertical Mosaic* (Porter, 1965) becomes horizontal or discrimination free. Thus, whereas the stratification or hierarchisation of ethnic groups is frequently identified with ethnic cultures (who are "minority cultures" in the sense that they are non-official), not all ethnic groups are minority groups in the sociological sense of the word.[11]

This is partly because not all immigrant groups arrived in Canada "on the same boat" but at different historical and economic periods, with rather different physical and human resources, and not the least, because they receive unequal treatment from mainstream society.[12] In fact, as Satzewich (1993) remarks, through immigration regulations (e.g. policies of family reunification), the Canadian state has played a major role in family formation, the reconstitution of kin ties and consequently controls family continuity and rupture. Its policies have either facilitated or hindered the integration of some populations, all of which affect their family lifestyles, and in that sense are at the essence of the multiethnic character of our society. Surely the historical endorsement of ethnic identification and the survival of ethnic groups has contributed to our contemporary pluralism, yet that may be regarded more as a recognition of the "unmeltable" character of ethnicity (see Novack, 1971) than as a social privilege accorded by the Canadian state.

Noticeably, "ethnicity" like "family' has been and is bound to remain the major source of group and individual identification. However, as Morgan remarks (1991, p.122) "Marriage and family as 'central life interests' are held to override class or ethnic divisions." In other words, because ideological constructions of "the family" stress universality, they help "smooth over or minimize social divisions." This reminds us that family life experiences often transcend ethnicity, and consequently, that ethnic families need to be assessed both in terms of their differences as of their similarities. On this feature, Morgan further points out (1991, p.133) that "there is a construction of difference or 'otherness'" to the point that even when the presumed differences are admired, ethnic families are still seen as strange and aliens. Therefore, as he suggests, an emphasis on distinct family practices or lifestyles usually ends up reifying the ethnic group. In reverse, such a category serves also to reify the existence of ethnic families.

Furthermore, let us not forget that since it is the dominant culture which sets the norms and the normative family practices, ethnic family variations are easily problematized. If not because of their "problems," at least because such families nourish a distinct ethnic identification, seen as problematic for "integration" or social cohesion. Surely, in reproducing themselves, these families also reproduce their minority group status, namely the disadvantages of one generation onto another. Yet it is undeniable that a fading away or disappearance of ethnic differentiation implies the adoption of the dominant culture's family life-worlds, itself a disrupture of one's private universe and psyche. For, if all variations in family patterns and practices are culturally-based, in the case of ethnocultural minorities, such practices reinforce and sustain a sense of belonging to another ethnicity.

Our last comment on the relationship between ethnic group and ethnic families concerns their codependence. Briefly, while all families are affected by the decline of "the community," the strength and dynamics of ethnic families are related to that of their ethnic communities. For example, in more ethnically cohesive communities, traditions are more easily maintained, networks function as social control against marital dissolution and other family issues, and the role of identity transmission, generally attributed to immigrant mothers (Taboada-Leonetti, 1983) is shared with community organizations. This means that within more extensive, active, or let us say "institutionally complete communities" (Breton, 1964), we may expect more cohesive family groups displaying more traditional family practices.

Of course, all along the processes of resettlement and acculturation, ethnic communities play a fundamental supportive role to families. The reverse is self-evident. The Little Italies, Jewish neighbourhoods, and Chinatowns are to a large extent a corollary of family reunification policies, reconstituted family networks and strong intergenerational family ties. In addition, these communities, of which ethnic entrepreneurs and businesses are a vital part, are usually made up of family enterprises whose very existence and success rely on family relationships and kinship. Here also, analysis in the opposite direction would likely show that family businesses help members obtain economic security and to keep a certain degree of autonomy, not without reinforcing strong family relationships amongst the coworkers.

Despite our limited knowledge of the economic relationships amongst intergenerational immigrant families,[13] there is evidence that substantial differences exist between these and dominant group families, although such patterns might be better explained in terms of class position than cultural background. For example, unlike portrayals of middle class Canadian families in which actors presumably relate to each other more in affective ties than material transactions, we found that, within three generations of working-class Portuguese-Canadian families, obligations of providing financial and social assistance prevail over choice and emotional ties (Noivo, 1992).

Unquestionably, the tempo of cultural adaptation and convergence to dominant norms and family lifestyles by ethnocultural minorities does not appear to satisfy the expectations of many Canadians. The "why can't they be, dress, or act more like us" perspective finds a parallel in scholars, for whom changes in roles and attitudes are slight even in the more established groups. On the other hand, many immigrants point to substantial changes, particularly across generations. Within many of these families, the pressure to maintain their ethnic heritage runs alongside an imposition of new family practices presumed to procure their youth greater social opportunities and upward mobility.

However paradoxical, this population is hardly alone in articulating concerns with losses in their cultural identity and traits. Despite Canadian pluralist ideals, differences tend to be tolerated or "accepted" insofar as minority cultures do not challenge nor "threaten" dominant cultures and or their symbols.[14] Schools are increasingly one institution at odds with this issue. Expected to act as an homogenizing force and to foster the integration of dominant values, they are becoming battlegrounds of ethnic alliances and marginalization among students.[15] In this regard, the new increasing diversity of racialized and ethnoreligious family groups represents new challenges and potential conflicts. However, clashes, like discriminatory practices are not confined between the above and the dominant group(s) but are likely to involve the Euroethnics (4 million in 1991), many of whom oppose multiracial immigration or interethnic co-residence.

Insofar as different family values are seen as breeding interethnic conflicts, emphasis is placed on the challenges or problems posed by the coexistence of presumed distinct value orientations, taken as if dissenting norms. Accordingly, it is often argued that school and family socialization enforce opposing social values and norms to children and youth. For many, ethnic families are inescapable sites of intercultural tensions, as parents are said to belong to one immigrant culture and their children to the dominant culture they experience at school and through peer contact. Consequently, the younger ethnic generations are depicted as "divided, marginalized and more susceptible to gang formation" mostly in reaction to their parents' imposition of cultural values prevalent elsewhere or in times passed.[16] An adequate critique of these postulates is beyond our scope, however, we suggest that conflicting cultural value orientations are more hypothesized than empirically substantiated.[17]

Far from neglecting the miscellany of ethnic family socialization practices, our point is that one cannot take different norms for values, as a shared value can take a variety of expressions, some more culturally based and others more influenced by age or gender. Without a strictly comparative analysis of the value systems of Canadian ethnic groups, such suppositions seem more detrimental than beneficial to foster cultural pluralism. It is possible that, within some ethnic minorities, parent-child relationships may appear more hierarchical or that those parents impose strict obedience and respect. Some such families may also hold a more familist orientation, display relatively extensive supportive ties, and represent a microcosm of their ethnic solidarity ties and community networks. Yet, such "differences" need to be understood in terms of interethnic relations, according to patterns of acculturation, and not the least, given ethnic and social inequality.

This means that several traits are often nonexistent or imperceptible in their cultures of origin but are activated or devised as coping mechanisms and social strategies. For example, immigrant family members may pool their resources due to economic deprivation, or co-reside due to inaccessible housing and not because of family norms. Minority group families may be more child centred because their jobs provide little gratification. Married children may conform to elderly parents more out of economic dependency than of actual choice. Briefly, minority group conditions not only affect ethnic enclaves, they may also help generate a greater diversity of family forms and lifestyles, mainly as reactions to structural factors. In addition, let us remember that some enforced attitudes and behaviours, like familism, have more than a material basis. In our study of intergenerational immigrant relations, we found that the older members use familism as a means to enforce some stability and continuity in their fragmented lives and within a context of reduced kin ties. From our understanding of family life as an unachieved entity always in the making—namely constructed, reinforced and intergenerationally reproduced through the interiorization and enactment of obligations and roles (Laing, 1962),—we can add that members use various means, including complex family arrangements and intergenerational transactions, to strengthen their family ties.

The argument that a differential pace of cultural adaptation by ethnic family members induces family tensions and ruptures has not been restricted to intergenerational relations alone. This "problem," according to many, is also found in marital relations as men are said to resist adopting dominant values and norms of gender equality, whereas women presumably embrace Canadian-like attitudes and practices wholeheartedly. The rationale is that as migration induces stress and insecurity, husbands attempt to hold onto their traditional powers and enforce submission. But because immigrant women assimilate new norms and gain greater autonomy and economic independence, they challenge old patterns and seek an end to their oppression: the anticipated outcome is divorce.

Decidedly, the adaptation to new cultural settings is an idiosyncratic process, and different family members may in fact be in different stages of acculturation or assimilation. The presumption that this nonlinear process induces marital conflict is nevertheless faulted on several accounts, namely by the belief that immigrant women identify with the struggles of women from the dominant group(s), or even that the former's newly "gained" autonomy and independence allows them the choice.[18] In fact, while some ethnic groups display divorce rates equivalent to the Canadian average, the vast majority show substantially lower levels, which disproves this part of the argument. Our ultimate point then, is that the emphasis on culture to explain family conflicts disregards the diversity in ethnic groups and assumes that intergenerational and marital conflicts are inevitable in bicultural-ism. This largely constrains our knowledge of these families, insofar as issues resulting from changing economic position, gender and age power differences are all reduced to and lumped together as "cultural clashes".

Concluding Remarks

If we cannot equate marital stability with family continuity, neither can we equate ethnocultural (family) diversity with social instability or interethnic tensions. Thus, we have argued that instead of opposing diversity to continuity, we should perhaps consider, that, given major global, social, political and economic transformations, the only possible continuity lies in diversity. Family forms, patterns, roles and lifestyles will continue to change drastically, but at the core, family life prevails. "The family" and families have shown an historical resilience comparable to ethnicity and let us keep in mind that both facts assure that in the third millennium Canadian society will remain pluralist. Decidedly, these two issues are intimately bound for "our ethnicity cannot be separated from our families" (McAdoo, 1993, p.3). In claiming that our ethnic attributes are not just mediated through and transmitted by our families, it was held that because immigrant and ethnic families form linkages with others—including with dominant group families in many ways including through inter-marriage—they are actually at the centre of interethnic relations.

In addressing widespread concerns over new family patterns, we insisted that the recent changes and current variety of family patterns are basic evidence that families are adjusting to social change. The greater challenges in the transition into the 21st century might be to have other institutions—namely schools, employment, health and social services—adapt to the "new families" and to accommodate their specific needs. By that we mean that public institutions must attend to the multiple stresses of all families: ethnic families, dual-career families, working-class families, single-parent families. In addition, in order to prepare for tomorrow, minority group families, like all other Canadians, need to know what that future will look like or what to prepare their children for.

Accordingly, we hold that greater links between policy makers, economic and social planners, and ordinary families need to be established. Surely, such tasks cannot be carried out by state agencies alone, but must be taken up by community services, the (ethnic) media, educators and so on. Moreover, the challenges confronting all Canadian families are tied to the future of our economic life, namely to resource distribution, structural unemployment and impending changes in the work process. To a large extent, several of the new family forms are already reactions or indirect consequences of the above, and have not, as is often presumed arisen singly out of ideology or of individual choice.

In the new millennium, we should see closer intergenerational relations. Several factors account for that, including the reduced number of kin members—more accentuated in foreign-born groups and internal migrants—along with changes in the concept and role of grandparenthood. Also, not only are economically inactive grandparents changing their attitudes and becoming more involved in the family lives of the other economically inactive members (children and youth),[19] but young families, hit by economic decline and deprivation, are also likely to turn to the aged for assistance and support. In the end, given life span increases, bridging the generations is as much a new challenge as an enrichment for all families.

Finally, given the established pluricultural makeup of Canadian society, with its commitment to anti-racism and to multicultural education, increasing demands from minority groups, and an expanding intercultural convergence is foreseeable. Also, let us remember that the transformations in one generation are frequently only noticeable or acted upon in the next generation. Clearly, intermarriage between Canadians of all ethnic backgrounds is rising, and, depending on our collective success in fighting ethnic and racial discrimination and minority group status, exogamy is likely to flourish. That alone will add new dimensions to current views of diversity. In other, words, the Canada of tomorrow can only be *de facto* pluralist insofar as a plurality of family forms and ethnocultures coexist and cohabit in amity. No doubt, in the year 2000 and beyond, family members will be as involved in the ageless task of intergenerational re-creation of cultural identities and family life as they are today.

Endnotes

1.   It has forcefully been argued by Bernardes (1985, 1986) this term reifies, gives family a sense of naturalness, and endorses conservative ideologies of one central family model. It is suggested that quotation marks around it or "family life" be used instead.

2.   Remarkably, the first ten leading source countries were all European.

3.   Of European background, Jews formed the second major
        religious group (nearly three hundred thousand in 1971).
4.   Whether, according to family historians (e.g. Laslett,
        1972), the nuclearized family preceded industrialization
        is relevant here since it is less its emergence as its world-
        wide predominance and idealization in industrialized
        settings that are at issue here.
5.   For a discussion of these, see Elliot (1986, chapter 5).
6.   On this issue see Morgan (1985), Harris (1990:69-83),
        and Stack and Burton (1993).
7.   *In Canadian Families* (1994:3).
8.   Ibid., note that such paradoxes must also be understood
        in terms of class differences.
9.   For reasons already given let us not equate marital
        stability with family stability. Divorce rates may
        destabilize certain relationships but generally not the
        strong bonds and sense of family.
10.   Obviously, there are significant class and gender related
        differences both in the expectations and skills to
        achieve such ideals. On this see for example, Rubin
        (1983) and Cancian (1989).
11.   According to Wirth (1956), it refers to a group, based
        on ethnicity, "race" or gender, that is either disadvantaged,
        excluded or discriminated against and which occupies a
        subordinate status in society.
12.   See for example the racist discrimination affecting the
        Chinese, presented by Satzewich, (1991).
13.   This is not to say that we know more about non-
        economic relations, namely supportive mechanisms.
        Indeed, research is particularly needed in non-
        traditional difficult situations, such as in divorced
        immigrant women with children, parents of drug-addicts
        and the like.
14.   Examples of this are the RCMP's resistance to accept
        the turban in lieu of the conventional stetson, and more
        recently, the refusal of schools to accept the Muslim
        "hijab."
15.   See for example, Fahlman's study of Muslim students
        in Edmonton (in McAdoo, 1993) and Bibeau et. al's
        (1992) study of the situation in Quebec.

16.   In Noivo (1993:14-16). Also see Jacques et. al. (1985).
17.   A nation-wide analysis of the representation of ethnic
       youth in street gangs, criminal activity or "deviant"
       behaviour is difficult to find (an opposition to collecting
       data based on racial origin is found in the C.C. Report,
       1991). Nonetheless, there is evidence the overall
       immigrant and ethnic youth population are
       underrepresented in law breaking behaviours (in
       Chalom and Kousik, 1993). However, a few groups do
       seem overrepresented, particularly those most affected
       by racism and minority group conditions (namely Blacks,
       Latinos and Asians. On this see *The Globe and Mail*,
       November 9th, 1994. P.A.2-3 and P. Blondin in Chalom
       and Kousik, 1993:91-103).
18.   For a discussion of women's struggles against sexism
       and racism see Kline (1989). Also, like Hochschild and
       Machung (1989) we found that immigrant women
       dissatisfied with their family roles and conditions sense
       that an eventual divorce would burden and impoverish
       them yet more.
19.   On the changing role of grandparents see Royal (1987).

References

Bellah, R. (1990). "The invasion of the Money World" in
       Rebuilding the Nest, edited by D. Blankenhorn.
       Milwaukee: Family Service America.

Bellah, R. et al. (1985). *Habits of the Heart: Individualism and
       Commitment in American Life*. Berkeley: University of
       California Press.

Bernardes, J. (1986). "Multidimensional Development Pathways:
       A Proposal to Facilitate the Conceptualization of "Family
       Diversity." *Sociological Review* 34, 3:590-610.

_____.(1985). "Do We Really Know What "The Family" Is?" Pp.
       192-211 in *Family and Economy*, edited by P. Close and R.
       Collins. London: MacMillan.

Bibeau, G. et. al. (1992). *La santé mentale et ses visages. Un
       Quebec pluriethnique au quotidien*. Montréal: Gaëtan
       Morin.

Breton, Raymond. (1964). "The Institutional Completeness of Ethnic Communities and the Personal Relations of Immigrants" in *American Journal of Sociology* 70:193-205.

Cancian, Francesca. (1989). "Gender Politics: Love and Power in the Private and Public Sphere." Pp. 219-230. in *Family in Transition*, edited by A. Skolnick and J. Skolnick. Boston: Scott, Foresman and Company.

Castles, Stephen. (1989). *Migrant Workers and the Transformation of Western Societies*. Center for International Studies, Cornell University, Ithaca, N.Y.

Centre de Criminologie. (1991) "Colloque sur la collecte des données concernant l'origine raciale et ethnique dans le système de justice pénale." Université de Toronto, October 16th, 1991.

Chalom, M. and J. Kousik eds. (1993). *Violence et Déviance à Montréal*. Montréal: Liber.

Clulow, C. (1991). "Making, Breaking, and Remaking Marriage." in *Marriage, Domestic Life and Social Change. Writings for J. Burgoyne*, edited by D. Clark. London: Routledge.

Eichler, Margrit. (1988). *Families in Canada Today: Recent Changes and Their Policy Consequences*. Second Edition. Toronto: Gage.

Elliot, Faith R. (1986). *The Family: Change or Continuity?* Atlantic Highlands, NJ: Humanities Press International.

Goldscheider, Frances and Linda Waite. (1991). *New Families, No Families? The Transformation of the American Home*. Berkely: University of California Press.

Goode, William J. (1963). *World Revolutions and Family Patterns*. New York: Free Press.

Hareven, T.K. (1986). "Historical Changes in the Social Construction of the Life Course" in *Human Development* 29, 3:171-180.

Harris, C.C. (1990). *Kinship*. Minneapolis: University of Minnesota Press.

Hochschild, A. and A. Machung. (1989). *The Second Shift: Working Parents and the Revolution at Home*. New York: Viking.

Jacques, R.L. et al. (1985). *"L'intégration des jeunes des minorités visibles*. Montréal: CIDIHCA.

Kline, Marlee. (1989). "Women's Oppression and Racism: A Critique of the "Feminist Standpoint". Pp. 37-64 in *Race, Class and Gender: Bonds and Barriers*, edited by Jesse Vorst et al. Toronto: Society for Socialist Studies.

Laing, R.D. (1962). "Series and Nexus in the Family" in *New Left Review* 15:7-14.

Lasch, Christopher. (1977). *Haven in a Heartless World.* New York: Basic Books.

Laslett, Peter. (1972). "Mean Household Size in England Since the Sixteenth Century" in *Household and Family in the Past Time*, edited by P. Laslett, and R. Wall. Cambridge: Cambridge University Press.

McAdoo, H. (1993). *Family Ethnicity: Strength in Diversity*. Sage: Newbury Park.

Mellman, M. et al. (1990). "Family Time, Family Values" in *Rebuilding the Nest*, edited by D. Blankenhorn. Milwaukee: Family Service America.

Morgan, David. (1991). "Ideologies of Marriage and Family Life." Pp. 114-138 in *Marriage, Domestic Life and Social Change. Writings for Jacqueline Burgoyne (1944-88)*, edited by D. Clark. London: Routledge.

_____. (1985). *The Family, Politics and Social Theory*. London: Routledge.

Nisbet, Robert. (1953). *The Quest For Community*. New York: Oxford University Press.

Noivo, Edite. (1993). "Ethnic Families and the Social Injuries of Class, Migration, Gender, Generation and Minority Group Status" in *Canadian Ethnic Studies* 25,3:66-75.

_____. (1993). "Les valeurs familiales et les relations intergénérationnelles des familles immigrantes au Québec." Report presented to the Direction des études et de la recherche, Ministère des Communautés culturelles et de l'Immigration, Gouvernement du Quebec.

_____. (1992). "Family Life-Worlds and Social Injuries: Three Generations of Portuguese-Canadians." Doctoral Dissertation, Department of Sociology, University of Montreal.

Novack, M. (1971). *The Rise of the Unmeltable Ethnics: Politics and Culture in the Seventies*. New York: MacMillan.

Orthner, D. (1990). "The Family in Transition" in *Rebuilding the Nest*, edited by D. Blankenhorn. Milwaukee: Family Service America.

Parsons, Talcott. (1971). "The Normal American Family" in *Readings on the Sociology of the Family* edited by B.N. Adams and T. Weirath. Chicago: Markham.

Porter, John. (1965). *The Vertical Mosaic*. Toronto: University of Toronto Press.

Reitz, J. (1980). *The Survival of Ethnic Groups*. Toronto: McGraw-Hill Ryerson.

Royal, S. (1987). *Le printemps des grand-parents. La nouvelle alliance des âges*. Paris: Robert Lafont.

Royce, A.P. (1982). *Ethnic Identity*. Bloomington: Indiana University Press.

Rubin, Lillian. (1983). *Intimate Strangers*. New York: Harper & Row.

Statistics Canada. (1993). *Census of Canada 1991*: The Nation. Catalogue 93-316. Ottawa: Statistics Canada.

_____. *Census of Canada 1991*. Catalogues: 93-831, 92-905, 93-106. Ottawa: Statistics Canada.

_____. (1993). *A Portrait of Families in Canada: Target Groups Project*. Catalogue 89-523E. Ottawa: Statistics Canada.

_____. (1991). *Canadian Social Trends*. Spring Pp.11-13 and Winter, Pp. 26-28. Ottawa: Statistics Canada.

Satzewich, Vic. (1993). "Migrant and Immigrant Families in Canada: State Coercion and Legal Control In the Formation of Ethnic Families" in *Journal of Comparative Family Studies* 24,3:315-338.

_____. (1991). *Racism and the Incorporation of Foreign Labour: Farm Labour Migration to Canada Since 1945*. London: Routledge.

Sennett, Richard. (1974). *The Fall of Public Man*. Cambridge: Cambridge University Press.

Stack, Carol and L. Burton. (1993). "Kinscripts" in *Journal of Comparative Family Studies*. 24,2:157-170.

Taboada-Leonetti, Isabelle. (1983). "Le Rôle des Femmes Migrantes dans le Maintien ou la Destructuration des Cultures Nationales du Groupe Migrant" in *Etudes Migration* 20:214-221.

The Globe and Mail. "Black criminality danger to Toronto, Tubman Group says." November 9th, 1994.

The Vanier Institute of the Family. (1994). *Canadian Families*. Ottawa: The Vanier Institute of the Family and the Canada Committee for the International Year of Family.

Voydanoff, Patricia. (1991). "Economic Distress and Family Relations: A Review of the Eigthies." Pp. 429-445 in *Contemporary Families: Looking Forward, Looking Backward*, edited by Alan Booth. Minneapolis: National Council on Family Relations.

Walczak, Y. and S. Burns. (1984). *Divorce: The Child's Point of View*. London: Harper and Row.

Walker, J. (1994). "Children of Divided Worlds: Promoting Post-Divorce Cooperative Parenting." Paper presented at the International Conference, "Today's Families: A Bridge to the Future." Montreal, October 13, 1994.

Wallerstein, J. (1985). "The Overburdened Child: Some Long-Term Consequences of Divorce" Pp. 116-123 in *American Journal of Social Work*. March-April.

Wallerstein, J. and S. Blakeslee. (1989). *Second Chances. Men, Women and Children a Decade after Divorce*. London: Bantam.

Wirth, Louis. (1956). "The Problem of Minority Groups" Pp. 237-260 in *Community Life and Social Policy*. Chicago: University of Chicago Press.

Zigler, E. and E. Gilman. (1990). "An Agenda for the 1990s: Supporting Families" in *Rebuilding the Nest* edited by .D. Blankenhorn. Milwaukee: Family Service America.

CHAPTER 11

SOCIAL POLICY AND
ETHNO-CULTURAL DIVERSITY

Roopchand B. Seebaran

INTRODUCTION

Before the arrival of European explorers, the land we now call Canada was inhabited by many different Aboriginal people. The existing diversity among the various tribes was expressed in a range of areas, including their customs and culture. Diversity in the population increased as a result of the many waves of immigration to this part of the globe. These movements of people from different countries of the "Old World" to Canada helped to define us as a land of immigrants.

At the beginning of the new millennium, it is clear that we have a population that is already very diverse in terms of religion, ethnicity, and cultural backgrounds. As well, this diversity is in flux. Before 1961, for example, 90 percent of immigrants who arrived in Canada were born in Europe; today, the percentage of such immigrants is less than 25 percent. Currently, the vast majority of immigrants are from China, India, Hong Kong, Vietnam, and the Philippines. Internationally, Canada is already "seen as the most multi-ethnic nation on the planet". (*Vancouver Sun*, April 27, 1999)

For a variety of reasons, this diversity will increase in the 21st century. First, Canada has a huge land mass, a relatively small population, a low birth rate, and an aging population that is increasing. All of these factors indicate that we must have not only a larger, but also a younger population to meet the social security needs of our citizens. Fortunately, this will be facilitated by our current immigration policies.

Second, Canada is a destination of choice for millions of would-be immigrants. For the past three years, the United Nations has named Canada as the best place in the world in which to live. Partly because of this, millions of people in other countries see Canada as a land of opportunity, and the place that they would like to make their home. Every year, hundreds of thousands of people pursue their dreams and immigrate here, often at great sacrifice to themselves and their families. Others also come as legitimate refugees, and still others enter illegally.

Third, the diversity that is currently invisible in the population of Canada will become increasingly visible as more and more citizens claim their cultural rights; preserve their languages, traditions and customs; and affirm their individual and group identity. All of these factors will ensure that the ethno-cultural diversity of the population will increase, both in size and range, and that it will be a characteristic demographic feature of our society as we enter and move through the 21st century. This current reality and projected diversity for Canada have important implications for social policies in this country.

SOCIAL POLICY IN CANADA

In this discussion, social policy is defined as those broad goals and objectives that are developed by government and public institutions to achieve desired social goals. They include strategies and measures that point the society in a desired direction. Social policies are based on values and ideologies that generally reflect the vision of the policy makers of the particular society. They are statements that articulate goals and objectives, and the instruments to achieve these objectives. Some definitions of social policy by respected scholars in the field suggest the following:

> Social policy is all about social purposes and the choices between them. The choices and the conflicts between them have continuously to be made at the government level, the community level and the individual level. At each level, by acting or not acting, by opting in or contracting out, we can influence the direction in which choices are made. (Titmuss, 1974, p. 131)

> Social policy is not essentially interested in
> economic relations but is very much concerned with
> the extent to which economic relations and
> aspirations should be allowed to dominate other
> aspects of life; more specifically, that social policy
> addresses itself to a whole range of needs—
> material, cultural, emotional—outside the wide
> realm of satisfaction which cannot conveniently be
> left to the market. (Lafitte, 1962, pp. 8-9)

> Social policy is concerned with the public
> administration of welfare services, that is, the
> formulation, development and man-agement of
> specific services of government at all levels...Social
> policy is formulated not only by government, but
> also by other institutions...Social policy is to be
> understood within the frame-work of societal ends
> or objectives and means. (Yelaja, 1987, p. 2)

Regardless of the content and objectives of social policies,
it is important to understand that they are rooted in, and arise from,
particular ideologies and values. In Canada, social policies are
grounded in an environment and context of conflicting ideologies.
One view, generally conceptualized as residualism, considers the
private market as the appropriate instrument to achieve individual
prosperity and social development. Its proponents argue that
government intervention stifles individual initiative and promotes
dependency on the state. This ideology suggests that intervention
by government should be a last resort.

An alternative ideology, held mainly by social and liberal
democrats, contends that government intervention in the market
place is necessary and desirable. Advocates of this institutional
concept of social welfare claim that intervention by the state is
needed, both to protect the casualties of the market system and to
guide the society in a specific direction. This perspective sees the
social, economic, and political structure of the society as having a
distinct impact on its members. Thus, the society has a responsibility to provide opportunities for both individual and social
development. The tension created by these two polar ideologies,
and the range of intervening values between them, is part of the

conflicting and competitive context in which our social policies are initiated.

In Canada, we have social policies that cover areas such as health, housing, education, employment, social services, access to justice, immigration and so on. In addition, social policies are developed to address particular needs of specific population groups or categories of people. Examples of these include policies related to Aboriginal people, the disabled, the elderly, women, youth, refugees, new immigrants, and the unemployed.

An analysis and discussion of social policy as it relates to the full range of diversity in Canada is a monumental task, and would be a very valuable contribution to the Canadian social policy literature. In this chapter, however, the discussion is limited to diversity as it relates to ethnicity and cultural heritage. Current social policy initiatives and their impact, as they pertain to people from diverse ethno-cultural backgrounds, will be examined. In addition, alternative ideas on social policy initiatives and practices to effectively address and engage this diversity will be offered. This focus is of fundamental significance and considerable urgency because, in this country, we have too many incidents of racism and violence directed towards people of a different colour or culture. Indeed, the social and economic health and well-being of our society depends on how competently we acknowledge and embrace the ethno-cultural diversity within the population.

POLICY RESPONSES TO ETHNO-CULTURAL DIVERSITY

This section will review social policy responses from a broad perspective and discuss their attempts to address the ethno-cultural diversity in this country. These will be considered in chronological and historical sequence.

Firstly, there are the social policies that pre-date the introduction of the policy of multiculturalism by the Trudeau government in 1971. These social policies were clearly designed to keep Canada "white". A striking example is immigration policy of this period. Policies were deliberately put in place to prevent "non-white" immigrants from coming to this country. In the field of education, textbooks and curricula clearly reflected the history and values of the dominant "white" culture. The social policy objectives of the curricula can be described as assimilation, colonialism, and indoctrination. In the areas of health and social services, the situation was no different. Social policies reflected the superiority of the ideas and values of the dominant "white" culture. Models of health and social services did not appreciate or value the resources and traditions of other cultures. A classic example is social policy related to Aboriginal people. Social policies in this period could be regarded as colonialistic and paternalistic.

Secondly, in the period immediately following the introduction of the multicultural policy, social policies and, in particular, institutional practices tended to be tentative and tolerant in their response to ethno-cultural differences. An example of this type of response is the introduction of a range of policies, such as employment equity and admission equity, in a variety of educational institutions. The defining problem with these policies has been their emphasis on recruitment of members of different cultural groups into particular systems, with little or no attention to policies and practices focusing on support and retention of the new recruits.

A more important factor in the failure of these policies is their lack of impact on the overall institutional culture in terms of its structure, process, and practices. The changes that occur, if any, are at the periphery of the system, not at the core or the centre. Efforts focus essentially on developing cultural sensitivity and raising awareness on the part of policy makers and service providers. Procedures and practices place emphasis on gaining ethno-specific information about different cultural groups in the population, and subsequently using this information in the development of policy and the delivery of services. As a result, we have seen initiatives and strategies such as "multicultural health, "multicultural education", "culturally sensitive social services", and so on. In the case of social services, for example, Aboriginal control of child welfare became a high priority in many jurisdictions across this country.

Thirdly, as different cultural and ethnic groups began to claim and affirm their rights of citizenship and make demands for services to which they were entitled, organizations and institutions scrambled in a rush to acquire knowledge and skills for the provision of culturally relevant services. In this response, more aggressive efforts were made by agencies to reach out to, and involve, different cultural groups within their service domains. Initiatives and strategies to move beyond cultural sensitivity and awareness to cultural competence were now in vogue. Members of different cultural groups were viewed as valuable resources in the training and education of policy makers and service providers. Training and educational institutions also made attempts, with varying degrees of success, to develop curricula that would be culturally responsive to addressing the needs of the diverse population. Here, again, the policies and practices were of an additive nature and did little to transform the institutions themselves.

Fourthly, as part of the attempt by social service agencies to provide culturally sensitive services, many of them made efforts to bring about change, not only at the service delivery level, but also at the level of the organization as a whole. These institutional change initiatives were often carried out through project funding, with the objective of bringing about multicultural organizational change. Here, the entire structure and operation of the system was seen as the target of change, including mission statements, board and staff composition, policies, practices, and procedures. Examples of this type of response in the non-government sector include the Agency Access Development Project sponsored by the United Way of the Lower Mainland in Vancouver, British Columbia; and the Manitoba Planned Parenthood Multicultural Organizational Development project in Winnipeg. Both the Vancouver and Winnipeg projects developed tools to help agencies to identify their current responsiveness to diversity, and to assess their progress towards multicultural organizational change. This response recognizes that multicultural organizational development cannot be accomplished by simply providing cultural sensitivity training for staff in the organization. It also requires bringing about change in the entire culture of the agency, and developing commitment to making the organization culturally competent.

In the public sector, as well, similar initiatives were being undertaken as government departments and agencies made efforts to bring about multicultural organizational change. Many used a framework developed by the Hastings Institute of Vancouver, which includes a set of principles and indicators to assistorganizations to evaluate their developmental process towards cultural competence. These principles are:

- Inclusiveness
- Reflecting the diversity of the community being served
- Valuing cultural differences
- Employment Equity
- Service Equity
- Adopting a participatory model/method

Finally, there has been the emergence of separate or parallel ethno-specific agencies to serve people of different cultural and ethnic backgrounds. These agencies came into existence largely because members of ethno-cultural minority groups experienced difficulty in accessing the services delivered by generic community-wide agencies. According to Johnston (1996), barriers to using services for these groups included language, lack of cultural sensitivity on the part of service providers, and perceived discrimination or racism within the service system. In addition, a significant barrier was fear of possible consequences of seeking services, such as loss of immigrant status.

ANALYSIS OF POLICY RESPONSES

In order to analyze the policy responses, it would be useful to consider models and frameworks relating to culturally competent and responsive systems. Five of these models and frameworks are identified and briefly described here: Elements of Ethnic Competence, Cultural Competence Continuum, Institutional Responses to Multiculturalism, and two Aboriginal Frameworks.

1. Elements of Ethnic Competence

This set of characteristics, developed by Green (1982, 1995), identifies five elements of ethnic competence, which pertain specifically to the delivery of culturally competent services. They are, nevertheless, quite applicable to the policy making process as well. The elements are:
- awareness of one's own cultural limitations
- openness to cultural differences
- a client-oriented, systematic learning style with the worker as learner
- appropriate utilization of cultural resources

- acknowledgement of the cultural integrity of other people's culture and acceptance of a multitude of lifeways

2. Cultural Competence Continuum

This model, developed by Cross (1989), suggests that the level of cultural competence of systems can be assessed along a continuum of responsiveness as follows:

Cultural Destructiveness: This beginning of the continuum is characterized by attitudes, policies, and practices that are destructive to cultures and individuals within the culture. This type of system assumes the superiority of one ethnicity and supports the eradication of "lesser" cultures.

Cultural Incapacity: At this level, the system is not intentionally destructive, but lacks the capacity to effectively serve ethno-cultural minority communities and their members. The system remains extremely biased, supports the superiority of the dominant group, and reinforces a paternalistic posture.

Cultural Blindness: This type of system believes or attempts to convey that it is unbiased and that culture or colour makes no difference. Such a system is based on the belief that traditional mainstream approaches are universally applicable and effective. Cultural strengths of ethnic minorities are not utilized and assimilation is encouraged.

Cultural Pre-Competence: The culturally pre-competent system recognizes its weaknesses in serving minorities and attempts to improve some aspect of its services to specific minority populations. It begins to take specific steps to remedy the situation.

Basic Cultural Competence: Agencies and systems operating at this level understand, accept, and respect cultural differences. They develop and implement effective strategies for serving members of ethno-cultural minority populations, do continuous self-assessment, incorporate the different cultural values in their service delivery models, and work closely with different cultural communities in the development of policy and practice.

Cultural Proficiency/Advanced Cultural Competence: At this level, the system and its practitioners represent the most advanced end of the continuum. They add to the knowledge base by conducting research and developing new approaches and service innovations for the different groups with which they work. They advocate for cultural competence throughout the system.

3. Institutional Responses to Multiculturalism

An analysis of human service organizations carried out by Seebaran (1996) suggests that they tend to respond to ethno-cultural diversity in one or more of the following modes: denial, paternalism, tokenism, partnership, and acknowledgement.

Denial: In this response, the system acts as if the person or community brings nothing that is culturally relevant or useful to the development of the society. In fact, they might be viewed as standing in the way of progress, and as barriers to the achievement of the system's goals and objectives. The culture, values, and resources of the person or community are essentially ignored and considered irrelevant in the development and promotion of a healthy and progressive society. There is no effort, therefore, to include or involve members of these different cultural groups in the affairs and activities of the system. Indeed, such participation is deliberately discouraged.

Paternalism: In this response, there can be an awareness that the person, group, or community that is ethnically and culturally different actually has values and resources. But these resources and values are not respected, and are viewed as inferior to those of the system. This oppressive response is similar to that of colonialism.

Tokenism: The system, in this case, grudgingly accepts that there is validity to the different cultural values, resources, skills, and traditions of members of other cultural groups. However, only token efforts are made to include and incorporate these ideas, resources, and values. The tokenistic response is often made for "political" and survival reasons, not from a genuine belief in the integrity of the different culture. This is an expediency response.

Partnership: The system recognizes and accepts the value of, and role that, the ideas and resources of different cultures can play in building a socially just and progressive society. There is a deliberate focus on efforts at inclusion and integration of these values and resources into the structures and processes of the system. Development of the system reflects genuine collaboration and partnership with culturally different communities and their members.

Acknowledgement: This response by the system is characterized by both a respect for, and a deference to, the values, ideas, skills, expertise, customs, traditions, and technology of different cultural groups. Here, particular cultural communities can have maximum input and participation in the structures, processes, policies, and practices of the system, including the design and delivery of relevant and appropriate programs. The acknowledgement model of response can involve various forms of partnership, collaboration and integration, but these are always based on mutual respect for cultural differences.

4. Aboriginal Framework (I)

Morrissette, McKenzie, and Morrissette (1993) have developed an Aboriginal framework which was proposed specifically as guidelines for social work practice with members of Aboriginal communities. However, the framework can be used for policy analysis and has relevance for other cultural communities. The framework consists of the following principles:
- recognition of a distinct Aboriginal worldview
- recognition of the impact of colonialism
- recognition of cultural knowledge and traditions as an active component of sustaining Aboriginal identity and collective consciousness
- empowerment as sustained through Aboriginal participation and control

5. Aboriginal Framework (II)

Graveline (1998) has used an Aboriginal framework in offering a course on "cross cultural issues" which is instructive for the development and implementation of social policy. In this framework emphasis is placed on learning through experience and voice. The elements included:

- First Voice, "Don't talk about what you don't know"
- Storytelling, "Transmission of the 'Gifts of the Cultures'"
- Talking Circle, "Speaking from the Heart/Listening Respectfully"
- Taking Action, "Doing more than Saying"

The five frameworks presented above can be used to assess the relevance and responsiveness of social policies and institutional practices to the ethno-cultural diversity in our population. Using Green's model of Ethnic Competence, social policies in Canada are definitely not characterized by an acknowledgement of the cultural integrity of other people's culture and acceptance of a multitude of lifeways. Applying Cross' (1989) framework, policy and institutional responsiveness can be generally described as wavering between Cultural Incapacity, Cultural Blindness, and Cultural Pre-Competence. When the Aboriginal framework is used as a template to examine social policy relating to Aboriginal people, it is clear that these policies are characterized by cultural destructiveness and irrelevance. According to Seebaran's (1996) Institutional responses to Multiculturalism, the majority of our institutions seem to be responding at the level of Tokenism or Paternalism. There seems to be a fundamental ambivalence, reluctance, and hesitancy to move toward Cultural Competence and Partnership or Acknowledgement.

FACTORS CONTRIBUTING TO CURRENT RESPONSES

In any country, there are a range of forces and factors that combine in dynamic interaction with each other to shape the society. Observation and analysis of the social, economic, political, and cultural context suggest that the following factors influence the content of social policy regarding ethno-cultural diversity in Canada.

Confusion about the concept of multiculturalism: This confusion exists not only among ordinary citizens in the society, but also among policy makers, including senior bureaucrats, government ministers, and service providers. For some people, the term applies to ethno-cultural minorities, particularly visible minorities, in our society. For others, it is a set of programs and services separate from the mainstream of our society that should be funded and managed by the ethno-cultural groups themselves. Still others see multiculturalism as an ideology and philosophy that not only values cultural diversity, but also promotes and celebrates it. Finally, there are those who see multiculturalism simply as an official policy of government that is causing social division and, therefore, should be abandoned as swiftly as possible.

Many Canadians still do not realize that we already have a very culturally diverse society. They do not understand that even without new immigrants, we are a multi-ethnic, multicultural society.

View of cultural diversity as a problem: In many sectors of the society, the range and extent of our cultural diversity is viewed as a weakness, and the cause of many of our social, economic, cultural and political problems. It is cited as the reason for a host of our societal ills, such as high unemployment rates, violence between youth groups in schools, the high cost of housing, the increasing rate of traffic accidents, crime, family violence, and drug or substance abuse. There is an attitude that we need to eliminate diversity and homogenize the society.

The existence of widespread of racism: One only has to listen to the daily news or read the local newspapers to become aware of the range and extent of racism that exists in our society. Many of us gain this awareness from personal experiences in the workplace, in our neighbourhoods, or when we seek the services of someone in a community agency or government department. These experiences inform us that racism is rampant throughout the society. Even more disturbing is the fact that racism seems to be spreading, especially among our youth. Consider the following examples:

- A 15-year-old student who was suspended from school and faces charges for uttering threats told his friends that he wanted to kill minority students at his high school because he is a white supremacist. Search warrant documents relating to the investigation in this matter state that the youth "disclosed to several students that he had access to guns and would attend the school and shoot some people". Less than two months after this particular student's threats, violent racist graffiti, including swastikas, racial slurs and phrases...spray-painted at the school. The day after the graffiti incident, two students made bomb threats, one over the phone and the other by computer. (*Vancouver Sun*, January 26, 2000)

In 1998, Justice Ronald Barclay of the Court of Queen's Bench, backed by the authority of the Supreme Court of Canada, stated:

Widespread anti-aboriginal racism is a grim reality of Canada and in Saskatchewan... It exists openly and blatantly in attitudes and actions of individuals. It exists privately in the fears, in the stereotypes held by many people and it exists in our institutions.

In responding to the judge's comments, Doug Cuthand, a Cree commentator, said that racism was deeply ingrained in the social fabric of the province of Saskatchewan. Kent Roach, Dean of the University of Saskatchewan Law School, noted that racism was as big a problem in Canada as it was in Saskatchewan. He suggested that racism exists in the common everyday assumptions often held by the well-meaning just as much as the mean-spirited. (*Vancouver Sun,* August 29, 1998)

- A poll conducted for the B.C. Human Rights Commission found that British Columbians "see themselves as quite tolerant of people who are different, but more so of elderly people than gays, lesbians and people of different colour." A woman of colour, in responding to the results of the poll, said that she still sees a lot of prejudice and that she did not want people to just put up with her. She observed that there is a growing level of intolerance and hate. The B.C. Human Rights Commissioner said that as a society we are still at "tolerance", and that we must move beyond that to a goal of acceptance. As well, the Attorney General of the province publicly stated that just

tolerating minorities or people with differences is not good
enough and that acceptance is much better than tolerance.
(*Vancouver Sun*, December 11, 1999)

• While out on a school skiing trip an elementary school student
from a school district in British Columbia, was taunted by his
school mates for over 40 minutes with racist remarks such as:
"You are Jewish, and in the First World War you would have
been the first to be shot". The father of the youth, on learning
about how his son was treated, went to the school and reported
the matter to the principal. The school principal handled the
situation by having the youth, who was the victim of the racist
remarks, sit with the boys who taunted him. He was told to
come up with alternative ways in which he could have dealt
with the situation. What is worse, according to the father of the
victimized boy, is that schools are silent about these kinds of
incidents. (*BCTV Newscast*, February 2000)

Lack of commitment on the part of policy makers: In numerous
workshops and conferences across this country, lack of
commitment is often cited as a reason for in both the absence of, or
weak policies related to effectively addressing the needs of the
culturally diverse population. This lack of commitment is present
at both the political and bureaucratic level. It is one thing to
develop policy; it is another to have the political will to implement
it. Implementing policy requires taking action to ensure that clear
objectives have been set; harnessing the resources to support the
achievement of policy objectives; identifying and removing
barriers, as necessary; and building mechanisms for on-going
monitoring and accountability.

In seminars and training workshops, staff in a number of
social services across the nation, regularly identify barriers and
obstacles to the provision of cultural services. These include lack
of corporate commitment to the goals of multiculturalism;
resistance on the part of executive and front-line staff to consider
multiculturalism as part of the organization's mandate; and a
prevailing view that the provision of culturally responsive services
requires additional resources. These views are held by executive,
management, and front-line staff in systems where policies are not
being implemented. There is little or no effort to consider the use

of existing resources, such as staff and regular annual budget allocations, in different ways. Planning and implementation seems to follow a linear and additive mind-set and approach.

This issue of commitment is directly related to another factor: the lack of adequate knowledge and skill on the part of service providers for culturally sensitive practice. On the whole training institutions have only tinkered with curriculum change; and service agencies have not given staff training and development sufficiently high and ongoing priority to this area.

The identity and location of the policy makers themselves: Social policy is developed largely by government and its related institutions. In Canada, it is developed through a variety of structures and processes including Parliament or the Legislature, the Cabinet, Ministers, Deputy Ministers, and other senior ranking officials within government. The policy makers, as a group, are not reflective of the diversity in the population. They reflect homogeneity of values and interests rather than diversity and difference. Several groups, including the poor, the marginalized, and the disadvantaged, are shut out of the process.

As Wharf and Cossom (1987) suggest:

> ...it is important to establish that the social policy makers are not only few in number but homogenous in nature. They are middle-aged men, with a business or professional background. The reality is that our elected representatives make policies which protect and promote their own interests and the interests of the groups that support them. (p. 273)
> ...Policy makers are a relatively small group of people who make policy which favours their own and their friends' best interests. (p. 274)
> ...The policy making process is largely dominated by govern-ment ministers, senior bureaucrats, and their elite counterparts in the private sector who are content to maintain the status quo as long as it continues to serve their social, economic and political interests. (p. 275)

The focus of policy analysis: According to Wharf and McKenzie (1998), approaches to policy analysis can place emphasis on both content and process issues:

> A content approach stresses the actual ingredients of the policy, that is, the substance of the policy, its goals and value preferences, and the types of benefits it provides...A pure content approach to policy analysis also tends to reinforce an elitist approach to policy analysis in that the policy expert, as armchair critic, gathers data on the policy issue, subjects these data to critical scrutiny, and draws conclusions about the impact of the policy. (pp. 52, 53)
> ...A process approach to policy analysis pays more attention to who influences the development of policies, how action is generated, and who makes decisions. (p. 53)

One of the weaknesses of policy analysis in Canada is that its emphasis is primarily on a content approach, and the focus of the analysis is not on those who make policy.

The global policy-making context: Social policy does not spring from a vacuum. It is usually responsive to the social, economic, cultural, and political environment in the particular country. More recently, it is increasingly responsive to, and dictated by, the impact of globalization, and especially by international bodies such as the World Trade Organization (WTO), and international agreements such as the General Agreement on Trade and Services. As we have sadly come to realize, this organization has the power to override legislation and policies of member countries that do not abide by its rules. And, it has used its power to do so on many occasions. In one sense, therefore, social policy in this country is influenced by the WTO, since Canada is a member of this organization. Following their November 1999 meetings in Seattle, Murray Dobbin, a Vancouver-based writer and social activist warns us about the comprehensive power of the WTO and its impact on the policies of governments:

...The WTO remains the most powerful governance institution ever devised. Its existing agreements have an enormous impact on governments's ability to make public policy. More importantly, for those concerned about social programs, the agreement that threatens these programs was already scheduled for a new round of negotiations before Seattle. Those negotiations have, in fact, already begun. in Geneva. The agreement in question is the General Agreement on Trade and Services and trade officials in Canada, the European Union and the U.S. are determined to open up public services including health and education to corporate investment. (pp. 1-2)

These agreements could ultimately affect the way in which health and social services are provided in this country and, therefore, have significant implications for social policy. In many respects, globalization is the antithesis of diversity. It is an instrument of hegemony and homogenization.

DEVELOPING SOCIAL POLICIES
THAT ADDRESS DIVERSITY

The observations and analysis in the previous sections suggest that our current social policies in relation to cultural diversity are tentative and tokenistic in their design, implementation, and impact. So, what might be more appropriate or preferred social policies for the future?

Following Green's model of ethnic competence, there needs to be a fundamental focus on the "acknowledgement of the integrity of the cultural diversity of other people's culture and an acceptance of a multitude of lifeways". Using Aboriginal frameworks as a guide (Morrissette, McKenzie, and Morrissette 1993; and Graveline 1998), it is clear that policies must demonstrate recognition of the impact of colonialism. They must also show recognition of cultural knowledge and traditions as an active component of sustaining Aboriginal identity and collective consciousness". They must fully respect First Voice.

Applying Seebaran's (1996) analysis of institutional responses to multiculturalism, social policies need to move beyond "tokenism" response to "partnership" and "acknowledgement" responses. Referring to Terry Cross' (1989) Cultural Competence Continuum, social policies need to advance from the "cultural incapacity", "cultural blindness", and "cultural pre-competence" levels of response to the "basic cultural competence" and "cultural proficiency" levels. Perhaps a deliberate and definitive move towards these models of social policy would go a long way in sending a message to the population at large that "tolerance" of cultural differences is not good enough; and that the societal goal is acceptance and mutual respect of cultural differences. The following processes and strategies are offered as steps for moving towards this goal.

Adherence to principles regarding cultural diversity

The principles presented here are adapted and draw substantially from the cultural frameworks described earlier. Principles relevant to the social policy making process for addressing diversity would include:
- awareness of one's cultural limitations as a social policy planner
- openness to and valuing of the range of diversity
- recognition of knowledge and traditions of the different ethno-cultural groups
- appropriate utilization of the resources of the various cultural communities
- acknowledgement of the cultural integrity of different cultures
- acceptance of different ways of achieving social goals
- promotion of equity
- respect for First Voice

Social inclusion in the policy-making process

This is the systematic and ongoing identification and inclusion of members of diverse cultural groups in the social policy process. A significant weakness of past, and many current, social policies is that they have been developed and implemented through a process of social exclusion of ethno-cultural groups. Indeed, policies have often been designed for particular cultural groups without their participation in the development or implementation process. This is what Byron Kunisawa (1999) has identified as "designs of omission". The challenge for social policies for the future is to concentrate on and create designs of inclusion in all stages of the policy process, including: initiation, formulation, development, implementation, monitoring and feedback, and evaluation of outcomes and impacts.

According to Wharf and McKenzie (1998):

> ...attention to the principle of inclusiveness is the single most important reform needed in the human services. It is important because policies that exclude the knowledge of those who receive services and of practitioners will be incomplete and inappropriate. Services users experience the reality of living in poverty and in unsafe neighbourhoods, a reality unknown and foreign to those who have traditionally made policy. (p. 127)

Appropriate utilization of policy committees

Deborah Rutman (1998) has chronicled the use of this strategy in the development of legislation related to adult guardianship in British Columbia in the early 1990s. She relates the story of "the formation and ongoing activities of a coalition of individuals and community groups across BC who worked with government representatives to shape and ultimately draft four interrelated Acts." (p. 97)

The stages in this process were:
- establishment of a joint working committee
- legislative drafting and policy planning
- community-based legislative response committees

The idea of policy communities can be of enormous value in the development of policies relating to the range of ethno-cultural diversity in the society. However, such structures require unwavering commitment to the principle of inclusiveness. Also, for this strategy to be effective, social policy communities need to be involved in all stages of the policy process, from initiation through formulation, execution, implementation, and evaluation. Partnership between community and government must be genuine and equal.

Balance between universalism, positive selectivism, and particularism

Thompson and Hoggett (1996), in a paper on postmodern social policy, discuss these three concepts. Universalism "seeks to apply the same standard to all individuals"; positive selectivism "aims to provide additional services and resources for certain disadvantaged groups"; and "particularist theories contend that different standards are appropriate in different circumstances for different individuals and groups" (p. 21). It may be useful to consider the above values in the development and implementation of universalist, positive selectivist, and particularistic policies to meet the common and special needs of the diverse population.

Move from segregation to integration

A current and pervasive perspective is that in the society there is a "mainstream", and a number of minority groups that exist on the periphery, including the wide range of small ethno-cultural communities. This conceptualization is both inaccurate and dangerous. Indeed, in many regions of the country, these so-called "minority" communities far outnumber the population that is considered the "mainstream". Social policies need to correct this misconception, and vigorously promote the view that ethno-cultural diversity is an integral component of the mainstream of our society. Thus, social policies need to explicitly and forcefully convey that multiculturalism applies not to cultural minorities, but to the population at large.

In efforts to achieve objectives in multiculturalism, policy planners and service providers, whether intentionally or otherwise, have actually promoted and perpetuated segregation. The responsible parties in this area include ethno-specific agencies, government funding bodies, and ethno-cultural groups themselves. One of the major causes of this problem is confusion and misunderstanding about the concept of multiculturalism.

Current social policies have permitted and encouraged the allocation of funding to a number of agencies that serve specific cultural groups. This has contributed to the emergence of ethno-specific agencies which operate separately from generic agencies that are expected to serve the community as a whole. In many communities, therefore, we have a system of parallel and segregated agencies serving diverse ethno-cultural groups. It should also be noted that many of these agencies also develop bridging programs and services with generic agencies in order to facilitate their clients' access to a wider range of services not available at the ethno-specific agency.

The existence of ethno-specific agencies in itself is not inappropriate, but their role and function need to be examined. These agencies should appropriately be in place to meet the needs of community members on a temporary basis. They should fill the needs of people who are in transition in their process of settlement and re-settlement in their new country. The role of these ethno-specific agencies should be three-fold: to encourage and facilitate the capacity and ability of citizens to use the general service systems in the community; to assist community-wide service agencies to become more responsive to the needs of the culturally diverse society; and to advocate for policy changes that may be needed to better serve the community at large.

The purpose in funding these agencies should be to acknowledge this role. Where necessary, funding should also be available for bridging programs, that is, programs that enable clients to use services of both ethno-specific and generic agencies. Funding from government should not be allocated to these agencies to provide parallel services for members of specific ethno-cultural groups on a continuing basis. Where particular ethno-cultural groups wish to provide such services, they should do so without automatically expecting government funding.

Making exclusive institutions inclusive

Currently, the personnel of many institutions that serve the public are not reflective of the range of ethno-cultural diversity in the community. By circumstance or design, these institutions are exclusionary both in their structure and process and, consequently, cannot claim to be adequately responsive to the diverse needs of the various cultural groups. Social policies need to emphasize the development of inclusive institutions in terms of philosophy, organizational structure, policies, personnel, procedures, and practices.

To some extent, the proliferation of ethno-specific service organizations has created an environment in which community-wide and generic institutions have not been compelled to restructure and transform themselves. The pressure to change in order to meet the needs of ethno-cultural groups does not exist since many of these demands for services are deflected to ethno-specific service agencies.

Regardless of the existence of ethno-specific service agencies in our society, community-wide and generic institutions have a public responsibility to be reflective of the culturally diverse population in all aspects of their organizational structure and process. Social policies need to facilitate and advocate for such institutions; and developing them will require policies that have clear consequences for non-compliance. Equally important are the facilitating and nourishing aspects for building these types of organizations. They include:

- competent leadership at all levels of the organization
- mentoring mechanisms for executive and management staff
- incentives or rewards for the achievement of desired structural changes
- the creation of diversity-friendly environments at the workplace

Inclusiveness of institutions should be an accreditation criteria. There are many agencies in our society today, such as hospitals, child welfare agencies, and educational institutions, that are required to undergo reviews in order to initially acquire, and subsequently maintain, their accredited status. The standards for accreditation for any institution in the society should include criteria that take into account the competence of the institution in acknowledging and addressing the ethno-cultural diversity within the communities being served. An example of some pioneering work done in this area is the accreditation requirements of the Canadian Association of Schools of Social Work (CASSW). As a result of a national task force study on multicultural and multi-racial issues in social work education, CASSW has included new accreditation criteria related to the responsiveness of curricula to diversity.

Culturally appropriate service development and delivery

The development and delivery of culturally responsive services will need to be supported by policies that provide for the following:

a)   Declared organizational commitment to culturally respons-ive services. These can appear, for example, in organ-izational mission statements and other policy documents.

b)   Staff training and development in the acquisition of knowledge and skills for culturally responsive practice.

c)   Opportunities for staff to learn about the range of different cultures within the communities they are mandated to serve. This would include gaining knowledge about different models of service delivery that the various ethno-cultural groups might have to offer, and using this knowledge in the provision of services.

d)   Active outreach to the different cultural communities being served, both to seek their consultation, and to develop partnerships for their involvement in planning and decision-making with regard to service development and delivery.

(e)   Regular evaluation of services to determine relevance, adequacy, accessibility, effectiveness, and equity.

(f)   Developing structures and processes of accountability to ethno-cultural communities.

Inclusive social policy research

Social policies need to provide opportunities for research that is inclusive of culturally diverse groups. This point was stressed at the 1997 seminar on Inclusive Social Policy Development in Ottawa. As one participant suggested:

Research is ultimately about who has the power to define the social reality, and what counts as knowledge. The power relation that is embedded in the research process and the standpoint of the researcher must be made explicit in any research that attempts to include marginalized and disadvantaged. (p. 8)

People being served must be involved in the research in order to assess the relevance and impact of policies. In addition, they need to be engaged as active participants in measuring program outcomes; giving feedback on best practices; and identifying issues and negative effects, where indicated. Others advocating this view include Tsang and George (1998), who contend that many of the conventional outcome measures and the constructs measured may not be culturally appropriate or relevant. They further state that what constitutes successful outcomes may vary considerably between different cultural groups.

Moving from tolerance to acceptance and acknowledgement

According to Canadian novelist Robertson Davies, "tolerance" implies putting up with people of colour, whereas "acceptance" requires going the step beyond to understanding them as equals (*Vancouver Sun,* February 7, 2000). Seeing members of culturally diverse groups as equals is a consequence of attitudes grounded in respect for people no matter their ancestral or ethnic origin. It is embedded in values that acknowledge the dignity and worth of every human being, regardless of race, colour, or creed.

We need to initiate and implement social policies that encourage and promote these attitudes and behaviours. Such policies will regard diversity, not as an irritant or impediment, but as a most valuable asset and resource for the continued social, economic, cultural and political development of our society. This fact is already being realized in the business community, for example, banks and the hospitality industry, as they consider both the positive impact on customer service and financial profits to be gained. Similarly, the benefits of valuing and acknowledging diversity are also being experienced in many other areas, such as education, health, and social services.

Primary focus on the elimination of racism

Across this country, many institutions and agencies direct an enormous amount of energy and activities on the elimination of racism. Despite their efforts, the problem persists at the individual, institutional, and systemic levels. Incidents of racism in this country leading to extreme violence and death are occurring at an alarmingly frequent rate. Consider these recent examples from the *Vancouver Sun* (February 25, 2000):

- In Saskatoon, police have been accused of carting inebriated men out to the city limits where they get dumped without suitable clothing to find their own way back in sub-zero temperatures.
- In Winnipeg, Mayor Glen Murray made a tearful speech promising a full inquiry concerning the deaths of two Métis women whose 911 calls may have been ignored because of the women's ethnicity. The mayor directly acknowledged that we live in a racist society.
- In Surrey, British Columbia, five youths beat a 65-year-old Sikh man to death outside the temple for which he was the caretaker. None of the killers knew the man, but they knew that he was a Sikh. And to emphasize their point, one of them extracted the steel bracelet, a symbol of the Sikh religion, from the battered man's wrist. The presiding judge called the assailants racists and misfits.

To be sure, racism is not only an issue of "whites" being racist towards non-"whites", as the following incident reveals:

- In Vancouver, a 20-year-old Indo-Canadian, who was delivering doughnuts to a 7-Eleven, was approached by six to seven Asian men in the parking lot and asked if he wanted to fight. He was punched and kicked repeatedly by the group of thugs, one of whom was armed with a piece of plywood. During the fight, the suspects made racist comments, which the police are investigating as a possible motive. [Police say] there is no indication that the suspects and victim knew each other. (*Vancouver Sun,* March 7, 2000)

Social policies and strategies for the elimination of racism must concentrate on at least these five areas:

First, a continuous and persistent effort at educating the population at large about the different ethno-cultural groups in the society and the positive contributions they have made, or potentially can make toward our social, economic, and cultural development.

Second, continuous efforts to engage different ethno-cultural groups in intercultural events and activities that promote awareness, understanding, and respect for each other.

Third, the mobilization and support of citizens in every local community in the country to visibly convey that racism is not acceptable. This message must be conveyed not only during Multiculturalism Week or the International Day for the Elimination of Racism, but throughout the year, every year.

Fourth, the development of strategies and structures to deal decisively with incidents of racism.

Fifth, the elimination of racism must be reflected in the curricula of all educational institutions.

All of these strategies for combating racism must have high priority and should be reflected in social policies at the national, provincial, and municipal government levels.

IMPERATIVES FOR ACTION

The development of social policy must take into account the above-mentioned processes and strategies for the following reasons.

The legislative imperative

Reference is made here to the many pieces of legislation at the national and provincial government levels that require institutions to provide services to members of the society in a manner that is respectful of their culture. Examples of such legislation include the 1981 Canadian Charter of Rights and Freedoms, the 1988 Canadian Multiculturalism Act, the 1984 British Columbia Human Rights Act, and the 1993 British Columbia Multiculturalism Act; as well as Human Rights Acts in other Canadian provinces.

The demographic imperative

There is a wide range of diversity in the ethno-cultural profile of communities served by institutions in our society. Indeed, as mentioned earlier, Canada is one of the most multi-ethnic nations in the world. Therefore, if they claim to serve communities, institutions must take into account this multi-ethnic and multicultural fact. To do otherwise, to provide programs and services that are monoculturally derived would relegate such institutions to irrelevance and paternalism. To maintain their legitimacy, institutions need to be responsive to the needs of the populace, as identified and experienced by them. To be responsive requires that service development and delivery include broad participation of the different ethno-cultural groups in the service community. Their ideas and resources need to be acknowledged and applied, as appropriate, in service provision.

The global imperative

Several countries around the globe are currently struggling with issues related to ethnic, religious, and cultural differences. In many of these countries, ethnic and cultural differences give rise to serious conflict, resulting in extreme violence that includes murder and mass destruction. Indeed, military approaches, including civil wars, are commonplace in efforts to resolve disputes and conflict emanating from ethnic and religious differences. Canada is strategically positioned, both in terms of geographic location and historical time, to show the rest of the world that cultural diversity can be a country's richest asset in nation building. To be sure, this is a challenging task, but it is also an exciting and unique opportunity. We have the people, the resources, and the talent for the task; we need the political courage and the commitment.

The development imperative

The future health and well-being of our society depends on the extent to which we maximize and use the capacity of all citizens in contributing towards our social, economic, cultural, and political development. This ultimately means the development and implementation of social policies that view and engage the diversity in the population as one of the country's most valuable resource. Differences in culture can be seen as the ingredients for creativity, for change and progress. The alternative is to view difference as a deficiency that must be stamped out or assimilated. Attempts to do so will largely result in underdevelopment, divisiveness, confrontation, alienation, and unproductive conflict.

The professional service imperative

In the human services field, many service providers belong to professions with codes of ethics that require their members to provide services in a manner that maintains the best interest of the service seeker (client) as the primary professional obligation. Consider an example from the Social Work Code of Ethics:

> A social worker in the practice of social work shall not discriminate against any person on the basis of race, ethnic background, language, religion, marital status, sex, sexual orientation, age, abilities, socio-economic status, political affiliation, or national ancestry. (Canadian Association of Social Workers, Code of Ethics, Chapter 1, Section 1.2)

Clearly, maintaining the best interest of the client should involve understanding and accepting the client's definition of issues or difficulties and ways of addressing them. And, these might be determined from a cultural context that is very different from that of the service provider.

CONCLUSION

As Canadians, we should be justifiably proud of the fact that we have been rated as the best country in the world in which to live. We can be proud also of the fact that we are the only country in the world with a national Multiculturalism Act, as well as equivalent legislation at the provincial government level. These pieces of legislation recognize and affirm that the cultural diversity of Canadians is a fundamental characteristic of the society. They also encourage the full and free participation of all citizens in the society; and recognize that government services and programs must be sensitive to the multicultural reality of the population.

Despite these policies, institutional responses have been far from culturally relevant or responsive. Indeed, the foregoing discussion suggests that social policy and institutional responses to serving members of diverse ethno-cultural backgrounds have been tentative and tokenistic. Several reasons have been advanced for this response, including the exclusive nature of the policy-making process, confusion over the concept of multiculturalism, lack of political will, and the existence of widespread racism in the society.

It is argued that in order to effectively address ethno-cultural diversity, social policies need to go beyond tokenism to full acceptance and acknowledgement of the diversity in the population. This will mean adopting principles of social inclusion and integration in all aspects of the policy-making process, as well as in the tasks of institution building and service delivery. It will mean provision of the needed support in terms of resources and political commitment. It will mean seeing our cultural diversity as one of our greatest resources, not only in terms of nation building at home, but also on the international stage in a variety areas, such as international trade, foreign policy, peace promotion, and human rights.

Whatever is done, there has to be a serious and sober realization that racism is pervasive and rampant in our society, and that this is cause for deep concern and collective shame. Out of this realization must emerge a firm and abiding conviction to develop nation-wide strategies to eradicate racism.

There will be many opportunities, like The United Nations Conference on Racismfor example, in the new millennium for Canada to show that it is serious about this issue. Our social policies should boldly convey the message that racism is not acceptable in our society. The future health and well-being of our society depends on it.

REFERENCES

Baker, H.R. , Draper, J.A. and Fairbairn, B.T. (1991). *Dignity and Growth: Citizen Participation in Social Change*. Calgary: Detselig Enterprises Ltd.

B.C. Advisory Council on Multiculturalism (1995). *Anti-Racism Forum Proceedings*. Victoria, B.C.: Ministry Responsible for Multiculturalism.

Canadian Council on Social Development (1984). *Issues in Canadian Social Policy Reader*. Ottawa: Canadian Council on Social Development.

Canadian Council on Social Development (1997). *Inclusive Social Policy Development: Ideas for Practitioners, Summary Report*.

Dobbin, M. (2000). WTO still lurching ahead after Battle in
    Seattle. *B.C. Association of Social Workers, Perspectives*,
    22(1), 1-2.
Dominelli, L. (1993). *Anti-Racist Social Work*. London:
    MacMillan.
Drover, G., Kerans, P., and Williams, D. (1985). "Administering
    the Welfare State: Bipartism and Worker Management of
    Social Programs." Report to The Canadian Association of
    Social Workers.
Drover, G. and Kerans, P. (Eds.) (1993). *New Approaches to
    Welfare Theory*. Aldershot, Hants, England: Edward Elgar
    Publishing.
Dye, T.R. (1972). *Understanding Public Policy*. Englewood
    Cliffs, NJ: Prentice-Hall.
Graveline, F.J. (1998). *Circle Works: Transforming Eurocentric
    Consciousness*. Halifax: Fernwood Publishing.
Green J.W. (1995). *Cultural Awareness in the Human Services*.
    Boston: Allyn and Bacon.
Guest, D. (1980). *The Emergence of Social Security in Canada*.
    Vancouver: University of British Columbia Press.
Hanna, M.G. and Robinson, B. (1994). *Strategies for Community
    Empowerment*. Lewiston, NY: Edwin Mellen Press.
Johnston, S.P. (1996). *Culturally Sensitive Mental Health Care:
    Communities Creating Change*. Vancouver: Culture and
    Health 2000.
Lafitte, F. (1962). "Social Policy in a Free Society." Lecture
    delivered at the University of Birmingham, Birmingham,
    England, May 18, 1962.
Littrell, W.B. and Sjoberg, G. (Eds.) (1976). *Current Issues in
    Social Policy*. Sage Publications: Beverly Hills, CA.
Morrissette, V., McKenzie, B. and Morrissette, L. (1993).
    Towards an Aboriginal Model of Social Work Practice.
    Canadian Social Work Review, 10(1), 91-108.
Moscovitch, A. and Drover, G. (Eds.) (1981). *Inequality: Essays
    on the Political Economy of Social Welfare*. Toronto:
    University of Toronto Press.
Pulkingham, J. and Ternowetsky, G. (Eds.) (1996). *Remaking
    Canadian Social Policy*. Halifax: Fernwood Publishing.
Ramcharan, S. (1989). *Social Problems and Issues: A Canadian
    Perspective*. Scarborough: Nelson Canada.

Rein, M. (1970). *Social Policy: Issues of Choice and Change*. New York: Random House.

Rutman, D. (1998). A Policy Community: Developing Guardianship Legislation. In B. Wharf and B. McKenzie (Eds.), *Connecting Policy to Practice in the Human Service*. Toronto: Oxford University Press. pp. 97-115.

Schwartz, M.A. (1991). *The Environment of Policy-Making in Canada and the United States*. Montreal & Calgary: C.D. Howe Institute and Washington, DC: National Planning Association.

Seebaran, R. (1996). "Rethinking the Approach to Health Care. *Keynote Address at the Annual Conference of the Northwest Territories Registered Nurses Association*. Yellowknife, May, 1996."

Splane, R. (1996). *75 Years of Community Service to Canada: Canadian Council on Social Development, 1920-1995*. Ottawa: Canadian Council on Social Development.

Titmuss, R. (1974). *Social Policy, An Introduction*. London: George Allen and Unwin.

Tsang, A.K.T. and George, U. (1998). Towards an integrated framework for cross-cultural social work practice. *Canadian Social Work Review*, 15(1), 73-93.

Wharf, B. (Ed.) (1990). *Social Work and Social Change in Canada*. Toronto: McClelland and Stewart.

Wharf, B. (1992). *Communities and Social Policy in Canada*. Toronto: McClelland and Stewart.

Wharf, B. and Cassom, J. (1987). Citizen participation and social policy. In S.A. Yelaja (Ed.), *Canadian Social Policy*. Waterloo: Wilfred Laurier University Press.

Wharf, B. and McKenzie, B. (1998). *Connecting Policy to Practice in the Human Services*. Toronto: Oxford University Press.

Yelaja, S.A. (1987). *Canadian Social Policy*. Waterloo: Wilfrid Laurier University Press.

Chapter 12

AGING IN A MULTICULTURAL SOCIETY:
PUBLIC POLICY CONSIDERATIONS

K. Victor Ujimoto

A stroll down any major street in Vancouver, Edmonton, Winnipeg, Toronto or Montreal today will reveal that contemporary Canadian society is characterized by its multicultural diversity. Indeed, the 1991 Census of Canada revealed that 31 percent of the population had ethnic origins which were neither British nor French (Statistics Canada, 1993). This was an increase from 25 percent as compared to the 1986 Canadian census reporting non-British or French ethnic origins. In some major urban areas such as Toronto and Vancouver, the percentage of those who are of neither British nor French ethnic origins are considerably higher than the national figure of 31 percent. Changes in Canadian demographic characteristics such as age and ethnicity require that social policies developed in the past, particularly education and health policies, must now be reassessed.

There are several areas of contemporary gerontological research in Canada that must be addressed as part of this reassessment process. First, it is now slightly over a decade since the first set of articles on ethnicity and aging was published as a special issue of *Canadian Ethnic Studies* (1983) and many of these articles require another look at the changing demographic profile of Canadian society. Second, with the exception of a relatively few Canadian gerontologists, (Driedger and Chappell, 1987), policy issues on ethnic minority aging have not been adequately examined. Third, given the changing demographic processes of fertility, mortality, immigration and their concomitant impact on the social characteristics of contemporary Canadian society, health care providers must be provided with sufficient training to meet the socio-cultural needs of ethnic minority elders. A brief overview of these three areas will now be presented followed by future research and social policy relevant issues.

Ethnicity and Aging: An Overview

The changing nature of the aging Canadian population was first reported in the early 1980s soon after the publication of the 1981 Census of Canada. At that time, 2.4 million Canadians were aged 65 years and over. This figure represented approximately 9.7 percent of the total Canadian population. A point of interest to specialists of ethnicity and aging was the fact that 11 percent of the older population spoke neither of the official languages of Canada. Ujimoto (1983) noted from his examination of immigration statistics for 1980 that over 60 percent of the immigrants to Canada came from third world countries in Asia, Africa, South America and the Caribbean.

More recently, Samuel (1992) reported his demographic projections for the year 2001. He noted that the Chinese population alone will constitute 23 percent of the visible minorities, 19 percent by both South Asians and Blacks, 13 percent by West Asians/Arabs, 6 percent by Latin Americans, and 7 percent by others. An important implication of these data is that as our population ages, special issues related to ethnicity and aging may become more pronounced unless educational and social policy considerations are addressed prior to issues becoming more serious social problems.

The study of ethnicity and aging in Canada has been relatively underdeveloped. There are several reasons for this situation. The first reason is that gerontological research in Canada has been dominated by certain assumptions such as the homogeneity of the population as well as the relevance of existing theories to the concerns of aging ethnic minorities. As a result of these assumptions, gerontological research to date has been conducted employing theoretical perspectives and methodological techniques that did not consider the cultural and inter-generational diversity of Canadian society.

The second reason is that most gerontological research has been linear in scope rather than systemic. Linear research examines a given problem or objective from a very narrow perspective. In contrast, systemic research includes several independent and intervening variables in order to account for the variations in the observed phenomenon to be examined. To be fair, part of this lack of emphasis on systemic research can be placed on the financial constraints imposed on many research projects in the first place. However, it can be argued that the curricula in gerontological studies do not adequately reflect the pluralistic nature of contemporary Canadian society.

A more compelling reason for the slow recognition of including ethnicity related factors in the study of the aging process stems from the fact that there are extremely few ethnic minority faculty associated with gerontological research and teaching at Canadian universities. Unlike many universities and professional organizations in the United States, there has been scarcely any effort to encourage and to train ethnic minorities to enter the field of gerontology in Canada. Nevertheless, given the limited resources, some progress has been made in the study of ethnicity and aging.

Early Canadian studies on ethnicity and aging owe much to the studies already undertaken in the United States. Dowd and Bengtson (1978), Gelfand and Kutzik (1979), Moriwaki (1976), Kalish and Moriwaki (1973), Osako (1979), Wu (1975), Fujii (1976) and Jackson (1980) all recognized the salience of ethnicity in gerontological studies. Furthermore, these researchers all argued for a systemic examination of socio-cultural and demographic factors in relation to the aging process in ethnic minority groups. Similarly, Holzberg (1981) alerted us to the importance of cultural beliefs, religion and symbolism to account for differential aspects of human behaviour. The failure to distinguish cultural factors from situational or socio-environmental factors often lead to incorrect assumptions about the aging process.

In Canada, it was not until 1983 that a collection of articles on ethnicity and aging first appeared in a special issue of *Canadian Ethnic Studies*. In this volume, various articles examined ethnicity and culture as independent variables in addition to the standard demographic variables, thereby furthering our knowledge about the diverse patterns of aging in a multicultural society. It was argued by Ujimoto (1983, p.iv) that individual studies must be placed within some theoretical context that were more or less recognized at the time in the field of social gerontology. Only then, it was noted, could we adequately assess the extent to which theories on aging were appropriate or not for the study of aged ethnic minorities. A key point raised by Ujimoto was the question of whether or not the theoretical inadequacies arose mainly because of the level of abstraction of the key concepts, or because of the cultural and ethnocentric biases implicit in the underlying assumptions of the theory.

One of the key issues to be dealt with in the study of ethnicity and aging was the many ways in which ethnicity was defined. Rosenthal (1983) notes that some scholars equated ethnicity primarily with culture whereas others viewed ethnicity as a determinant of social inequality. Rosenthal demonstrated the significance of the diverse meanings attached to the concept of ethnicity by examining the modernization theory of aging. This model on aging equated the traditional/modern dichotomy in terms of "ethnic/non-ethnic" dimensions. For example, ethnic families were placed in the traditional end of the traditional-modern continuum and were presumed to receive greater family support.

At issue with this overly simplistic notion of fitting ethnic groups into established theoretical categories was the fact that some groups such as the Chinese and Japanese Canadian minority groups were stereotyped as "model minorities" and thus seldom included in discussions on the needs of the elderly. It was assumed that traditional cultural attributes were sufficiently strong to meet the contemporary needs of the aged. What this argument failed to recognize were the inter-generational differences within a given ethnic group. Diverse needs of the aged first generation immigrants are considerably different to those of ethnic minority Canadians who were socialized into the cultural norms of the dominant groups in Canada.

The issue of stereotyping ethnic groups into a simple category may have sufficed at one time in Canadian history. However, with continued immigration and the establishment of third, fourth, and in some cases fifth generation Canadians, it became necessary to account for the validity in stereotyping aged ethnic minorities. Factors such as the impact of immigrant life histories, degree of racial discrimination encountered not only during the initial immigrant adjustment period, but continued denial of access to improving one's economic and social position had considerable bearing on one's well-being in later life. Chan (1983), for example, viewed ethnicity and culture as variables which can hinder or facilitate the adjustment to the social and psychological constraints of aging.

Another aspect of ethnicity and aging that has not received much attention in Canada is the role of socialization and maintenance of cultural duality. Sugiman and Nishio (1983) examined the dynamics of Japanese Canadian social relationships by comparing the traditional norms of the aged as manifested by the *issei* or first generation Japanese Canadian immigrants and the *nisei* or Canadian born second generation. They examined those elements of traditional Japanese culture that resulted in inter-generational conflict. Such conflict was based mainly on differences in the interpretation of traditional social values and their relevance in contemporary Canadian society.

The study of the socialization processes of the *nisei* provides an interesting case study as it illustrates social conflict between the inculcation of traditional social values and the desire for complete assimilation and acculturation by the Canadian born. Perhaps this was predominantly a reflection of the times as all Japanese Canadians were affected by the forced removal from their communities along the coastal areas of British Columbia to inland internment camps. The economic, social, and psychological damages of this experience are still vividly recalled today by many Japanese Canadian seniors.

The importance of understanding the socio-cultural and psychological aspects of ethnicity and aging may be better understood if one considers how health care services are organized and administered today in long-term institutions. In many such institutions, health care is still primarily focused on meeting the needs of the dominant anglophone group. An aged ethnic minority member in such an institution experiences added stress in attempting to cope with the demands of daily living (p. 6).

Practical issues arising from ethnic minority residents in institutions organized for another cultural group have been examined by MacLean and Bonar (1983). Their research confirms that potential negative institutional effects exist in settings in which familiar support systems such as friends and family members are lacking. In addition to the loss of family and friends, MacLean and Bonar note that an elderly ethnic person in an institution of another dominant culture results in other losses such as the loss of one's own culture and community. It is possible to compensate for some of these losses by providing at least some symbolic support to meet the psychological needs of the minority ethnic elderly.

An example of meaningful symbolic support may be provided by the presence of a Black Canadian nurse or Registered Nursing Assistant in an institutional setting that is predominantly White, but nevertheless has a few residents who are from one of the Caribbean islands. Symbolic presence in many instances is sufficient to enable ethnic minority residents to face their daily challenges which may stem from within their own institutional setting. Similarly, a Japanese Canadian social worker assigned to assist in an institution with one Chinese elderly person may provide the symbolic or spiritual encouragement to cope with daily tasks although the Chinese language may not be spoken by the social worker.

With the passing of time, the issue of providing symbolic reference personnel in health care settings may eventually disappear as members of minority ethnic groups gradually increase and various service sectors of Canadian society become institutionally complete. As Gerber (1983) has observed, many ethnic groups are experiencing old age in different ways. It remains for future research to document the diverse ways in which members of minority ethnic groups reach their retirement years.

Ethnicity and Aging: Policy Considerations

The ultimate aim of any research on ethnicity and aging should be to utilize the knowledge gained to assist in the maintenance of one's health as well as to facilitate improvements in one's well-being as the aging process occurs. However, research results to date on ethnicity and aging that is considered to be of any significance in the development of social policies appears to be limited. The art of developing social policies are often politically motivated and are developed in reaction to existing problems rather than as a preventative measure.

An important aspect of a social policy designed as a preventative measure is that it must be viewed within a time frame that is considerably longer than the customary duration of five to ten years. Instead, the social policy framework should be based on a time frame of at least fifty years that is nested with periodic evaluations at five year intervals to make adjustments as required.

The availability of information technologies today will greatly facilitate the inclusion of many key variables for the policy development process.

The crucial role of information technology for creative purposes in the development of policies on future scenarios is still in its infancy, but rapidly advancing in various areas of social science research. One example is that of demographic projections. Here, key variables that influence the population size of Canada at any given period such as immigration, emigration, births, and mortality are used to make predictions of future labour force needs. Another example of a demographic projection is that of estimating future revenues that will be required to meet the social security needs of a rapidly aging population.

In contrast, policies related to old age security payment is based on the age criterion, the age of 65 years. Other programs such as the guaranteed income supplement is based on an additional variable, that of total income. Similarly, other social programs are based on eligibility criteria for services such as drug prescriptions, various types of therapy, and laboratory tests. It is in this latter area of medical service provision that ethnicity factors become important, not only for one's well-being, but also in reducing health care costs for unnecessary medical tests and services.

An understanding of the relationship between ethnicity and ethnic minority attitudes and behaviour towards health and health care services can be facilitated by existing information technology. Information technology usually refers to computers capable of storing vast quantities of data, a communication network system that provides easy access to this data and a printer capable of presenting the required data in various formats. A data system which has stored ethnic and cultural differences on perceptions and behaviour regarding personal health and illness, utilization of health services, and coping responses will assist considerably in developing alternative choices of health care for different ethnic groups. Today, information on various aspects of ethnicity, aging, and health are available and access to this information is gradually improving because of much wider use of information technology.

The influences that ethnic and cultural factors have on health and health care have been noted by many: Masi (1988), Lorens (1988), Ujimoto (1988), Gallagher, Grudzen and Wallace (1989), Waxler-Morrison, Anderson and Richardson (1990), Hikoyeda and

Grudzen (1991), Masi, Mensah and McLeod (1993), and Ujimoto (1994). Masi (1988, p.2173) argues that "culturally sensitive health care is not a matter of simple formulas or prescriptions that provide a single definitive answer; rather it requires understanding of the principles on which health care is based and the manner in which culture may influence those principles. That influence may affect or bias physicians, patients, and institutions serving the community". By culture, Masi means the patterns or standards of behaviour that one acquires as a member of a particular group. The standards of behaviour are influenced or modified through one's language use and values and beliefs held by the individual. Ethnocentric biases can only be reduced if access to relevant bodies of information is provided and a re-educative policy is put in place.

One approach in addressing cultural sensitivity issues in the health professions is through the educational process. This process must be, by necessity, a two prong approach; first, to direct more attention to the re-educative needs of those health care providers and professionals who were trained in a previous era in which ethno-cultural health topics were not an integral part of their professional training, and second, the inclusion of culturally sensitive educational material in the curricula of various health professions at the college and university levels.

These very recommendations were in fact advanced in 1988 when a national workshop on ethnicity and aging was convened in Ottawa (Canadian Public Health Association 1988). Workshop participants made a variety of recommendations "to create a society in Canada in which there is greater public understanding and acceptance of cultural diversity and of the special needs of ethnic seniors". In order to achieve these goals, there were 33 separate recommendations which covered six general areas of policy as follows:

1. Public understanding and acceptance,
2. Access to information,
3. Establishment of a national resource centre on ethnicity and aging,
4. Access to services,
5. Special needs groups, and
6. Independence issues common to all seniors.

Follow-up on these recommendations has been limited to a few specific areas. Efforts to educate the public on cultural diversity have been initiated at several major Canadian universities that have medical and nursing faculties. Also, the federal Seniors Independence Program has funded a few research projects, however, results of these projects have not been widely distributed. A more effective utilization of information technology is obviously in order.

Ethnicity and Aging: Training Needs

With rapid changes in the demographic composition of Canadian society, there is a growing demand for more health professionals who are familiar with ethno-cultural health issues. In order to approach this demand, it is necessary to develop a long-range strategy rather than relying on short-term, partial solutions. In this regard, the Gerontological Society of America (GSA) provides an excellent model on how they tackled a similar issue. About a decade ago, the Council of the GSA established a Task Force on Minority Issues in Gerontology. Eventually, similar task forces were set up in each of the sub-sections, for example, the Behavioral and Social Sciences Section, the Biological Science Section, the Clinical Medicine Section, and the Social Research, Policy and Practice Section. The Task Force came up with the following three goals (Gibson 1988, p.559):

1. To increase the quantity and quality of gerontological research on minority aging questions
2. To increase the number of minority researchers in gerontology, and
3. To increase the number of minority members in the Society and participation of minority members in Society activities and governance.

Gibson argues that there are two important reasons for improving the quality and increasing the quantity of minority aging research. First, high quality research provides a more solid foundation for new research and social interventions. Second, the larger the number of studies and through systematic replication, greater confidence can be achieved in the findings. Gibson's emphasis was on integrated knowledge based on cumulative theory building and research.

The Gerontological Society of America has continued to promote greater attention to minority issues in gerontology. Recently, the GSA (1994) published an important document entitled

Minority Elders: Five Goals Toward Building A Public Policy Base.
In his preface, Dr. James S. Jackson (1994), Chair, Task Force on
Minority Issues, makes the observation that "at every point in the life
span, most racial and ethnic minority groups are at greater mortality
and morbidity risks than Whites. On the other hand, based upon
current demographic projections, older minority populations have
grown at a greater rate than non-minority elderly and will continue to
do so for the foreseeable future". For these reasons, Jackson argues,
that there is an urgent need to include racial and ethnic minority
content in research on aging.

Another very significant observation made by Jackson
(1994) is that "race, ethnicity, and cultural distinctiveness have to be
considered as resources, providing psychological, social and personal identity and group connectedness and facilitating tangible sources
of family and friend support. Although there is a convergence of the
need for a resource based, life-span model of ethnicity and minority
status that transcends traditional notions of culture and assimilation,
the empirical literature has not kept pace". This observation clearly
provides him with a research agenda that is organized around public
policy goals as follows:

1. Improving the data base on minority aging populations
2. Improving the economic status of minority persons as they
   enter old age,
3. Increasing longevity and improving the health status of
   minority older persons,
4. Strengthening family support systems for minority older
   persons, and
5. Increase health and longevity, economic status, and family
   support of American Indian Elders.

These five goals are also most relevant for the development
of Canadian public policy which spans areas other than ethnicity and
aging. An understanding of diverse cultures, attitudes, and behaviour
is becoming important in almost all daily transactions today because
of the globalization of knowledge. While this globalization of
knowledge is occurring mostly in the economic and commercial
sectors, other areas of contemporary research have also taken on a
global perspective. Thus, cross-cultural communications has become
an extremely important aspect of the globalization phenomenon.

The impact of globalization has provided an added stimulus
for cross-cultural understanding and research. Some ethnic groups in

Canada, particularly Asian Canadians, do not constitute a very large population, however, given the global perspectives of today's economic transactions, some Asian Canadians have taken on the role as international citizens. In this role, they serve as facilitators in assisting cross-cultural interaction. Unfortunately, such roles exist only in the commercial area, and not in the educational sphere. Canadian credentials and appropriate experience in Canada appear to be major stumbling blocks. Surely a person capable of communicating in Cantonese or Mandarin but possesses only a Bachelor's degree is much more useful in a health care setting in an urban area than a social worker with a Master's degree but does not have the linguistic skills other than in English!

Another aspect of the globalization of knowledge is the proliferation of Japanese ways of social organization as manifested in contemporary management style which appears to be occurring in the health care field. Government responsibilities are gradually shifting to the community levels and greater cooperation between various health care services is expected. Unfortunately, Canadians have been socialized to be individuals first, and while the concept of teamwork may appear feasible in theory, actual practice is much more difficult to achieve. What aspects of culture, then, facilitate group cohesion? Given the declining financial resources for health care, public policy should look to those areas that maximize aspects of ethno-cultural cooperation.

Conclusion: Implications of Cultural Diversity on Public Policy

Demographic changes in Canada have promoted researchers to examine more closely the challenges presented by an aging society. More people are living longer and in different ways. As the population ages, the diversity in lifestyles places a heavy burden on health care providers who are governed by outmoded social policies which appear to be more reactive rather than forward looking.

As noted earlier, gerontological research in Canada has been influenced by false assumptions that as the population ages, the needs of the elderly become similar. Consequently, researchers have treated their elderly subjects as being homogeneous in nature when addressing their needs. The primary task for gerontologists today is to recognize the cultural diversity of our elderly population. There are positive benefits to be gained from an aging heterogeneous population if the elderly are perceived as resources for social change instead of viewing them as a group always in need to compensate for deficits brought about by the process of aging.

Taeuber (1990) has argued that the complexities associated with the social and economic diversity of an heterogeneous population cannot be understood by generalizations. It is now necessary to recognize the fact that each age, gender, race and ethnic group has distinctive characteristics that impact on aging. With reference to the age variable alone, it is important to understand changes in the age structure of Canadian society and public policies must be developed to reflect the long-term implications of this age structure.

It is necessary to consider the long-term implications of the age structure because all too often, social policies are developed in reaction to a given crisis. If we continue to develop policies in reaction to fiscal crises associated with the elderly, for example pension benefits, retirement savings investment plans, etc., there is a distinct possibility that there will be repercussions for the younger generation as well. Today's youth will be tomorrow's elders. Because of fiscal constraints today, financial resources for educational and training programs are being reduced. Do we really expect those youths who experience difficulties in entering the labour force today will be sufficiently prepared for their own retirement?

In addition to the problem of reduced financial resources for education and training to prepare today's youth to meet the challenges of the future, it should be noted that the globalization of the economy is shifting labour intensive jobs offshore to countries where wages are a fraction of that in Canada. Accounting firms now utilize information technology to transfer their data to places such as Taiwan and Singapore for processing. Similarly, software manufacturers have targeted India as a place for low cost yet highly creative environment for computer program development. Multinational firms have relocated their manufacturing plants to Third World countries where an industrious labour force can produce quality goods at a fraction of North American costs. Such labour intensive activities obviously will have an immense impact on the current as well as future generations of youth.

Bass, Kutza and Torres-Gil (1990, p.178) make the observation that our changing economy may not benefit future seniors because one's work history is very closely related to later retirement income. They argue that because of the globalization of the economy, it will be the women and minorities who will be most directly affected. They have fewer opportunities for job experience and this will impact on later life. An interesting perspective to this issue is provided by Moody (1990, p.133) who links the issues of international competitions, national deficits, and persistent poverty to the policy on aging.

Today, government bureaucrats are examining ways to reduce medical health and pension costs and their arguments are based on individual needs rather than on benefits based on universal age criteria. An alternative strategy is proposed by Moody who argues that instead of viewing the elderly as a group in need and of entitlements based on age, older people should be seen as a resource. Moody accepts the fact that some old people may be in need, however, there are others who are able to make a contribution to society through their productive role. Thus, not everyone should retire at a pre-set age of 65. What this means is that existing policies must be redesigned to provide alternative choices for people who are not only enjoying a productive role, but can serve as effective members of society either as role models for the next generation or by not becoming a welfare burden on the state.

Perhaps the most important advice for future policy planners is provided by Torres-Gil and Kmet (1990, p.167) who reason that today's senior citizens are best positioned to provide the political leadership that will be required to take us into the next century. Torres-Gil and Kmet observe that older people have "the wisdom and experience to know why and when reforms require public sacrifice and commitments." It is argued that this new leadership by older persons will promote policies that will serve the interests of the future generation and not just narrow political interests. It remains to be seen if this leadership from the ranks of the "new elderly" can move beyond self-serving narrow interests.

References

Bass, Scott A., Kutza, E.A., and Torres-Gil, F.M. (1990). *Diversity in Aging.* Glenview, Illinois: Scott, Foresman and Company.

Bengtson, Vern L. (1979). "Ethnicity and Aging: Problems and Issues in Current Social Science Inquiry." In D.E. Gelfand and A.J.Kutznik (eds.), *Ethnicity and Aging*. New York: Springer Publishing Company, pp. 9-31.

Blakemore, K. and M. Boneham. (1994). *Age, Race and Ethnicity, A Comparative Approach*. Buckingham, UK: Open University Press.

Canadian Ethnic Studies (1983). Special Issue: *Ethnicity and Aging*. Calgary: Canadian Ethnic Studies Association.

Canadian Public Health Association (1988). *Ethnicity and Aging. Report of the National Workshop on Ethnicity and Aging*. Ottawa: Canadian Public Health Association.

Chan, Kwok B. (1983). "Coping with Aging and Managing Self-Identity: The Social World of the Elderly Chinese Women." *Canadian Ethnic Studies*, Vol. XV, No. 3, pp. 36-50.

Dowd, J. and Vern L. Bengtson (1978). "Aging in Minority Populations: An Examination of the Double Jeopardy Hypothesis." *Journal of Gerontology 33* (3), pp. 427-436.

Driedger, L. and N. Chappell (1987). *Aging and Ethnicity, Toward an Interface*. Toronto: Butterworths.

Fu, F.Y.T. (1975). "Mandarin-Speaking Aged Chinese in the Los Angeles Area." *Gerontologist* 15, pp. 271-275.

Fujii, S.M. (1976). "Elderly Asian Americans and Use of Public Services." *Social Casework* 57, pp. 202-207.

Gallagher, D., Grudzen, M. R. and Wallace, M. (1988). *Creative Coping with Caregiving: Clinical and Policy Making Areas*. Stanford: Stanford Geriatric Education Center.

Gelfand, Donald E. and Alfred J. Kutzik. (1979). *Ethnicity and Aging*. New York: Springer Publishing Company.

Gerber, Linda. (1983). "Ethnicity Still Matters: Socio-Demographic Profiles of the Ethnic Elderly in Ontario." *Canadian Ethnic Studies,* Vol. XV, No. 3, pp. 60-80.

Gerontological Society of America (1994). *Minority Elders. Five Goals Toward Building A Public Policy Base*. Washington, D.C.: Gerontological Society of America.

Gibson, Rose C. (1988). Guest Editorial. Minority Aging Research: Opportunity and Challenge. *The Gerontologist*, Vol. 28, No. 4, pp. 559-560.

Hikoyeda, N. and M. Grudzen. (1990). *Traditional and Non-Traditional Medication Use Among Ethnic Elders.* Stanford: Stanford Geriatric Education Center.

Holzberg, Carol S. (1981). "Cultural Gerontology: Towards an Understanding of Ethnicity and Aging." *In Culture,* Vol. 1, No. 1, pp. 110-122.

Jackson, Jacqueline J. (1980). *Minorities and Aging.* Belmont, CA: Wadsworth.

Jackson, James S. (1994). Preface and Introduction, *Minority Elders. Five Goals Toward Building A Public Policy Base.* Washington, D.C.: Gerontological Society of America.

Kalish, R.A. and Moriwaki, S. (1973). "The World of the Elderly Asian American." *Journal of Social Issues* XXIX, pp. 187-209.

Llorens, L.A. (1988). "Health Care for Ethnic Elders: The Cultural Context." Stanford: Stanford Geriatric Education Center.

MacLean, M. J. and R. Bonar. (1983). "The Ethnic Elderly in a Dominant Culture Long-Term Care Facility." *Canadian Ethnic Studies*, Vol. XV, No. 3, pp. 51-59.

Masi, Ralph. (1988). "Multiculturalism, Medicine and Health" *Canadian Family Physician* 34:2173-8; 2429-34; 2649-53.

Masi, Ralph, L. Mensah, K.A. McLeod (1993). "Health and Cultures, Exploring the Relationships." *Policies, Professional Practice and Education. Vol. 1.* Oakville: Mosaic Press.

Moody, Harry R. (1990). "The Politics of Entitlement and the Politics of Productivity." In Scott A. Bass, Elizabeth A. Kutza, and Fernando M. Torres-Gil (eds.), *Diversity in Aging.* Glenview, Illinois: Scott Foresman and Company, pp. 151-173.

Moriwaki, S. (1976). "Ethnicity and Aging." In I. Burnside (ed.) *Nursing and the Aged.* New York: McGraw-Hill.

Osako, Masako M. (1979). "Aging and Family Among Japanese Americans: The Role of Ethnic Tradition in the Adjustment to Old Age." *The Gerontologist* 19, pp. 448-455.

Rosenthal, C. J. (1983). "Aging, Ethnicity and the Family: Beyond the Modernization Thesis." *Canadian Ethnic Studies,* Vol. XV, No. 3, pp. 1-16.

Samuel, John T. (1992). *Visible Minorities in Canada: A Projection.* Toronto: Canadian Advertising Foundation.

Statistics Canada (1993). *Ethnic Origins, Catalogue 93-315.* Ottawa: Industry, Science and Technology.

Sugiman, Pamela and Nishio, H. K. (1983). "Socialization and Cultural Duality Among Aging Japanese Canadians." *Canadian Ethnic Studies,* Vol. XV, No. 3, pp. 17-35.

Taeuber, Cynthia. (1990). "Diversity: The Dramatic Reality" In Scott A. Bass, Elizabeth A. Kutza, and Fernando M. Torres-Gil (eds.), *Diversity in Aging.* Glenview, Illinois: Scott Foresman and Company, pp. 1-45.

Ujimoto, K. Victor. (1983). "Introduction/Ethnicity and Aging in Canada." *Canadian Ethnic Studies,* Vol. XV, No. 3, pp. iii-vii.

Ujimoto, K. Victor. (1988). "Aging, Ethnicity and Health." In B.S. Bolaria and H.D. Dickenson (eds.) *Sociology of Health Care in Canada.* Toronto: Harcourt Brace Jovanovich.

Ujimoto, K. Victor. (1994). "Racial and Ethnic Dimensions of Aging: Implications for Health Care Service." In B. Singh Bolaria and Rosemary Bolaria (eds.) *Racial Minorities, Medicine and Health.* Halifax: Fernwood Publishing.

Waxler-Morrison, N., Anderson, J. M. and Richardson, E. (1990). *CrossCultural Caring: A Handbook for Health Professionals in Canada.* Vancouver: University of British Columbia Press.

Wu, F.Y.T. (1975) "Mandarin-Speaking Aged Chinese in the Los Angeles Area." *Gerontologist 15*, pp. 271-275.

Chapter 13

PROMOTING CANADIAN COMPETENCE: THE EDUCATION OF A DIVERSE PEOPLE

Deo H. Poonwassie

In the year 2000, there will be many analyses of the past and present with some predictions for the future; indeed it happens with every impending decade, but the scope of current writing will be wider and deeper because of this significant chronological benchmark. One sure question to emerge will be what is Canada?

The simplest answer is: Canada is a sovereign nation with a population of 31 million people. But, as we probe deeper, a stultifying complexity emerges because Canada may be seen as a mosaic—vertical, lateral, and circular; a cosmopolitan community; an officially bi-lingual nation with a multicultural population; an immensely rich country in natural resources and human potential; a people who believe in and practise human rights and peace-keeping; and, above all else, a nation with a bright and promising future for all its people. In addition, a major asset that makes Canada an attractive and progressive country is its **diversity.**

From the Arctic to the Atlantic and Pacific Oceans, the landscape and climate vary markedly, and so does the fauna and flora. The population is composed of many peoples made up of Aboriginals and every other "colour" and "race" to be found on this globe, speaking many languages, and representing a variety of cultures. Such is the diverse nature of our country. The term **diversity** refers to differences and variations, but it also includes some commonalities whether these be in goals, beliefs, space, allegiances, values, or political ideologies. It is important to distinguish this concept from **multiculturalism** which refers to cultural diversity; in other words, diversity is the all-encompassing term referring to differences and variations, whereas multiculturalism is particular to cultural differences and denote only one type of diversity. **Education** and **schooling** will be used interchangeably to mean learning in a prescribed setting.

The focus of this chapter will be on cultural diversity and education; we will explore and analyze (a) the current issues, (b) developments and challenges, (c) directions for education, (d) working through schools, and (e) the beginning of a new century. This chapter will provide arguments for the position that cultural diversity must be a key consideration in the provision of education in any Canadian public school (although private educational institutions should opt for this provision also).

Canada is comprised of Aboriginal peoples and descendants of immigrants. Indeed the pattern of immigration has determined the demographic variations of the Canadian population. We will return to the issue of immigration later, but suffice it to say that cultural, ethnic, and racial diversity has been determined by immigration from various parts of the world, largely from Europe. Patterns of diversity seen globally are mirrored in Canada. As Street (1992) points out: "... the social reality that we are observing when we look closely at life on the ground, is actually of diversity... Once we have decided that in reality the world is becoming more, not less, diverse, then the policy issues become harder not easier." (p. 61)

Current Issues

Some 95% of Canada's population is non-Aboriginal; British-only and French-only origins make up 51% of this country's population. In 1991, 83.1% were Canadian-born and 16.1% were immigrants (Statistics Canada, 1994, p. 19). Of the top ten countries of birth for all immigrants to Canada only four are non-European, namely, the USA, India, People's Republic of China, and Hong Kong; however, between 1981 and 1991 only three European countries (Poland, UK, and Portugal) are ranked in the top ten (Statistics Canada, p. 14). Clearly, there was a shift from Europe to other countries; in fact the 1996 Census, (Nation Tables) indicate that the top 10 source countries for immigration to Canada are: Hong Kong (13.33%), India (9.45%), China-mainland (7.8%), Taiwan (5.88%), The Philippines (5.77%), Pakistan (3.45%), Sri Lanka (2.73%), United States (2.58%), Iran (2.58%), and the United Kingdom (2.48%) (James, 1999. p.183). Here is evidence that Canada is becoming more culturally diverse; the ethnic and racial mix of Canada is showing an increase in peoples of non-European origin.

This shift in the ethnic and racial composition of Canada's population brings with it diversity in language, values, religion, expectations, levels of training, and political ideology. How are the schools responding to these changes? In assessing the example of Aboriginals and the school system, the failure of the current schooling arrangements to meet the needs of this population becomes clear. For centuries the imposed system of education has been insensitive to the needs of the Aboriginal peoples. Now the trend is to facilitate total control of education of Aboriginals by their own people. In other words the system was rigid; will the same happen for minority ethnic and social groups again?

Schools in Canada are classified as public, private, or separate. For our purposes, we will deal with the public schools only, which are totally funded by a publicly elected government. Generally, most parents are satisfied with public schools in Canada. (*Canadian School Executive*, Nov. 1990, p. 27). Efforts are being made to include components of various cultures in the school activities, especially in the curriculum. In some cases this is seen as tokenism, in others serious attempts are promoted through legislation by establishing administrative units for multiculturalism within ministries of education.

In March, 1984 the Special Committee on Visible Minorities in Canadian Society submitted its report *Equality Now* to the House of Commons. This report contains six chapters; the sixth focuses on education. This chapter includes fourteen recommendations ranging from the establishment of race relations policy and an examination of the hidden curriculum to "the establishment of research centres and chairs of study." Most of these recommendations are directed to the proposed Ministry of Multiculturalism (Canadian Government Publishing Centre, 1984, pp. 140-141). The Government of Canada endorsed each of these fourteen recommendations (Minister of Supply and Services, 1984). However, all recommendations pertaining directly to schools are outside the jurisdiction of the Federal Government because education is a provincial responsibility! In other words, the Federal Government has little power to implement these recommendations, except to provide funds for specific projects, and to act in an advisory capacity. Most urban school boards (for example, Toronto, Ottawa, Winnipeg, Vancouver) have accepted and implemented some of these recommendations. Although great strides have been made to accommodate diversity in the public schools, a great deal is still left to be initiated and implemented. Recent incidents arising from systemic racism have erupted in schools in many provinces such as New Brunswick, Ontario, Alberta, and British Columbia; some of these incidents are organized by racist groups.

Some of the major current issues about cultural diversity in schools today include the organization of appropriate curriculum and materials, the development of policy on equality and equity, the hiring of committed staff, and the establishment of effective parent-school collaboration. Above all else is the cultivation of a school culture for fairness and justice.

Based on the Canadian Charter of Rights and Freedoms, many minority ethnic and racial groups are seeking their rights to their chosen type of education, not through privately funded schools, but from the public schools. Provincial and federal policies on multiculturalism recognize and promote cultural differences for those who choose this route. This is a hotly debated issue that is potentially explosive and can create deep chasms in our society.

Schools today are faced with the major task of designing and implementing an **inclusive curriculum.** Diversity in our population, apart from race and culture, includes the handicapped, women, and homosexuals. All special interest groups are demanding recognition in the educational system, and every effort must be made to accommodate them. How and what share of the school curriculum should be allotted to various interest groups will be determined according to the political ideology of the decision-makers; the decisions will be difficult to make in these times of a shift to the political right.

With the implementation of national examinations (School Achievement Indicators Program), the effects of geographic diversity and economic inequity will be seen. Do the poorer provinces have the resources to provide education at acceptable levels in the public schools? Do the rural public schools have proper facilities (including skilled teachers) to enable students to approach achievement at their maximum levels? Are inner-city students receiving the best instruction under optimum conditions for success? The answers to these questions are generally negative, and the provinces and the federal government must consider forms of equity that will allow all Canadians an equal chance to obtain meaningful education.

The current state of education in Canada varies according to geographic location, economic development, and political ideology. Cultural differences play an important part in procuring opportunit- ies for education both for groups and individuals. Within cultural, racial, and ethnic groups social class plays a key role in taking advantage of, and creating, opportunities in education. While educational opportunities are created and available, there is no reason to be complacent; there are many who are still unable to benefit from the current systems: these persons must be identified and accommodated.

Developments and Challenges

Canada has a long history of diversity beginning with the many First Nations peoples who spoke their own languages and practised distinct ways of living. With the arrival of Europeans and Americans of diverse ethnicity, the Canadian population began to reflect a variety of religions and languages. As conflicts occurred in other countries within the last three decades, people came to Canada as refugees, especially from Africa (Uganda), Bosnia and South East Asia (Vietnam); in addition peoples from South Asia (India), Latin America, and the Caribbean sought opportunities for a better life by migrating to this country. Indeed Canada has actively recruited affluent immigrants from South East Asia, especially Hong Kong; government action is taken to encourage business people to settle in this country in order to enhance the economy. As pointed out earlier, in recent years the majority of immigrants to Canada are arriving from non-European countries.

A brief history of Canadian diversity is included in *Multiculturalism: Building the Canadian Mosaic* (1987), a report of the standing committee on multiculturalism, House of Commons, Canada (pp. 13-19). Canadian diversity is recognized through legis- lation and government policies. Religion and language have played major roles in determining the nature of this country. For example, as early as 1869 New Brunswick witnessed religious conflicts over schools; in 1870 similar problems surfaced in Manitoba. The Canadian government responded in various ways to the growing uneasiness derived from diversity: in 1960 the *Bill of Rights* was introduced; in 1969 the *Official Languages Act* was proclaimed making Canada an officially bilingual country—English and French—not including the other languages spoken in this country. As opposition to this Act was voiced, the Government produced the *Multiculturalism Policy of 1971* (which became an Act in 1988) recognizing the cultural diversity of this country. In 1977 the *Canadian Human Rights Act* was passed; this act outlawed discrimination based on "race, national or ethnic origin, colour, religion, age, sex, marital status, family status, disability or conviction for an offence for which a pardon has been granted." This was a deliberate attempt to recognize Canada's diversity and to ensure a measure of equal opportunity and social justice, through legislative authority.

The most recent government action to recognize and promote Canadian diversity is the entrenchment of the Charter of Rights and Freedoms in the Canadian Constitution, 1982. It preserves and enhances basic rights and freedoms for all citizens including mobility and minority language rights regardless of "race, national or ethnic origin, colour, religion, sex, age or mental or physical disability" (Section 15). The development of legal measures to ensure the rights of citizens has produced many formal safeguards; indeed Canada is seen globally as an example of high moral ground in human rights and the promotion of cultural diversity.

Within Canada there will be many challenges to traditional practices based on the Charter of Rights and Freedoms. Quite recently we have witnessed court cases dealing with the rights of Sikhs to wear their religious headdress as part of their uniform in the RCMP and in Legion Halls; litigation in cases of hate mongering against targeted minority groups; and gay and lesbian rights in the form of social benefits for spouses. The Charter will be severely tested as individuals and groups become more conscious of their rights in a diverse Canada.

Education is instrumental in creating a heightened consciousness of one's rights and responsibilities; as Paulo Freire (1971) points out, education is not neutral; it is either for liberation or domestication. The process of conscientization becomes an on-going vigil for critical awareness of one's reality, and praxis invokes a sobering empowerment. This level of analysis poses a great challenge for educators, and it is seen in various forms both in and out of educational institutions; these challenges will now be explored.

National unity has been questioned in light of cultural diversity. The argument often presented on this issue goes somewhat like this: if cultural diversity is promoted and supported by the public and governments, then we will have ghettoized ethnic groups; this situation will prevent the formation of national character and a unified country. However, if immigrants were forced to use only an official language of choice and were penalized for using their mother tongue and customs from their country of origin, this would lead quickly to assimilation and the enhancement of national unity. Both scenarios are false and unacceptable, and indeed the arguments are invalid. (For a detailed consideration of this issue, see Magsino, in Chapter 16) So the challenge is how to make immigrants "comfortable", productive, and law-abiding citizens, yet allowing them to maintain their values, customs, and language if they so desire. The situation need not be polarized, yet common ground must be found. It is possible to retain the language of one's ethnic group and nurture the realities of life in Canada simultaneously without being forced to abdicate all sense of self, acquired in another culture. In other words, accommodation can be made by immigrants of the new situation if only because they **chose** to come here for a better life; national unity can be forged from diversity as seen in Switzerland.

The **sharing of power** is at the root of all arguments about diversity; and we should not see diversity as a characteristic of immigrants only, especially those of colour. The French in Quebec and in other provinces such as Manitoba, Ontario, and New Brunswick, constitutes part of this diversity; so too do the Ukrainians, the Germans, the English, the Irish, the Scottish, the Filipinos, the Indians, the West Indians, the Africans, etc. To what extent should organized ethnic or racial groups be allowed to share power in this country? Can the Ukrainians' or the Jews' powerful lobby groups change the course of legislation in this country? A view often expressed about the policy on multiculturalism is that the policy is a mechanism for the federal government to control the activities of immigrants and minority groups. While the accuracy of this claim is contestable, it is clear that the federal government (and others) will create any structures necessary to maintain power over any potential "disruptive" elements. The Canadian Secret Service, the RCMP, and the War Measures Act, are all instruments for protection (against whom?) and maintenance of the status quo; and these powers work well when they are invoked.

The question of **official languages** will continue to be a challenge for this country. Many individuals, groups, and voices from geographic regions (Western Canada) are criticising the policy of two official languages; they advocate English as the only official language. Of course, Quebec will not consider such a proposal unless French is the chosen language! Diversity on this large scale has always divided the soul of Canada and it will continue to do so.

The maintenance or destruction of cultural diversity is complex and has its casualties. The federal and some provincial governments have opted for supporting and maintaining this diversity; the financial cost to Canadians is negligible (compared to our GNP), and participation in most programs is voluntary. However, a major challenge arises when these **two levels of government are required to work co-operatively** for the benefit of immigrants and minority ethnic groups. The problems appear in the forms of power struggles, duplication of services, and lack of a unified vision for our nation. In addition, there are regional disparities which are exacerbated by political allegiances—is it the province or Canada that should come first?

Many people regard Ottawa as the symbolic (and sometimes real) centre of power; but all too often the location of the federal capital is seen as remote; therefore, the real power that affects the everyday lives of common people is the province. Ottawa, however, exerts real power in the form of social programs, and indeed the present "safety nets", such as unemployment insurance, are being reconstituted. Ottawa provides the finances in many areas such as Medicare, the military, social assistance's, etc. Ottawa determines many areas of development through tax breaks for businesses, the level and type of training, and direct funding. While Ottawa does not have jurisdiction over education, it influences directions in the provinces through transfer of payments, direct funding of certain programs such as heritage languages, student loans, and language programs for immigrants. The federal government (Ottawa) is in fact directly involved in education, if education is seen as a means of providing information for the purpose of changing people's actions. For example, public hearings, the media, and government papers on social programs, the budget, fisheries, and national unity are all forms of the Federal presence in education. According to Heather-

Jane Robertson (1994) there are seventeen departments and agencies in the federal government that have admitted involvement specifically in education programs at the elementary and secondary school levels. This creates the "phantom presence" of the national government in educational matters. Education in its broadest sense is a key instrument for the enlightenment of the people, the propagation of ideology, and the maintenance of a superior quality of life in our country. It has not been, and will not be, the sole responsibility of any one government or of any one institution.

Directions for Education

School is one of the most important institutions in our society; it serves as a vehicle for the transmission of our accumulated knowledge and our culture; a place for training both youth and adults; an instrument for the perpetuation of the status quo; and a form of social control through curriculum decisions. In many cases, schools are blamed for the ills of society—the drug problem, violence, delinquency, poor training for the work force, and inadequate preparation for entry to post-secondary education. As pointed out earlier, most people have positive feelings about public schools, but when problems arise, the quick response is to blame this multi-dimensional institution. With the increase in immigration to this country since the turn of the century, the goals and missions of schools have become increasingly complex.

Education for a diverse population has raised very serious questions about the ability of our schools to provide equal opportunity for all Canadians. In developing a school program for a multi-ethnic setting, Wright and Coombs (1981) suggest six areas that may form the basis for dealing reasonably with this very complex task. First, "a conception of person or humanity" must be developed. This involves the recognition of needs—physical, mental, emotional, and moral—which are common to **all** people. Second, "developing a sense of self-worth" in people must be considered so that their values, abilities, and contributions are appreciated in our society. Third, "developing a sense of society" is important because collective rights and responsibilities are key to the cohesion of any community. While there are differences among individuals and groups (even within families) based on any number of factors, there must be shared realities in order to have common goals and a common direction. This is where Canada shines as an example of a successful multicultural society, for even though there are many cultures in this nation, the common threads of rights, responsibilities, productivity, and respect for others bind its people together. Indeed, political ideology also plays an important role in this complex society to the point of threatening the mosaic pattern that now exists. This is the controversial nature of democracy in a diverse society.

Fourth, "developing an understanding of the concepts of 'prejudice', 'stereotyping', and 'racism'" is important. Anyone in any school should (a) understand these terms, (b) know how to detect these phenomena, and (c) know how to deal with them. Fifth, it is suggested that "developing an understanding of what harms people" must be considered because most people get hurt by the same things such as racism, colonization, lack of opportunity, poverty, etc. Psychological harm can be compounded by derisive treatment based on ethnic or cultural background. Finally, "promoting good reasoning" is key because it is important that individuals are convinced about the requirements of social justice through sound reasoning and valid arguments. The proper treatment of others regardless of race, colour, or gender must be grounded in a firm and substantiated belief about the worth of people; a superficial replication of cultural recipe knowledge, often without understanding, leads to a blinding hypocrisy.

The above six principles cut across all cultural and ethnic groups when designing programs. Variations within each principle will be determined by the constraints of community values, goals, and directions. While we must move on to build this nation facing the realities of diversity, we must also be aware of the challenges of multiculturalism.

Friesen (1993) draws our attention to four problem areas regarding the desirability of ethnic diversity. First, ethnic diversity hinders unity; this issue has been reiterated from time to time in spite of the fact that Canada has never been a uniform or homogeneous country even before the European invasion. Yet Canada as a nation has survived and developed into one of the best in the world; is it in spite of, or because of our vibrant diversity? It is probably time to put this criticism behind us and continue to work in developing the just society to which we all aspire.

Second, the political manipulation of the "ethnics" is seen ultimately as a ploy to get votes. Offering grants for cultural festivals, feasts, and heritage language programs are often regarded as "softening up" the immigrant groups for ideological indoctrination. Third, support of cultural diversity through a policy for multiculturalism draws out differences between individuals and groups and emphasizes dissimilarities; this moves us towards ghettoization and setting up barriers between individuals and groups. Yet, in a democratic society there is the basic principle of individual development that clearly leads to disagreement and diversity which form the essence of a culturally rich and creative society.

The fourth criticism of Canada's multicultural policy is directed at the elevation of immigrant groups to the level of "founding nations", the English and the French. In the first place, Aboriginals have major problems with this because they are left out of the "founding nations"; and secondly, Quebec does not subscribe to the concept and principles of multiculturalism because the French do not want to be equated with a minority ethnic group fearing cultural and political devaluation of their current status.

From the above principles (Wright and Coombs, 1981) and criticisms (Friesen, 1993) of cultural diversity one can begin to see the complexity of forging a nation that can practise the virtues of social justice. The uniqueness of Canada is, up to this point, the ability of its people to negotiate and compromise, and to produce principles that allow its people to have a superlative quality of life. Indeed this is not to deny that our "vertical mosaic" which differentiates hierarchical social class is in full operation; one only has to examine the socio-economic situation of Aboriginals and Blacks, for example, to see that intra-nationally, we have many areas that urgently need decisive action.

Working Through Schools

Schools are powerful institutions in the lives of people; they can be used for shaping the attitudes, minds, and directions of individuals and groups. How can schools promote the ideals of a culturally diverse society?

Schools are associated with learning governed by curricula. Curriculum decisions must reflect the knowledge of the cultures represented in the community being served—first the common knowledge and second the differences. How is knowledge constructed? Is the knowledge contained in textbooks taken as truth without questioning the basic assumptions? Teachers must assist students to analyze, evaluate, and criticize the prevailing taken-for-granted cannons of conventional wisdom. This will allow students to construct and legitimize knowledge based on their cultural values, gender, and social class. Banks (1993) identifies five types of knowledge that can be used in structuring the curriculum. These are (a) personal/cultural knowledge which includes concepts derived from home, community, and cultural experiences; (b) popular knowledge that reflects the values and perceptions shaped by the mass media, such as stereotypes of racial and minority groups; (c) mainstream academic knowledge which consists of Eurocentric interpretations of history, social and behaviourial sciences; (d) transformative academic knowledge which questions the basic assumptions and construction of Eurocentric traditional interpretations as seen in the research of postmodernists and feminists; and (e) school knowledge which is the officially sanctioned and legitimized concepts, truths, and half-truths included in subject curricula, overtly and covertly.

Using Banks' typology for constructing curriculum in schools leads us to believe that personal/cultural knowledge should be included in curriculum at all times. Popular knowledge, on the other hand, must be screened for bias regardless of how seductively it is presented; critical thinking skills must be taught to students so that they can do their own analysis of everyday, taken-for-granted beliefs. Mainstream academic knowledge must be examined from the individual's experiences, for example the use of such words as **victory, massacre, settlement**, and **development** in history textbooks must be seen from perspectives other than European. Transformative academic knowledge will help students to see that there are other interpretations of "facts", and to question whether certain statements often taken for granted are "facts" or "truths". Students should be encouraged to investigate the changing criteria for what constitutes knowledge. School knowledge must be questioned, not only its construction, but how it is distributed, packaged, and promoted.

Curriculum is a form of social control (Apple, 1979) and in many cases reproduces the values of the status quo. Cultural diversity in Canada can be promoted by pursuing the construction of **inclusive** curricula. The centrality of curriculum in schooling is of vital importance, because it influences what is taught and learned; this is a key point of intervention in the school system if cultural diversity is to be pursued and practised effectively in this country now and in the future.

Antiracist education is a relatively recent approach to tackling the problems of schooling in a diverse society. This approach is actively concerned with changing institutional policies, structures, and systems that allow or promote racism. Further, it acknowledges the results of racism and other forms of oppression (such as gender and class), and questions the assumed power and privilege of whites; in addition, it seeks to establish an educational system that is more inclusive of minority and Aboriginal concerns. Antiracist education includes students' backgrounds as key to learning, and examines the negation of valuable experiences and knowledge of subordinate groups in the educational system (Dei, 1994).

Policies about education in schools are chiefly developed by school boards with general directions from provincial or territorial governments. Although Canada is a multicultural society emphasis is not placed on making policies that acknowledge or reflect that reality. Sometimes there is a token office with few experts who have responsibilities for race relations, community liaison, or public relations, such as in the Winnipeg School Division and at the Toronto Board of Education. If school boards seriously recognize the need for understanding the complexity of educating people in a diverse society, they will put more resources into developing strategies for demystifying diversity (and its false contradictions) and implementing curriculum that enhances equity, excellence, and self-esteem for all in their jurisdictions.

Providing education for a diverse cultural population is multi-dimensional and must be approached from various vantage points. Some of the main stakeholders in this challenging enterprise are parents. Generally, the parents of immigrant students take the education of their children very seriously. But all too often these parents are ignored or marginalized because school personnel do not believe that they have anything to contribute (Lee, 1985). The bureaucratic structure of schooling must be reorganized to allow all parents to exert influence on what happens to their children; this should not be on a volunteer basis, it should be built into the structure as powersharing; an example of this is in the Province of Manitoba.

Teachers are an integral part of this struggle for equity in education. As a result teachers must first be well-trained in methods and content for teaching a diverse student population. Second, they must have an opportunity to seriously examine, question, and change (if necessary) their own assumptions about students from different racial and ethnic groups. All too often teachers are expected to implement curriculum for which they are not trained. It should be necessary for teacher-training institutions to provide compulsory and elective courses in cross-cultural/multicultural education, both at the pre-service and in-service levels. Teachers' societies and school boards can be of great help in providing workshops that are helpful to teachers. Structural barriers for hiring teachers representing different racial and ethnic groups should be removed in **all** school boards, not only in those that serve a culturally diverse population; programs and courses about cultural diversity are not for "ethnics" only but for the entire population.

Students are the largest group of stakeholders in the educational enterprise, yet they have the least power. Students of colour and from non-English/French speaking countries have even less power. Although some are born here, students of non-European descent tend to suffer from the consequences of negative stereotyping and racism. Self-esteem and pride in one's cultural values are seriously jeopardized; learning suffers, performance levels drop, and those affected either drop out of school or are labelled a "behaviour problem". We then have a situation of dominant and subservient groups rather than social equality, and sometimes the subservient groups organize gangs for self-protection. This situation leads to disruptions in the social system; Adler explains this as follows: "equality (is) a fundamental prerequisite for the logic of social living; without it, there can be no stability or social harmony" (Dreikurs, 1971, p. x). While this provides a simple analysis of the development of disruptive forces beginning with school, the variables affecting this type of outcome are much more complex and entangled. However, the fact is that school plays an important role in shaping the behaviour of all students, especially minority students.

Can education solve the problems and meet the challenges of a culturally diverse society? Not by itself. Even if education did meet its ideals of equity, equality of educational opportunity, and the development of students' potentials to the fullest, it would not do it alone, because education is only one factor that enables the realization of goals. Equally important are other factors such as economic welfare (jobs, stable income), social welfare (access to services and opportunities), sharing of power in the social structure, and self-esteem (pride, respect, self-worth). The combination of all these factors in producing a harmoniously working society will depend on the socio-political, cultural, and economic environment for success; even then, the very nature of democratic societies will produce tensions and contradictions—hopefully these will also provide creative and dynamic solutions.

This New Century

"Quietly the message is being driven home: recent immigrants are Canadians too, and we are here to stay." (*Indo Caribbean World*, 1994, p.4). This quote, from an "ethnic" local newspaper in Toronto, expresses clearly and succinctly a reality that is shared by most immigrants. There are very few immigrants who return to their original homeland, and those who do so, return mostly for retirement. Canadians—especially those in powerful decision-making positions—must take this statement seriously, because it reflects the development of Canada and it could have been made anytime after Europeans first established settle-ments here. What is different today is that Canada has many non-Europeans of colour and this raises serious questions about racism.

In a *Winnipeg Free Press* article, "Immigration policy racist", Jim Carr quotes Tom Denton, head of the Citizenship Council of Manitoba:

> What we have here is a classic example of systemic racism. The current and intended immigration policies, while appearing to be uniform and hence fair for all, in reality, in their application will tend to impact negatively on non-white would-be immigrants. (Nov. 15, 1994, p. A6)

Carr's argument was based on a $500 immigrant applicant fee which most people from Third World countries could not afford. Ponting (1994) argues that although racism in Canada has long been covert and slavery in Canada was not abolished until 1833, "racism has been a long standing feature of Canadian society... (and) for many generations racial discrimination has been structured into key institutions of Canadian society, such as the Immigration Act and other laws, the schools, the ideology, the economy, the real estate market, and the criminal justice system." (pp. 86, 88). Generally Canadians do not wish to face the truth of these statements; instead they wish it would simply go away. However, if immediate radical surgery is not performed to remove the cancerous tumours of systemic racism in our society, the future of this country will see race riots, more police action, a sinister secret service, and an unsafe environment; tensions will rise between racial and ethnic groups, productivity will decline, and the vision of a just society will be eclipsed. How can we begin to prevent such doomsday scenarios?

As an educator I believe that schools have an important role to play in solving this problem. In the new millennium, decision makers will have to **share power** with people of different racial and ethnic groups. The school must be required to promote the intrinsic worth of all people, and this must be done in a very conscious and sensitive way through the curriculum by emphasizing the positive contributions that diverse people make to society (Knight, Smith & Sachs, 1990). Who controls and legitimizes the production of knowledge will become a major issue; this has already started in Halifax, Toronto, and Vancouver. Minority and oppressed gender groups are contesting established ways of knowing, traditional perceptions, and "historical facts". Institutions of learning will be forced to open up their closed systems to new knowledge and research methods in the near future. Ladson-Billings (1994) reports that research shows:

> ... that five areas matter a great deal in the education
> of a multicultural population: teachers' beliefs about
> students, curriculum content and materials, instruct-
> ional approaches, educational settings, and teacher
> education. (p. 22).

While there is some progress in each of these areas, the demands far outweigh the present rate of change. These demands are based on the Charter of Rights and Freedoms; people are now demanding public support for schools to include their religious values and languages; gays and lesbians are demanding their rights according to the law of the land. We are a relatively reasonable and peaceful people, but the future will see many court battles based on the **Charter**; Canada will become even more conscious of individual and group **human rights**.

An issue raised over time by educators and politicians about a federal role in education will be discussed openly and seriously on a larger scale. Indeed, the federal government is already involved in many aspects of education and training throughout the country. The challenge will be how to affirm differences/distinctiveness without separation as in the case of Quebec and First Nations.

Conclusion

The Canadian economy drives all other areas that affect learning and living; in the 1990s, the national debt was over 700 billion dollars, some 40 per cent is owed to foreigners. The media (*Wall Street Journal*, CBC TV, *Winnipeg Free Press*) reported that Canada could easily be an honorary member of the third world, and if the deficit was not reduced, the International Monetary Fund (IMF) would determine fiscal policies in this country. The obsession with deficit reduction and the negative effects of market forces impacted heavily on social/cultural programs. Programs in multicult-uralism, including programs in schools, were adversely affected.

In the year 2000, the Federal Government indicated that the surplus will be in the range of $75 billion. How will this windfall be spent? The bulk will be in the form of tax relief for middle income earners and small businesses. Little of this is actually allocated for social programs such as poverty alleviation, Aboriginal land claim, settlements, appropriate housing for the homeless or refugee assistance. The multicultural secretariat is not even mentioned in spite of potential racial conflicts in several parts of the country. Programs such as English (French) as a second language for immigrants and refugees that were previously cut are not reinstated. This increases the difficulties of newcomers, from countries where English or French is not the first language, to contribute to Canadian society.

Regardless of high levels of education and training, ability, and desire to work, and political ideology, individuals of ethnic minority groups—especially those who are visibly different—will be the majority of the unemployed. The adverse psychological effects that this will have on families will be damaging and may lead to social disruptions in the form of protests, class/race struggles, and violence.

Educators will have great pressures placed on them to "do something" about this situation of discord. There will be less funds, but the public schools will be required to do more in the area of multicultural education. Schools will pay more attention to cultural diversity through curriculum changes although the basic disciplines will take precedence. The inclusive curriculum will become recognized as part of schooling; even so, there will be many more private schools based on race, religion, and political ideology.

The whole effort by the Federal government in multiculturalism will be downplayed. However, the Federal government **will** continue to play a role in promoting cultural diversity, if only to have information about these groups so as to control disruptive activities. As the digital economy expands and globalization becomes cancerous, Canada will be forced to harness the talents of skilled immigrants to maintain our economic competitive edge.

REFERENCES

Apple, Michael. (1979). *Ideology and curriculum.* London: Routledge and Kegan Paul Ltd.

Banks, James A. (Sept. 1993). "Multicultural education: development, dimensions, and challenges." *Phi Delta Kappan.* Vol. 75. No. 1. pp. 22-28.

Carr, Jim. (1994). "Immigration policy racist". *Winnipeg Free Press.* Nov. 15. p. A6.

Dei, George. (1994). "Anti-racist education: Working across differences. Introduction." *Orbit.* Vol. 25., No. 2. pp. 1-3.

Dreikurs, Rudolf. (1971). *Social equality: The challenge today.* Chicago: Contemporary Books, Inc.

Freire, Paulo. (1971). *Pedagogy of the oppressed.* New York: Herder and Herder.

Friesen, J.W. (1993). "Implications of ethnicity for teaching" in Stewin, L. and McCann, S. (Eds.). *Contemporary educational issues the Canadian mosaic.* Second edition. Toronto: Copp Clark Pitman Ltd.

Government of Canada. (1984). *Response of government of Canada to equality now"* . Ottawa: Minister of Supply and Services.

Government of Canada. (1984). *Equality now: Report of the special committee on visible minorities in Canadian society.* Hull, Quebec: Canadian Government Publishing Centre.

Government of Canada. (1987). *Multiculturalism: Building the Canadian mosaic*. Report of the standing committee on multiculturalism. Ottawa: Supply and Services, Canada.

Indo Caribbean World. (July 20, 1994). "*Multicultural signs*". p. 4.

James, Carl E. (1999). *Seeing ourselves: exploring race, ethnicity and culture*. Second Edition. Toronto: Thompson Educational Publishing.

Knight, J.; Smith, R.; and Sachs, J. (1990). "Deconstructing Hegemony: Multicultural policy and a populist response." in Ball, S. (Ed.) *Foucault and education disciplines and knowledge*. London: Routledge pp. 133-152.

Ladson-Billings, G. (May 1994). "What we can learn from multicultural education research". *Educational Leadership*. Vol. 51. No. 8 pp. 22-26.

Lee, Enid. (1985). *Letters to Marcia*. Toronto: Cross Cultural Community.

Magsino, Romulo F. (2000). *The Canadian Mulitculturalism Policy: A Pluralist Ideal Re-visited*. Chapter 16, In this Volume.

Ponting, Rick (1994). "Racial conflict: Turning up the heat". in Glenday, D. and Duffy, A. *Canadian society understanding and surviving in the 1990's*. Toronto: McClelland & Stewart, Inc. pp. 86-116.

Poonwassie, D. H. (August, 1994). "Challenging society through anti-racist education". *Native Issues Monthly*. Vol. 2. No. 7 pp. 44-46.

Robertson, Heather-jane. (1994). "Is there a national role in education? A rationale for the obvious." in Nagy, P., Lupart, J. (Eds.). *Is there a national role in education?* Toronto: The Canadian Education Association and the Canadian Society for the Study of Education.

Statistics Canada. (1994). *Canada's changing immigrant population focus on Canada*. Scarborough, Ontario: Prentice Hall Canada, Inc.

Street, Brian V. (1992). "Literacy and culture" in *Language, policy, literacy and culture*. Paris: UNESCO. pp. 55-61.

Wright, I. and Coombs, J. (1981). *The cogency of multicultural education*. University of British Columbia, Vancouver: Centre for the Study of Curriculum and Instruction.

Chapter 14

IDENTIFYING HUMAN RIGHTS ISSUES FOR THE NEXT DECADE*

John Samuel, Constantine Passaris, Lloyd Stanford, Cyril Dabydeen

I. INTRODUCTION.

The year 1998 marked the 50th anniversary of the *Universal Declaration of Human Rights* adopted by the United Nations General Assembly. The *Declaration* is considered to be the most important and far-reaching document of this century setting the direction for subsequent work in human rights. It is described as "an inspirational cornerstone document in the evolution of human rights in Canada, including the development of the *Canadian Charter of Rights and Freedoms*" (as stated in a release by the Department of Canadian Heritage).

This is an occasion to reflect upon human rights issues which still lie ahead of Canada, seen in the forefront of nations in its human rights record and practices, as evidenced by the United Nations award of the Nansen Medal for the treatment of refugees in the past and recently (March 2, 1998) for the Franklin Delano Roosevelt International Disability Award for the country's policies on persons with disabilities. During the last six consecutive years, Canada has also received the designation by the UN as the best country in the world to live in on the basis of social indicators that take into account the quality of life. While we can rejoice at our success and celebrate the recognition we are receiving for our human rights record, it is also appropriate to attempt to foresee some of the changes in our environment that will be brought about by demographics, globalization, the new economy and the financial constraints on Canadian human rights commissions and their work in the next decade. At the same time, the budgets of federal and provincial human rights commissions in Canada have not increased in proportion to population growth, and in some jurisdictions, they have, in fact, declined.

At the annual conference of Canadian Association of Human Rights Associations in June 1997, it was pointed out by pollster Angus Reid that **human rights organizations are swimming against the current in the new economy of "swim or sink".** His advice was: **"it is better to swim together than alone."** It was also warned at the Conference that human rights organizations are facing a double whammy (Samuel, 1997). On the one hand, complaints related to human rights violations are increasing because of two reasons: (1) the orgy of downsizing due to technological changes and corporate mergers in the private sector, and deficit cutting in the public sector; (2) Canadians are becoming more aware of their human rights and with higher levels of education, the possibility of approaching a human rights agency for redress is increasing. At the same time, the resource base to deal with the complaints is either shrinking or not expanding commensurate with the demand for human rights redress.

This is the context of the current effort to look at some of the issues that Canada would face in the next decade in order to help the human rights organizations to better prepare themselves for changes ahead. The authors of this paper do not pretend to have made a comprehensive survey of all the issues that might come up in the next decade or so. Their purpose is to help to lead appropriate human rights agencies to address fundamental questions rather than supply answers during this phase of the exercise. It is expected that a subsequent phase can provide some of the answers to the questions posed. If the idea of "swimming together" is accepted, answers to those questions using a methodology that is appropriate in consultation with interested human rights commissions can be provided.

This paper has six main sections: performance of Canadian human rights commissions in recent years in terms of complaints, and budgets; human rights and the projected demographic picture; the new economy and its directions; human rights and societal trends; conclusions; a list of questions to be developed in cooperation with the Canadian Human Rights Commission (CHRC) to be answered in any future work. What this paper tries to do is to provoke thoughts among human rights policy and program officials and other interested parties to formulate some of the appropriate questions related to the emerging environment. In this paper, we have chosen to focus upon the following:

II. Performance of Human Rights Commissions in Canada

The number of complaints received or accepted by human rights agencies could be compared for periods 1989-90 and 1995-96, bearing in mind that some of these agencies did not accept all the complaints that were received for lack of resources. If the number of such complaints accepted by the federal agency and one provincial agency from each of the five regions (Ontario, Quebec, BC, Alberta and Nova Scotia) are added up, during the period in question the number of complaints rose about 68 percent (Samuel, 1997, p.11).

An analysis of the resources available to meet such an increased demand for their services might be appropriate. Between 1991 and 1996, Canada's population grew by 11 percent. The growth of the groups that require interventions by statutory human rights agencies was much higher than 11 percent. However, resources allocated for human rights agencies during approximately the same period decreased by 16 percent for CHRC. The resources base shrunk 23.1 percent for Ontario, 11.1 percent for Quebec, and did not grow at all for Nova Scotia. Only BC, and to some extent Alberta, showed an increase.

II.1 Human Rights Challenges

Human rights commissions will be confronted with significant challenges during the coming decade. Their success will depend on their ability to redirect their resources, adopt a new agenda for human rights, and embrace a proactive strategy for achieving their objectives. This decade should be viewed in the context of doing more with less, widening the circle of human rights protection, identifying new priorities, and enhancing the efforts of human rights commissions toward a proactive approach to human rights education and community awareness about human rights issues. In short, human rights commissions will be required to go through the fundamental process of renewal in order to enhance their ability to protect and promote human rights in the next decade.

II. 2 Leadership, Vision and Strategy

The three essential ingredients for the efficient and effective operation of human rights commissions in the next decade are **leadership, vision and strategy development**. More specifically new ideas, new directions and new initiatives must become the fundamental building blocks for an innovative style of effective and capable leadership, an inspiring and proactive vision for human rights and sound, workable strategies.

Human rights commissions have an important leadership role in setting the agenda for human rights discourse and practice. It is worth noting that the human rights agenda has been evolving during the last two decades and will continue to do so in the next decade. It is anticipated that the human rights agenda at the beginning of the new century will require leadership from human rights commissions in response to the structural changes in the Canadian economy and society. Demographic trends, globalization, and the advent of the information society and rapid advances in information technology and urbanization, have raised new issues in the definition, interpretation and implementation of human rights policies and programs. These are just a few examples of the issues that will become increasingly more prominent in the human rights agenda of the next decade. This will require all Canadian human rights commissions to provide enlightened leadership in addressing these issues. They will also be called upon to provide capable leadership in finding a balance between individual and collective rights and advancing the human rights agenda regarding economic and social rights.

II. 3 Proactive Approach

Articulating an inspired and proactive vision for human rights in the next decade should become a major pre-occupation of human rights commissions. It should be a vision that enhances public awareness about the many significant features that unite Canadians across this vast and diverse country. The vision should affirm the fundamental principles and values of human rights.

Leadership and vision should be accompanied by the development and implementation of effective strategies. The strategies should be designed to deal with the national and international economic, social and cultural environments. The policies and programs developed should be realistic and down-to-earth. The experience gained in the last 50 years and lessons learned both nationally and internationally must be taken into account in the development of such strategies.

Human rights commissions ought to become a powerful force promoting a human rights culture in a continually evolving Canadian society. The implementation of a proactive and purposeful vision for human rights will require commissions to have innovative strategies to combat discrimination and promote equality empowered with a more effective arsenal of tools. This cannot be accomplished in a passive and reactive manner. It requires becoming strong advocates of an inspiring vision that promotes the fundamental human rights principles of justice, fairness, tolerance, equality, acceptance, inclusion, respect, accommodation and humanity as the centrepieces of social, economic and educational policies. Ultimately, it is these human rights principles and values which are the most enduring foundation upon which nation-building can flourish and prosper in a Canada that will advance leadership in the world.

II. 4 Workloads and Resources

The next decade will be a defining one for Canadian human rights commissions. This decade will demand from human rights commissions innovative and creative solutions to the paramount challenge of meeting their mission and mandate in an era of financial restraints and human resource downsizing on the one hand, and on the other, an increased work load of complaints' adjudication and a more prominent role in public education. This will most likely result in the evolution of human rights commissions from considering themselves as sole champions of human rights toward an emphasis on building partnerships (except in adjudicating individual complaints) with the public, private and non-government/volunteer sectors in the adjudication of individual complaints of discrimination and the delivery of their public education programs.

During the past two decades, human rights commissions have had to contend with a substantial increase in workloads at a time when these government agencies have had to absorb restraints in the appropriation of government financial and human resources. There is no denying that the general public has become better informed about human rights and has turned in increasing numbers to human rights commissions to redress grievances of discrimination and inequality. The complaint adjudication process, in addition to a quantitative increase in complaints, has also faced a qualitative increase in workloads.

More specifically, the addition of new grounds of discrimination in human rights legislation has broadened the scope of human rights protection for the more vulnerable disadvantaged and minority groups. Furthermore, the emergence of a larger number of complaints dealing with "compound" discrimination, such as that of a black woman who has experienced discrimination as a woman and as a black person, is another feature of the qualitative increase in workloads. At the same time, the complex nature of recent complaints has made the conciliation process more challenging and consequently more labour-intensive.

As the next decade is anticipated to increase the quantitative and qualitative workloads of all Canadian human rights commissions as vulnerable groups demand and achieve human rights protection, the evolutionary process of widening the circle of protection will bring about increased demands on the already strained human and financial resources allocated to human rights commissions. The qualitative difficulties enveloped in the interface and complexity of human rights complaints is also anticipated to become more intense and result in an increased workload. The consequence of all this is the likelihood of backlogs and long delays in the complaint adjudication process and a strong affirmation of the maxim that "justice delayed is justice denied" unless innovative and creative solutions are found. The scope, complexity and rapidly changing nature of human rights issues will require appointed commissioners and full-time staff to undertake retraining and skill enhancement on a regular and frequent basis.

As a consequence of workload pressures and fiscal restraints applied by governments, an imbalance in the appropriation of funds and resources between the complaint handling and educational functions of human rights commissions has developed. It is a sad commentary that, at a time when educational branches are being provided with dwindling financial resources, they are experiencing an increase in the demand for their expertise and resources by employers, unions, government departments, comm-unity groups, volunteer organizations, educational institutions and a host of other institutions that turn to human rights commissions for support and guidance.

II. 5 Education and Compliance Strategies

In the short-term and more expedient solution practiced by human rights agencies has been to allocate proportionately more resources to their complaint branches at the expense of their educational agenda. This is a short-term band-aid solution that is not conducive to a longer term and ultimately more cost-effective solution. The next decade will require a competent and far-reaching resolution of this dilemma in favour of a more appropriate balance in resource allocations for the complaint and educational branches that is effective and efficient to provide sustenance to the proactive educational approach. The next decade must also develop a new strategy for human rights commissions that encompasses the interdependence and complementarity of their compliance and educational agendas. Human rights commissions should be guided by three objectives in the resolution of human rights complaints: 1) simplify the process, 2) streamline the administrative functions, and 3) speed up the conciliation and adjudication phase. All of this must be done without compromising the confidentiality of the system and at the same time reducing the hurt and trauma experienced by individual complainants seeking redress. Educational branches on the other hand need to develop a proactive educational agenda whose implementation will require building partnerships with the private and public sectors as well as educational institutions and community organizations. All of this should reflect the regional differences in human rights issues within the context of the Canadian diversity of the twenty-first century.

III. Human Rights and the Demographic Picture

The different human rights commissions in Canada were not unanimous in their mandate regarding the areas in which to receive complaints on human rights violations. Focusing attention on the two largest human rights commissions—the Canadian and Ontario Commissions—according to statistics available the most common bases for complaints to the CHRC were (in 1994) in order of importance: disability, sex, age, race/colour, national/ethnic origin, family/marital status, sexual orientation and religion. For the Ontario Human Rights Commission (1988-89) they were disability, sex, race/colour, age, family/marital status and ethnic origin, and creed in that order.

A good knowledge of the demographic characteristics of a population, the basis of evaluating any society, is necessary in order to analyze and determine issues that could lead to development of policies and programs that produce results. When one tries to examine potential issues of the future, this information is vital. The size and characteristics of the population relevant to human rights violations and consequent complaints can be gleaned from population projections. In this section we will examine the projected growth for the total population of Canada with gender breakdowns; of the Aboriginal population, visible minorities, persons with work disabilities, seniors, foreign born, selected religious groups, and others such as poverty and homosexuality trends during the next decade or so.

III. 1 Projected Canadian population

Canada's population is projected to grow from 29.9 million in 1996 to 35.4 million in 2011, an increase of 18.4 percent in 15 years (George, M.V. et al., 1994, p.67). Normally, a larger population would create more human rights complaints than a smaller population, other things remaining the same. This level of population growth is occurring more because of international migration and not because of natural increase (births minus deaths). For instance in 1993-94, natural increase contributed 47.6 percent of the population growth while by 2011 this will only be 14.3 percent. Such a change in the components of population growth has important implications for human rights, as will be seen later.

In the context of human rights issues, the sex distribution of the population is very important. During the period 1996 to 2011, the female population is projected to grow by 20.0 percent compared to a growth of 16.2 percent for males. For a better appreciation of the issues to be faced, the age distribution of the female population needs to be looked into. Issues of gender discrimination generally, pregnancy and pay equity-related issues in particular would loom larger in the years to come.

III. 2 Projected aboriginal population

The projections, prepared by Statistics Canada, for the Aboriginal population are to the year 2016 (Norris, 1995). The numbers used here are projections of the population with Aboriginal origins or ancestry based on the 1991 Census. In 1991, 1.1 million persons (adjusted by Statistics Canada for incomplete enumeration and undercoverage) indicated at least one Aboriginal ancestry.

The population with Aboriginal ancestry is expected to increase from 1.1 million 1991 to 1.6 million by the year 2016 under a medium-low growth scenario, almost a 50 percent increase. This scenario reflects a continuation of the current trends: that is "a rapid decline in fertility and a decline in mortality combined with a continuation of current residential and regional migration patterns" (*Ibid*, p.252).

Between 1991 and 2016, given the continuation of current trends, the registered Indian component of the Aboriginal population is expected to grow by 64 percent, from 254,000 to 418,000. The Aboriginal population is much younger than the Canadian population in general and is becoming more educated. When the Canadian population had a median age of 34 in 1991, the Aboriginal population had a median age of 22.5 (*Ibid*, p.255). Ontario, BC and Alberta had, and will continue to have, the highest number of Aboriginal Canadians. However, in terms of proportions they would be most numerous in the Northwest Territories (63%), the Yukon (25%), Saskatchewan and Manitoba (15% each).

III. 3 Projected visible minority population

The visible minority population in Canada has grown by leaps and bounds after changes in immigration policy in the sixties. The immigration levels have increased annually from 84,000 in 1985 to 225,000 in 1996. Though some changes are in the offing for the immigration program, according to official statements, the levels are not likely to be affected.

According to Statistics Canada projections, the visible minorities are likely to increase in numbers from 3.2 million in 1996 to 6.3 million in 2011, an increase of almost 100 percent in 15 years (Dai, S. Y. and George, M.V., 1996).

III. 4 Projection of persons with disabilities

In 1991, one out of six Canadians had one or more

disabilities. Up to 80 percent of those who wanted to join the labour force could not do so. The unemployment of Canadians with a disability is twice that of able-bodied Canadians. Over half of all the working age persons with disabilities had incomes under $10,000. They also face additional expenses related to these disabilities.

Statistics Canada has projected Canada's population with work disabilities. According to the medium projections (considered to be most likely), their numbers are to rise from 1.4 million in 1993 to 2.0 million in 2011, a 43.7 percent rise in 18 years (Statistics Canada, 1996, p.29).

Ontario is expected to have 41.7 percent of persons with work disabilities, distantly followed by British Columbia with 15.8 percent, Quebec with 15.4 percent and Alberta with 11.7 percent (*Ibid,* p.33).

III. 5 Projected number of seniors

As is well known, Canadian society is aging and issues related to aging should become more important for Canadians. The median age of the population in 1996 was 35.1, and this is expected to rise steadily to 37.0 in 2001, 38.4 in 2006 and 39.5 by 2011 (George *et al.*, 1994, p.71).

The number of seniors (the 65 and over age group) will rise from 3.2 million in 1991 to 5.0 million in 2011, an increase of 56.3 percent (*Ibid*: p.73). This is much higher than the rate of growth of the total population during the same period.

The baby boomers are now entering the 50 plus age group. The group will grow from 14 percent of the labour force to 28 percent in the next 20-30 years. We have not seen its impact as yet, but will very soon. At the same time the downsizing in the economy has affected the older persons much more than the others. Even in a low-unemployment economy as that of the US, of the 10 million or so unemployed older workers, a quarter are willing and able to work. The vast majority of them have substantial skills and education, could work in high-demand occupations, and are flexible about conditions of employment. Unfortunately, they cannot find work. A higher-unemployment economy in Canada would be much worse for older workers.

III. 6 Projected number of foreign born

In 1996 there were about 5 million foreign born in Canada of whom over a million had come during 1991-1996. The arrival of the over one million during that period raised their proportion in the population from 16.0 percent in 1991 to 17.4 percent in 1996. In the period 1997-2011, it is assumed that the average annual level of immigration would be 225, 000. This takes into account the fact that the average level of immigration for 1994-1997 was 225, 000, and that is the level envisaged for 1998 as well. Official pronouncements indicate that this level may continue in future years. Assuming that their mortality (though the mortality rate may have declined a little, it is not significant enough to make a great deal of difference) and re-migration rates are the same as for immigrants who came during the period 1961-1996, the 3.6 million or so immigrants who would arrive during the period 1997-2011 would raise the proportion of the foreign born in the population somewhat significantly, given the low fertility rate. Ontario and BC will be the main provinces of their concentration.

III. 7 Projection of persons in selected religious groups

Liberalized immigration policies have brought several non-Christian religious groups to the shores of Canada. The major groups are Islam, Hindu, Sikh and Buddhist. An examination of the 1981 and 1991 censuses (latest available) shows that their numbers have increased significantly during the period. Their numbers were very small in 1971 and almost non existent in censuses before 1971.

There are no available official projections for these religious groups. However, if one assumes that their numbers will continue to increase at the same rate as they did in 1981-91 period, Canada could have the numbers shown in Table 1. The projected numbers in the columns for 2001 and 2011 assume that the Buddhist will grow two fold every decade (as they did in 1981-91), the Hindus and Sikhs will grow 2.2 times in a decade and the Muslims (those who follow Islam) by 2.6 times per decade.

It is obvious that these religious groups will show very high growth rates based on the assumption that immigration levels and sources will continue to remain the same as before. It should be remembered that the growth will come also as a result of natural increase within these religious groups. They are expected to add up to about 11 percent of Canadian population—roughly the same proportion as visible minorities in Canadian population in 1996.

Table 1. Projections of selected religious groups to 2011

		Actual		Projected	
Religious Group	1981	1991 (000s)		2001	2011
Buddhist	52	163		326	652
Hindu	70	157		345	759
Islam	98	253		658	1710
Sikh	68	147		323	711
Total	**288**	**720**		**1652**	**3832**

(Statistics Canada, *1981 Census: Population: Religion*, Cat. 92-912, pp. 1-9 to 1-11; *Religions in Canada: The Nation, 1991 Census*, Cat. 93-319, pp. 14-15; Projections by John Samuel & Associates Inc.)

III. 8 Poverty trends

Michelle Falardeau-Ramsey, Canadian Human Rights Commission's Chair, soon after taking office had suggested that poverty be considered for inclusion as a factor that would cause discrimination. It is only too well known how the poor do not get a fair treatment in society. In 1993, about 1.4 million children alone were caught in the poverty trap. A Metro Toronto task force on services pointed out that young children living in poorest neighborhoods suffer a disproportionate share of the City's recorded incidents of abuse, school absenteeism, teen-aged parenthood and attempted suicide (Samuel, 1997, p.5).

The definition of the term "poverty" has not been easy. There is no internationally accepted definition of poverty unlike for terms such as "employment", "unemployment", "gross domestic product", "consumer prices", as Canada's Chief Statistician Ivan Fellegi pointed out (*The Daily*, Dec. 8, 1997). In Canada, Statistics Canada's Low Income Cut-Offs (LICOs) has been used as demarcating the poverty line. Statistics Canada explains LICOs "as income levels at which families spend 20% of their income more than the average family on food, shelter and clothing" (Clarke, 1991: i). "They reflect consistent and well-defined methodology that identifies those who are substantially worse off than the average" (*Ibid*, p.2).

The following table shows the number and proportion of low

income persons in Canada from 1989 to 1996.

Table 2. Low Income Persons in Canada, 1989-1996

Year	No. of persons (000s)	Percentage
1989	3,779	14.1
1990	4,179	15.4
1991	4,543	16.5
1992	4,757	17.0
1993	5,143	18.0
1994	4,941	17.1
1995	5,205	17.8
1996	5,294	17.9

(Statistics Canada, *The Daily*, Dec. 26, 1997, pp. 8-9)

As seen in the table above, the proportion of the poor has been in the range of 14 to 18 percent of the population. Among the significant variables that affect poverty are the rate of growth of the economy, unemployment rate, social programs to ameliorate poverty, the tax system, and other relevant socioeconomic factors. It is not easy to predict any of these in the context of the New Economy and the international competition for goods and services through globalization. At best one could only estimate that the percentage of those below the poverty line could be somewhere between 14 and 18 percent. In order to arrive at a single percentage for projection purposes, the average of the two (somewhat optimistically) at 16 percent is assumed to be the proportion of the poor in the year 2011. Applying this to the total population we arrive at 5.7 million as the probable number of the poor in 2011 indicating that the poor will be always in our midst. Their numbers would have risen by 7.5 percent over 1996.

III. 9 Trends in Homosexual Population

There are no projections for the homosexual population available. Even their current proportion in the total population is not known. What is known is that "homosexuality is immutable, and non-pathological, and a growing body of more recent evidence implicates biology in the development of sexual orientation" (Burr,

1993, p.65). When more and more people are coming out the so-called closet to declare their homosexuality openly, one is forced to look at sexual orientation in a more open light. It is certain that the human rights of homosexuals would require more attention too. It is difficult to estimate how fast the homosexual population would grow, however.

IV. Human Rights and the Economy

The single most important defining feature of the Canadian economy during the first decade of the twenty-first century will be the growth of the information technology sector and in consequence the human rights issues congruent with a vibrant and dynamic information society. The advent of the information technology sector as the engine of economic growth for the Canadian economy in the twenty-first century is also a vivid illustration of the confluence of economic and social policy from a human rights perspective. These changes will also require closer cooperation between human rights commissions and the privacy commissions.

Information technology sector will emerge in the next decade as the principal economic sector to generate the largest number of employment opportunities. In this regard, human rights commissions can anticipate an increase in workplace-related complaints of discrimination from the information-technology sector. Furthermore, the nature of the product and wider dissemination of the services of the information-technology sector will require a more avant-garde interpretation of existing human rights legislation as well as demands for the introduction of new legislation to confront the human rights abuses and discriminatory practices of the information age.

IV. 1 Globalization

An adjunct of the predominance of the information technology sector will be the continued emphasis on the economics of globalization. International economic relations and the affirmation of free trade initiatives between trading partners, trading blocks and geographic regions from a global perspective will contribute to the debate on human rights. The Canadian economy in the next decade will be susceptible to the economic emphasis on globalization. Indeed, Canada will be under increased scrutiny to choose between the two prevailing schools of thought: The first school of thought that promotes the vision that countries should engage in international trade despite the divergence in human rights protection with a view to encouraging those countries with a poor human rights record to a higher level of human rights enforcement. The second school of thought which emphasizes the need to adopt an economic embargo against countries that do not comply with international standards of human rights compliance. However, Canadian human rights commissions will not have to deal with these issues directly.

IV. 2 Workplace-Related Complaints

By far, the largest number of individual complaints filed with Canadian human rights commissions concern discrimination in the workplace. The range of human rights violations and abuses that surface in the workplace include sexual harassment, sexist or racist behaviours in the form of slurs, jokes, graffiti or expression of hate; denial of equal opportunity for women or minority groups; discrimination on the basis of sexual orientation; refusal to make a workplace accessible to an employee or a client with a disability; unequal treatment because of a pregnancy; denial of employment opportunities for visible minorities; and pay disparity between men and women. Workplace related complaints are expected to increase during the next decade.

IV. 3 Economic Rights

The next decade will require human rights commissions to provide more capable leadership and a more enlightened vision regarding economic rights. The increasing number of complaints about discrimination in the workplace suggest that the passive and reactive approach practised by human rights commissions during the recent past has been ineffective. Furthermore, the large number of complaints arising out of abuses of workers rights points to a disturbing pattern of overt and covert discrimination in the workplace and a poisoned work environment with negative side effects in terms of weak economic performance. It is therefore incumbent on human rights commissions to endorse a more proactive approach in the promotion and protection of economic rights in order to achieve a more positive record of accomplishments in this vital area of provincial and national economic prosperity.

The rights of labour unions to protect and enhance their interests are among the economic rights. In the US particularly and also in Canada, some multinationals have moved aggressively against unions aiming to tame them or maim them. In Canada, the employment earnings of workers under age 35 have declined substantially since the late 1970s. Those who lost their jobs were believed to be those who could not deliver "a fair day's work for a fair day's pay".

IV. 4 Social and Economic Linkages.

Human rights continue to be perceived as an appendix of social policy. The fact of the matter is that human rights are a prime example of the interlinkages and interdependence between social policy and economic policy. The respect and promotion of human rights principles and values in the workplace and the economy in general are the only guarantees of cohesion and harmony in a multicultural and multiracial workforce, of a greater acceptance of gender equality, of the enhanced participation of persons with disabilities, and of the accommodation of other disadvantaged and vulnerable groups that have been the targets of historical and systemic discrimination. In short, the strong endorsement of human rights in the workplace is the most effective guarantee for the full and efficient utilization of our human resources with all their talents, creativity and expertise and the promotion of a work ethic that is conducive to economic success and prosperity.

Worker and employer education in human rights and the promotion of a human rights culture in the economy are fundamental prerequisites in establishing an economic synergy that promotes a dynamic, productive, respectful and harmonious work environment. Human rights commissions must be prepared to assume the role of an economic catalyst and a proactive agent for the promotion and development in the workplace of sexual harassment policies, employment equity programs, affirmative action plans, policies on reasonable accommodation and pay equity. Indeed, one cannot emphasize enough the need for adopting and respecting human rights principles and values in the workplace.

IV. 5 Human Rights Culture in Business

The protection and promotion of human rights in the workplace are no longer simply a moral or ethical issue; within the demographic realities and financial constraints of the next decade, it is a fundamental prerequisite for business and economic success. Indeed, the degree to which the workplace is sensitive and responsive to gender equality and the various forms of diversity will determine success or failure in the highly competitive environment of the next decade. There is no denying that customer preferences and services demand from business corporations and government departments and agencies require a higher level of conformity to human rights principles and values. In short, respecting and promoting a human rights culture in the workplace is essential to safeguarding one's competitive edge in the domestic and global markets and ensuring qualitative excellence in the services provided.

IV. 6 Managing Diversity

In the next decade, managing diversity effectively will be a key precondition for economic success. Globalization and economic interdependence have forced us to deal with people of different cultures and languages. Canada's workforce is becoming increasingly heterogeneous and demographic projections reveal that our population and workforce in the next decade will be significantly more culturally and racially diverse. The deepening and broadening of Canada's ethnic, cultural and religious diversity in the workforce offers unique challenges and magnificent opportunities. The ability to cope with diversity and use it to economic advantage is a skill that is becoming increasingly more important.

Diversity is a unique economic asset and a powerful force that can contribute to our competitive edge. Our future economic well being will require that special attention be given to those who find themselves at the margins of the working population: women, certain groups of immigrants, visible minorities, persons with disability, people with low levels of education, the poor and aboriginal people. Discrimination in the workplace against such persons is a violation of their economic rights. It represents a significant loss to the nation of the potential talents, creativity and contribution of our valuable human resources.

IV. 7 Employment and Pay Equity Strategies

Human rights agencies must assume the educational role of promoting a greater awareness that employment equity programs are not about preferential treatment but rather about creating a level playing field that affords equal opportunity. Effective strategies for employment equity policies must promote the full and equal participation of all in the economic opportunities and rewards. It must contribute toward breaking the glass ceiling, dispersing the clustering of women and minorities in some occupations and sectors, and correcting the under-representation of women, minority groups, persons with disabilities, and Aboriginal persons from the decision-making process and from the corporate boardrooms. The recent federal court decision on pay equity is probably an indication of the change in the direction in which the wind is blowing for human rights agencies.

IV. 8 Government and Corporate Downsizing

The process of public and private sector downsizing, re-engineering and restructuring contributes to economic stresses that often find recourse to human rights commissions for alleged human rights violations. These conditions are likely to continue into the next decade with the consequential increase in workplace-related human rights complaints. The overall economic malaise particularly in terms of weak employment opportunities is also conducive to an increase in human rights complaints. In short, the next decade will result in human rights commissions facing increasing pressures to make greater advances in economic rights, the new frontier of human rights. The role of the Canadian Human Rights Commission as Canada's dominant human rights agency, both multi-laterally and bi-laterally, promoting the creation and strengthening of national human rights institutions needs to be noted.

V. Human Rights and Society

The areas that will be looked into here are the international context, public education, school curriculum, human rights in schools, the media and human rights tribunals.

V.1 The international context

As a signatory to the UN convention on human rights, Canada bears an enormous moral and legal responsibility. Because, despite the fact that such instruments of emerging public international law do not have the force of national law and the sanctions that give domestic law its coercive power, the reputation Canada enjoys in world affairs as a civilised and progressive middle power obliges it to be a model in its human rights record.

This global context in which Canada's human rights record and current initiatives is to be viewed is at once universal—the UN's declaration which covers political and economic rights—and "regional". Specifically, Canada is an active participant in the UN's human rights activities, as evidenced by Dr. Maxwell Yalden's membership of the UN Human Rights Tribunal. Canada also was one of the chief architects of the Harare Declaration of 1991 which provides the normative framework for good "governance" in Commonwealth countries. Indeed the principles enshrined in this document are meant to guide the actions of the respective countries of the Commonwealth in their treatment of their residents, notably of their minorities. At the operational or "functional" level, Canada has integrated human rights considerations into the conduct of its foreign policy, notably in the field of aid to developing countries. On the non-governmental front, prominent Canadians are active in organisations like Human Rights Watch that endeavour to keep countries on their toes.

V.2 Public Education about Human Rights

One of the imperatives of good governance is active education of the general public about human rights. A corresponding obligation falls on governmental authorities to ensure that their military and civilian personnel are sensitised to the human rights dimension of their services to the public and the administration of their organisations.

In practical terms for Canadians, the three levels of government should be involved in active public education campaigns, primarily through their respective departments of citizenship and the human rights commissions. This task assumes greater urgency as the population becomes more diverse, mostly because of governments' liberalized immigration policies (referred to above) and increased international migration of peoples. This diversity affects both the clientele and the staff of public service agencies and private companies. The most palpable outcome of the exercise of these rights is that of earning a living. The challenge of employment equity remains paramount, especially when more highly educated immigrants and their progeny enter the work force. It is perhaps noteworthy that human rights commissions typically have an explicit mandate to engage in public education and advocacy of human rights.

V.3 The School Curriculum

One potential forum for increasing awareness of human rights issues is the school curriculum. It could even be argued that it is the quintessential medium for public education as it is practised. Educators will probably differ about philosophy and approach as well as on technical points of pedagogy, but there is likely to be agreement that some elements of "multiculturalism in education" might profitably be introduced early in the curriculum—ones that would at least attenuate if not eradicate stereotypes and prepare pupils to be more conscious of the worth and dignity of their classmates of different colours, and of cultural and religious backgrounds from their own. The idea of introducing courses in human rights in university courses, or offering a B.A. in human rights is being mooted in some quarters. Human rights commissions may have at least an employers' interest in such a development in curriculum planning, particularly in the new millennium.

V. 4 Human Rights in Schools

A corollary of the attempt to inculcate notions of fundamental human rights in the minds of the young would be advancing the best human rights practices in educational administration. This is an area that will require increased attention, both at the administrative and the classroom levels. Some commissions have already been hearing from teachers about alleged discrimination on the job. This could become exacerbated. Nevertheless, it appears that the greatest challenge will come in sensitising the "mainstream" teachers to the importance of their wards of minority origin having equal access to a first-class education and, thereby, enhancing their prospects of finding good employment. This issue should not be considered as being a mere "immigrant" one. It seems to be one central to the training of First

Nations youth and youngsters of colour. (It is difficult to envisage how some of these complaints would be formulated and how they would be handled but class actions emanating from parents or student councils are not inconceivable.)

V. 5 Human Rights Tribunals

The tribunals have a potential for enhancing the enjoyment of human rights in Canada. They could, for example, help in the 'oversight' of governmental implementation of legislation, as in the case of the regime contemplated for the new federal *Employment Equity Act.* However, two aspects of the way these administrative tribunals operate bear scrutiny: the length of time spent on cases, and the number of lawyers who serve on them. Some observers see a direct causal relationship between the two. Furthermore, the courts are being increasingly called to review tribunal decisions and therefore the presence of a lawyer on tribunals is a necessity.

It is possible that tribunals will lose credibility if they proceed no faster or different than the courts, and because of the predominance of lawyers in the process, make their decisions based on narrow legalisms. The result could be that, justice delayed is justice denied, especially when the backlog in cases at most commissions is considerable.

VI. Conclusions

In the paradigm shift currently taking place in a "swim or sink" kind of economy and society, the predictions made at one time that discrimination will decline does not seem to be true any more. Employment discrimination in particular has become worse for many groups. It is increasingly becoming difficult to achieve equality of employment opportunities in a society that is becoming more conservative and more likely to turn a blind eye on rights violations. As noted by the Chief Commissioner of the CHRC, "technological developments and other wonders of modernization have failed to reverse growing disparities between North and South, rich and poor, those who can afford rights and those for whom the world has little practical meaning" (Falardeau-Ramsay, as quoted by Samuel, 1997, p.13).

Acknowledgments

*This article was originally submitted in 1998 as a Report to the Canadian Human Rights Commission. The authors gratefully acknowledge the funding provided for this work by the Canadian Human Rights Commission in Ottawa.

REFERENCES:

Burr, Chandler. (1993). "Sexual Orientation", *The Atlantic Monthly*, 272:3

Clarke, Michelle. (1991). *Fighting Poverty Through Programs*. Ottawa: CEJY.

Dai, S.Y. and George M. V. (1995). *Projection of Visible Minority Population Groups, Canada, Provinces and Regions, 1991-2016*, Ottawa: Statistics Canada.

Fellegi, Ivan. (1997). "On Poverty and Low Income", *The Daily*, December 8.

Norris, Mary Jane. (1995). *Projections of Aboriginal Populations in Canada, 1991-2016: Trends and Issues*, Ottawa: Statistics Canada.

Samuel, John. (1997). "The Changing Workplace: Downsizing, Reightsizing and Rights", Presentation to CASHRA, Toronto, June.

Statistics Canada (1997). *The Daily*, Ottawa.

----------------(1996). *Projections of Persons with Disabilities (Limited at Work/Perception), Canada, Provinces and Territories, 1993-2016*. Ottawa.

----------------(1995). *Annual Demographic Statistics, 1994*, Ottawa.

Chapter 15

CONTESTING THE FUTURE:
ANTI-RACISM AND DIVERSITY

George J. Sefa Dei

I. INTRODUCTION

This article is arguing for the necessity of a new paradigm with which to analyse and deal with Canadian diversity. In presenting an analytical model that stands as an alternative to the dominant liberal-multicultural approaches employed today, I attempt to acknowledge the significance of, as well as examine, issues concerning Canadian diversity. In the current political and ideological climate of Canadian nationhood and 'democratic citizenship' there are several discursive tropes to articulate the rights and responsibilities of belonging to the collective. Anti-racism as a discursive and political practice offers one possible trope for those who maintain that race and difference (ethnicity, gender, class, sexuality, ability, language, religion and culture) provide the context for power and social domination. Thus, anti-racism is presented in this essay as an educational approach to social change; an approach that is not to be seen as a liberal methodology. It is not simple ignorance, behaviors, or attitudes that anti-racist education focuses upon, rather, herein, education is seen as a pedagogy of empowerment. A pedagogy that provides people with the analytical, tools, methods to contribute to making structural change in society. Anti-racist education attempts to broaden hegemonic understandings of education. It expands the realm of education to every area of knowledge production and organization. My academic and political project is to use anti-racism to articulate a broad-based political coalition that will transform the social, political and economic agenda and priorities of the Canadian 'nation' in the face of social diversity. My objective is driven by three main questions: First, an understanding of the current state of race relations in our diverse society. Here, I am specifically interested in questioning the 'denial of the significance of race' in society. Secondly, what I see as the preferred future in terms of the creation of an open and equal opportunity society: that is, creating challenges to ensure that equity and justice transcend the rhetoric and lip service into concrete political action. Equal opportunities cannot be achieved without equal conditions, and unequal starting points for people cannot be absolved as easy as making everybody equal under the rhetoric of meritocracy. And thirdly, how we go about achieving that ideal, the preferred future state for the 21st century; that is, the imperative of working collectively and the approaches required for this endeavour.

In this discussion I purposely use the collective 'we' to implicate all who read the paper and join in the politics being pursued. It is often said that a history must teach us something otherwise it is not a history worth talking about. Any academic work on anti-racism builds on a long history and tradition of intellectual scholarship and community politics. Using history as a starting point my objective is not to rehash existing knowledge, but to extend the discussion of anti-racism to think through issues of 'diversity and difference' as we engage the new Millennium. There is the long history of community struggles and battles waged by Canadian parents, students and educators of diverse racial, ethnic, religious, class, sexual and gender backgrounds to ensure that society responds concretely to the ideals of 'democratic citizenship Within local communities there exist rich accounts of coalition political organizing informed by academic and intellectual discourse to effect social change. Today, the desire to share and create a new 'community' has ushered in critical and alternative ways of understanding 'diversity and difference'.

Each and everyone of us is affected by racism and other oppressions. Dyer (1997) argues that while we may not all necessarily invent racist thoughts, we are affected by racist ideologies and practices. We must, therefore, always speak out and challenge race and power hierarchies that maintain oppressions in society. In seeking to create a new community we must focus on the collective responsibilities and complicities in the production, maintenance and sustaining of oppressions. Any discourse that excludes discussions of individual and collective complicities and responsibilities in the maintenance and removal of injustices cannot be truly transformative. Dominance is achieved through the maintenance of invisibility. Therefore, political change must make visible that which is rendered invisible.

Park (1999) notes that race identity and power are multi-relational. Equity cannot occur when politics exclude. Progressive politics must therefore focus on the "construction of interlocking power hierarchies". A critical discourse of anti-racism cannot 'exclude'. The understanding of the specific ways social groups are differentially racialized in Canadian contexts allows us to develop an effective politics for equity and social change. The complex and contradictory constructions of racial hierarchies reveal how we are all implicated in the perpetuation of racism. The minoritized can be guilty of internalizing racist tropes. But as Park (1999) correctly notes, the supposed racism of the racially minoritized is transferred racism. It is a direct result of being powerless. On the other hand, white racism is a reaffirmation of power. How do we then work with such knowledge and understanding?

To begin to work together we must first acknowledge that we are differentially privileged and oppressed. We are constructed through relations of power and domination. Social oppression is effected through visible and invisible systems of privilege. Marginalized groups are also active agents who act beyond the confines and constraints of institutionalized power. Therefore, in theorizing about anti-racist change, marginalized groups must be presented as active subjects, creators and resistors. For example, it is through the stories of marginalized resistance that we learn about the development of collective consciousness (see also Park, 1999).

Anti-racism is not neutral, innocent nor apolitical knowledge. It is a politicized education for social transformation. It is an interrogation of how discourse and politics can shape the construction of so-called 'objective' knowledge. It is about producing knowledge for empowerment and resistance. Anti-racism connects research and political action. Given on-going technological, political, social, spiritual, economic and material developments of the Millennium, there are powerful new questions that evoke the current state of race relations in society. For example, Yuval-Davis (1999) asks: What new modes of identification and belonging are being formed in this Millennium? How does the 'nation' respond to the multilayered 'global' in a new era? How do we understand contemporary modes of identification and belonging, and their self-relations to dominant conceptions of 'citizenship' in pluralistic nation states? What new forms of relations can be structured between 'homelands and the diasporic spaces'? In affirming difference how do we avoid reifying identities and cultures? (see Yuval-Davis, 1999). I would also add: How do societies today respond to the multiple and often competing and contradictory needs and concerns of a collective? How do governments ensure that social goods and services are not simply accessible to all but also equitably distributed? Whom do we hold officially accountable for the persistence of inequity? In other words, how do we move beyond the bland/seductive politics of inclusion to the pointed discourses of transparency and accountability? Can we build a common view of justice based on a critical understanding of difference? Or can we work with different models of equity and justice (beyond simply treating everyone the same)? If well-meaning intentions are to translate into action, then how do we ensure that what is theoretical does not stand in opposition to what is pragmatic? And can we avoid the vilification of theory in the privileging social practice?

I will not attempt to broach all these questions. But suffice to say that within our communities today, groups are competing for access to resources. The differential positions of social groups in terms of their access to societal resources have fostered an atmosphere of mistrust among groups disadvantaged in the process about the unfairness of the system. Racial minorities generally feel left behind in a political climate of harsh conservatism in which the state has shirked its societal responsibilities to the weakest in promoting a culture of social greed and the 'survival of the fittest'. While empty rhetoric of 'caring' and 'common sense' cannot diminish the brutal realities of the capital markets, I think it is important that we always hang on to the possibility of changing society through the power of ideas. Given appropriate and relevant knowledge, identities can be transformed as sites of resistance and action. We just need to avoid the political paralysis of simply intellectualizing transformative political projects. Thus, anti-racism should not just be a discourse but a political practice. It should be about developing a philosophical view of the world and acting within it to produce change. Anti-racism demands a power of language to articulate a sense of person and self-worth, and to develop a collective and shared understanding of what it means to work for change. I enter the discussion of some of these questions from the ontological stance of presenting resisting[ant] knowledge to highlight the invisibilities and exclusions in knowledge construction about difference and diversity.

II. Personal And Subjective Location

My personal politics are influenced by a 'philosophy of hope'. It is a philosophy that informs my understanding that although the pace of social change can be slow, one should not give up believing that change will eventually happen. In this respect, change should not be seen as a matter of superficial evolutionary growth. Rather, it should be made clear that change will happen but only if we make it happen. This philosophy of hope lays down a firm commitment to and belief in the power of the people to make change. This "will" power is based on love—in the form of the spirit/energy that cannot be shaken once focused. Just as people have lead to the construction of inequality in society, it will be people who will inevitably lead to making advances towards equality in society.

As a pedagogue I have often told my graduate students that if I did not believe in the possibility of change I have no business discussing social transformation in class. It smacks of hypocrisy and intellectual grandstanding if I laid out possible conditions for social change and yet entertained doubts about it happening. As a middle-class, heterosexual, Black male I see myself as invested and colluding in the maintenance of domination as I struggle to shed the cloak of oppression. If change is to happen I must draw on my own responsibility and complicity.

Our personal journeys, educational histories and lived experiences all inform how we make sense of our world. Personal events and occurrences inform how we interpret the world in which we live and act within it. Identities are not simply imposed: they are also claimed and resisted. We constantly create identities as much as we resist them. There is a personal struggle to constantly identify. It should be understood that in particular specificites and contexts, identities are performed. Through these struggles we produce knowledge which is located and contextualized in a particular history, politics and identity. The power of subject[ive] identity, lived experience and social history is that these collectively help shape how we produce knowledge. Every knowledge is thus linked to culture, identity and social practice. As Hall (1991) opined, we all speak from a particular place, context, history and experience. There are limitations of knowledge.

As an 'implicated subject', I ask what understandings do I bring to the notions of 'difference and diversity'. I know full well how bodies are marked differently in society along lines of race, class, gender and sexuality. Some markers connote privilege and others punishment. Other cultural markers bring with them a pressure to fit and become 'normal'. But the gaze of normalcy has some consequences. I remember vividly my early years in Canada when as a graduate student at the University of Toronto my attention was drawn to a flyer on a campus notice board. It was an advertisement urging international students to enrol in a speech language class 'guaranteed to change your accent'. I struggled with the dilemma of what my response would mean in future years. Of course, there was a fee for this 'service' and that might have been the reason why I said 'No thanks'. But the sub-text was clear: if one wanted to 'fit in', then speaking 'like a Canadian' was a good start. This is one message constantly repeated in myriad ways to so-called immigrants. There may well be pragmatic/practical reasons for this particular advertisement. After all, language has a powerful currency in society. The power of language is that it can mark people differently to the extent that a racial minority can be advantaged by language while disadvantaged by race, class, gender, sexuality, culture or religion. This realization has implications for how we come to acknowledge, interrogate and understand 'difference'. Difference challenges the "liberal belief in a universal subjectivity", the claim that "we are all just people" (hooks, 1992, p.167).

III. Race As A Signifier Of Difference

As with other forms of difference, race is a contested notion. There are tensions, ambiguities and contradictions in knowing about race as 'difference'. Race is constituted in multiple ways through discourse and discursive politics in the claiming of history and culture. Michael Omi and Howard Winant (1993) stress that race is "a significant principle of social organization and identity formation". They further argue that North American society is so racialized that to "be without a racial identity is to be in danger of having no identity" (p. 5). To varying degrees our social institutions and systems are racially coded. Writing for the U.S. context, Fine, Weis, Powell, and Wong (1997) also note that race hierarchies shape our schools, legal courts, criminal justice system and workplaces. We live our anxieties, fears, desires and aspirations in racial terms. Powerful racial demarcations persist even with the knowledge that the individual is not just 'one thing' (Said, 1993).

While race may be 'scientifically' meaningless (and it depends on a definition of science) the term still possesses material and social consequences for people. There is both a market and social value of race (Li, 1998). Race achieves its significance when it is systematically paired with rewards and punishment (Li and Bolaria, 1988). There are groups in society that have been historically constructed as fundamentally different on the basis of skin colour. In a very troubling reading, Davies and Guppy (1998) subvert critical thought by arguing that the framing of social "disparities and cultural [in]compatibility" in racial terms is itself the source of problems as far as schooling in concerned. They decry the racialization of the Canadian schooling context. They ask: 'Where do these racialized perceptions come from? (p.145). They see a trend towards racialization of contemporary education as a particular politics of racial minority scholars that create problems rather than find solutions. While the two authors note that the changing racial composition of society has influenced institutions, nevertheless they claim that it is social activists and critical educators who have influenced how race is perceived and institutionalized in schools. I differ in asking: When African-Canadian students speak of differential [negative] treatment by race, how can this be attributed to the educational politics of racializing schooling contexts? Students' concerns must not be naively dismissed as mere 'perceptions', unproven scientifically or objectively.

I see a worrisome trend for particularly dominant scholars to critique those who stress the importance of knowing race as 'difference'. It is as if to say the less said about race the better it is for society. But we cannot wish race away. The intellectual dancing around race can only take us so far. Race is a significant form of difference and highlighting this significance is not a politics of racializing [schooling] contexts. Memmi (1971, p.187) astutely observed that "making use of the difference is an essential step in the racist process...[however]... it is not the difference which always entails racism; it is racism which makes use of difference" (cited in Rothenberg, 1999, p.281). It is the process of devaluing difference (or assigning negative value and meaning to difference) that must be interrogated. Rothenberg (1999, p.294) also notes that difference is created by racism and other forms of oppression, not simply reflected by them. But it is important to acknowledge that anti-racist practice does not seek to create difference for the sake of maintaining dominance. Rather anti-racist politics seeks to interrogate difference and offer alternative and empowering readings and meanings to difference. This understanding of difference attempts to demonstrate that the meaning of this phrase isn't "simply there in all its meaning for us to see." Meanings that are attached to the term difference must be interrogated to deduce why "common-sensical" understandings are not sufficient. Reclaiming language, complicating meanings are part of the process of decolonizing language to avoid hegemonic reification. Historically the disadvantaged have had their identities defined and imposed upon them. The marginalized have often reacted to this imposition by asserting, redefining and reconstructing difference in positive (solution-oriented) ways. Through this process race has been affirmed as significant difference that must not be denied.

Therefore, anti-racist practice does not create a racialized system simply by accentuation of racial identities structured along the lines of difference. A Eurocentric reading sees difference simply in terms of a hierarchy of superior and inferior. It sees difference in terms of decadence and deficiency in moral character (see also Rothenberg, 1999, p.290) In this narrow conception it is 'difference' that makes people unequal, serving to justify social inequities.

For many the use of skin colour as a demarcation of racism is without question, except for those bent on denying skin colour privilege. We have also known how, throughout history, groups have been racialized through a process that allows people to be subjected to differential or unequal treatment because of some real, imagined or presumed phenotypical, physical or other cultural traits (e.g., skin colour, language, culture, religion, etc.). While critical race theorists have looked at this 'racialization' as happening through a labour migration process (as the case of early Chinese immigrant workers in Canada), it is an overstatement to argue that to speak of racialized contexts is to create a problem that never existed in the first place. As argued elsewhere (Dei and Calliste, 2000), in the discourse of anti-racism change, an important clarification needs to be made regarding the evocation of race. This is crucial in order to focus anti-racist political work.

Working with the race concept means acknowledging the power of constructing racial differences. But the anti-racist politics requires that we disassociate [negative] meanings from race. Rather than deny race as meaningless, anti-racist workers must problematize and disassociate the injurious and negative meanings attached to race. The struggle for racial equality cannot be predicated on abolishing or minimising race. Some may find this observation disappointing. But Benedict (1999, p.43), speaking about racial persecution, pointed out that "race is not in itself the source of conflict". Rather, it is the institutional and social practices that create and sustain injustice and inequity among groups and individuals defined in racial terms. Race, whether as a concept or idea, does not signify a difference of inferiority or superiority. As a term, race need not imply any supremacist assertions. Race is not causally connected to racism except through the deliberative human action and response.

It is the affective, cognitive and material meanings embedded in the race concept that have served to create the invidious distinctions or hierarchy of superiority and inferiority. In one of his works, John Rex (1999) argued that "sociology... has ideological and political competitors whose speeches and writings are so influential that it is difficult for sociologists to ignore them and to insist upon pure academic discourse. If their work is to have any influence on public debate they are bound to take up the terminology of the ideologies and politicians, even if in so doing they seek to use it with greater precision" (pp. 149-50). In fact, Rex (1999) has cautiously stressed that we "might for example, eliminate the use of the term "Jew" or "black" in its current meaning and see that its implications have to do with universally shared rights of [hu]man[kind]. What we cannot do is to eliminate culture and meaning altogether" (p. 148).

Where I am going with this? I am of the view that race must remain an important concept in dealing with social change if we are to promote peace, social equity and fairness among all groups. Social inequities are structured along the lines of race, class, gender, sexuality and other forms of difference. The bland talk of diversity has served to sustain power hierarchies in the understanding that we can acknowledge our differences and not deal with the fundamental questions of power, representation and identity. Yet we cannot hope to address socioeconomic inequities by denying the power of race as difference. For example, what does it mean to celebrate and respect all diversity? If it means simply affirming that we are all different and we can get along and not deal with power issues of society then achieving social equity is simply a dream.

It is argued that the theoretical orientation highlighting the saliency of race in anti-racist practice is to shift the talk away from tolerance of diversity to the pointed notion of difference and power (see Dei, et al, 1999). Race and racism is central to how we claim, occupy and defend spaces. The task of anti-racist practice is to identify, challenge and change the values, structures and behaviours that perpetuate systemic racism and other forms of oppression such as patriarchy, capitalism and homophobia. An anti-racist discourse and practice should highlight persistent inequities among communities focusing on relations of domination and subordination. This discourse sees the issue of exclusion/inclusion starkly as entrenched inequities and power imbalance. Anti-racism views the mechanism of redress through a fundamental structural change. The assumption underlying empathy, commonality and goodwill promoted by multiculturalism is that we start from a relatively level playing field, that we have access to similar resources and that we have comparable values, aspirations and concerns. Nothing could be further from the reality of those racially minoritized in our communities (see also Price, 1993).

Eaton (1999) has asked that we rethink the ways we theorize domination and mobilize for resistance. She reminds us that we cannot amputate particular identities in order to gain a coherent analysis of our social positions. She questions whether social theories that are unable to speak to the complexities of lived lives and experiences have any valuable information to offer about the simultaneity of oppressions. Engaging these questions present a new stance in the search for understanding social oppression and working for change. Acknowledging difference is interrogating the power behind the construction of difference. It is asking critical questions about what differences are named, constructed, negotiated by whom, for whom and for what purposes. It is about understanding the construction of difference as itself situated within the broader macro-structural and political processes that create social meanings to regulate people's lives. The world today is about difference and the collectivity that guides the shaping of difference and commonality. We are all differentially privileged and simultaneously oppressed. We are all shaped or scripted by the broader social and political forces of colonialism, capitalism and transnationalism. How then do we balance between avoiding grand narratives and the fragmentation or paralysis of difference? Would a shift of analytic emphasis away from oppressions to privilege be useful in the transformative politics of change? Rather than focus on who is oppressed do we seek to ask who is privileged? (See Eaton, 1999). These questions call for a rethinking of the strategies for mobilizing against domination. We must examine how race, class, gender and sexuality work together to benefit particular groups, to the detriment of others in society.

IV. Anti-Racism: From Diversity To A Pointed Notion Of Difference

Winant (1997) has alluded to current developments in public discourse and social policy pertaining to race: There is the denial of the significance of race in academic discourses. Many educators are reluctant to talk about race. It is argued that to bring up the subject is to open a can of worms. Thus race is still a taboo subject (Tatum, 1992) and many find racial discussions very unsettling. Yet we know and understand our worlds differently through the lens of difference. There is also the open renunciation of racial differences in progressive politics. This denial can be seen in the call for a transracial politics devoid of a politics of identity. However, transracial politics without a politics of identity should not be misunderstood to be the same as collectivities of different identities. Also, collectivities of different identities are not to be correlated to problematic coalitions representing "communities". There is a recourse to strictly class-based criteria in the formulation of social policy for equity and justice. Many ultra-conservative governments would grudgingly acknowledge class distinctions at best while blaming the poor for a lack of work ethic and individual responsibility. Structures and policies are beyond critique and interrogation. Conservatives and some liberals deny race as relevant for social policy focus. Amidst these developments, racially minoritized youth continually experience a loss of a sense of entitlement and belonging in educational institutions. It is important to ask then: What is citizenship about? It is about a sense of duty, responsibility and entitlement. It is about rights, privileges and a sense of belonging.

To address this disturbing trend in public discourse, we must first acknowledge the varied evocations of difference and bring a critical, politicized and unromanticized reading/meaning to difference. To be raced is to be different. It is not the mere acknowledgement of difference but how difference is engaged, acknowledged and negotiated in discursive and political practices (Mohanty, 1990). Difference needs to be explored in the context of its relation to power. That is, who has the power to construct and name difference, why, when and for what purposes and to what ends? There are also many sites of claiming difference. For example, race must be understood as difference of different kinds. Golberg, (1993) Gillborn, (1995) and many others have enthused about the importance of drawing on broader definitions of race and racism extending beyond skin colour as the only signifier of difference. Goldberg in particular, examines the concept of "different racisms", pointing to the myriad ways racism is manifested in society. Borrowing from such an analysis, Dei (1995) uses the notion of 'anti-different racism' to refer to the historical specificities of racisms and the use of culture, language, religion, as powerful markers of differentiation. Such understandings of different racisms can be a discursive and political practice that moves beyond a simplistic Black/White duality. Equally important, the notion of 'different racisms' also gestures to the discursive and practical distinction to be made between the possibility that all peoples can hold racist beliefs as a form of ideological conditioning (e.g., non-Anglos can hold certain beliefs about whites; whites hold certain racist beliefs about racial minorities), and the actual practice of racism with significant material consequences for people (those with power to differentiate and discriminate against others for material benefits). For example, it can be argued that there can be a distinction between social practice that constitutes a mechanism of oppression and one which is a mechanism of resistance. The discourse of difference can unmask unequal power relations, positions and structures. In fact, I find very useful Park's (1999) observation that the racism of minorities is transferred racism, a direct result of being powerless and the racism of the dominant as a reaffirmation of power.

Race like class, gender and sexuality is not an absolute conception of difference. Race, gender, class and sexuality are not fixed or bounded categories. They are relational concepts. Their meanings change depending on contexts and location of deployment. Furthermore, racism, as with sexism and classism, works differently for people depending on history, class, race, gender, sexuality and ethnicity. Given these nuances, there are bound to be differences in the ways racism is experienced.

Difference can both fracture and strengthen the community. Understanding difference within a collectivity is crucial so as not to erase the diverse histories of oppression and resistances of the members of a collective. However, caution must be exercised so that we are not mired in a politics of claiming difference that only creates a political paralysis. Buenaventura (1996) has asked: if each individual has a different experience, how can we speak of a group-based oppression? How do we talk about group-based oppression without negating or erasing differences? I believe we can if we point to the connections of history, culture and politics, and to the fact that we are collectively scripted by the powerful historical and structural forces of colonialism, racism, patriarchy, sexism and hetero-sexism. Difference is not simply about individual experience. It is about how history, culture and politics shape experiences for different subjects and collectivities. Therefore, difference must be engaged as relational, contextual and interdependent. Difference is a connecting web meaning that we are co-implicated since we share histories, experiences and responsibilities. As Glenn (1984) alluded, our histories are not simply diverse; they also intertwined, interdependent and independent. This knowledge of difference is helpful in the forming of collective identity and political solidarity.

The acknowledgement of difference must always be historicized and contextualized given the varied meanings we bring to difference. While a discursive practice of racial and cultural diversity may work with a liberal understanding of difference, it can also problematically assume difference without noting embedded power relations. This happens when ethnic realities within the racial canopy become safe and comfortable spaces to speak about all forms of difference except race. This is a depoliticization of discourse which ends up with a celebratory mode of difference. Similarly, the bland talk of pluralism does not deal with the pointed notion of difference anchored in power relations. Thus, representation is understood simply in terms of including multiple voices without addressing the fundamental question of physical representation (i.e., bodies) meaning power sharing.

Another important dimension to a critical discussion of difference is to challenge the normality of whiteness and the pervasive effects of white privilege. White privilege is performed in relation to the social construction of whiteness as significant difference. White privilege is a relational phenomenon that has arisen out of a series of social, political and historical contexts (see Frankenberg, 1993; Dyer, 1997, Roediger, 1994).

This should be our vision of the 21st century, one in which no group has an automatic right to privilege, supremacy and a disproportionate share of the valued goods and services of society.

V. Models Of Change: Anti-Racism And Multi-Oppression

How do we go about achieving the preferred future state in the 21st century? How do we promote change in the midst of diversity and difference? Foremost, justice is not accomplished simply with good intentions. Justice requires a political commitment to act to remove all forms of oppressions. Since oppressions interlock, the understanding of one form of oppression necessarily entails coming to know other oppressions. Oppressions also have things in common. They work with power. They operate within structures and institutions. All oppressions are intended to establish material and symbolic advantage and consequences.

Oppressions achieve their effects through a process of 'Othering', including the making of an invidious us/them distinction). The idea of multiple oppressions eschews the embeddedness of race, class, gender, sexuality and the multiplicative nature of social identities and relationships (Brewer, 1993, p.16), yet oppressions differ in their consequences depending on situation and context. Hence oppressions are not equal. To examine this position race, gender, class, and sexual oppressions must be historicized and contextualized. This means a critical anti-racist approach must work with the idea of situational and contextual variations in intensities of oppressions. It must problematize competing marginalities which end up serving dominant interests. Similarly, there are relative saliency of different identities and depending on contexts, social identities produce varying effects. Despite the rhetoric of individual merit and achievement, it is a fact that race, gender, class and sexuality demarcate life chances for individuals and groups on differential terms. Although seen as categories of analysis, race, gender, class and sexuality are not closed concepts. They are inextricably linked with one another to refract on our multiple and fluid identities and the simultaneity of social oppressions (see also Lorde, 1983; Dua and Robertson, 1999).

There is no one model of anti-racism. There are different approaches to equity and social justice. This paper argues for an anti-racist model that emphasizes the saliency of race in oppression work while acknowledging the intersections of race and other forms of difference. Depending on the context, situation and history, race becomes salient. Elsewhere (Dei, 1999) I have elaborated on my use of the word 'saliency'. It gestures to the notion of situational and contextual variations in intensities of oppressions. It is also a political practice of affirming an identity without necessarily constructing hierarchies. The understanding of the saliency of race also alludes to a degree of political pragmatism that at least acknowledges the messiness of social movement politics. Both intersecting and interlocking analysis (see Dei, 1999) must be approached at the level of discourse as purely a discursive practice. Race can then be presented as a separate analytical category even as we recognize its intersections with other forms of difference. A particular form of identity can be an entry point for pursuing politics, knowing full well that such identity is relational and interdependent on other forms of identity.

This stance is informed by Hall's (1999) use of the concept of 'articulation'. It is asserted that in different contexts a particular identity could be grounded (as salient) without necessarily arguing that other identities disappear. Therefore, progressive practice would treat equality and difference as an articulation. While differences are connected there can be a strategic recognition of one form of difference in a given context for political purposes.

Anti-racism is about simultaneously affirming differences and commonalities. There are numerous conceptions of difference. Each of the varied conceptions of difference is not mutually exclusive of each other. Particular forms of difference cannot be understood in isolation of each other. They are articulated with others. Besides the material issues of equity there is also a right to difference and to be different. Again, as Hall (1999) notes, the 'rights' to difference must be negotiated to allow those who choose to remain with the majority to do so or to opt out. The state must enable diversity since the state belongs to all groups and not just to one powerful interest (e.g., the dominant). The implication is that dealing with difference must also acknowledge that desire to claim difference and a requirement that such right be respected and acted upon.

Zine's (1999) work also points to the importance of distinguishing discourse from social policy. For example, there can be a policy model for equity, targeting specific social groups as the focus of change. This approach serves to acknowledge the severity of issues for certain bodies. Thus, there can be race, class or gender-centred approach to change with identifiable bodies as the primary targets. This approach is multi-centric in the sense that social policy can be simultaneously effected through the lens of race, class, gender, sexuality, language, religion or culture. The approach distinguishes practice from discourse given the unique histories and experiences of subjects. Social policy must be focused so as to achieve intended outcomes. More specifically, given the severity of educational issues for certain groups in the school system (e.g., First Nations, Black, Portuguese students and the noted high rates of dropouts, school disengagement and disaffection—see Brown, 1993; Dei, et al, 1995; Daenzer, 1995), an approach to change may target these groups of students. Within schools there are groups for whom language, culture and religion present additional challenges. Policy specifically aimed at addressing the unique needs and requirements of these groups should be respected. This does not mean that in the approach to inclusive schooling, racial minorities be [re]presented, taught, and reinforced as discrete, valued entities operating in separate settings, enclaves or as separate entities.

However, anti-racist practice for change could also move beyond specificities to reach all social groups. This means having an alternative approach to change that is 'all inclusive' and may be termed an 'anti-oppression model'. A truly inclusive practice will have implications for all social groups. An anti-oppression model espousing the inseparability and the interlocking nature of oppressions would insist that no one oppression could be dealt with without the others. This model will address the question of physical representation broadly ensuring that different identities structured along race, class, gender, sexual, religious and language be brought onto the table for discussion in order for change to materialize. The lesson of physical representation is that equity is fundamentally a question of power. But in order to be truly transformative, this approach to change must acknowledge the lessons of history and the practices that have excluded others. The lessons of history is that many times in supposedly 'inclusive approaches' to change, race issues are least discussed because there is some discomfort and pain. As already pointed out, race is an unsettling issue for many North Americans. The dominant would rather acknowledge an access model to change that highlights class and economics but downplays the relevance of race.

VI. Doing Anti-Racism: Acknowledging Privilege And Collective Complicity.

An entry to genuine anti-racist work is to acknowledge our relative privileges and collective complicities in the maintenance of dominance. There is a tendency for the subject to cast her/his gaze on the site of oppression but not on the site of privilege. Acknowledging differential privilege is crucial to successful ant-racist politics. There are relative complicities in the maintenance of dominance and fighting oppressions is an exercise in self-criticality. It is a decolonizing project of implicating the self and becoming self-reflective. We must continually reflect and act on our beliefs and practices without claiming innocence and creating a moral distance.

Anti-racist work also requires dealing with the risk and consequences of progressive politics. Those who speak of issues of race, racism and other forms of oppression are bound to face physical, emotional and symbolic assaults, attacks and violence. For the dominant there will be questions of credibility and legitimacy. For the minoritized, politics will always be suspect and be deemed self-serving. Claims to knowledge will be questioned and experience will be seen as offering an insufficient basis for producing knowledge. Thus, today, the question is no longer who can do anti-racist work, but whether people are prepared to face up to the risks and consequences that come with doing anti-racist work.

VII. Conclusion

A truly transformative anti-racist practice in the new Millennium must situate equity within the broader definition of everyday social practice. It requires working towards a broader definition of equity (race, gender, class, sexuality, language, culture and religion) while acknowledging the severity of issues for specific groups. It also means knowing the limits of theory and the material conditions which structure discursive practices. All rights have accompanying responsibilities. That is, as students and learners of change, the right to education means developing a responsibility to ask critical questions about the omissions, negations and absences. As a teacher, the privilege to teach is also a responsibility to be humble and show humility.

Part of the contemporary challenge of anti-racism is to subvert Eurocentric definitions of rights, citizenship and justice. Rights are not just individual issues but those of a collective as well. Rights should be contextualized in societal responsibilities. Citizenship is not defined in a homogenous identity but within the terrain of differentiated subjects with split and conflicted interests. And, justice is not about fairness to all or simply treating everyone the same. Justice is recognizing the different ways individuals and groups have been historically disadvantaged and developing remedial measures that work with the lessons of history.

The process of minoritization can end up liquidating difference and identity. Thus, to affirm difference and identity is not to homogenize the collective. Generally, the process of minoritization denies access to power and resources to the 'other'. The state has traditionally been opposed to notions of 'collectivity' and 'collective rights'. In fact, resistance to collective rights would often accomplish such questions as: who speaks for whom? Such a question is never applied to the state. For example, who speaks for Canada? For those who have been minoritized there is a thin line to cross for the individual right to become a collective right. The state cannot simply defend individual rights. It has other responsibilities. Hall (1999) argues that there are prohibitions to enter the public sphere so the state can ease the entrance of those who have been historically excluded. This is the state fulfilling its responsibility to the disadvantaged.

As we engage the Millennium, we must see anti-racism as being about the differentiated (and not homogenised) collective and their rights and recourse to social power. Anti-racism must posit a critique of the liberal ontology that over-privileges individual rights. The individual is never completely discrete, autonomous, or independent. The individual may exist in relational autonomy and dependent on the larger collective. In critiquing the dominant discourse of rights as individual rights, anti-racism must situate the notion of 'responsibility' within its critical practice. Anti-racism must foreground questions of collective responsibilities rather than individual rights. Anti-racism must ask questions about the responsibility of the larger collective (e.g., the state) to its disadvantaged/subordinated members. It should also ask questions about our collective responsibilities to each other to ensure that justice is not only done but is seen to be done.

Thus, as we fight for equitable access for social groups to valued goods and services of society, anti-racism will bring a broader understanding of rights involving the enhancement of respect, dignity, and cultivating the capacity for individual and collective agency and reciprocity. For those who are forced to occupy marginal positions, hooks (1991) extols the site of marginality as being a site of resistance. Anti-racism recognizes that institutional resources may be needed for minorities to exercise their collective economic, cultural, political and legal rights to exist and resist. But just as we caution against homogenizing rights we must also be careful not to equate all rights. Rights are understood in a given context and within a history.

Disrupting the power of Eurocentrism should also be a central focus of any transformative anti-racist practice. Since Eurocentrism is intertwined with sexism, classism and homophobia, disrupting oppression based on race must simultaneously address sexism, classism, homophobia and other forms of oppression that work to bolster and reinforce racism. This paper has presented some of the challenges and possibilities of pursuing anti-racism for meaningful change in a new Millennium. The goal is to achieve a radical disruption of the status quo. While I am interested in pursuing the issue of 'social access for all' equity is more than a question of access. There are other fundamental issues at stake: the production, validation and dissemination of multiple knowledge forms; the affirmation of individual and collective identities and social practices, and the pursuit of meaningful power-sharing that destabilizes the dominance of hegemonic power.

As a political and discursive practice to decentre and derail exclusive white nationalist projects, anti-racism deals with difference and diversity. The nation is not simply diverse but also differentiated. An approach to social equity and justice must reflect the differences and commonalities that subjects of the nation share. All institutional settings/sectors (e.g., law, education, media, criminal justice system and the arts) are implicated in the struggle for social change and transformation. As an anti-racist pedagogue, I would end this discussion with words directed at formal education. Instruction, curricular, textual and pedagogical practices must reflect the diverse histories and bodies of students who enter or fail to enter today's classrooms. Where classrooms are socially diverse (in terms of the operational definition of race, class, ethnicity, gender, sexuality, religion and culture), educators (and governments) have a strong ethical responsibility to represent the diverse histories, knowledges, values and aspirations of all children. The responsibility is directly related to the presence of bodies (hearts, minds, senses of self-worth and belonging, aspirations for futures, quality of life, etc.).

For those who claim that their classrooms are not "significantly" diverse, or where schools are primarily of the dominant population, it is also essential that diverse knowledges, ideas and values are represented. The reason is simple. As Thielen-Wilson (1999) argues, for the benefit of those who have been minoritized, educators have a moral obligation to challenge racism of Eurocentric knowledges, attitudes and ways of life among dominant groups because doing so is to acknowledge the minoritized whether or not they are physically present within the classroom. Dominant groups need to expand their knowledge base and be anti-racist. They need to know and act on diversity, and be self-critical, not primarily because it benefits the dominant, nor because the presence of a critical mass of minoritized bodies demands it (i.e., a "fairness" resulting from "numbers"). Rather, it is because it lessens the likelihood that individuals will enact racism towards racial minorities. Further, it lessens the likelihood that whites will endorse a political and social system that perpetuates white nationalism. For the benefit of dominant groups, inclusive education helps expand existing knowledge bases and gives a more accurate understanding of the sources of knowledge, to place the dominant in touch with the reality of global and local diversity, and to render people as 'better' human beings for being anti-racist, and inclusive.

Acknowledgements:

I would like to thank the students in my graduate level course, SES 1921Y: "Principles of Anti-Racism" for sharing ideas and engaging in critical discussions which helped shape my thoughts as I wrote this essay. I would like to thank Leeno Karumanchery for his assistance in preparing the final draft of this paper. And finally, I thank Gurpreet Singh Johal of the Department of Sociology and Equity Studies, Ontario Institute for Studies in Education, University of Toronto, for reading and commenting on an initial draft of the paper.

REFERENCES

Benedict, R. (1999). "Racism: The ism of the Modern World". In Harris, R. (ed.). *Racism*. New York: Humanity Press, pp. 31-49.

Brewer, R. (1993). "Theorizing Race, Class and Gender: The New Scholarship of Black Feminist Intellectuals and Black Women's Labour". In R. Brewer and A. Busia (eds). *Theorizing Black Feminisms*. New York: Routledge, pp. 13-30.

Brown, R. (1993). *A Follow-Up of the Grade 9 Cohort of 1987*: Every Secondary Student Survey Participants. Toronto: Board of Education, Research Report #207.

Buenaventura, L. (1996). Class presentation: Chandra Mohanty *"On Race and Voice"*. Department of Sociology and Equity Studies, OISE/UT.

Chater, N. (1994). "Biting the Hand that Feeds Me: Notes on Privilege from a White Anti-Racist Feminist". *Canadian Woman Studies*. 14:100-104.

Daenzer, P. (1995). Black High School Dropout in Four Ontario Urban Centres. A Report prepared for the Canadian Alliance of Black Educators (CABE) Toronto.

Davies, S. and N. Guppy. (1998). "Race and Canadian Education". In V. Satzewich (ed.). Racism & Social Inequality in *Canada: Controversies & Strategies of Resistance*. Toronto: Thompson Educational Publishing Co., pp. 131-156.

Dei, G. J. S. (1995). "The Integrative Anti-Racism and the Dynamics of Social Difference". *Race, Gender & Class*. 2(3): 11-30.

Dei, G. J. S. (1999). 'The Denial of Difference: Reframing Anti-Racist Praxis". *Race Ethnicity and Education*. 2(1): 17-38.

Dei, G. J. S., L. Holmes, J. Mazzuca, E. McIsaac and R. Campbell. (1995). Push Out or Drop Out? The Dynamics of Black/African-Canadian Students' Disengagement from School'. *Final Report submitted to the Ontario Ministry of Education and Training, Toronto.*

Dei, G. J. S., I. James, L. Karumanchery, S. James-Wilson, and J. Zine. (1999). *Removing the Margins: The Challenges and Possibilities of Inclusive Schooling*. Toronto: Canadian Scholars' Press.

Dei, G. J. S., S. James-Wilson and J. Zine. (1999). *Inclusive Education: A Guide To Teacher Development'*. Toronto: Canadian Scholars' Press.

Dei, G. J. S. and A. Calliste. (2000). "Introduction". *Knowledge, Power and Anti-Racism: A Critical Reader*. Halifax: Fernwood Publishing.

Dua, E. and A. Robertson. (1999).(eds.). *Scratching the Surface*: Canadian Anti-Racist Feminist Thought. Toronto: Women's Press.

Dyer, R. (1997). *White*. New York: Routledge.

Eaton, L. *(1999)*. Class Presentation: Davia Stasiulis "Theorizing Connections: Gender, Race, Ethnicity and Class". Department of Sociology and Equity Studies, OISE/UT.

Fine, M., L. Weis, L. Powell, and L, Mun Wong (1997). "Preface". In Fine, et al., (eds.). *Off White: Readings on Race, Power, and Society*. New York: Routledge., pp. vii-xii.

Frankenberg, R. (1993). *White Women, Race Matters: The Social Construction of Whiteness*. Minneapolis: University of Minnesota Press.

Gillborn, D. T. (1995). *Racism and Anti-Racism in Real Schools*. Philadelphia: Open University Press.

Giroux, H. (1997). "Rewriting the Discourse of Racial Identity: Towards a Pedagogy and Politics of Whiteness". *Harvard Educational Review* 67(2): 285-320.

Glenn, E. N. (1985). "Racial Ethnic Women's Labour: The Intersection of Race, Gender and Class Oppression". *Review of Radical Political Economics*. 17(3): 86-108.

Goldberg, D. (1993). Racist Culture. Oxford: Blackwell,

Hall, S. (1991). "Ethnicity, Identity and Difference". *Radical America* 13(4): 9-20.

Hall, S. (1999). "Personal Reflections and Closing Plenary Remarks" Delivered at the International Conference on 'Nationalism, Identity and Minority Rights: Sociological and Political Perspectives". University of Bristol, England, September 16-19.

Harris, C. (1993). "Whiteness as Property." *Harvard Law Review*. 106(8): 1710-91.

hooks, b. (1984). *Feminist Theory: From Margin to Center*. Boston: South End Press.

hooks, b. (1992). *Black Looks: Race and Representation*. Toronto: Between the Lines.

Li, P. (1998). "The Market and Social Value of Race". In V. Satzewich (ed.). *Racism & Social Inequality in Canada*:

Controversies & Strategies of Resistance. Toronto: Thompson Educational Publishing Co., pp. 115-130.

Li, P. and S. Bolaria. (1988). *Racial Oppression in Canada.* Toronto: Garamond Press.

Lorde, A. (1983). "Age, Race, Class, and Sex: Women Defining Difference". In Lorde, *A. Sister Outsider: Essays and Speeches.* New York: Crossing Press, pp. 114-23.

Lorrain, J. (1996) "Stuart Hall and the Marxist Concept of Ideology". In D. Morley and K-Sing Chen (eds.). *Stuart Hall: Critical Dialogues in Cultural Studies.* London: Routledge.

McIntosh, P. (1990). "White Privilege: Unpacking the Invisible Knapsack". *Independent School Winter* 1990, pp. 31-36.

McLaren P. (1997). "Unthinking Whiteness, Rethinking Democracy, or Farewell to the Blonde Beast: Towards a Revolutionary Multiculturalism". *Educational Foundations* 11(2): 5-39.

Mohanty, C. (1990). "On Race and Voice: Challenges for Liberal Education in the 1990s". *Cultural Critique* 14: 179-208.

Omi, M. and H. Winant. (1993). "On The Theoretical Concept of Race". In C. McCarthy and W. Crichlow (eds.). *Race Identity and Representation in Education.* New York: Routledge., pp. 3-10.

Park, H. (1999). "Whiteness as Property: The Politics of Critique". *Unpublished paper*, Department of Sociology and Equity Studies, OISE/UT.

Post, R. and M. Rogin (eds.). (1998). *Race and Representation*: *Affirmative Action.* New York: Zone Books.

Price, E. (1993). "Multiculturalism: A Critique". *Unpublished paper,* Department of Sociology and Equity Studies, OISE/UT.

Rex, J. (1999). "Racism, Institutionalized and Otherwise". In Harris, R. (ed.). *Racism.* New York: Humanity Press., pp. 141-60.

Roediger, D. (1994). *Towards the Abolition of Whiteness: Essays on Race, Politics and Working Class History.* London: Verso.

Roman, L. (1997). "Denying [White] Racial Privilege: Redemption Discourses and the Uses of Fantasy". In Fine, M., L. Weis, L. Powell, and L. Mun Wong (eds.). *Off White: Readings on Race, Power, and Society.* New York: Routledge., pp. 270-282.

Rothenberg, P. S. (1999). "The Construction, Deconstruction, and *Reconstruction of Difference". In. L. Harris (ed.). Racism: Key Concepts in Critical Theory.* New York: Humanity Books, pp. 281-296.

Said, E. (1993). *Culture and Imperialism.* New York: Alfred Knopf.

Stoik, E. (1999). Class presentation: Peter McLaren "Unthinking Whiteness, Rethinking Democracy, or Farewell to the Blonde Beast: Towards a Revolutionary Multiculturalism". Department of Sociology and Equity Studies, OISE/UT.

Tatum, B. (1992). "Talking About Race, Learning About Racism: The Application of Racial Identity Development Theory in the Classroom". *Harvard Educational Review* 62(1): 1-24.

Thielen-Wilson, L. (1999). Review of Paper, "Rethinking Schooling in Euro-American Contexts" by George J. Sefa Dei. Unpublished paper, Department of Sociology and Equity Studies, OISE/UT.

Winant, H. (1997). "Behind Blue Eyes: Whiteness and Contemporary US Racial Politics". In Fine, M., L. Weis, L. Powell, and L, Mun Wong (eds.). *Off White: Readings on Race, Power, and Society.* New York: Routledge.

Wray, M and R. Newitz (eds.). (1997). White Trash: Race and Class in America. New York: Routledge.

Yuval-Davis, N. (1999). "The Multi-layered Citizen, the 'Politics of Recognition' and the Right for "Self-Determination". Abstract of paper for presentation at the International Conference on 'Nationalism, Identity and Minority Rights: Sociological and Political Perspectives". University of Bristol, England, September 16-19.

Zine, J. (1999). "Negotiating 'Equity': The Dynamics of Minority Community Engagement in Constructing Inclusive Educational Policy". Paper read at the International Conference on 'Nationalism, Identity and Minority Rights: Sociological and Political Perspectives". University of Bristol, England, September 16-19.

Chapter 16

THE CANADIAN MULTICULTURALISM POLICY:A PLURALIST IDEAL RE-VISITED*

Romulo F. Magsino

INTRODUCTION: MULTICULTURALISM UNDER SIEGE

After decades of checkered existence in Canada, multiculturalism remains in search of better fortunes. Despite noteworthy efforts by both federal and provincial governments, implementation of the federal Multiculturalism Act (Canada, 1988) and several pieces of provincial legislation officially adopting multiculturalism as government policy remain subject to changing political and economic tides. Though S.27 of the Constitution Act, known as the Canadian Charter of Rights and Freedoms (Canada, 1982), requires the interpretation of its provisions to conform to the multicultural heritage of Canadians, its political and legal implementation is uneven and its ramifications uncertain.

In this chapter, I re-visit the Canadian policy of multiculturalism, whose meaning and justification were analyzed in my writings about a decade ago (Magsino, 1989, 1991). I briefly survey the current criticisms concerning the policy and attempt to demonstrate that they do no damage to the policy as a set of values and principles governing not only the Canadian government's interaction with cultural groups but also the interrelationships among themselves. My view, that the policy remains defensible nothwithstanding a detectable backlash against it, is anchored in my belief that the policy's values and principles dimension has not been fully understood and appreciated. The lack of understanding and appreciation of the policy and, worse, its distortion, are illustrated through a survey of the criticisms directed against multiculturalism. To meet these criticisms, I present the various values and principles embedded in the notion of multiculturalism by quoting directly from federal government documents, which are echoed in the policy statements or legislation in the various provincial jurisdictions in the country. Following some commentary on these values and principles, I comment briefly on the programmatic implementation dimension of the policy.

THE CRITIQUE OF MULTICULTURALISM

Egalitarian Concerns Against the Policy. Since its popularization in the late 1960s and early 1970s, multiculturalism has been subjected not only to severe criticisms but also to outright rejection. Certainly regarded as a serious reason for objecting to multiculturalism is the view that it condemns members of ethnic groups to a life of perpetual isolation and disadvantage in a land of opportunity and affluence. Such a view has found support in the writings of Porter (1965, 1979), Clement (1975), and Bissoondath (1994). Using Canadian census data on ethnic occupational distribution, as well as other considerations, Porter observes that "the idea of an ethnic mosaic, as opposed to the idea of the melting pot, impedes the processes of social mobility" and that "(W)here there is strong association between ethnic affiliation and social class, as there almost always has been, a democratic society may require a breaking down of the ethnic impediment to equality, particularly the equality of opportunity" (1965, pp. 70, 73). In the same vein, and following Steinberg's (1981) lead, Li (1988, p. 9) likens multiculturalism to pluralism which "unduly emphasizes the transplanted culture from the old country as the principal antecedent and defining characteristic of ethnic groups... and ... overlooks the structural conditions of the host society in shaping ethnic inequality." Despite former Prime Minister Trudeau's intent, "there is little indication that racial prejudice has been less prevalent, or ethnic inequality less evident. The policy has failed to combat racism and discriminatory practices. Indeed the persistence of ethnic inequality in the labour market is well documented..." (ibid.). Thus presumably because it compromises equality for minority groups, multiculturalism's encouragement of cultural retention based on ethnic affiliation has proved odious to people with egalitarian pretensions. For some, multiculturalism is doubly objectionable because it serves to distract ethnic minorities from the task of politicized participation in society in pursuit of equality (Li, 1988; Moodley, 1983; Peter, 1981).

The Concern for National Unity. Equally objectionable for critics of the multiculturalism policy is its perceived harmful impact on national unity. Such impact allegedly arises in different ways. Bibby (1990, pp.10-11), for example, believes that multicultural-ism insidiously compromises unity because it induces a narrow sense of loyalty among ethnic members. For Gairdner (1990, pp. 392-393; also, Granatstein, 1998), multiculturalism needs to be scrapped because it works toward the silent destruction of English Canada by undermining the country's core values and way of life which undergird the nation' stability and unity. The foundation of national unity and stability, Gairdner asserts, is natural similarity or homogeneity. Against this, multiculturalism emphasizes equal acceptance of natural differences and, imposed by government on the majority, breeds fear and hostility.

Still another way by which multiculturalism allegedly promotes disunity is the policy's encouragement of divided loyalty. For Bissoondath (1993), it is disturbing enough that some Canadians are doggedly monarchists, that others are pro-American, and that still others are Francophone. Worse, "To such fracturing must now be added a host of new divisions actively encouraged by our multiculturalism policy...." Multiculturalism, "in encouraging the wholesale retention of the past" (p. 375), not only makes it impossible for immigrants to develop wholehearted commitment to the new land and its ideals and visions but also encourages them to import with them ethnic, religious, and political hatreds from their countries of origin.

The Concern for the Cultural Ghettoization of Minority Groups. Not surprisingly, multiculturalism has also been attacked for its encouragement of cultural retention. Brotz (1980) has painted the policy as muddled in its concern for such retention. The reason, in his view, is that, in a fundamental sense there is no cultural diversity in Canada. Whatever was diverse belonged "to the workings of a privately organized social life or a privately organized market" which catered to no more than differences in taste (p. 44). Even the Natives and the French, two groups seen to differ most from the English, fundamentally agree with the latter about "the desirability of the bourgeois-democratic way of life" (p. 43). Roberts and Clifton (1982) extended this critique by insisting that all that ethnic groups possess in Canada is symbolic ethnicity rather than true ethnic cultures because of the absence of institutional structures needed to maintain the traditional mosaic version. Insofar as symbolic ethnicity is on the same plane as the identity of voluntary organizations, government should simply allow or protect its voluntary and private practise by ethnic groups, instead of promoting it.

Some critics, however, are less benign in their criticisms. For Bissoondath, multiculturalism assumes "that people, coming here from elsewhere, wish to remain what they have been; that personalities and ways of doing things, ways of looking at the world, can be frozen in time. ... It treats newcomers as exotics and pretends that this is both proper and sufficient" (1993, p. 372). In his view, one deleterious consequence of this is that mainstream Canadians find it easy to dissociate from new Canadians; "differences, so close to the surface, are seized upon; are turned into objects of ridicule and resentment" (p. 379. Also, see Meghji, 1991).

Needless to say, the preceding survey does nothing more than represent the thrust of significant criticisms against multiculturalism. (For additional survey of critiques against multiculturalism, see Friesen, 1991, 1993; Fleras & Elliott, 1992). Given a surfeit of criticisms, why defend the policy?

I believe that most of these criticisms, perhaps well-meaning despite their virulence, are misdirected or misguided, in part because of a lack of understanding of the policy of multiculturalism. The next section therefore addresses this problem.

MULTICULTURALISM:
DEFINITION, GOALS, AND PRINCIPLES

Canadian multiculturalism has two dimensions. As a statement of **values and principles** to be pursued in a culturally diverse society, the policy of multiculturalism certainly deserves a much better reception from governmental authorities, political leaders, moulders of opinion, and the public at large. As explicit espousal of fundamental Canadian values, it ought to be entrenched and implemented in different aspects of public life, particularly in terms of governmental action and programs. However, as a statement of a **programmatic plan** for implement-ation purposes, it is not impervious to valid criticisms. If it is to be true to its intent, it should be examined critically and monitored closely to determine how seriously and effectively its values and principles are, or are not, promoted in societal institutions. Quite clearly, then, analysis or critique of multiculturalism is superficial, at best, if it makes no distinction between the two dimensions of the policy.

Multiculturalism as a Distinctive Canadian Concept. Despite a plethora of definitions for "multiculturalism", and despite some critics' sense of futility in ascertaining one acceptable definition, a distinctive Canadian notion is clearly evident. Burnet (1983) appears justified in her claim that the term "multiculturalism" first arose in the 1960s in Canada to focus on a new reality in contrast with the officially accepted policy of biculturalism in the country (Magsino, 1989, pp. 54-57). As a notion, it was not defined as explicitly or directly as academics or government planners would have preferred. Nonetheless, its two dimensions (values/principles and programmatic plans for implementation) are explicitly evident. Thus the first dimension can be gleaned from the following passage concerning the policy's general intent:

> Such a policy should help to break down discriminatory attitudes and cultural jealousies; national unity, if its to mean any thing in the deeply personal sense, must be founded on confidence in one's own individual identity; out of this can grow respect for that of others and a willingness to share ideas, attitudes and assumptions... It can form the base of a society which is based on fair play for all (Trudeau, in Mallea & Young, 1984, p. 519).

The values and principles become even more evident in the government's implementation strategies, stated as follows:

First,... to assist all Canadian cultural groups that have demonstrated a desire and effort to continue to develop....

Second,...(to) assist members of all cultural groups to overcome cultural barriers to full participation in Canadian society.

Third,... (to) promote creative encounters and interchange among all Canadian cultural groups in the interest of national unity.

Fourth, (to) assist immigrants to acquire at least one of Canada's official languages in order to become full participants in Canadian society.

The principles aimed at in the first three implementation strategies are quite clear. The first strategy relates to the principle of freedom to retain and develop one's culture (henceforth, "cultural retention' will be used for brevity); the second, to equality; and the third, to cultural sharing for cultural under-standing and appreciation. The last strategy, aimed at full participation in society, obviously falls under the second principle, that is, equality. These principles are already discernible in the statement of general intent quoted earlier. They are also implied in the following:

> The policy I am announcing today accepts the contention of the other cultural communities that they, too, are essential elements in Canada (note equality), and deserve government assistance in order to contribute to regional and national ways of life (note unity) in ways that derive from their heritages (note cultural retention) yet are distinctively Canadian (note unity).

The passing years and changing governments have not altered the values and principles in the original conception of multiculturalism in the country. Thus, the federal Multiculturalism Act of 1988 (Canada, An Act for the Preservation and Enhancement of Multiculturalism in Canada) states, among others, as follows:

3.(1). It is hereby declared to be the policy of the Government of Canada to

(c) promote the full and equitable participation of individuals and communities of all origins in the continuing evolution and shaping of all aspects of Canadian society and assist them in the elimination of any barrier to such participation....

(e) ensure that all individuals receive equal treatment and equal protection under the law, while respecting and valuing their diversity;

(f) encourage and assist the social, cultural, economic and political institutions of Canada to be both respectful and inclusive of Canada's multicultural character;

(g) promote the understanding and creativity that arise from the interaction between individuals and communities of different origins.

In fact the provincial governments have not been outdone in institutionalizing multiculturalism. Earlier pieces of legislation in other provinces, such as Alberta and Saskatchewan, and the policy statements of the other Canadian governments which have not legislated multiculturalism, embed multiculturalism's principles, namely, cultural retention, equality, and cultural sharing. Manitoba's Multiculturalism Act (Manitoba, 1992) is, perhaps, a model of explicitness and clarity in expressing these principles. Consistent with the original statement and with subsequent official statements on the policy of multiculturalism, we may briefly define it—if a definition is called for—as the policy which promotes and supports cultural retention and enhancement, cultural sharing, and equality among cultural groups in order to achieve national unity and development through a program of government support.

Unity: The Valued Goal of the Multiculturalism Policy. Unity has been an overriding preoccupation in Canada since its inception as a state. Its regional and/or provincial allegiances and identities have rendered unity problematic since Confederation, and the influx of immigrants particularly from non-European countries has exacerbated the situation. The need to resolve the problem is urgent. The very existence of society presupposes at least some degree of unity. Societal processes—whether political, economic, social, educational, and the like—cannot effectively operate in the absence of stable conditions that unity makes possible. It is clear, from Trudeau's statement and from subsequent federal and provincial acts and policy statements, that multi-culturalism is intended to attain the goal of unity. Yet, it is perplexing that multiculturalism has been attacked for fomenting divisiveness in society.

Perhaps the reason is all too obvious. Critics see unity from their narrow, biased lenses. Gairdner (1990), as we have seen, is quite straightforward about his conception of unity. It is not coop-eration and harmony among equally respectful and appreciative cultural groups; it is, rather, through the predominant sway of the English traditional way of life and values, which has been so imposed on all minority ethnic groups that peace and harmony are achieved. However, now that ethnic minority groups are conscious of their entitlement in democratic societies, this view is surely being contested. The present drive for equality by ethnic groups, even as they strive to retain elements of their cultural heritages, has engendered a politics of recognition that cannot be ignored or underestimated (Taylor, 1992). Where peoples profess their difference, yet demand equal opportunities and participation in society, the imperial imposition of cultural and political hegemony by one particular group—even a predominant majority—is clearly not the way to attain unity. It is sad that multiculturalism critics like Gairdner and Bissoondath remain myopic to the lessons of past and present societies where atrocities and warfare have been waged due to the powerful group's imperialistic policies over the others. As Gurr has recently pointed out on the basis of research on politically active ethnic and communal groups, "grievances about differential treatment and the sense of group cultural identity provide the esssential bases for mobilization..." (Gurr, 1990, p. 124. Also, see Brass, 1985; Hall, 1979; Maybury-Lewis, 1982; Sigler, 1983). It is not that, in Canada, ethnic groups are bound to rise in arms if multiculturalism were scrapped. It is to insist, however, that the goal of unity will be difficult to attain in this country if the principles of equality and freedom of cultural retention were denied to minority ethnic groups in this country.

In view of the explicitness with which multiculturalism is presented as a strategy to attain unity, it is odd that it has been criticized for promoting disunity. If criticism is made by those whose vested interests are apparently threatened by other groups' or individuals' attaining equal socio-economic and political status, receiving equal cultural respect, or interacting openly with their established counterparts, then it does not appear that multi-culturalism is the culprit. In any culturally diverse society, composed as it is of peoples with different beliefs and values, the road to unity is paved not by unbending resistance to others but by mutual understanding and appreciation and by accommodation of one another. This, precisely, is what the multiculturalism policy has explicitly advocated. If there remains ethnocentricity among ethnocultural members (as Bibby maintains) or if they remain blindly committed to their original values, beliefs, and ways such that they carry on with their reprehensible hatreds and conflicts originating from their homelands (as Bissoondath claims), then it certainly is not a failure of intent or of the principles dimension of the policy. In fact the policy, with its principles, is intended to combat individual or group discord arising from ethnocentricity. Thus it may be that its programmatic implementation does not include properly conceived strategies, effective enough programs, and/or adequate financial outlay; or those of us who ought to suppport its implementation may not be serious enough in our efforts. But to charge the policy as the cause of disunity, and to blame it for contributing to ethnocentricity or to continued conflicts among former enemies in their new homeland, is certainly an ignorant and inexplicable failure to understand what the policy, with its embedded principles, is all about.

The Principles Animating Multiculturalism. It is ironic that the policy is ignorantly criticized for its lack of concern for principles or values which, in fact, are the component elements of the Canadian notion of multiculturalism itself. Thus, the principle of **equality** has been an explicit element of the multiculturalism policy since its proclamation in 1971. Equality, together with freedom, has been the moral and political principle or value pursued by democratic societies everywhere. Based on human worth which the human person possesses, and insistent that each person deserves respect and equal concern (Dworkin, 1977), equality, at least in terms of having access to what one justly deserves as a human being, is difficult to dispute. The reality in Canada, however, is that this entitlement has not been fully enjoyed by members of ethnic minority groups. After more than three decades, since Porter decried the vertical mosaic characterizing the country's socio-economic and political landscape, the disadvantage experienced by these groups remains. Whatever has been achieved in improving their lot, it remains that "visible minorities face earning penalties in the labour market" and are still subject to exclusion from political, social, and economic institutions, as well as other aspects of ethnic and racial inequality (e.g., prejudice, hate and violence, and discrimination in recruitment, interviewing, hiring, promotion, training, and termination practices (Lautard and Guppy, 1998, p. 247. Also, Ramcharan, 1982; Li, 1988; Kallen, 1996; Alladin, 1996). The concern of critics for promoting the socio-economic and political parity of minority ethnic groups is unquestionable. What is problematic is that they automatically assume that minority groups and their members have to pay a price for this parity over and above what the privileged and advantaged groups need to pay. The price they exact is high: renunciation of the cultural heritage which has given them the identity that they bring with them. What is expected of them is complete transformation so that linguistically, cognitively, and in most other ways, they are able to compete on equal terms with mainstream Canadians. Their original culture is presumably a burdensome baggage which ethnic members had better discard if they are to succeed in life. Indeed, it appears so, because having the intellectual abilities and skills equal to, and even better than, those possessed by their counterparts in the mainstream society fails them in their aspiration for income parity. In one study, Lautard and Guppy note that, of the top one-third of groups studied, five of the six groups with the most post-secondary education credentials are visible minority groups, yet this study, and others, report "ethnic penalties," "brutal income inequality" or "financial penalties" when it comes to translating education into occupational position and income attainment (Ibid., p. 223, and Breton, 1998, pp. 105-106). However, why cultural background or ethnicity should be a liability has not been explained or justified. In any case, because both multiculturalists and critics subscribe to the principle of equality, the latter are well-advised to search for scapegoats other than the policy.

Freedom of cultural retention has been the focus of widespread, yet misleading, attack against multiculturalism by critics, such as Bibby (1990), who presume that the justification for cultural retention is grounded on the doctrine of relativism.

Granting, for the sake of argument, that relativism blurs the distinction between right and wrong, good or bad, worthless and worthwhile, and the like, this doctrine is indeed disturbing and ought to be resisted. But this is a pseudo-problem capitalized upon by the enemies of multiculturalism. Far from having to appeal to cultural relativism, cultural retention is anchored on a strong moral ground. As some writers (Coombs, no date; Wright & LaBar, 1984; Magsino, 1989) have insisted before, the policy is justified in terms of the most fundamental moral principle of the dignity of and respect for human beings or persons, from which other principles are drawn. As an ethical axiom, respect for persons arises from the ineluctable fact that human beings have certain characteristics, namely, susceptibility to suffering and frustration and the capacity to form and act on intelligent conceptions of how their lives should be lived (Dworkin, 1977, p. 272; also, Quinton, 1973; Milne, 1986). Based on these human characteristics, respect for each person demands that each being be accorded equal concern: the right to equal treatment, "that is, to the same distribution of goods or opportunities as anyone else has or is given"; and the right to treatment as an equal, that is, "the right, not to an equal distribution of some good or opportunity, but the right to equal concern and respect in the political decision about how these goods and opportunities are to be distributed" (Dworkin, 1977, p. 273). But respect for persons also implies treating them as ends and never only as means. As a being with human potentialities and capacities, each person must be regarded as an agent, capable of formulating and pursuing purposes of her own (Milne, 1986, p. 82). As an autonomous agent, she is entitled to demand freedom from interference by others in relation to her choices, being, and property. Given that freedom to choose and to determine one's pursuit of life is a deeply embedded value in our democratic political structure, cultural retention by those who choose it, in a way that does not harm other individuals or groups or obstruct their own aspiration toward attainment of equal or acceptable conditions of life for themselves, is an eminently rational and defensible stance for ethnic members to take. In doing so, they need not be seen to undermine the notion of unity. As Kymlicka (1996, p. 118) perceptively points out,

The ethnic revival has essentially been a matter of self-identity and self-expression, disconnected from claims for the revival or creation of a separate institutional life. People want to identify themselves in public as members of an immigrant group, and to see others with the same identity in prominent positions of respect and authority.... They are demanding increased recognition and visibility within the mainstream society. The ethnic revival, in other words, involves a revision in terms of integration, not a rejection of integration.

Cultural retention could easily be a threat to unity if cultural groups were to be encouraged to preserve their cultural heritages in isolation from one another. Clearly, however, the policy explicitly encourages cultural sharing, which is vitally important if cultural groups are to understand and appreciate one another. This follows from the justified moral assumption that individuals, and the group that they make up, are persons with human worth and dignity and who are therefore worthy of our respect and attention. Moreover, no matter how different from ourselves, they have their beliefs, values, and ways that we may profit from. Webber (1996, pp. 274-275) shares with us his insight as follows:

Minority communities may follow practices we find incomprehensible, perhaps objectionable. We may reject general conversion to their ways. But we can nevertheless acknowledge that from their different perspectives, they have grasped something about the world that we have missed. They may have something to teach us, or they may at least compel us to reflect on the justification of our own practices.

The problem raised against cultural sharing arises from the common perception that public expressions of symbolic ethnicity— in the form of dance, song, food, costumes, and the like—do nothing whatsoever, or little, toward the promotion of true and meaningful cultural understanding or, much less, toward any deep appreciation of different cultural groups and their heritages. However, multiculturalists need not deny that, for a while, the multiculturalism policy implementation was subject to this criticism. But policy implementation has evolved beyond the "song and dance" stage (Fleras and Elliott, 1992), and multiculturalists need to conceive of appropriate ways to attain the policy's intent to generate enriched, meaningful, and satisfying interaction among cultural groups. The important point to note, however, is that this is not a criticism of the intent or principle of cultural sharing, but of implementation strategy.

THE MULTICULTURALISM POLICY:
SOME REAL PROBLEMS

Trudeau's political instincts enlisted the principles of equality, cultural retention, and cultural sharing in his drive for the value of unity. But the value of unity draws its compelling character for the ultimate value of respect for persons. Unity is indispensable in society because it establishes the conditions under which interaction among human beings, and between human beings and their institutions can flourish in ways that conform to the value of respect for persons. It is in this sense that the moral justification for pursuing unity and institutionalizing the three principles in governmental policy lie in a higher value. Ultimately, it is respect for persons, which we presuppose as the fundamental, over-arching value in society. Assuming that this claim can be justified, and also that honoring respect for persons by promoting equality, cultural retention, and cultural sharing has the effect of promoting unity, there is little to quarrel about concerning the values and principles dimension of the policy. It is clear that many criticisms are levelled against multiculturalism because of the perception that it is exclusively concerned with one principle or value or another, such as cultural retention, to the neglect of other equally important principles needed to show respect for persons and to attain Canadian unity. Indeed, multiculturalism as a notion embeds compelling values and complementary principles which critics themselves are arguing for. Realization that this is the case should allay some of the critics' worries. Unfortunately this is not the case in relation to the policy's program implementation dimension.

Nothwithstanding his many misdirected and misconceived criticisms, Bissoondath (1993, 1994) understandably expresses fear that the policy, for lack of explicit guidelines, encourages unbridled cultural retention and gives the impression that cultural groups may import, in a wholesale manner, their cultural ways into the country. Now, some intensely ethnocentric immigrant groups, due to their unreflective and unrealistic claims to cultural retention, could raise valid concerns on the part of the Canadian mainstream. Were the policy to acknowledge such claims, Gairdner's and Granatstein's criticisms would be vindicated. Surely this is tantamount to undermining the goal of unity and the principle of cultural sharing which the policy is meant to achieve. But this much trumpeted problem is more imagined than real. Clearly, individuals who apply of their own free will to immigrate to another country realize that cultural adjustment is required on their part. This is true even in the case of refugees forced out of their own countries by circumstances beyond their control. In any case, even if we allow Bissoondath's over-blown claim and agree that some ethnic groups wish to import their traditional ways in a wholesale manner, sooner or later they realize that they do not have either the institutional resources or the power to do it, and that existing societal institutions will not allow this preposterous idea. Closer to reality, ethnic groups themselves do not expect to live in the host country in much the same way that they lived in their country of origin. All that they ask is that elements of their culture, which they hold dear and sacred, are preserved and perpetuated, albeit in some modified way to fit their new circumstances (Kymlicka, 1998, pp. 40-59). Indeed, Bissoondath's problem is not likely to be a real one.

Nonetheless, some real difficulties need to be conceded. One such difficulty is that some things which people hold dear or sacred from their original culture may conflict with fundamental values or principles held in the host culture. For example, the controversy between the Sikhs, on the one hand, and the Legion of Veterans, on the other, involving the use of the former's headgear in the latter's Legion halls, is a reminder that passions are aroused by the conflict of traditions, beliefs, or values. Practices from Muslim countries that run counter to Christian religious and moral perceptions among mainstrean Canadians are bound to produce confrontational situations. However, it should be pointed out that, no matter how alike, groups within the mainstream society also have their own conflicting beliefs, values, and practices. Thus, unless we wrongheadedly insist on the unattainable dream of cultural homogeneity, we must realistically countenance the occasional occurrence of conflictual situations. In this regard, multiculturalism may properly be viewed as a policy of realism rather than illusions in its attempt to insure more understanding among, and mutual appreciation of, different cultural groups who recognize the inevitability of cultural and other differences. In any case, inevitable as the occurrence of such conflicts may be, our democratic system provides for means of resolution. At the first instance, the political system may offer possibilities for compromise or accommodation through legislative action following public discussion and debate. Failing this, the legal system is available as a final resort.

However, serious problem related to the policy's implementation is undeniable. The policy is a multi-principled one, which requires different but coordinated thrusts simultaneously. Yet multiculturalism has generally been implemented as a single-track policy which focuses at different times on a single principle (e.g., cultural sharing through "song, food, and dance") in a piecemeal, inadequate way. Though the policy's intent is to promote a united society marked by freedom of cultural retention and equal participation on the part of all cultural groups and individuals who mutually relate to, and appreciate, one another, its implementation thus far has been limited, ill-focused, and inadequately funded. Its early implementation in the 1970s concentrated on (symbolic) cultural retention, to the justified dismay of those who rightly believe that equal participation by ethnic groups and members, as well as unity, needed no less attention. However, realization of the extent of discrimination and racism in Canada has resulted in the subsequent thrust toward equity and anti-racism strategies. Following the Meech Lake Accord and Charlottetown Accord debacles, the need to directly pursue unity more energetically and singlemindedly has come to the fore. Such unilinear, single focus approach, rather than a systematic, simultaneous, and multifaceted, implementation of the policy, has distorted the true nature of multiculturalism in the public view, and the chorus of criticism against it is understandable. That the policy's focus on "song, food, and dance" in the 1970s was very disquieting cannot be denied. If multiculturalism is to command the credibility that it deserves before the public, it has to be implemented, and seen to be implemented, adequately, rigorously, and systematically as a multi-thrust policy.

Apparently governments have attempted to pursue the policy in appropriate ways. Their changing implementation foci over the years (Abu-Laban, 1994; McRoberts, 1995; Pal, 1993) signify their sensitivity to public criticism. Policy implementation has responded to well documented studies and evaluations (e.g. Special Committee on Visible Minorities in Canadian Society, 1984; Standing Committee on Multiculturalism, 1987; Canada, Citizens' Forum on Canada's Future, 1991; Canadian Heritage, 1996). Yet it appears that these studies themselves respond to the changing perceptions of the day and fail to demonstrate that the implementation of the policy of multiculturalism requires multi-pronged programs which are systematically linked and coordinated to attain objectives flowing from its values and principles.

Worse still, the implementation process has become exceedingly circumscribed for lack of funding. Challenging economic circumstances have given Canadian governments the arguments, if not the pretext, for stringent, ever-diminishing government resource allocation for multicultural programs. The shrinking funding, which was insufficient to start with, has forced the continuing contraction of government offices or departments charged with the limited implementation of a wide-ranging policy.

THE MULTICULTURALIST AGENDA:
A VIGOROUS POLICY IMPLEMENTATION

Difficult as governmental circumstances have been, the fact remains that, with its goal of unity and its three fundamental principles, multiculturalism is a policy that demands greater attention from governmental institutions. More than ever, as disadvantaged ethnic members continue to find that opportunities in the land of promise remain beyond their grasp, and as majority groups exhibit their underlying sense of fear or resentment of new and different peoples in their homeland, a more effective, committed, and encompassing implementation of the policy of multiculturalism is required.

Unfortunately, now that the backlash against multiculturalism has succeeded in painting a negative picture of the policy in
the public mind and intimidated ethnocultural groups from
pursuing their entitlements implied in federal and provincial
statutes and policies, it is doubtful that governments are eager to
place the cause of multiculturalism on its political and financial
agenda. Indeed lack of governmental action, even as governmental
fiscal capacity improves, will prove discouraging, particularly for
those who believe that lack of governmental support for
multiculturalism is due simply to budgetary constraints, to which
government constantly appeals, when charges of inadequate
funding are leveled against it.

A further discouraging reality is that, in their current form,
statutory enactments or governmental statements on multiculturalism are largely a political declaration to which little, if any,
specific programmatic mandates are attached. Thus, if the policy is
to get implemented, government at all levels must have and
exercise its political will. This, as we know, is evidently nowhere.
Given a disaffected Canadian mainstream, the burden surely falls
on ethnocultural minorities themselves. As Binavince (1997, p.
100), a prominent ethnocultural community leader, puts it,

> ...We (minority groups) need a new strategy
> to mobilize ... Canadians. Further, minorities have
> to stress to political leaders and other Canadians
> that our efforts are not driven by a will to get power
> or special protection. The community must, in the
> future, be more aggressive in making itself heard. It
> can contribute creatively to Canada in the
> multicultural and constitutional debate.

Needless to say, if a new strategy is to work, the policy
which it advocates should be, in the public eye, transparent,
justifiable, and worthy of substantial resource allocation. It is truly
unfortunate that the uniquely Canadian conception of multiculturalism has not been presented with clarity and decisiveness, and
that it has been confused, in the minds of so many, with hazy,
ambiguous, or problematic conceptions peddled or criticized by
popular Canadian writers who should know better (Magsino, 1998,
pp. 7-21), and even by minority groups or members themselves

(Binavince, 1997, p. 100). One task in front of multiculturalists is therefore that of ensuring—through dialogue in different forums and through the various media—that the appropriate Canadian conception of multiculturalism is understood and its moral justification appreciated (Magsino, 1989; 1998) by ethnocultural members and the Canadian mainstream. In this regard, educational institutions at all levels may be expected to do their part. Multiculturalism advocates need to persuade schools and post-secondary institutions that multicultural education is included in their educational mandate. In a culturally diverse society, the development of educated citizens requires an understanding of the cultural pluralism and its implications not only for interpersonal and group relationships, but also for the workings of societal institutions. Moreover, insofar as multiculturalism, as well as multicultural education, is an established policy in most provinces, the propriety of tactfully reminding educational institutions of their obligation to pursue multiculturalism and multicultural education cannot be questioned.

Beyond educational institutions, multiculturalists must enter the political arena in its various sites, if they are to make an impact on the government and its institutions. Whether it is through lobbying in the Parliament, provincial legislatures, town halls, or constituency offices of politicians; at public meetings, political rallies, and the like, the cause of multiculturalism needs to be raised energetically and intelligently. In this, multiculturalists have the full justification for their advocacy: multiculturalism is not only an established policy but also a constitutionally recognized principle in the country. More compellingly, it is also one policy that is indisputably worthy of implementation because of its grounding in an overriding moral principle accepted in a humane, democratic society: the principle of respect for persons. Their advocacy has also a wealth of instruments, in the form of reputable reports based on solid research and wide-ranging consultation, which have recommended programs and measures intended to attain the goals of multiculturalism in a diverse society.

The case for multiculturalism, and thus for its adequate, properly planned, and efficiently executed implementation, is unexceptionable and strong. Dare ethnocultural minority members, and their multiculturalist friends, to demonstrate their political will as full-fledged Canadian citizens through a concerted advocacy of multiculturalism?

Acknowledgements

* An earlier version of this article was published in *Canadian and International Education,* Volume 28, Number 2. We wish to thank the Volume's Guest Editor, Dr. Rosa Bruno-Joffré; and Editor, Dr. Jack Y. Lam for permission to reprint this article.

REFERENCES

Abu-Laban, Y. (1994). The politics of race and ethnicity: Multiculturalism as a contested area. In J. Bickerton & A-G. Gagnon (Eds.), *Canadian politics.* Peterborough: ON: Broadview Press.

Alladin, M.I. (1996). *Racism in Canadian schools.* Toronto, ON: Harcourt Brace & Company, Canada.

Binavince, E.S. (1997). The role of ethnic minorities in the pursuit of equality and multiculturalism. In A. Cardozo & L. Musto (Eds.), *The battle over multiculturalism.* Ottawa: PSI Publishing.

Bibby, R. (1990). *Mosaic madness.* Toronto: Stoddart Publishing.

Bissoondath, N. (1993). A question of belonging: Multiculturalism and citizenship. In W. Kaplan (Ed.), *Belonging: The meaning and future of Canadian citizenship.* Montreal & Kingston, ON: McGill-Queen's University Press.

Bissoondath, N. (1994). *Selling illusions. The cult of multiculturalism in Canada.* Toronto: Penguin Books.

Brass, P. (1985). *Ethnic groups and the state.* Totowa, NJ: Barnes and Noble.

Breton, R. (1998). Ethnicity and race in social organization: Recent developments in Canadian society. In R. Helmes-Hayes & J. Curtis (Eds.), *The vertical mosaic revisited.* Toronto: ON: University of Toronto Press.

Brotz, H. (1980). Multiculturalism in Canada: A muddle. *Canadian Public Policy*, VI(1): 41-46.

Burnet, J. (1983). Multiculturalism. In J.H. Marsh (Ed.), The
    Canadian Encyclopedia. Edmonton, AB: Hurtig
    Publications.

Canada. (1988). *An Act for the preservation and enhancement of
    multiculturalism in Canada.* (Bill C-93). House of
    Commons.

Canada. (1882). *Constitution Act, 1982*. R.S.C. 1985, Appendix II,
    No.44. (The Canadian Charter of Rights and
    Freedoms).

Canada. Citizen's Forum on Canada's Future. (1991). *Report to the
    people and government of Canada (Spicer Report).*
    Ottawa: Minister of Supply and Services Canada.

Canadian Heritage. (1996). *Strategic evaluation of
    multiculturalism programs. Final report*. Ottawa:
    Corporate Review Branch.

Clement, W. (1975). *The Canadian corporate elite*. Toronto:
    McClelland & Stewart.

Coombs, J. (No date). *Multicultural education and social justice*.
    Xerox copy.

Dworkin, R. (1977). *Taking rights seriously*. Cambridge, MA:
    Cambridge University Press.

Fleras, A. & Elliott, J. (1992). *Multiculturalism in Canada.*
    Scarborough, ON: Nelson Canada.

Friesen, J. (1991). Multiculturalism in Canada: Hope or hoax?
    Multicultural Education Journal, 10(1): 1-36.

Friesen, J. (1993). When cultures clash. Calgary, AB: Detselig
    Enterprises.

Gairdner, W. (1990). *The trouble with Canada*. Toronto: General
    Paperbacks.

Granatstein, J.L. (1998). *Who killed Canadian history?* Toronto:
    Harper-Collins.

Gurr, T. (1993). *Minorities at risk: A global view of ethnopolitical
    conflicts*. Washington, D.C.: United States Institute for
    Peace.

Hall, R. (1979). *Ethnic autonomy*. New York: Pergamon Press.

Kallen, E. (1995). *Ethnicity and human rights in Canada*. Toronto:
    Oxford University Press.

Kymlicka, W. (1996). Social unity in a liberal state. In E. Paul, F.
    Miller, & J. Paul (Eds.), *The communitarian challenge
    to liberalism*. Cambridge: Cambridge University Press.

Lautard, H. & Guppy, N. (1999). Revisiting the vertical mosaic: Occupational stratification among Canadian ethnic groups. In P.S. Li (ed.), *Race and ethnic relations in Canada.* Don Mills, ON: Oxford University Press.

Li, P. (1988). *Ethnic inequality in a class society.* Toronto: Wall & Thompson.

Magsino, R. (1989). Multiculturalism in schools: Is multicultural education possible and justifiable? In S. Morris (Ed.), *Multicultural and intercultural education: Building Canada.* Calgary, AB: Detselig Enterprises.

Magsino, R. (1991). The immigrant student and multicultural education: Exploring the bases of legal entitlement. In W. Foster & F. Peters, *Education and law: Strengthening the partnership.* Montreal: Soleil Publishing.

Magsino, R. (1998). Multiculturalism in Canadian society: A re-evaluation. Paedeusis. *Journal of the Canadian Philosophy of Education Society,* 12 (2): 7-21.

Manitoba. (1992). *The Manitoba Multiculturalism Act.* (Bill 98). Manitoba Legislative Assembly.

Maybury-Lewis, D. (1984). *The prospects for plural societies.* Washington, D.C.: American Ethnological Society.

McRoberts, K. (1995). Living with dualism and multiculturalism. In F. Rocher & M. Smith (Eds.), *New trends in Canadian federalism.* Peterborough, ON: Broadview Press.

Meghji, A. (1991). Multiculturalism in the new Canada. In J.L. Granatstein & K. McNaught (Eds.), *"English Canada" speaks out.* Toronto, ON: Doubleday Canada.

Milne, A. (1986). *Human rights and human diversity.* London: Macmillan Press.

Moodley, K. (1983). Canadian multiculturalism as ideology. *Ethnic and Racial Studies,* 6(3): 320-332.

Pal, L. (1993). *Interests of state. The politics of language, multiculturalism, and feminism in Canada.* Montreal & Kingston, ON: McGill-Queen's University Press.

Peter, K. (1981). The myth of multiculturalism and other political foibles. In J. Dahlie & T. Fernando (Eds.), *Ethnics and education.* London: Allen & Unwin.

Porter, J. (1965). *Vertical mosaic.* Toronto, ON: University of Toronto Press.

Porter, J. (1979). *The measure of Canadian society.* Toronto, Gage.

Quinton, A. (1973). *The nature of things*. London: Routledge & Kegan.

Ramcharan, S. (1982). *Racism: Non-white in Canada*. Toronto, ON: Butterworths.

Roberts, L. & Clifton, R. (1982). Exploring the ideology of Canadian multiculturalism. *Canadian Public Policy*, VIII(1): 88-94.

Sigler, J. (1983). *Minority rights: A comparative analysis*. Westport, CT: Greenwood Press.

Special Committee on Visible Minorities in Canadian Society. (1984). *Equality now*. Ottawa: Queen's Printer.

Standing Committee on Multiculturalism. (1987). *Multiculturalism: Building the Canadian mosaic*. Ottawa: Queen's Printer.

Steinberg, S. (1989). *The ethnic myth*. Boston: MA: Beacon Press.

Taylor, C. (1992). *Multiculturalism and the politics of recognition*. Princeton, NJ: Princeton University Press.

Trudeau, P.E. (1984). Statement by the Prime Minister in the House of Commons, October 8, 1971. In J. Mallea & J. Young (Eds.), *Cultural diversity and Canadian education*. Ottawa: Carleton University Press.

Webber, J. (1996). Multiculturalism and the limits to toleration. In A. Lapierre, P. Smart, & P. Savard (Eds.), *Language, culture and values in Canada at the dawn of the 21st century*. Ottawa: Carleton University Press.

Wright, I. & LaBar, C. (1984). Multiculturalism and morality. In S. Shapson & V. D'Oyley (Eds.), *Bilingual and multicultural education: Canadian perspectives*. Clevedon, Avon, England: Multilingual Matters.

Chapter 17

UNITY IN DIVERSITY: NOT UNIFORMITY

John Sahadat

Historical Realities

There was a time when we could refer to Canada as a Judaeo-Christian society without being challenged. The Judaeo-Christian world-view played a dominant role in shaping our socio-political and educational institutions, our code of ethics and our legal system. However, this should not lead to the false assumption that Christianity was the only religion in Canada at any given time in the history of this country. At its earliest advent through explorers, settlers and missionaries, Christianity encountered the indigenous peoples of this land who had their unique religious beliefs, practices and customs; but that encounter became confrontational. The scars of that confrontation have persisted through the centuries and they appear more and more visible today as the indigenous peoples struggle to recapture their identity and to reconstruct their world-view. The critique that Christianity is imperialistic and exclusivistic is not uncommon, notwithstanding its great contributions to world and particularly western civilization.

But Christianity's commitment to evangelization must be understood in the context of its early sense of call and mission. The exhortation to go out into the world and make disciples was taken with deep concern. Moreover, it was believed that there was an urgency for the proclamation of the gospel message as preparation for the **Second Coming**. There was also the belief that Christianity was the only path through which salvation could be attained and only believers would be saved. In 1302, the position of Pope Boniface VIII on this issue was made quite clear and was reaffirmed by the Council of Florence (1438-1445), in the often quoted phrase: *extra ecclesiam nulla salus*—outside the Church no salvation. From the Protestant side a more recent declaration of exclusivism is brought out in the Congress on World Mission at Chicago in 1960, which states that since the war over one billion souls have inherited eternal life while more than half that number passed on to hell with no knowledge of who Jesus Christ was, what he stood for, or why he died.[1] Right here at home, the report of the United Church's Commission on Christianizing the Social Order (1934) states that the goal of the United Church is to initiate the interpenetration of our civilization and the transformation of institutions and agencies with the Spirit of Jesus Christ so that Christians may realize the Christian life more fully and others may also be led to the same realization.[2] And there is the dogmatic and exclusivistic position of Karl Barth, the towering Protestant theologian, regarded by many as the greatest in the modern era. Barth is emphatic in his contention that the revelation of God in Jesus Christ is the abolition of religion, and on the basis of this revelation the Church is "the locus of true religion."[3] But times have changed and so have attitudes. In its declaration on the relation of the Church to other religions, Vatican II, *Nostra Aetate*, emphasizes that all men and women comprise one community under one God who is the Creator of all; and furthermore, we all share a common ultimate destiny which is God whose loving kindness and saving grace are extended to all. Moreover, the Catholic Church does not deny or reject those teachings that are "true and holy" in other religions. Vatican II also goes a long way to encourage and support inter-faith dialogue.[4] Today the role of the Catholic Church in seeking the rights and freedoms of the oppressed and justice for all is a highly recognized fact. The emphasis of the Society of Jesus, for example, on becoming persons for others and on seeking the restoration of human dignity has brought the Church *in media res*, so to speak. From the Protestant standpoint, the World Council of Churches comprising the United Church of Canada, the Anglican Church and other denominations share similar concerns. We can correctly say that mainstream Christianity has undergone fundamental attitudinal changes to grasp the existential fact of one humanity under one God in one world community, putting to a great extent the emphasis on caring for the poor, the stranger, the sick and the oppressed. In spite of attitudinal changes in many Christian Churches, however, fundamentalism and evangelicalism still persist in several denominations, whose primary concern is to present Christianity as the only authentic path to salvation.[5]

For obvious empirical reasons no one today can speak of Canada as a Judaeo-Christian society and not expect to be contradicted, not only because of the empirical data depicting diversity; but also because the indigenous peoples as well as other visible minorities have a heightened sense of their rights and freedoms to live out their unique traditions with dignity and to take much pride in doing it. Never before in the history of Canada has this country been so characterized by diversity. From Vancouver to St. John's one will find not only in large cities like Vancouver, Calgary, Toronto, etc.; but also in smaller ones, peoples of different racial and religious backgrounds. It is not surprising, therefore, that within short distances of Christian churches there are synagogues, mosques and temples. The vast Christian population is dotted by Amerindian, Jewish, Hindu, Buddhist, Islamic, Sikh, and other communities. All of these communities have been contributing to the richness of the multi-racial and multi-religious mosaic of Canada. What is it, then, to be Canadian? The answer to this question is certainly not determined by any **one** of the following factors of race, colour, creed, language, manners or customs. On Canada Day, which is observed on July 1st each year, we notice at celebrations throughout the country the coming together of diverse ethnic groups with their unique dress codes, cultural performances and varieties of culinary display. Underlying this diversity there is a sense of unity which transcends racial, cultural and religious particularities and which gives to us a sense of patriotism and nationalism as **Canadians** united under one constitution, one flag, one currency, two official languages, one national anthem, and one democratically elected government. But we can also speak about unity in diversity from a metaphysical level, which will lead us to explore the question of our ontological structure and its corollary existential challenge. This issue will be explored below from the vantage point of a **Vedantic Model**. Canadians of diverse racial and religious backgrounds comprise the population of this nation; and they are given the opportunity to be educated and trained in our various institutions for service in every walk of life and profession. Freedom and equality of opportunity have made the **rainbow picture** a common phenomenon throughout our **workplace** from coast to coast, and it is no longer surprising to encounter visible minorities working alongside their white Canadian fellow citizens, contributing to the general good of the whole country.

Today science and technology have broken the barrier of distance through modern means of travel and communication, thus making the confluence of peoples a common sociological phenomenon. Through immigration there is a shifting trend in population. People are migrating from their homeland either because they are forced to do so in search of refuge in foreign countries, or because they leave of their own accord in search of greater opportunities or to rejoin family members, etc. Canada has been the host country of many such immigrants over the years, though not always with open arms, for example, one recalls the unpleasant experience of the Sikhs in **the Komagata Maru incident** in 1914 when four hundred of them were denied entry into this country and were forced to return to India from off the coast of Vancouver.[6] A confluence of peoples means a meeting of traditions with their unique beliefs, manners and customs. Canadian society is an excellent example in the western world of this kind of mosaic. The appropriate response of the host country is neither assimilation nor mere tolerance, but understanding with empathy, and tolerance with acceptance of one another through respect, on-going dialogue and cultural reciprocity.

Metaphysical Unity in Phenomenal Diversity:
A Vedantic Model

A country as vast as Canada in its geographical dimensions and in its racial and religious diversity is a good example of what is meant by a global community. Any effort towards religious/ cultural reductionism can only be an exercise in futility, for the roots of religion/culture run deep into a people's history and heritage. Their beliefs, manners and customs are dear to them as expressions of loyalty to ancestors, tradition, and as essential ingredients for determining their ultimate destiny. A melting-pot scenario is well intentioned, but it is an unnatural and superficial response to diversity. For example, should it be compulsory for Sikhs to cease wearing turbans to become members of the Royal

Canadian Legion or to serve in various capacities in order to maintain uniformity in dress code, as some insist? To argue that the answer should be in the affirmative is to miss the profound religious significance of the turban for the Sikh tradition and its community. Religious symbols have deep roots, not only for Sikhism, but for all religions; and whereas some **may appear** strange to the outsiders of a tradition is no justification for demanding their removal. A melting-pot scenario does not hold as much significance for the Vedantic model as does the sociological phenomenon of religious pluralism and the challenge of parallelism in peaceful co-existence. Seeking to grasp and understand the unity underlying diversity is taking a significant step beyond religious and cultural particularities.

From the Vedantic standpoint unity in diversity is characteristic of phenomenal existence. The Vedantic attitude is deeply rooted in the primary and foundational religious and metaphysical consciousness of the seers in the *Rig Veda*, the *Upanishads* and the *Bhagavadgita*. Brahman is the absolute truth (*paramartha satya*), the reality of all realities (satyasya *satyam*), and devoid of all attributes (*nirguna*); but for the sake of humanity, the Absolute, Impersonal Brahman phenomenalizes **Itself** by taking on various attributes (*saguna*). Thus the *Gita 4:7-8* explains the purpose of *avatara* (the descent of God: incarnation) in human history. **Whenever** and **wherever** there is a decline in *dharma*, that is, in the natural order of things, in righteousness and morality (*dharmasya*), the Divine Being incarnates **Itself.** Incarnation, therefore, is the historicization of the Divine for the restoration of *dharma* in the welfare of humanity. In the same chapter of the *Gita, verse 11*, the Lord declares that all paths belong to him and thus accepts all devotees regardless of the path by which they seek him. From the metaphysical standpoint, it is the One Reality that takes on different **names** and **forms** in different historical and cultural contexts, but for the same purpose. From the phenomenal point of view religions are many, and are to be taken as diverse pathways leading aspirants from different racial and cultural backgrounds to ultimate liberation in the One. While Hindu thinkers such as Sri Ramakrishna, Swami Vivekananda, Mahatma Gandhi, Sarvepalli Radhakrishnan and others of the East make this Vedantic model a basic platform for dialogue and acceptance, Christian thinkers such as Ernst Troeltsch, Arnold Toynbee,

Wilfred Cantwell Smith, John Hick, Ninian Smart and others of the West have gone beyond western parochialism to speak of the One in the many,[7] and to steer clear of the false assumption that because God has revealed himself in **our** religion the claim to revelation by any other people or religion is false.

The Vedantic model removes the following erroneous claims: that my religion has a monopoly on truth, hence the claim to truth by any other religion must be either partially true or false; that revelation in my tradition is the culmination of all God's revelations and it is the final disclosure of truth to humanity, hence all other claims to revelation before mine must be either partially true or false, and all claims after mine must be false; that my religion is the only true and authentic path to salvation, hence all other religions must be either deficient or false. At this point in our history neither Judaism, nor Christianity, nor any other religion for that matter can afford to take any of the above positions unless it deliberately wishes to brand itself exclusivistic, or unless it wishes to exist in isolation; but isolationism can be nothing more than abstractionism in a shrinking world. The foundational experience of the seers and prophets of the world's religions was initially enunciated in their native language and lived out within their historical and cultural milieu, hence Hinduism has that Indian cultural flavour to it, as well as Buddhism which later took on the cultural garb of Southern and Northern Asia in its Theravadian and Mahayanic expressions, respectively. Islam, proclaimed by the Prophet, Muhammed, in the sixth century A.D., was shaped by its indigenous Arabic language and culture; and so likewise were Judaism and Christianity in their Hebraic-Greco-Roman background. Despite the variations in the primordial experiences of these early seers and prophets, and despite the diverse historical and cultural contexts in which their religions originated, there are fundamental beliefs which they all hold in common. First, that they had an experience of the Ultimate Reality. Second, from that enlightening experience they understood the human existential crisis and, third, that they found a way that can lead out of that crisis to a state of ultimate meaning and total well-being, the *summum bonum* of all existence. There is no religious tradition that will deny that it is an authentic path to salvation. There are some people, however, who, even today, will deny that other religions are authentic paths to salvation except their own. The real problem arises when religions compete with one another for absolute and exclusive authenticity. The argument of any religion, based on either revelatory claims or hermeneutical ingenuity or both, to assert itself as the most authentic path to salvation puts the truth—claims of all other religions into question and itself into a dogmatic dilemma.

In Canada the challenge to fundamentalism and exclusivism has come from primarily two angles, the **socio-practical** and the **theoretical-academic**. First, the flow of immigrants into Canada especially from Asia and the Middle East has affirmed with the presence of the indigenous peoples of this continent that there are other religions, many of which predate Christianity, and that Christianity is only one among many. The second challenge comes from a **theoretical-academic** angle and, this, like the flow of immigrants is a fact not only in Canada; but also in the United States, the United Kingdom and wider Europe. Many Canadian Universities, for example, have established departments of Religious Studies, Asian, African, and Middle Eastern Studies etc., at the undergraduate and graduate levels. The music, painting, sculpture, literature and religions of these geographical regions testify to the fact that the sense of aesthetics, creativity, mystical insights and philosophical reflections are not the exclusive gifts of the fathers of western civilization. Courses in **World Religions** and in **The Comparative Study of Religions,** for example, are studied from a historical and phenomenological perspective without bias or allegiance to a particular religious tradition. Such a methodology coupled with the hermeneutical analysis of sacred texts indicate two things among many. First, that all religions claim to have their origin in the One, Eternal and Absolute Reality. The ancient text of Hinduism, the *Rig. Veda I-164-46* declares, "Truth is One, the wise call it by different names," hence *Brahman* for the Hindus, *Dharmakaya* for the Buddhists, *Tao* for the Taoists, *God* for the Christians and *Allah* for the Muslims. The point is, there are not many truths, hence we cannot meaningfully speak about the Christian truth, or the Buddhist truth, or the Muslim truth, etc. We can, however, make sense by speaking about the Christian apprehension and interpretation of truth, the Hindu, the Buddhist, or the Muslim apprehension and interpretation of truth within their respective historical and cultural milieu.

Any religion that makes exclusive and absolute truth-claims about the revelation of God, and on that basis asserts itself as the only authentic religion seeks to do the impossible by putting a limit on the infinite love of God and on his powers of manifestation. The Vedantin, Ramakrishna, explains that the manifestations of God are many and through anyone of them, he can be known.[8] The celebrated Muslim poet and mystic, Rumi, wrote in his poem entitled "The One True Light," that God is the core of Existence but the disagreement between the religions of the world are due to different points of view.[9] And from the Judaeo-Christian perspective, the Prophet Malachai poses the timely, soul-searching question when he asks, "Have we not all one father? Has not one God created us? Why then are we faithless to one another...?"*(Malachai 2:1).*

The second thing that this methodology indicates is that structurally the religions of the world hold a common ultimate intent in so far as they provide a passage to their aspirants for a transformative and fulfilling experience of the ultimate reality. It is a methodology that exposes the invalidity of any religion's claim to have a monopoly on truth, and it simultaneously affirms the validity of Hinduism for the Hindus, Sikhism for the Sikhs, Islam for the Muslims, Christianity for the Christians, etc. On the one hand, it is a methodology that negates the superimposition of the assumptions and beliefs of one's own tradition upon another and avoids the pitfalls of distorted value judgment and prejudiced conclusions. On the other hand, it challenges an outsider to a tradition to become an insider, for example, a Christian or anyone else who wishes to study Hinduism, or any other religion for that matter, can become an insider by entering the world-view of Hinduism or any other religion through an analysis of its theological and philosophical beliefs and assumptions as they are contained in its sacred literature.

Unity in Intent but Diversity in Approaches

To Christianity religion is **christocentric**, to Zoroastrianism, Judaism, Islam, Bhakti Hinduism and strands of Mahayana Buddhism religion is **theocentric**; but whereas the christocentric model excludes all other religions, the theocentric model includes Christianity. But the christo-theocentric models

exclude all non-theistic religions, for example, Theravada
Buddhism, and are thus also limited and exclusivistic. They fall
short of giving a complete picture of the whole range of religions.
From a phenomenological and hermeneutical perspective it can be
deduced that religions are **salvificentric**. This must not be taken to
mean that the religions of the world are the same, and that their
teachings are identical. The **salvificentric model** is more
comprehensive and it accommodates the entire spectrum of
religions as historical phenomena. It indicates their common intent
within a tri-functional structure, notwithstanding their varied
historical and cultural backgrounds and their doctrinal differences.
As we cut through to the core of religions we find that they all
have a common goal, which is salvation/liberation; however, the
approaches to realize this ultimate goal are as many as there are
religions.[10] The use of the terms **salvation** or **liberation** raises
three basic questions: (a) salvation from what? (b) salvation to
what? (c) by what means can one make the passage from (a) to (b)?
All religions realize that there is an existential crisis in the human
condition (Q); they prescribe a method of passage (R) from (Q)
to an experience of ultimate meaning and certainty of total well-
being (S). This tri-dimensional structure can be applied as a
paradigm for a cross-cultural study of the inherent salvific intent of
religions and can be diagrammatically illustrated as follows:

---------------------------->R----------------------->
Q _____ S

| The human condition | Passage via precepts and practices | Experience of the ultimate reality and certainty of total well-being. |

Even Theravada Buddhism falls within this tri-dimensional
structure, though it is one of the most unorthodox religions because
of its refusal to postulate the existence of God, soul or eternality,
and because of its deontologization of nirvana. From its perception
of the human condition, Buddhism concludes that the existential
crisis is suffering, caused by selfish craving and ignorance which
hold human beings in bondage to empirical existence; Hinduism

concludes that human beings are held in bondage to empirical existence and to the sufferings that go with it, because they are under the influence of spiritual ignorance which leads them into mistaking the selfish ego for the real self (*atman*); and for the Semitic religions the existential crisis is alienation from God because of sin/disobedience exemplified in human beings' deliberate contradiction of the will of God. We can delineate from these perceptions of the human condition that the selfish ego, the **empirical-I**, functions as a centrifugal force that pulls human beings away from the absolute reality and thus from ultimate meaning and total well-being. Religions, however, are cartographical and centripetal in structure and function in so far as they map out a course that leads from the existential crisis to an experience of the ultimate reality. For Buddhism, the course is the Noble Eightfold Path which promises liberation from suffering/bondage to *Nirvana;* for Hinduism, it is either the path of knowledge, the path of selfless action or the path of devotion (depending on one's choice) that will lead from bondage to liberation in moksha; and for Islam, it is the Five Pillars that will lead to Paradise. A cross cultural, hermeneutical study of terms such as **nirvana, moksha, paradise** in Christianity and **paradise** in Islam will show different meanings, but in the final analysis they indicate the **summum bonum** as perceived by the various traditions.

While loyalty to one's own religion is understandable, in a pluralistic society neither ethnocentricity nor religiocentricity should dim our vision of the crucial existential fact that we are all in need of deliverance from our predicament, and that the human soul longs to fulfill its quest for ultimate meaning and total well-being. Who then can answer the question, which religion is most fulfilling? Neither a Christian could answer for a Muslim nor vice versa, nor a Hindu for a Christian, etc. The most authentic answer can only come from a Christian for Christianity, a Muslim for Islam, a Buddhist for Buddhism etc. The authentic answer can be given only by the practitioners of a religion and not by outsiders. The response to religious pluralism is to think not in terms of **we** and **they** but, with regard to fundamental existential questions as presented by religions, to think in terms of **we** and **all of us** as **travelers** seeking the common goal of ultimate reality and the fullness of being. Moreover, the response to religious pluralism should not be hierarchialism which would put us into an archaic, prejudicial and self-righteous situation to give first place to our own religion and classify others as less authentic with lesser degrees of truth. The appropriate response should be an attitude which would allow **me** to accept Christianity as **my way** to ultimate reality and total well-being, and simultaneously accept the fact that Hinduism, Buddhism, Jainism, Islam, Sikhism, etc. are alternative ways, authentic and fulfilling for Hindus, Buddhists, Jains, Muslims and Sikhs, respectively. The fact of diversity at the threshold of the 21st century leaves us with two responses: to acknowledge a metaphysical unity at the depth of empirical diversity, and to accept the fact that it is **we** (**all of us**) as members of the whole human race on a single planet who are seeking the Ultimate through diverse beliefs and practices. The **we** and **us** factor is a significant social denominator that will help us value diversity without losing our identity. It will steer us clear of the limited vision of ethnocentricity and religiocentricity to a wider and deeper sense of a human family within a global community.

Meeting the Challenges

Racial and cultural diversity can be an enriching sociological phenomenon, but although it provides a fertile milieu and a timely challenge for understanding our world, our neighbours, our common problems, our ultimate destiny and ourselves more fully, it arouses fear and suspicion, discrimination and injustice, bigotry and hostility. Religions can undoubtedly play an important role in this complex situation, but religions themselves have been the cause of bigotry and hostility. For religions to make their full, positive impact, they must be willing to face the following challenges: to go beyond parochialism; to cease from making exclusivistic and absolute truth-claims against one another; to shift the emphasis from orthodoxy to orthopraxy; to recognize a common ontic source as the *sine qua non* of their very existence and of unity in diversity; and to recognize the validity of a passage from the human condition to the fullness of being as an open existential challenge for all peoples through the religion of their personal choice. This is the first set of challenges that religions have to meet, if they intend to become an effective, consolidated force for harmony and well-being. In other words, religions have some house cleaning to do: self-criticism, self-evaluation and self-understanding in relation to one another and in relation to the general good. The challenge of the future is not a mega-religion, but as Harold Coward contends religious pluralism should be acceptable and people should be allowed the freedom to follow the religion of their choice and to draw closer to the **One** that underlies religious diversity.[11]

Among the many other challenges that religions face today, there are two that will be our main concern in the following discussion: **alienation and dialogue**. Alienation must be understood in a tri-dimensional sense and religions must be prepared to face this challenge with a more comprehensive view of reality compared to that of classical theism and a metaphysics of being. The selfish ego, a mechanistic view of the universe, the abuse of science and technology, the compartmentalization of God, nature and humans as independent realities are some of the reasons for a tri-dimensional alienation so characteristic of the twentieth century and so highly pronounced in industrialized and pluralistic societies. The first dimension of alienation arises from an internal conflict between the selfish ego and the real self.[12] As human beings succumb to the greed and pride of egocentricity, they alienate themselves from their true being, their ontic centre. This is mankind's first encounter with alienation and it is experienced at the psycho-spiritual level. The second dimension of alienation is experienced at the social level. It manifests itself in various forms of discrimination and it operates on the principles of how one looks, what one believes, what one has, and not on the more profound principle of who or what one **is** and **needs**. In such circumstances one lives in a mechanical society with superficial relationships and little or no sense of community spirit. Visible minorities, the poor and under-privileged are alienated and they become victims of humiliation and dehumanization. The third level of alienation is experienced between human beings and nature. Our desire to dominate and possess, and our misuse of advanced science and technology have led to the exploitation of nature to the extent that we have created one of mankind's most disastrous ecological crises. Underlying this tri-dimensional structure of alienation: alienation from God, from our fellow human beings and from nature is the selfish ego, the empirical-I, and a misconception of reality.

Life is an organized whole in which **interdependence**, **interrelatedness** and **interaction** are of vital importance for the general welfare of society. Alienation of any kind , therefore , is an extraneous factor on life and could only serve towards negative consequences. The problem of alienation cannot be properly addressed, if it is understood only from a socio-economic perspective. It has to be grasped in its primordial state as a religious problem manifesting itself at the psycho-spiritual, the socio-economic and the ecological levels. Fritz Pappenheim's thesis that the experience of alienation in the modern world is the result of "economic and social trends" must be challenged.[13] Socio-economic trends are not the **root cause** of alienation. The same can be said about scientific, technological and racial trends. The cause/effect relationship does not necessarily follow that because of advanced science and technology the rape of nature is a logical effect; or because Canada is a multi-racial society, discrimination is the result. If such were the case, then it would follow that we have no choice but to accept a kind of scientific/technological and racial determinism. The point is we do have a choice because we can make decisions, build and create. Pappenheim contends that it is possible to overcome the forces of alienation, but only if we are prepared to work towards a "new foundation of society" and to initiate changes at the "roots of our social system".[14] We may agree with Pappenheim that the victory over the forces of alienation is a new foundation of society. Our major contention, however, is that the new foundation of society can never be ushered in through the establishment of new socio-economic institutions. These will only treat symptoms of the malady and not the cause.

As long as we are alienated from our ontic centre, we will be dominated by the **empirical-I** and can never tackle the problem of alienation at its root cause. To return to our ontic centre and to live from that depth of reality means that we must be willing to sacrifice egocentricity. This is the transformative challenge of religions. We have to exercise our choice to become co-workers with our fellowmen, with nature and with God in the general welfare of the whole. The change has to occur in us who are the true foundation of society and its institutions. Raimundo Panikkar contends that the remedy can be found in what he calls "a radical **metanoia**", and in a cosmotheandric vision of reality that constitutes God, nature and the human being.[15] The world view of the native peoples of Canada, Taoism, and process philosophy/theology have contributed much towards an understanding of a holistic view of reality, which takes us beyond classical theism and a metaphysics of being to accommodate mutuality and the process of becoming. As Religions face the challenge of alienation in the 21st century, they will have to become more open to the organic and holistic view of reality by emphasizing interdependence, interrelatedness and creative interaction between God, nature and human beings, and by extending their ethical concerns beyond human life to all of nature and its various life-forms. The poet, Rabindranath Tagore, brings out the organic and holistic view when he states that the same life which flows through him also flows through the world and through the "dust of the earth in numberless blades of grass and breaks into tumultuous waves of leaves and flowers..."[16]. The emphasis has to be on stewardship, responsibility and accountability. Thus, indeed, we must be our brothers' and sisters' keepers regardless of race, colour or creed; and we must be the guardians of nature and our environment. Religions have to place a greater thrust on the horizontal dimension of existence without losing sight of its vertical and transcendental dimension.

In our complex, pluralistic society religions must face the challenge to dialogue. But for dialogue to be creative and effective, it must go beyond the theoretical and academic levels of understanding similarities and differences and the reasons for them, to the level of challenging us with a praxiological imperative to accept one another as **persons** regardless of our racial and religious differences, to share our truth-claims, to build trustworthy relationships and to foster co-operation for the purpose of dealing with discrimination poverty, ecological disasters, growing materialism, the erosion of the family structure, ethnocentricity, religiocentricty and the threats to national unity. We must be willing to dialogue in a sprit of open-mindedness and empathy to learn from one another. The major prerequisite for this pursuit calls upon every tradition to free itself from the false assumptions that it exclusively possesses the absolute truth, and that its apprehension and interpretations of it are the only authentic ones. Either at the inter-personal or inter-cultural level such exclusivism can be a deterrent to meaningful dialogue and relationship. Wilfred

Cantwell Smith contends that pluralism poses an epistemological challenge. The encounter of individuals and communities necessitates communication and relationship from which we can learn about **us** and not only about **them**.[17] In the final analysis we are really learning about all of us as the **we** and **they** dichotomy narrows.

Partners in dialogue must steer clear of becoming polemical or dialectical for the former functions on the basis of confrontation and refutation, the latter on the basis of systematic reasoning for the juxtaposition of opposing views and beliefs in order to find a resolution to conflicts. In a pluralistic society there will always be differences, but these should be recognized for what they are and should not be emphasized to create tension and division between groups; nor should similarities be pushed to the extent of obliterating differences. They should help build bridges for stronger relationships. The fact of diversity is pivotal to Canadian society and it is here to stay. We have to find our places within this milieu by respecting and talking with another and by seeking harmony without attacking one another's traditions or cultures. The radical dialectic of the Madhyamika system which pursues the demolition of every ideological position and point of view has no place in dialogue. Anthony Gaultieri contends that people are nurtured by their different cultures and traditions. The attack or condemnation of a culture or tradition, therefore, is on people themselves. He makes the very timely and challenging observation that the preservation of a "viable culture" is an expression of love for persons whose "sacred quality" is assumed in biblical teachings.[18] Dogmatic loyalty to **our** own race and tradition on the assumption that they are superior can stifle our growth by restricting us within the boundaries of our own **way**, and thus deprive us of the valuable insights that are beyond the threshold of our neighbour's. Although the eternal, divine reality is **One**, Ernst Troeltsch observes that the divine life is not one but many, and the unique feature of love consists of our apprehension of the One in the many.[19]

The **yin** and the **yang** which are the two creative principles in the Chinese world-view, though different and opposite to each other, are not polarized. They complement each other in the process of creativity. On their own as independent realities, they are ineffective and non-creative. From this metaphysical insight of

Taoism we can deduce a practical lesson that differences do not necessarily presuppose polarization of peoples, but provide the possibility for complementarity, for recognizing our sacred quality whether we call it the **image of God**, the **Buddha-nature**, the **atman** or the **yin-yang,** and for consolidating our potentials in the welfare of the general good. Dialogue should lead us from attitudes of segregation and discrimination to complementarity, the richness of which should be felt in a **consolidated drive toward harmony in diversity without the threat of uniformity.** In his teachings on relationships, Confucius stresses the importance of *li*, which is action in accordance with propriety, and *chung-shu*, which is conscientious reciprocity. Five centuries before the birth of Christ, he anticipated the **golden rule** in his exhortation **not to do to others what we do not want done to ourselves**. In the Taoist and Confucian teachings, in the great compassion (*mahakaruna*) of the bodhisattva, in the golden rule and love of Jesus Christ, and in the Gandhian teachings on non-violence *(ahimsa)* there is an existential appeal to peoples of diverse backgrounds to conscientiously apply themselves in a spirit of community for the welfare of the general good. To encourage dialogue on the basis of this appeal will keep plurality intact and will not deny individuals their rights and freedoms to pursue the religion of their choice with confidence and integrity.

As religions face these challenges with the appropriate attitude, pluralism will not be seen as a threat. It will make our complex society more viable as we move beyond the threshold of the 21st century. It will continuously be a source of enrichment to the life of our nation; and our sense of unity without the threat of uniformity will be good reason for hope of a brighter future with deeper understanding and trustworthy relationships.

Endnotes

1.   A succinctly penetrating account of the Christian vision of other religions is given by John Hick, *God Has Many Names,* (Philadelphia: Westminister Press, 1982), pp. 29-39. For a concise description of the Amerindians' responses to evangelization, cf. Cornelius J. Jaenen, "Amerindian Responses to French Missionary Intrusion", 1611-1760: A

Categorization" in William Westfall, et al (eds.) *Religion and Culture: Comparative Canadian Studies*, (Association for Canadian Studies, 1985), pp. 183-196; and for a study of the impact of Christianity on Canadian society, cf. Roger O'Toole, "Society, the Sacred and the Secular: Sociological Observations on the Changing Role of Religion in Canadian Culture", *ibid.*, pp. 102-11.

2.   Roger Hutchinson argues that the transformative view of a denomination is not without tension in a society of religious pluralism. Cf. his "Morality and Law" in Peter Slater (ed.), *Religion and Culture in Canada/Religion et Culture au Canada*, (Canadian Corporation for Studies in Religion, 1977), p. 200, *passim*.

3.   Karl Barth, "The Revelation of God as the Abolition of Religion", in Owen C. Thomas (ed.), *Attitudes Toward Other Religions*, (London: SCM Press, 1969), pp. 96-97.

4.   Austin Flannery, *Vatican II: The Conciliar and Post Conciliar Documents*. (Leominster: Fowler Wright Book Ltd., 1980), pp. 738-742 and pp. 1002-1006. The report of the XIVth General Assembly of the *International Federation of Catholic Universities* held in Toronto, August 22-26, 1983, states that our contemporary world is seeking "a new world-order" that goes beyond the boundaries of states and nations and to foster a family of all peoples; and of necessity we must "examine realistically the expressions, the meaning and implications of this new, planetary yearning, beyond the opposition of ideologies and the diversity of particular cultures." *The Catholic University and the Search for a New World Order: Thematic Report*. (Paris: Permanent Secretariat of IFCU, 1984), p. 1; and for a brief discourse on Peace and Justice, cf. pp. 89-94. These concerns of *Vatican II* and *IFCU* are not unique to the Catholic Church alone, but they go hand in hand with many Protestant denominations.

5.   For a detailed and informative study of the conservative and evangelical model of Christianity, cf. Paul F. Knitter, *No Other Name?: A Critical Survey of Christian Attitudes Toward the World Religions*, (New York: Orbis Books, 1990), pp. 75-96.

6. For a detailed account of this incident, see Hugh Johnston, *The Voyage of the Komagata Maru: the Sikh Challenge to Canada's Colour Bar*. Delhi: Oxford University Press, 1979. Those who have interest in the history of the British Empire with particular reference to immigration laws and race relations will find this book an interesting source.

7. Cf. V.S. Naravane, *Modern Indian Thought*. (Bombay: Asia Publishing House, 1967), Chs. III, IV, VI and VIII; also John Hick and Brian Hebblethwaite (eds.), *Christianity and Other Religions*, (Glasgow: Collins, 1980), Chs. I, V, IX. Ninian Smart, *The Religious Experience of Mankind*, (London: Collins, 1973), p. 31, *passim*: Arnold Toynbee, *Christianity Among the Religions of the World*, (New York: Scribners & Sons, 1957), p. 3. *passim.*

8. F. X. Max Muller, *Ramakrishna: His Life and Sayings*, (New York: Scribners & Sons, 1989), p. 99.

9. Reynold Nicholson (tr.) *Rumi: Poet and Mystic*, (London: Allen & Unwin, 1950), p. 166; cf. also Rumi's "All Religions are in Substance One and the Same", in his *The Masnavi*, tr. by E.H. Whinfield, London: Octagon Press, 1979), p. 139.

10. The term *salvificentric* is used to suggest that all religions are concerned with the salvation of human beings from the human predicament. The terms *salvation* and *liberation* will be used synonymously to denote the ultimate goal of religions though they hold different meanings for different religions. Cf. for example, Frederick Streng, *Understanding Religious Man* (Belmont: Dickenson Publishing Company, 1969), p. 3, *passim*; Huston Smith, *The World's Religions*, (San Francisco: Harper Collins, 1991), p. 12, passim; John Hick, *God and the Universe of Faiths*, (London: Macmillan, 1977), pp.108-147; and Raimundo Pannikar, "The Religion of the Future or the Crisis of the Notion of Religion: Human Consciousness", *Interculture*, Vol. XXIII, No. 2, (Montreal: Monchanin Cross-Cultural Centre, Spring 1990), pp. 3-21.

11. Harold Coward, *Pluralism: Challenge to World Religions*, (New York: Orbis Books, 1985), p. 96.

12. For an analysis of three kinds of conflicts: "Man and Nature, Man and man, Man and himself", see Bertrand

Russell, *New Hopes for a Changing World*, (London: Allen & Unwin, 1951), p. 18, *passim.*

13. Fritz Pappenheim, *The Alienation of Modern Man*, (New York: Monthly Review Press, 1966), p.109.

14. *Ibid.*, p.134

15. Raimundo Panikkar, "The New Innocence", *Cross Currents*, Vol. XXVII, No. 1, (New York: Cross Currents Corporation, Spring 1977), pp. 7-12; cf. also my "Mystical Experiences and Metaphysical Assumptions in a Cosmotheandroganic Conception of Reality", *Proceedings of the Fifth International Symposium on Asian Studies*, (Hong Kong: Asian Research Service, 1983), pp. 291-305; and my "Towards an Organic View of Society", *Religion and Society*, Vol. XXX, No. 1 (Bangalore: The Christian Institute for the Study of Religion and Society, March 1983), pp.28-36.

16. Rabindranath Tagore, *Gitanjali*, (London: Macmillan, 1913), poem 69.

17. Wilfred Cantwell Smith, "Comparative Religion: Whither and Why?" in Micrea Eliade and Joseph M. Kitagawa (eds.), *The History of Religions: Essays in Methodology*, (Chicago: University of Chicago Press, 1966), pp. 38-58. Smith contends that in order to know whether people find fulfillment in their religion we should speak of them, but we should keep in mind that in the final analysis **we** are speaking about **us**. He is one of the pioneers in the **we** and **us** factor, which is a significant contribution to dialogue.

18. Anthony R. Gaultieri, "Towards a Theological Perspective on Nationalism", in Slater, *op. cit.*, p. 515.

19. Ernst Troeltsch, "The Place of Christianity Among the Religions of the World", in John Hick and Brian Hebblethwaite *Christianity and Other Religions, op. cit.*, p. 31.

Chapter 18

DIVERSITY: A MATTER OF ETHICS

David J. Roy

Diversity is central to bioethics at the beginning of the 21st century. While many deplore the loss of diversity, for example as seen in the extinction of species of plant, insect and animal life on this planet others decry the presence of diversity, experienced as conflict, within the very foundations of ethical systems in our culturally pluralistic world. The most diverse views about how a human life, particularly about how human sexual life, should be lived draw people into tense social conflict over the place and the rights of homosexual people in Canadian society. Moreover, violent conflicts have occurred in Canada, elsewhere in North America, and in Europe over how similar or how diverse human fetuses are from human being who are recognized in law as persons. These conflicts, some involving shootings and even murder, have centred on abortion clinics in the United States and Canada. Similar scenes of violent opposition have featured research laboratories because people cannot agree about how different or diverse animals are or are not from human beings. On the frontiers of a rapidly advancing human genome project, people are beginning to fear that an expanding instrumentarium of diagnostic tests will uncover genetic diversities leading to possible genetic stigmatization and discrimination against people who may come to be seen as different from, and as generally inferior to, other people. And on the final frontiers of life, diversity has emerged as an ethical challenge of profound societal significance in current debates about euthanasia, debates that center on the question, "Is there only one right way to die?". Diversity in dying was the subject of study by a special Canadian Senate Committee in 1994, conducting hearings on this issue with people from across Canada.

This essay will explore and describe a selection among the many ways in which diversity is perceived in ethical discourse at the beginning of this century, either as a value to be cherished or at the very source of value conflicts that divide society or even threaten to split society asunder.

Diversity in the Foundation and Method of Ethics

The days are long gone when great thinkers pondering in solitary silence could work out the differences between right and wrong, the days when they could do this not only for themselves, but also for the rest of humankind.

Voltaire, that exemplar of the Enlightenment, marvelled at how it took centuries of collaboration among scientists to work out a single law of nature, whereas it took a wise person only a few hours of thought, a day at most, to work out what a human being's duties were in life.[1]

Now, at the beginning of this century, particularly in the context of our high technology but limited resources, we often do not readily perceive the differences between what is right, what is wrong, and what can be tolerated.

Within the classical notion of culture, ethics proceeded to distinguish right from wrong by an appeal to the governing concepts of human nature and the human good. Ethics in the classical mode assumed *three stabilities*: the unchangeability of the human condition; agreement about what constitutes the human good; and quite fixed temporal and geographical limits on the reach and impact of human action[2]. These stabilities no longer hold. Human nature is now no longer simply a governing principle of human action. Human nature is also an unanswered question, and an unfinished project. There is widespread disagreement on what is right and good, on what is wrong and bad, and on what is tolerable or not, among all the things we can now do to and with, if not always for, human beings.

In the classical notion of culture and ethics, there was one set of beliefs, ideals, and norms, and these were assumed to be the standard of thought, word, and act for all human beings in all places and at all times. The scope of human duty, obligations, and rights, and the recognition of reprehensible behaviour, were assumed to be readily accessible to, and comprehended by, the cultivated mind. It was within such a classical notion of culture and ethics that Voltaire could claim that little more than a few hours thought were needed for a wise person to work out the difference between right and wrong.

However public life in Western societies is no longer lived in the classicist mode. We have passed from an integrated, universalist culture to a culturally, philosophically and ethically fragmented and pluralist world. In this post-classicist world, ethics is neither a ready-made achievement nor a simple inheritance of principle, stored for all time in great books and great minds and waiting for universal application[3]. In Western society, we largely find ourselves in the difficult situation of having to strive and struggle together to reconstruct standards that enable us to distinguish right from wrong, when we differ as profoundly as we do on the level of beliefs and values.

A society, as Nicolo Chiaromonte has put in his *The Paradox of History*, is not merely a collection of individuals and cannot be reduced either to the sum total of the political and juridical institutions on which it rests or to its economic and cultural structures. Society also consists of the beliefs on which members of a community agree or clash.[4]

People in Western societies today clash profoundly on two levels: on the level of their world view beliefs, the beliefs within which people find the goals of life and the costs of death; and on their hierarchies of value against which people decide which values may be sacrificed, if need be, and which values must be maintained at all costs.

Diversity: From Aristotelian Dialectic Towards Fractal Ethics

In the context of such diversity, ethics requires a shift from divergent to a convergent method and mode of thought. The shift required is from the task of constructing arguments to the work of constructing practical judgements about what must be done, what must be prohibited, and what can be tolerated. This is the shift required to extricate bioethics, the ethics of research, and public policy ethics from the deadlock of interminable discourse about matters upon which people are likely never to agree.[5]

The shift from theoretical to practical reasoning in ethics emphasizes the importance of Aristotelian dialectic in ethics, and that dialectic utilizes diversity as ally rather than foe.

Aristotle's method to arrive at the best ethical judgements possible in any given situation was based on the assumption that people need *to learn* what they really think about a given issue. The dialectical method pits both the many and the wise, ordinary folk and experts, into discussion with each other. The aim is to unfold, to lay out, the values and judgements of people who come to an issue with definite intuitions and value commitments. The mutually corrective interplay of these views, achieved as people work through practical alternatives in dialogue, is what Aristotle's dialectic involves.[6]

This approach to ethics is what Gordon Dunstan has called a "new development in method"[7] And Paul Ricoeur has reached back to Aristotle's term *phronesis* to characterize this method as one based upon the practical wisdom of the many, as a method based on the prudence of the many (*une phronesis à plusieurs*) rather than on the persuasive brilliance in argument of the few.[8]

Where some would want to suppress diversity in belief and values as being a source of moral error, this dialectical approach respects diversity as a source of moral wisdom. In analogy with B. Mandelbrot's fractal geometry,[9] respect for the rich, if not infinite, diversity of beliefs about human life, and for the many diverse ways of living humanity, requires a *fractal ethics*. Fractal geometry was developed to explore and capture the form of structures in nature that seemed to be pathological because they failed to conform to the classical geometrical rules of Euclidean geometry. In an analogous way, fractal ethics seeks to explore, understand, and respect the very diverse ways of living a human life, a diversity that some find to be in contradiction with their classical view that there should be one ethic for all people in all places and all times.

When Diversity Is Endangered

Arnold Toynbee, the famous historian, organized his account and interpretation of the rise and fall of civilization in terms of challenge and response. The earliest civilizations sprung forth from the original responses some audacious peoples in primitive societies managed to mount against changes in the physical, geographical environment that threatened their habitual way of life. To survive and to thrive, they had to move, change their way of life, their often centuries-old way of life, or both. Later civilizations came into existence primarily out of responses to challenges from the human environment. When dominant minorities ceased to lead and became oppressive, people responded by breaking away from the failing civilization and founding a new one.[10]

People across the planet, at the beginning of the new century, are also facing powerful environmental challenges to their habitat, to their ways of life, and some are now facing environmental challenges to their lives. One need only think for a moment of the thousands of people in Southern regions of the planet who die yearly because they cannot mount adequate responses to the devastating challenges of drought, crop-failure, incompetent local government, and exploitation of their resources by powerful corporations and states of the planet's Northern regions.

The environmental threats that challenged early peoples to mount civilization-building responses came from natural changes in the environment, such as those that followed upon the end of the Ice Age. The devastating environmental threats characteristic of this late period of our century, quite to the contrary, come from a continuing stream of provocations mounted by human beings against the environment. The human environment has become the major threat to the geographical environment. The current environmental threats to human life and to ways of life have been caused largely by the way industrial and technological activities have damaged, and are still damaging, local environments and the global ecology. This challenge to ecological integrity, coming from the human environment, is calling forth a human response in the form of a large and growing movement, the movement of environmental and ecological ethics.

The disappearance of ecological and biological diversity is at the core of the challenge, and preservation of this diversity is the ethical and global goal of a late 21st century response. The challenge is massive and one can hardly be sanguine about the capacity of early 21st century human beings to mount and sustain an effective response. The practical ethic needed to preserve the diversity of life in Canada and in so many other places on this planet is a high and difficult achievement. That ethic requires, as Edward O. Wilson has stressed, "...vision reaching simultaneously into the short and long reaches of time. ... To choose what is best for both the near and distant futures is a hard task, often seemingly contradictory and requiring knowledge and ethical codes which for the most part are still unwritten."[11]

Sexual Diversity Within an Ethic of Love?

Human fertility and reproduction are beginning a new and decisive scene in the drama depicted in Gustav Vigeland's hundreds of sculptures that populate the Vigeland Park in Oslo, Norway. The sculptures represent human bodies at successive stages of the life cycle and depict the many poses and postures of the human body expressing the power of a human being's desire and quest for other human beings.

Sex is at the centre of the human drama and these last fifteen years or more have challenged Canadians and other people throughout the world to think again about the ethics of sexual diversity. What is the ethics of sexual diversity when it is developed in light of the historical length, breadth, depth, and richly varied reach of humanity?

The HIV pandemic, among other events, challenges people to liberate their minds from the constricting mold of narrow righteousness, from the totalitarian sexual orthodoxy that would blind us to humanity's basic facts: that we are all utterly unique and different; that we are humanly all utterly equal in worth; and that we all, to flourish and find our identity, need to live and be loved, to embrace and be embraced, to kiss and fondle, and to be bodily cherished in like manner.

Some, perhaps many, would deny these facts. They would believe that *heterosexual eros* is the only sexual way to express and realize *agape*, that increasingly unselfish love that wills the full flowering of another human being. But the ethics based on that view of sex falls far short of the full measure of tolerance and understanding humanity's demands. The ethos of humanity does not expect, nor does it demand, that a human being renounce being bodily and intimately cherished for a lifetime because his or her desire is for a human being of the same sex.

Within the full sweep of human sensitivity, sexual love or activity is reprehensible not because it is homosexual rather than heterosexual. It is rather so that sexuality, whether it be homosexual or heterosexual in expression, matches the demands of humanity when it offers comforting and supporting presence in the midst of loneliness; when it offers fidelity in the midst of lies; and when it liberates human beings from the need to sell or enslave themselves to obtain the companionship and sense of worth we all universally desire. The ethics of homosexual relations, as is equally true of heterosexual relations, is based on humanity's commands: do not trivialize, enslave, or betray another human being! Do not give death when you love! There are terms of the human drama when it is acted out in sex. This drama calls for a fractal ethics that can recognize and understand the humanity present in persons whose feelings and personal experience diverge from what many people believe to be "Euclidean" norm of sexual ethics.

When Animals, Though Splendidly Different, Are Like Us[12]

It is generally assumed that the ethical justifiability of research with human subjects depends on adequate prior experimentation on animals. Both the *Nuremberg Code* and the World Medical Association *Declaration of Helsinki* mention that animal experimentation should precede research with human subjects in the testing of new drugs and surgical operations. We also generally assume that our prime responsibility to animals in research is to minimize pain or discomfort. Beyond that, few would question, perhaps until recently, that we are ethically justified in inducing mortal illness into animals to produce animal models of human disease. Few would question that the needs of research to cure disease in humans justify the sacrifice of the lives of animals of other species.

These assumptions governing the ethics of research have been rooted within an even deeper, largely unquestioned, belief about the profound and unbridgeable chasm of experiential differences between human beings and all other species of animals. Following this belief, only human beings, ethically speaking, have to be treated as ends unto themselves. The conviction about the moral equality of all human beings, although violated repeatedly throughout history, has been deeply engrained in a number of the world's civilizations for centuries. Only humans, according to this conviction, belong to the community of beings who must be treated as ends unto themselves.

Over thirty years ago, Adolf Portmann, then director of the Institute of Zoology of Basle University, questioned this conviction. The principle of self-reproduction or self-display is central to his philosophy of the life process and that philosophy rejects the simplistic image of nature that would reduce the purpose and value of living beings to their functions.[13]

Portmann's analysis targets the role of colour in the worlds of the stickleback, the bee, the butterfly, and the parrot, in general, of fish, birds, and insects. Portmann's conclusion is that the marvellous displays of splendid colours in fish, insects, and birds can be only partially explained by natural selection principles of functional utility. Portmann distinguishes *"unaddressed"* from *"addressed"* phenomena to account for colour broadcasts in the bodies of living beings, broadcasts that are directed to no seeing eyes[14]. The *unaddressed* colour broadcasts, inadequately explainable in terms of the principle of functional utility, exhibit the principle of self-representation or self-display: the colour broadcast serves not as utilitarian signal, but seems to be an end unto itself.

The Portmann analysis expresses a transformation of our view of nature. It takes us beyond a reduction of living forms to their utilitarian functions. The implication is strong: those living forms are there for their own sake. Their very appearance is the sufficient reason for complexities of structure and for expenditures of energy that serve no identifiable utilitarian function.

An emerging current of thought, gaining momentum over the last several years, extends Portmann's philosophy and now challenges the basic assumption that even higher animals such as the great apes, are so different from human beings that they do not belong within a community of equals with human beings. The challenge emphasizes the striking similarities of mental capacities and emotional experience that bind chimpanzees, gorillas, and orangutans into solidarity with humans.[15]

The capacity of some of these higher animals to express their own individuality and to bond emotionally to an individual human being can profoundly shake, if not shatter, the long unquestioned assumption that they are "not one of us". Some higher animals behave in a fashion that seems to express their feeling that they "are one of us". Quite so, it would seem of the chimpanzee who gesticulated to a scientist passing by its cage one day, then took the scientist's hand firmly on its own and looked up into the scientist's eyes while the scientist held the chimp's hand as it died from the results of an invasive experiment. The tag on the chimp's cage gave it all away. This was the chimpanzee for whom the scientist had earlier been responsible, from its baby days on through its early rearing in the same research institute.[16]

Diversity challenges us ethically in many different ways. The challenge here is to look through the evident differences between humans and other higher animals to perceive the less obvious, but wondrously real similarities between some of these animals and ourselves. The perception that these animals, with their capacity for consciousness, recognition, and for emotional bonding with humans, are indeed "one of us" may come to be one of the most profound conversions in late 20th century ethics of diversity. If these animals are "one of us" we will have to change our behaviour toward them radically. If these animals really are one of us, then who are we really?

The Early Human Embryo: Diversity and Individuality

A wide range of research projects, considered by a number of scientists to be highly important both for basic science as well as for the eventual prevention and cure of disease, would require the study of the human embryo in ways that would disrupt its normal course of development, render the embryo unfit for implantation, or entail the embryo's destruction. Though the question of the moral status of the human embryo arises in the setting of laboratory fertilization and embryo transfer for the treatment of infertility, the ethical issue about the degree of respect and protection due to the human embryo is most acute in the setting of research.

The question of diversity, of a being's difference from or similarity to human beings, raised with respect to higher animals in the preceding section, arises with a special twist in the context of research with the early human embryo. The question here is not so much, "Is the early human embryo one of *us*?". The question is rather, "Is the early human embryo *one* of us?" The critical question is about the time when the early human embryo becomes an *individual organism*.

One current of thought asserts that the zygote resulting from human sperm fertilizing the human ovum has the biological identity of a new human individual. On this view, a unique and individual human being exists once the fertilization process is completed. Some findings of developmental biology, however, cast serious doubt on the assertion that the fertilized ovum or zygote (very early embryo or preembryo) is *biologically* an individual organism. While the cells after fertilization each contain a unique and new genome, the stabilizing of these cells into a single unique organism occurs later in the development of the early embryo or preembryo.

Individuals are differentiated one from another if it is impossible to combine two to produce a third or to divide one to make two individual of a kind. On this understanding, the early embryo cannot yet be an individual organism because division of these early cells can and does produce identical twins. If one group of human cells can, and does at times, split within the first 14 days after fertilization to form two individuals, then it is difficult to argue that this group of cells was one human individual prior to the split.

During the first two weeks of development after fertilization, most of the dividing cells deriving from the fertilized ovum are destined to form tissues and membranes, such as the placenta, that will provide supporting and nourishing connections of the future embryo to the mother. Toward the end of this preembryonic phase of development, up to 99 percent of the cells coming from the fertilized ovum are destined to form these extraembryonic tissues, and only a small group of cells deriving from the fertilized ovum will go on to form the embryo that will develop into the fetus and the baby. It happens often enough that no embryo at all forms from the preembryonic cells or that twin embryos emerge from these cells. The "primitive streak" is a longitudinal band of cells forming from the preembryonic cells about 13 to 16 days after fertilization. It is the formation of the primitive streak that marks the emergence of an individual embryo.[17]

The human preembryo, to take up the question raised above, becomes *one* of us only when the initial cluster of cells resulting from successive divisions of the fertilized ovum become sufficiently differentiated over the two to three weeks following fertilization. In this sense diversity is essential for the constitution of an individual human organism. The ethics of research with early human embryo is greatly dependent upon how adequately this role of diversity has been understood.

Normality: A Condition for Being Treated as Equal?

A recent study has shown that the DNA composition of the chimpanzee genome differs by only 1.6 percent from that of humans, and there is only a 2.2 percent DNA composition difference between the genome of human and gorillas. These findings have prompted Simon Easteal, a geneticist of the Australian National University to propose that apes should be regarded as a human species.[18] This proposal supports the idea discussed above that the great apes should be treated as members of the moral community of equals.

Should the same perception of equality extend to human fetuses that are discovered after prenatal diagnosis to have genetic mutations that will lead to diseases or abnormalities of varying degrees of severity at birth or later in life This question centers on the issue of eugenics. How normal does one have to be to be allowed to enter the human community? Once in the human community, how normal does one have to be treated as equal to all other human beings? This question centers on the issue of genetic stigmatization and discrimination, a threat many fear could turn into a reality, the reality of a genetic underclass created by those who would prize "genetic purity" above human equality within genetic diversity.

Some would define eugenics as any effort to interfere with individuals' procreative choices in order to attain a societal goal.[19] Eugenics, however, can result from the free workings of parental choice. There is no need for a state-inspired and state-organized and, by implication, coercive eugenics programme if voluntary parental uptake and utilization of prenatal diagnosis, with selective abortion of fetuses found to be defective, will, for all practical purposes, achieve the same result.

The first lesson of genetics, Albert Jacquard has emphasised, is that individuals are all different and cannot be classified, evaluated, or placed on a hierarchy.[20] That is not the first lesson of prenatal diagnosis, as it has functioned in Western societies over the last quarter century. The practice of prenatal diagnosis has taught that there are differences between human beings, differences in quality and value that some people find intolerable and that, in their view, justify selective abortion. Leaving all decisions to the discretion of parents, Angus Clarke stresses, indicates the low value our society places upon those with genetic disorders and handicaps.[21] The justification of this charge rests with the question of how free parental choice for selective abortion after prenatal diagnosis can really be if we have societally decided that the costs of caring for those who differ from the normal are too much to bear. Cost-efficiency considerations seem to make it advisable, as Benno

Müller-Hill has perceived, for both parents and state, to destroy the cost-intensive embryo and fetus.[22]

How will those with genetic diseases and congenital disorders, if they escape spontaneous or selective abortion, come to be seen in our society? Leon Kass fears they may be seen as persons who need not have been, and who would not have been, if only someone would have gotten to them on time.[23] It may well be true that only constant reinforcement of tolerance for differences will prevent such tragic eugenic devaluation of human beings.[24] But who will reinforce this tolerance for differences, if no one has the perception and the social courage to define the threshold beyond which selective abortions are intolerable?[25]

Unravelling and revealing a person's genomic secrets may release the brakes societies have set on the social process of stigmatization and ostracism. This process need not, but could, accelerate in tandem with the design of more and more molecular markers for presymptomatic testing and screening of individuals and families.[26] Stigmatization will occur if molecular markers become social markers that set off those with gene defects as being different from other human beings. Discrimination will occur if these social markers provoke the exclusion of people from goods, services, opportunities, and privileges to which they have as much a right as everyone else.

Will the benefits of presymptomatic genetic diagnosis, such as prevention of disease or timely treatment, be paid for with the social price of stigmatization, ostracism, and discrimination? Could an expansion of presymptomatic testing, contrary to the noblest of therapeutic intentions, lead to the social creation of a genetic underclass; a class of people who are, on the basis of their genotype alone, increasingly excluded from education, insurance, employment and other goods that are supposed to be open to all in an open society?

Diversity in Dying: Is There Only One Right Way To Die?

Over the last twenty years resistance has grown against technological zeal to prolong life at all costs and to the bitter biological end. There is today a solidly entrenched consensus both in clinical ethics and in law, in favour of allowing people to die in peace and dignity. Some physicians still seem to be unaware of this, and some particular cases will always provoke agonizing discussion, but the trend against senseless tethering of people to life-prolonging technology is generally serene and probably irreversible.

However, liberation from enslavement to life-prolonging technology is for some dying people not quite enough. So it was for a young man in the terminal stages of AIDS. He had a head full of projects and wanted to live. Yet, knowing he would inevitably die soon from AIDS, he asked for sufficient drugs and for instructions in how to use them so that he could time his death to occur before he wasted away and lost his mental competence and this is what he did one night after a going-away evening dinner with his friends. Recently, a young dying woman, utterly lucid, was driving her doctors into a corner of helplessness by her persistent demands for immediate death. She accepted her doctors' protestations that giving her death was something they just could not do. They were also unable adequately to relieve the young woman's constant pain in her legs and feet. She could not accept that pain and felt horribly diminished by the drowsiness she was experiencing from the drugs the doctors were using in their unsuccessful attempt to control her pain. And no, she did not want to be heavily sedated. She wanted to go home and use her freedom there, and her blender, to prepare that one last laced orange drink that would bring her death and relief from the intolerable days of dying through which she was having to live.

Sometimes a dying person's request or demand for death is ambiguous and ambivalent. Such requests, though tough to handle, leave space for maneuvering. She is asking for death, yes, but she is also asking for something else; she wants death, yes, but she also wants something of those experiences that make life worth living, however short the time for living may be. In these circumstances, doctors, nurses, family members have pathways they can explore. They can decode the request for death, uncover the other request the death demand is masking, and then set about achieving what the dying person "really" wants. When demands for death are ambiguous and ambivalent there are still enough pieces on the board for the game to go on. There are still moves that a doctor or nurse or family member, harassed by the dying person's demand for death, can make and, while there are still moves to be made, the dying person's time may run out while the game is still being played.

Some will dogmatically claim, and others will desperately hope, that *all* demands on the part of the dying for death are ambiguous and ambivalent. Wouldn't that be comforting! It would confirm a worldview within which we never have to face our limits, suffer our finitude, and acknowledge our helplessness. But that does not seem to be the way the world today actually works. Some demands of the dying for death are quite definitive, unambiguous and unambivalent. Death now is what they want and what they are demanding. Those who receive and confront such demands have no pieces left on the board and only two moves available: accede to the demand or refuse to do so while continuing to offer care and comfort that may well fall short of the anguish the dying are experiencing; a care and comfort that may well be rejected.

Many have had opportunities to grieve over deaths that have come too early, but death can also be untimely because it comes too late. Sometimes death is forced to wait because a powerful technology is marshalled to keep someone alive beyond the point when a person's time can be anything more meaningful than an unrelenting sequence of signals of one's own deterioration. At other times life-prolonging technology has nothing to do with death's delay. It is one's own stubborn biology that keeps one's brain and body alive long after one's mind is prepared and waiting to die. Death is at times so long and overdue that emptiness echoes within each moment of a dying person's day. Human time, though, is for life, not for the slow tasting of death.

There are many ways to die with dignity. Few today could assert that resigned acceptance of imminent death is more an expression of human dignity than is Dylan Thomas' admonition to rail against the dying of the light and to go raging into that gentle night.

A thanatological liberalism that respects diverse attitudes towards dying is relatively easy. However, the assumption still deeply rooted in our culture, though frequently challenged today, is that rectitude, if not dignity, demands of people that they accept—this means that they await—their time, their moment of death. Can we in our society tolerate, let alone accept, the same diversity of *acts* as we can of *attitudes* in the matter of dying? This is the core of the controversy, likely to dominate this last decade of the 20th century, over assisted suicide and euthanasia.

Diversity of Civilization: The Global Drama of 2001 and Beyond?

This chapter has considered diversity as the source or as the stage of ethical conflicts, but of ethical conflicts as occurring within the relatively unified Western culture and civilization as lived in Canada and North America. Samuel P. Huntington has advanced the hypothesis that conflict between civilizations will be the latest phase in the evolution of conflict in the modern world.[28] If the clash of civilizations does come to dominate global politics over the early years, if not centuries, of the next millennium, ethics itself will pass through a new phase in its evolution. People will be challenged, perhaps more profoundly and broadly than ever in the past, to confront the question of how will it be possible to live with respect for, and in peace with, radically different views of life when these threaten to collide in conflicts that transcend matters of economics, technology and national power. If, as the poet Seamus Heany has said, our unspoken assumptions have the force of revelation[29] the new millennium may provoke the emergence, and the sharing, of radically new insights into the meaning and the function of diversity within humanity. The alternative to that emergence hardly bears contemplation.

Endnotes

1.   Voltaire. Dictionnaire philosophique 1V. In: *Oeuvres complètes de Voltaire*. Paris: Garnier Frères, 1879, 195-96.

2.   Jonas H. Philosophical Essays: *From Ancient Creed to Technological Man*. Englewood Cliffs, New Jersey: Prentice Hall, 1974, 3.

3.   Lonergan B. Dimensions of meaning. In: Crowe F.E., Doran RM (eds). *Collected Works of Bernard Lonergan*, Volume 4. Toronto: University of Toronto Press, 1988, 241.

4.   Chiaromonte N. The Paradox of History. Stendhal, Tolstoy, Paternak and others. London: Weidenfeld and Nicolson (undated), 134.

5.   Toulmin S. How medicine saved the life of ethics. *Perspective in Biology and Medicine* 1982; 25:736-750.

6. Nussbaum M.C. *The Fragility of Goodness. Luck and Ethics in Greek Tragedy and Philosophy.* Cambridge: Cambridge University Press, 1986, 240-263.

7. Dunstan G. R. Two branches from one stem. In: Callahan D, Dunstan GR (eds). Biomedical Ethics: An Anglo-American Dialogue, *Annals of the New York Academy of Sciences* 1988; 530:4-6.

8. Ricoeur P. Lectures 1. *Autour de la politique.* Paris Éditions du Seuil, 1991, 268.

9. Mandelbrot BB. *The Fractal Geometry of Nature.* San Francisco: W.H. Freeman and Company, 1983.

10. Toynbee AJ. *A Study of History.* Abridgement of Volumes I-VI by D.C. Somervell. New York, London: Oxford University Press, 1947, 569-570.

11. Wilson EO. *The Diversity of Life.* Cambridge, MA: The Belknap Press of Harvard University Press, 1992, 312.

12. This subtitle is a somewhat modified version of a sentence in: Rollin BE. The Ascent of Apes - Broadening the Moral Community. Chapter 20 of: Cavalieri P, Singer P (eds). *The Great Ape Project. Equality Beyond Humanity.* London: Fourth Estate, 1993, 214.

13. Grene M. The Characters of living things. I. The Biological philosophy of Adolf Portmann. In: Grene M. *The Understanding of Nature. Essays in the Philosophy of Biology.* Boston Studies in the Philosophy of Science. Vol. XXIII. Dordrecht-Holland, Boston: D. Reidel, 1974, 267.

14. Portmann A. Colors of Life. *Main Currents in Modern Thought.* Retrospective Issue, November 17, 1940 - November 17, 1975;32:71.

15. Portmann A., op. cit., 73.

16. Editors and Contributors. A Declaration on Great Apes. In: Cavalieri P, Singer P (eds). *The Great Ape Project. Equality Beyond Humanity.* London: Fourth Estate, 1993, 4-7.

17. McLaren A. Prelude to embryogenesis. In: The CIBA Foundation. *Human Embryo Research. Yes or No?* London, New York: Tavistock Publications, 1986, 5-23.

18. Mclaren A. IVF: regulation or prohibition. *Nature* 1989;342:469-470.

19. Anon. Australian genetic study says ape should be regarded as human. *The Gazette* November 19, 1994:A17.

20. Holtzman NA. *Proceed with Caution: Predicting Genetic Risks in the Recombinant DNA Era*. Baltimore, London: The John Hopkins University Press, 1989, 223.

21. Jacquard A. In Praise of Difference. Genetics and Human Affairs. New York: Columbia University Press, 1984. Translated by M.M. Moriarty of the French original: Éloge de la différence. Paris: Éditions du Seuil, 1978.

22. Clarke A. Is nondirective genetic counseling possible? *Lancet* 1991;338:998-1001.

23. Müller-Hill B. Genetics after Auschwitz. *Holocaust and Genocide Studies* 1987;2:3-10.

24. Kass LR. Implications of prenatal diagnosis for the human right to life. In: Hilton B. et al. (eds). *Ethical Issues in Human Genetics. Genetic Counseling and the Use of Genetic Knowledge*. New York: Plenum Press, 1973, 189.

25. Holtzman NA., op.cit., 228.

26. Clarke A., op. cit., 998, 1000.

27. Markel H. The Stigma of disease: Implications of genetic screening. *The American Journal of Medicine* 1992;93:209-215.

28. Huntington SP. The Clash of civilizations? *Foreign Affairs* 1993; 72/3:22.

29. Heany S. *The Haw Lantern*. London, Boston: Faber and Faber, 1987: 19.

CANADIAN DIVERSITY IN THE TWENTY - FIRST CENTURY

Joseph E. Nancoo

As the Twenty-First Century dawns
Canada, Voltaire's "few acres of snow",
At its threshold heroically stands
Like its intrepid, inspired pioneers
Who braved the perils of the land
And blazed trails through rugged wilderness
To build a blessed country
Acclaimed universally:
The best place on earth to be.

Canada, promised land of the future,
At the new century's threshold stands
Seeking new, intrepid, inspired pioneers
Who look, listen, and learn life's lessons
From Nature's infinitely varied tapestry
And awaken and ignite
The minds of people everywhere on planet earth
To contemplate and embrace
The ennobling necessity
Of harmony in humanity's rich diversity.

Canada, gift of the St. Lawrence-
Magnificent river, for countless centuries
Facilitating, nourishing Nature's own diversity;
Fertile frontier for flourishing flora and fauna,
Friendly haven for migratory life-forms
Ages before the birth of our Inuit and Indians;
Its scenic grandeur the glittering setting
For Canada's Centennial centrepiece: Terre des Hommes
Extraordinary exposition of human exploits
Changing Canadians forever.

Canada, like the Aurora Borealis,
Spectacularly compelling mankind's admiration
Not, as of yore, for scarlet-coated Mounties
Instead, for a peaceful peace-keeping people
Creating, inspiring a virtual vision
Of our place in the universe.

Canada, cornerstone of the Twenty-First Century,
Formidable foundation for building a future
Egalitarian society, enriched enormously
With dynamic diverse cultures, cherishing
Shared visions and common soaring aspirations
For a heroic, humane, global community
Valuing the liberty, dignity and nobility
Of each and every human being!

CONTRIBUTORS

Dr. Pat Bradshaw is Associate Professor in the Schulich School of Business, York University.

Cyril Dabydeen spent the last decade as race relations specialist with the Federation of Canadian Municipalities. He is an award-winning poet and novelist.

Dr. George J. Sefa Dei is a Professor in the Department of Sociology and Equity Studies, Ontario Institute for Studies in Education, University of Toronto. He is the author of *Removing the Margins: The Challenges and Possibilities of Inclusive Schooling* and *Inclusive Education: A Guide to Teacher Development.*

The Hon. Stéphane Dion is Minister of Intergovernmental Affairs in the Government of Canada. Dr. Dion is a former Professor of Political Science at the Université de Moncton and Université de Montréal. He was also co-director of the Canadian Journal of Political Science, senior research fellow with the Canadian Centre for Management Development. He is the author of a number of books and articles.

Nahum Kanhai is an Assistant Professor of Native Studies at Laurentian University.

Dr. Romulo F. Magsino is Dean of the Faculty of Education at the University of Manitoba and Professor of Educational Administration, Foundations and Psychology. He has authored and edited several books and monographs, and his numerous articles have been included in books and journals published in Canada and the United States. He was president of the Canadian Philosophy of Education Society.

Joseph E. Nancoo is an educator and journalist. He was editor of *The Teachers' Magazine*, *The Sentinel*, and the *Montreal Teacher*.

He is a former President of the Royal Commonwealth Society in Montreal.

Robert S. Nancoo is a researcher and writer. He is co-editor of *The Mass Media and Canadian Diversity*, and the *Indo-Caribbean Canadian Profiles of Achievement.*

Stephen E. Nancoo is author-editor of *Community Policing in Canada, The Mass Media and Canadian Diversity and 21st Century Canadian Diversity*. He taught at the University of the West Indies and Carleton University, was Senior Training Officer with the Government of Canada, instructs at the Ontario Police College and was a journalist with Thomson Newspapers in Canada and the Caribbean.

Dr. Edite Noivo is Assistant Professor of Sociology at the Université de Montréal.

Dr. Constantine Passaris is Professor of Economics at the University of New Brunswick. He is the author of numerous articles on public policy, regional economic development, human rights and the economics of immigration and multiculturalism. He has served as Chairman of the New Brunswick Human rights Commission, President of the Canadian Association of Statutory Human Rights Agencies, President of the New Brunswick Multicultural Council, chair of the Ministerial Advisory Committee on Multiculturalism, President of the Atlantic Multi-cultural Council and Member of the Economic Council of Canada.

Dr. Deo H. Poonwassie is Professor in the Department of Adult Education, University of Manitoba. He is co-editor of *Education and Cultural Differences: New Perspectives, Adult Education in Manitoba* and *Adult Education: An Introductory Reader.*

Dr. David Roy is Director of the Centre of Bioethics, Clinical Institute of Montreal, Faculty of Medicine, Université de Montréal.

Dr. Roberta Russell is Director of Research in the Department of Justice, Government of Canada.

Dr. John Sahadat is Professor of Religion at University of Sudbury College, Laurentian University. He is the author of *Ways to Meaning and a Sense of Universality.*

Dr. John Samuel is President of John Samuel & Associates Inc. in Ottawa. His 26 years in the federal Government of Canada included being Director of Policy Development in Immigration, Director of Race Relations and Executive Director of Canada Employment and Immigration Advisory Council. He is an honorary research professor at Carleton University and has 70 publications to his credit in the form of books, monographs, chapters in books, and journal articles. He has done consulting work for the United Nations, the International Labour Office, several federal government departments (including the Prime Minister's Office) and the private sector.

Dieter Schachhuber is Senior Advisor, Diversity Management at RCMP Headquarters, Ottawa; and a lecturer at Algonquin College.

Roopchand B. Seebaran is Professor of Social Work at the University of British Columbia. He also taught at the University of Manitoba, King's College and at the University of Western Ontario. Professor Seebaran specializes in Social Planning and Community Development, and is the author of several related papers and articles. He was named Social Worker of the Year in 1984 by the B.C. Association of Social Workers and was also the recipient of the 1996 Canadian Association of Social Workers Distinguished Service Award. He is the recipient of the David C. Lam Award for promoting the values of multiculturalism. He serves on the Board of Governors of the Law Foundation of British Columbia and on the Health and Social Development Committee of the Vancouver Foundation, former President of the British Columbia. Association of Social Workers, and chair of the British Columbia Advisory Council on Multiculturalism.

C. Lloyd Stanford is president of the consulting firm, Le Groupe Stanford Inc. in Ottawa. A former senior public servant with the Government of Canada, he helped write its report *Equality Now!,* is co-editor of *Canada 2000: Race Relations and Public Policy;* and co-author of *Visible Minorities and the Public Service of*

Canada. He is a former president of the Royal Commonwealth Society, Ottawa.

Dr. K. Victor Ujimoto is Professor, Department of Sociology and Anthropology and Gerontology Research Centre, University of Guelph. He is co-editor of *Visible Minorities and Multiculturalism: Asians in Canada.*